Cases in Electronic Commerce

Second Edition

Cases in Electronic Commerce

Sid L. Huff
Scott Schneberger
Both of the Ivey School of Business Administration
University of Western Ontario; Sid L. Huff is also
Chair, Information Systems, Victoria
University of Wellington, New Zealand

Michael Wade
Schulich School of Business, York University

Boston   Burr Ridge, IL   Dubuque, IA   Madison, WI   New York   San Francisco   St. Louis
Bangkok   Bogotá   Caracas   Kuala Lumpur   Lisbon   London   Madrid   Mexico City
Milan   Montreal   New Delhi   Santiago   Seoul   Singapore   Sydney   Taipei   Toronto

McGraw-Hill Higher Education

*A Division of The **McGraw-Hill** Companies*

CASES IN ELECTRONIC COMMERCE

Published by McGraw-Hill, an imprint of The McGraw-Hill Companies, Inc. 1221 Avenue of the Americas, New York, NY, 10020. Copyright © 2002, 2000 by The McGraw-Hill Companies, Inc. All rights reserved. No part of this publication may be reproduced or distributed in any form or by any means, or stored in a data base or retrieval system, without the prior written consent of The Mc-Graw-Hill Companies, Inc., including, but not limited to, in any network or other electronic storage or transmission, or broadcast for distance learning.
One time permission to reproduce granted by Ivey Management Services on February 28, 2001. Some ancillaries, including electronic and print components, may not be available to customers outside the United States.

This book is printed on acid-free paper.

domestic   1 2 3 4 5 6 7 8 9 0 DOC/DOC 0 9 8 7 6 5 4 3 2 1 0
international   1 2 3 4 5 6 7 8 9 0 DOC/DOC 0 9 8 7 6 5 4 3 2 1 0

ISBN 0-07-245731-7

Publisher: *George Werthman*
Senior sponsoring editor: *Rick Williamson*
Senior marketing manager: *Jeff Parr*
Project manager: *Jill Howell*
Manager, new book production: *Melonie Salvati*
Media producer: *Greg Bates*
Coordinator freelance design: *Artemio Ortiz Jr.*
Lead supplement producer: *Marc Mattson*
Cover design: *JoAnne Schopler*
Typeface: *10/12 New Century Schoolbook*
Compositor: *Carlisle Communications, Ltd.*
Printer: *R. R. Donnelley & Sons Company*

Library of Congress Cataloging-in-Publication Data
Huff, Sidney Laurence.
    Cases in electronic commerce / Sid L. Huff, Michael Wade, Scott Schneberger.—2nd ed.
      p. cm.
    Rev. ed. of: Cases in electronic commerce / Sid L. Huff . . . [et al.]. 2000
    Includes index.
    ISBN 0-07-245731-7 (alk. paper)
  1. Electronic commerce—Case studies. I. Wade, Michael. II. Schneberger, Scott L. III. Cases in electronic commerce.

HF5548.32.H85. 2002
658.8′4—dc21   2001032699

INTERNATIONAL EDITION ISBN 0-07-112352-0
Copyright © 2002. Exclusive rights by The McGraw-Hill Companies, Inc. for manufacture and export. This book cannot be re-exported from the country to which it is sold by McGraw-Hill. The International Edition is not available in North America.

www.mhhe.com

Preface

Today, companies of all sized—from the world's largest to the shop on the corner—are still working hard to figure out what electronic commerce means for them, now and in the future. However, the period of "jockeying for position" is ending, and economic Darwinism (survival of the economically fittest) is beginning to make clear which business models work, and which do not, in the world of Internet business. The downturn in the stock market values for "dot coms" (companies whose sole, or primary, business is transacted over the Net) that began in mid-2000 has heralded the end of the period of wild speculation, when profits were deemed to be unnecessary and all that was needed for a successful IPO was to make sure the company's name began with an *e*. A new sobriety has entered the scene, along with the recognition that maybe some of the old business practices weren't so bad after all.

The purpose of this book is to provide a collection of case studies of companies operating in the broad domain termed *electronic commerce*. The cases are targeted for use in teaching programs such as business schools or commercial business programs. They also provide interesting and instructive reading for anyone seeking a deeper understanding of the electronic commerce phenomenon. Each case study provides a rich description of a real company at a particular point in time, and specifically focuses on the actual decisions faced by the manager or managers in the companies at that time. In this, the second edition of *Cases in Electronic Commerce,* nearly all the cases presented are new. A few cases have been carried over from the first edition—cases that are still current and that present a unique perspective on certain important and interesting issues. The cases in this second edition are also, on average, somewhat shorter than those in the first edition. Consequently, there are more of them: 29 in total, as opposed to 24 cases in the first edition.

This book was written for three audiences: first, for students; second, for e-commerce practitioners; and third, for general managers. The 29 cases included here describe in substantial detail a set of organizations "doing" e-commerce in a variety of different ways. The cases were written as *teaching* cases, as opposed to purely *descriptive* cases often found in books aimed principally toward managers (the nature and objectives of a teaching case are discussed further below). For this reason, the cases in this book are ideally suited for use in university or college courses on electronic commerce. As well, these cases will be of interest to people working in e-commerce–related businesses. Studying these cases will provide e-commerce practitioners with a multifaceted look at "how the other guys are doing it," and, in so doing, perhaps provide new ideas, approaches, or principles to apply in their own firms. Finally, general managers will also benefit from studying the cases in this book. Many managers in traditional companies have not yet truly absorbed the import of e-commerce, for themselves or for the companies for which they now work. An examination of the cases will help those managers to learn by example and extension what the future may hold for them.

WHY A CASEBOOK?

The Socratic method, upon which the case method of learning is based, has been understood and employed in some teaching/learning arenas (e.g., philosophy) from ancient times. However, it has only been since the Harvard Business School introduced case teaching to its curriculum in the first decades of the 20th century that the case method has been accepted as a tool for management education. Since that time, the case method has spread across North America and, more recently, to other parts of the world. Today, most management education programs use cases, either as the preferred approach to learning or as a supplement to other learning methods.

A case is a description of an actual situation, commonly involving a decision, a challenge, an opportunity, a problem, or an issue faced by a manager or managers in an organization. It represents an unbiased, textual "snapshot" of a company, with a decision/issue focus. In effect, a case challenges the reader with a question: What would you do here? Teaching with cases really amounts to assisting students to answer that question and to justify their answers. This teaching and learning approach is termed the *case method.*

The cases in this book are not hypothetical; rather, they are based on real situations faced by real managers in real businesses, practicing electronic commerce in some form. Due to the sensitive nature of the material, the names of individuals in a few instances have been disguised (although all the firm names are real). Other than that, each case in this book attempts to reflect accurately the reality in that organization at that time.

Cases give students an opportunity to practice management in real-life situations without any of the real-life corporate or personal risk. It has been said that cases are to management students what cadavers are to medical students: the opportunity to practice on the real thing, but harmlessly. The analogy is not perfect however: A cadaver is lifeless, whereas a case represents a vibrant company faced with a challenge. Cases are also an effective tool to test the understanding of theory, to connect theory with application, and to develop stronger theoretical insights. Best of all, cases frequently make learning more interesting and more fun.

A rapidly growing number of books are being published about various aspects of electronic commerce, ranging from traditional textbooks (e.g., Corbitt, et al., *Internet Commerce: Digital Models for Business)*, to "how to" books (e.g., Minoli and Minoli, *Web Commerce Technology Handbook)*, to books for general readers wishing to understand the phenomenon better (e.g., Tapscott, et al., *Digital Capital)*. Books of readings in electronic commerce are also appearing (e.g., Kalakota and Whinston, *Readings in Electronic Commerce)*. A few of the general business books in this area include a limited number of case studies. However, these case studies are not particularly useful as teaching cases; they are usually written from third-party sources as simple descriptions of what some company has done. They generally lack the richness, first-person credibility, and decision/issue focus of good teaching cases. The first edition of *Cases in Electronic Commerce* was the first book of teaching case studies in this field; this, the second edition, continues that trend by presenting a new collection of recent cases suitable for teaching, study, and general managerial perusal.

ORGANIZATION

This book is organized into nine chapters. The introduction provides a brief overview of electronic commerce, sets the stage for the remainder of the book, and provides a detailed look ahead. Chapter 2 examines the underpinnings of e-commerce—the infrastructure provided by the Internet, and cases about companies that focus on infrastructure. Chapter 3 focuses on the sourcing problem: Where and how should companies acquire the products and especially the services they need to conduct electronic commerce? Chapter 4 examines financial issues associated with e-commerce, including capitalization, payment systems, and online banking.

Chapters 5 and 6 constitute the core of the book, focusing on Internet-based commercial transactions. Chapter 5 addresses business-to-consumer e-commerce, while chapter 6 addresses business-to-business issues and also e-commerce strategy.

Chapter 7 concerns the issue of virtual work—utilizing the Internet and other information technologies to relax the temporal and geographical boundaries of conventional office-based work, and to enpower new types of organizations seeking to provide virtual work services. Chapter 8 focuses on a related topic, virtual communities. The Internet has proved to be an effective medium for enabling the formation of communities of people with common, share interests. While some virtual communities are managed by altruists, others have become commercial ventures, as the cases in this chapter illustrate.

The final chapter, Chapter 9, includes cases that emphasize social, legal, and other e-commerce issues. Among these topics are questions of privacy, ethics, legality, and culture, specifically Internet culture. The topic of virtual education is also addressed.

Because the primary audience for this book is comprised of students studying electronic commerce, we have prepared a set of teaching notes to accompany the cases. These notes—which provide suggested assignment questions, suggested class discussion questions, analyses of each case, and suggested detailed case teaching plans—are available as an Instructor's Manual from the publisher to instructors who adopt this book for their e-commerce courses.

ACKNOWLEDGMENTS

As well as the three of us, a number of other people have contributed to creating this book. Most, though not all, of the cases were drawn from field research conducted by the Richard Ivey School of Business, at the University of Western Ontario. We thank Dean Lawrence Tapp for supporting the creation of this book. We also thank Associate Dean Paul Beamish for his support, and the Ivey Publishing group for their assistance in the preparation of both the original cases and this book. Financial support for researching and writing most of the Ivey cases was provided through the Ivey Business School's Plan for Excellence.

Cases prepared by individuals outside the Ivey Business School include, "Banking on the Internet: Bank in Germany," written by T. Jelassi and A. Enders (INSEAD); "Autobytel and General Motore: David and Goliath," written by S. Dutta, A. De Meyer, and S. Kunduri (INSEAD): "Celebrity Sightings," written by A. De Meyer, S. Dutta, and L. Demeester (INSEAD); "Ford Motor Co.: Supply Chain Strategy," written by R. Austin (Harvard); and "Reuters' Internet Strategy (A) and (B)" by S. Rangan and B. Coleman (INSEAD). We are grateful to these individuals and their institutions for allowing us to include their cases in this book.

Finally, we thank the numerous managers who invited us into their companies, allowed us to ask dozens of pertinent as well as impertinent questions, and shared their time and resources with us so that we might create case studies of their organizations. Without their willing cooperation and assistance, this book would not have been possible.

Sid Huff
Michael Wade
Scott Schneberger

March 2001

Contents

Chapter 1

Introduction

In the past five or six years, the phrase "electronic commerce" has entered the popular vocabulary with a vengeance. This phrase and the basic principles underlying it were largely unknown prior to about 1995. That year, however, marked the beginning of a new era: the "age of the Internet." And with the Internet has come electronic commerce as we think of it today.

Computers and communications networks have been a part of business for decades. Today, however, information and communication technologies (ICT) are no longer just a support mechanism (for data processing or information systems); rather, they now have become the very *medium* of business. A few years ago, very few managers used electronic mail to communicate with business associates in other companies on a regular basis; *very* few people in organizations had ever even *heard* of a "Web page"; and almost nobody would have thought it possible to build a huge business, such as Amazon.com, based firmly upon something called the Internet.

We are seeing the beginning of a true paradigm shift. From the early stages of exploration in the mid-1990s, to the over-the-top intoxication associated with stratospheric valuations and willy-nilly IPOs of the late 1990s, to the cold reality bath of *de*valuations starting in the second half of 2000, the paradigm shift continues today. The growth in awareness of and use of the Internet may well be seen by future historians as the most incredible technology story of all time.

SOME BACKGROUND

The roots of electronic commerce developed over two decades ago, with what was then called "electronic data interchange," or EDI. EDI was driven primarily by the recognition that firms in transactional economic relationships were wasting time and money by printing, transferring, then having to re-key interorganizational transaction data from one firm's computer to the other's. To avoid this cumbersome process, a few firms worked together to agree on common formats and structures for exchanging computer-based data. For example, a company might write its payroll data onto a reel of magnetic tape, which would then be taken to the company's bank and read by the bank's computers, from which checks were printed out and mailed. Exchanging reels of computer tape was eventually replaced by the use of telecommunication networks, but the principle was the same: computer-to-computer electronic data interchange.

Following the early experimentation and adoption of ad hoc EDI, standards bodies—principally ANSI in North America and the United Nations in Europe, Asia, and elsewhere—came forward to create sets of data interchange standards, used by most organizations doing EDI today.

Originally, EDI was limited to nonfinancial transactions: for example, order placements and acknowledgments. Payments were still handled the old-fashioned way, usually by printing and mailing paper checks. Initially, there was sufficient uncertainty about the security and reliability of EDI that most managers could not stomach the idea of actually sending (or receiving) *money* electronically. Over time, however, it became clear that unless the financial side of a firm's business transactions were included in its EDI processes, it would only be reaping a portion of the potential benefit that EDI promised.

Hence, in recent years, more and more organizations have undertaken to combine their financial and nonfinancial business transactions together into complete electronic relationships with their business partners. Frequently this included employing electronic mail for unstructured communications, as well as EDI for structured transactions, and EFT—or electronic funds transfer—for financial payments. This larger concept—the complete business-to-business electronic relationship—became known as *electronic commerce*. But in those days, electronic commerce was solely a business-to-business endeavor. Consumers were not in the picture.

THE RISE OF THE INTERNET

The rise of the Internet as a business mechanism during the past few years has again changed the meaning of electronic commerce. Today the concept of electronic commerce is often equated with "doing business over the Internet." Interestingly, the Internet, which has existed in one form or another since 1969, has been used as a business medium for decades. But the scale of business was so small, and the participants so few and so specialized in their technical interests, that very few people noticed or cared. Two critical events changed this: One was the abolition of the so-called Acceptable Use Policy; the other was the invention of the World Wide Web.

The Acceptable Use Policy (AUP) was established in the late 1980s, when the U.S.-based National Science Foundation (NSF) assumed the responsibility for partially funding the Internet backbone. In return for providing public money to fund the Internet backbone, the NSF demanded that the Internet (specifically, the Internet backbone—which for practical purposes meant the entire Internet) *could not be used for commercial purposes.* The NSF relinquished its funding role in the early 1990s and soon after the AUP was dropped. This opened the Internet floodgates to the world of business.

However, the Internet as a medium for business would not have progressed very far if it had continued to be as user-unfriendly as it was in the 1980s or early 1990s. The world needed a new friendly Internet interface that was intuitive, graphical, and, above all, simple to use. Tim Berners-Lee, a computer scientist working at CERN high-energy physics lab in Geneva, thought so too. In 1991, he and a few of his colleagues invented what we now call the World Wide Web (WWW). Along with the basic architecture of the WWW, they also created a new kind of program for interacting with the Internet, the Web *browser.* Shortly thereafter, the first graphical web browser, Mosaic, was developed and introduced by a group working at a research center at the University of Illinois in 1993. One of the people involved in the early work on Mosaic was Mark Andreesen, who later, with his friend Eric Bina, left to form the company Netscape Communications Corp. and develop the groundbreaking Netscape Navigator web browser. Some time later Microsoft Corp. followed suit with its own browser, Internet Explorer. The Web browser quickly emerged as the key mechanism making possible mass access to, and acceptance of, the Internet.

The WWW and the Web browser were developed initially to make it easier for physicists and other researchers to more easily share technical information. As bright as they were, those pioneers at CERN had no idea that their brainchild would soon change the world of business. In fact they probably would have been aghast at the very thought. Nonetheless, during the past half-decade, their brainchild, the World Wide Web, has become *the* backbone for global electronic commerce.

People are sometimes confused about the difference between the Internet and the Web. Imagine a highway network as an infrastructure on which numerous services operate—such as shipping of goods (trucks), personal transportation (automobiles), exercise (bicycles), and so forth. The Internet may be compared to the highway network (an "information highway," to borrow an overused phrase) while the World Wide Web is a *service* that operates *on* the highway network. Numerous other services also operate on the Internet, including electronic mail, newsgroups, file transfer (FTP), and more recently Internet chat and Internet telephone (voice-over-IP). The service termed the World Wide Web, however, continues to dominate the Internet, in part because the other popular Internet services can be executed within the confines of a Web browser.

The WWW and associated software, mainly the well-known Web browsers, have made the Internet broadly accessible, enjoyable, and useful. Furthermore, the creation and growth of thousands of Internet service provider companies, or ISPs, have brought access to the Internet within local-phone-call reach of most people in developed countries; developing nations are also moving quickly to provide their citizenry with access to the Internet as well.

ELECTRONIC COMMERCE

These two streams—business-to-business, EDI-centered electronic commerce and individual use of the Internet and the WWW—came together in the mid-1990s. 1995 is usually cited as the year in which the Internet first began to be taken seriously as a basis for commerce. Today, the roots of electronic commerce in business-to-business EDI transactions are largely ignored by the business press; the WWW-based, business-to-consumer side of electronic commerce garners almost all of the popular attention, while Web-based business-to-business e-commerce actually accounts for most of the revenues.

The growth of electronic commerce has given rise to a plethora of new terminology. Figure 1 below illustrates the relationship among a number of the new terms.

FIGURE 1 Relationship among Terms and Concepts

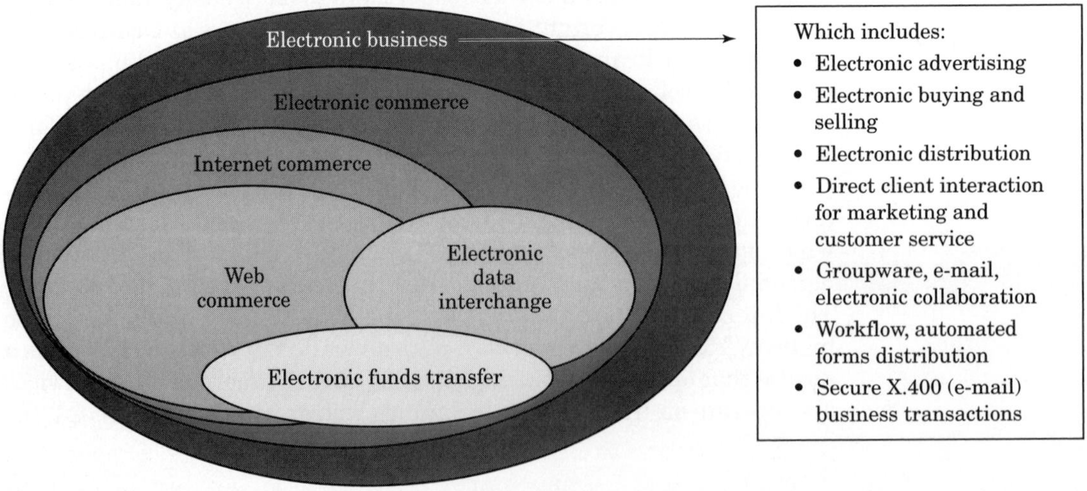
Electronic business
Electronic commerce
Internet commerce
Web commerce
Electronic data interchange
Electronic funds transfer
Which includes:
• Electronic advertising
• Electronic buying and selling
• Electronic distribution
• Direct client interaction for marketing and customer service
• Groupware, e-mail, electronic collaboration
• Workflow, automated forms distribution
• Secure X.400 (e-mail) business transactions

The largest oval is labeled "electronic business." Simply put, this includes everything having to do with the application of information and communication technologies (ICT) to the conduct of business between organizations or from company to consumer. Within the electronic business oval is a smaller oval labeled "electronic commerce." This highlights the fact that there are numerous forms of business-related ICT-based interactions that can occur between businesses, or between a business and an end consumer, which do not directly concern buying and selling (i.e., commerce). Only those forms of interaction having to do with commerce are included in the electronic commerce oval. This includes advertising of products or services, electronic shopping, and direct after-sales support. It would not include such things as interorganizational collaboration using ICT-based collaboration systems for the development of a new product.

Within the electronic commerce oval is a smaller oval labeled "Internet commerce." This reflects the fact that electronic commerce need not be conducted only over the Internet. In fact a great deal of business-to-business electronic commerce is still conducted over private networks, using primarily traditional EDI channels and value-added network (VAN) service providers. This is changing, as more and more companies adopt the Internet for some or all of their business-to-business electronic commerce, but it will be many years before the Internet totally displaces the VANs.

Within the Internet commerce domain lies an even smaller subset, termed "Web commerce." This is the component of electronic commerce conducted strictly over the World Wide Web. The WWW is not the only way of using the Internet for commercial interactions. Electronic mail, for example, serves well for certain forms of electronic commerce. As another example, software may be conveniently sold over the Internet using the file transfer protocol (FTP) for product distribution. Nevertheless, the Web is clearly the dominant medium for the large majority of Internet commerce today. Furthermore, since modern web browsers incorporate other Internet applications, including electronic mail and file transfer via FTP, all under one hood, users today have the perception that they are relying solely on the Web even as they send and receive e-mail, transfer files, and conduct other forms of Internet application that used to be conducted using separate application programs.

Two other important domains are represented in Figure 1. One is labeled "electronic data interchange." It is shown to lie fully within the electronic commerce realm, but it overlaps the other domains of web commerce, Internet commerce, and electronic funds transfer. As discussed earlier, EDI precedes modern-day electronic commerce by almost two decades. It is clearly a type of electronic commerce, since EDI comprises standard formats for a variety of business commercial transactions such as orders, invoices, shipping documents, and the like. But EDI can be conducted either over private networks or over the Internet. If conducted over the Internet, it may or may not make use of the World Wide Web. Also, it may or may not involve aspects of electronic funds transfer.

Finally, the oval labeled "electronic funds transfer," or EFT, bears much the same relationship with the other domains as does EDI. It is an aspect of electronic commerce, hence is represented as falling fully within the electronic commerce oval. It can be conducted over the Internet or over private networks, and, if over the Internet, may or may not be conducted over the Web. Also, EFT may be executed using EDI standards, or alternately may be done in non-EDI fashion.

With that as background, let us turn to the cases that comprise the main part of this book.

OVERVIEW OF THE CASES

The cases in this book have been grouped into eight segments:

- E-Commerce Infrastructure
- Sourcing of E-Commerce Capabilities
- Financial Systems and Choices
- Business-to-Consumer E-Commerce
- Business-to-Business E-Commerce and E-Commerce Strategy
- Virtual Work
- Virtual Communities
- Social and Legal Issues

E-Commerce Infrastructure

The first major section of the book addresses infrastructure issues. Building an appropriate technical infrastructure to support electronic commerce in a company is *sine qua non*—you simply cannot *do* electronic commerce without it. Making the appropriate choices is critical.

Case	Topic
HighWired.com: Hardware Decisions	Choosing an appropriate hardware solution/ configuration to support rapid growth
WaveRider Communications, Inc.: The Wireless Last Mile	Evaluating the business case for solving the "last mile" problem using a fixed wireless solution
Canadian Imperial Bank of Commerce Wireless Strategy	Developing a wireless banking strategy
Cisco Systems Inc.: Managing Corporate Growth Using an Intranet	Evaluating the strategic uses of corporate intranets

Sourcing of E-Commerce Capabilities

This section addresses the question of sourcing—in effect, whether to develop one's e-commerce facilities using in-house staff or to outsource the work. Part of the sourcing conundrum companies face today concerns the issue of ASPs—application service providers. ASPs are in the business of renting the use of certain software applications to other companies, usually charging a transaction-based usage fee.

Case	Topic
OP4.com: Choosing a Website Design Agency	Choosing an appropriate outsourcing partner for website design and development
Enerline Restorations Inc.: Stay with an ASP?	Choosing between using an ASP provider or bringing IT in-house
SalesDriver: The Lorimer Request	Selling ASP services in a rapid-growth environment

Financial Systems and Choices

A huge amount of interest and attention has been paid to the financial side of the new economy, including issues of securing venture capital, providing virtual financial services, and securing financial transactions done over the Internet. The cases in this section address the issue of financing e-commerce activities and other financial aspects of e-commerce.

Case	Topic
CYBERplex Interactive Media	Sourcing various rounds of financing options for an e-commerce start-up
Grocer Gateway.com	Evaluating a business plan from the perspective of a venture capitalist
First Virtual Holdings Incorporated (A)	Exploring online payment options and infrastructure
Banking on the Internet: The Advance Bank in Germany	Evaluating the strategic choices around setting up a virtual/branchless bank

Business-to-Consumer E-Commerce

Electronic commerce activities between businesses and consumers have achieved great public awareness over the past five years. Unquestionably the most notorious of all the business-to-consumer companies has been Amazon.com, which started as a Internet-based bookseller, then branched into many other lines of business, and more recently has scaled back its expanding operations toward a more manageable and more profitable core set of businesses. Thousands of other Amazon "wanna-bes" have been launched in the past five years, and many are now scaling back, reorganizing, or have gone out of business altogether. The retail end of electronic commerce is proving to be a great deal more difficult than people originally thought.

Case	Topic
Homegrocer.com	Evaluating an Internet grocery operation
Auto-By-Tel and General Motors: David and Goliath	Comparing strategies for online and offline automobile vendors
Looks.com (A): Building Asia's First Health, Beauty, and Fashion E-Tailer	Relating channel conflict and disintermediation in the Asian cosmetics market
Blinds To Go: Evaluating the BlindsToGo.com Retail E-Commerce Venture	Evaluating online performance through website statistics

Business-to-Business E-Commerce and E-Commerce Strategy

The business-to-business side of electronic commerce is much larger, in terms of both dollar and transaction volume, than is the business-to-consumer side. However, it receives substantially less press, presumably because it doesn't involve consumers directly. All the cases in this section address various aspects of B2B e-commerce.

Case	Topic
Ford Motor Company: Supply Chain Strategy	Using emerging technologies to integrate the supply chain
Metropolitan Life Insurance: E-Commerce	Developing an e-commerce strategy in the insurance industry
eLance.com: preventing Disintermediation	Controlling online transactions to minimize disintermediation
Reuters' Internet Strategy (A)	Assessing the impacts of e-commerce on large content provider (self-cannibalization)
Reuters' Internet Strategy (B)	Developing an e-commerce strategy for an information content supplier

Virtual Work

Web-based businesses have been accompanied by the development of Web-based working styles. Virtual work refers to the notion of incorporating information and communication technologies so thoroughly into an organization's workstyle that distance becomes irrelevant, company boundaries become vague or disappear altogether, and the concept of an office broadens to include airplane seats, hotel rooms, front seats of automobiles, and in fact anywhere a wireless-connected laptop computer can be used.

Case	Topic
eLance.com: Projects versus Personnel	Deciding on priorities and evaluating the tension between focus and flexibility
Guru.com: Power for the Independent Professional	Evaluating a virtual work firm's business model
Scantran	Understanding the costs and benefits of running an e-commerce from home

Virtual Communities

Virtual communities are collections of individuals who associate over an extended time period primarily using the Internet. Although virtual communities existed prior to the rise in popularity of the Internet (e.g., The "Whole Earth 'Lectronic Link" (WELL) has existed since the mid-1980s—see www.well.com), the recognition of virtual communities as a commercially important new organizational form is only a few years old.

Case	Topic
Stockgroup Interactive Media	Evaluating the business model of an infomediary and how to leverage a virtual community
Celebrity Sightings	Generating revenue from a virtual community

Social and Legal Issues

Finally, a number of issues concerning electronic commerce have arisen in the past five years. Dominant among the social issues is the question of privacy. Appropriately managing the privacy of virtual customers or business partners is of paramount importance to firms conducting e-commerce today. Also, numerous challenging ethical issues exist in the e-commerce domain: The trials of Napster, the music file-sharing company, mainly center on the ethics of freely sharing copyrighted content. Finally, there is a growing thicket of legal issues facing anyone venturing into the world of e-commerce.

Case	Topic
DoubleClick Inc.: Gathering Customer Intelligence	Generating value from customer information without contravening ethical or legal privacy standards
Canadian Imperial Bank of Commerce: Digital Employee Privacy	Assessing whether or not to monitor employee communications and how to deal with infractions
iCraveTV.com: A New-Media Upstart	Exploring the limits of intellectual property rights for online broadcasting
Open Text Preferred Listings	Exploring what is, and is not, acceptable behavior for content providers
Euro-Arab Management School	Investigating issues in running a virtual university

Chapter 2

E-Commerce Infrastructure

It must not be forgotten that the *e* in e-commerce is "electronic"—computer-based, digital electronics in almost all cases. Although e-commerce is often described as a new paradigm in business with vast new opportunities for innovation and application, it clearly did not occur, and could not occur, without the infrastructure electronically linking information systems and their users. Wonderment with e-commerce opportunities and the rate of innovation, adoption, and adaptation can overshadow the underlying technical infrastructure that gives it life and spawns newer opportunities. Technical innovations continue to amaze us and inspire novel business uses, and then just as quickly are taken for granted. Internet infrastructure features come at us at dizzying speed, in specialized technical language we struggle to understand, only to be rapidly eclipsed by follow-on innovations. But the magnitude of e-commerce dependence on Internet infrastructure continues to grow.

In the e-business world, managers need to know the fundamentals of e-commerce infrastructure—the terminology, the issues, and the industry. This knowledge will enable them to discuss e-commerce issues with technologists, identify business opportunities and threats, and plan and manage infrastructure procurement.

This chapter covers e-commerce infrastructure issues with four cases concerning hardware, software, data communications, wireless data communications, and intranets. The first case, "HighWired.com: Hardware Decisions," addresses e-commerce hardware infrastructure issues. HighWired.com, a provider of content generation tools and web space to high schools, was experiencing tremendous growth. The company wished to expand in a way that maintained its current service levels and minimized overall downtime (which was currently very close to zero).

What and how should its performance be measured? What technical and practical alternatives did HighWired have to improve response times? What were the issues it needed to consider?

The second case, "WaveRider Communications, Inc.: The Last Mile," addresses the powerful issue of broadband connectivity for residential users. Users are demanding higher bandwidth Internet access, e-commerce businesses are yearning for the features they could provide with widespread broadband, and communications conglomerates are hungering for the revenue those last-mile connections could bring. What's the problem? There are many hurdles—some technical, some financial, some architectural, some user-demand. This case presents one company with a technical option and a goal to capture 5 to 10 percent of the worldwide wireless Internet access market.

The third case, "Canadian Imperial Bank of Commerce Wireless Strategy," follows a large bank's decision-making process regarding the development and implementation of a wireless banking strategy. From being ahead of the curve, the bank finds itself playing catch-up because other financial institutions have already implemented competing wireless strategies. Among the decisions that have to be made are which wireless devices to support, which technical protocols to follow, which banking and nonbanking services to offer and with whom, if anyone, to partner. The case includes a technical primer and a glossary of technical terms related to wireless communications.

Finally, the fourth case in this chapter, "Cisco Systems Inc.: Managing Corporate Growth Using an Intranet," examines how an Internet-based infrastructure can be used to support corporate communications. The fact that Cisco popularized the routers and switches that enable the Internet to exist today is not a coincidence in this case. The case brings out why this infrastructure is ideal for Cisco's corporate organization and strategy.

HighWired.com: Hardware Decisions

By Professor Scott Schneberger and Ken Mark

Introduction

"Due to our blistering growth, we were approaching our peak load capacity in June," thought William (Bill) Doctor, vice president (VP) of product development for HighWired.com. Headquartered in Watertown, near Boston, Massachusetts, HighWired.com's network had grown from 1,000 member high schools to over 12,000 schools in 50 states and 72 countries in only 13 months.

> I expect that growth will continue at this pace and I want to ensure that we strike the right balance between low response time and minimal downtime, and acceptable hardware costs. Any changes we choose to make must be made by the time school starts in September 2000.

Doctor wanted to confirm that his recommendation to use multiple servers[1] with redundant network storage devices[2] attached was the optimal solution.

Background on HighWired.com

HighWired.com provided to high school students and teachers a range of free services to enable school interaction on a personalized school website. These free services included free, unlimited website hosting for high school home pages, a suite of publishing tools that simplified content publishing, e-mail and messaging capability, and a selection of sports-related team management tools that allowed for the tracking of high school sports-related statistics.

Launched in January 1998 as HighWired.net, the now renamed HighWired.com provided online publishing systems for the high school sector. Co-founded by Mark Johnson and Matthew Flaherty, High-Wired.com's goal was to aggregate the largest community of high school websites in order to attract corporate sponsors and vendors interested in accessing the high school market. HighWired.com's goal was to reach 30 million page views in the month of December 2000, up from its cur-

IVEY Ken Mark and Professor Scott Schneberger prepared this case solely to provide material for class discussion. The authors do not intend to illustrate either effective or ineffective handling of a managerial situation. The authors may have disguised certain names and other identifying information to protect confidentiality.

Ivey Management Services prohibits any form of reproduction, storage or transmittal without its written permission. This material is not covered under authorization from CanCopy or any reproduction rights organization. To order copies or request permission to reproduce materials, contact Ivey Publishing, Ivey Management Services, c/o Richard Ivey School of Business, The University of Western Ontario, London, Ontario, Canada, N6A 3K7; phone (519) 661-3208; fax (519) 661-3882; e-mail cases@ivey.uwo.ca.

Copyright © 2000, Ivey Management Services.   Version: (A) 2001-01-16

---

[1]Servers—received incoming data requests, retrieved the information from itself, a database or a network storage device, then "served" the request to the customer. Servers had limited, unscalable storage capacity.

[2]Network storage devices—acted much like hard drives in computers, storing information that could be accessed by any device on the network.

rent five to 10 million monthly page views. It anticipated revenues to grow from under US $5 million in 2000 to US $10 million to US $15 million in 2001, to US $30 million in 2002, reaching profitability between 2001 and 2002.

Because of the rapidly changing nature of its industry, HighWired.com had many competitors, although three seemed to stand out as direct threats: Ysource, NSchool, and HighSports. Each focused on their niche—either sports or publishing, but none competed against High-Wired.com as a "community" site.

"We are the only company that is approaching the high school online market from a comprehensive point of view," stated Don Young, president of HighWired.com. "We've decided to build our four communities—school, sports, alumni, educators—at the same time," continued Young. There were a few dozen companies that focused on serving the student markets (grade school, high school and university) and High-Wired.com's goal was, as articulated by Young, "to be the last one standing." Young believed that in order to survive as an e-commerce company in this space, one needed to be able to articulate, implement and finance a strategy. It was more about having staying power rather than any one particular performance metric. "Companies who simply do not have one of those three things will not survive," explained Young. He noted gravely, "Judgment Day comes really frequently in the Internet space."

By providing "online publishing tools," HighWired.com was designed to be easy for students and teachers to use. Needing no prior training in software or HTML, students would be able to post articles to their customized HighWired.com paper from any web browser, and within seconds, teachers could review and approve articles for publication.

According to Johnson, "Anyone can learn HighWired.com in 10 minutes. It's just point, click, publish. Plus, teachers have complete control every step of the way. Nothing goes on their site that they don't expressly approve." Once published, student articles could be viewed by other students, parents and the entire online world.

HighWired.com employed 120 people, 40 of whom were engineers. Of those engineers, five were in systems infrastructure (hardware), and 35 were in product development.

William Doctor, VP of Product Development

William Doctor is the vice president of product development. Doctor directed all technology-related initiatives at HighWired.com, including development, engineering, quality assurance, and network and database architecture. Prior to joining HighWired.com, Doctor was vice president and chief technology officer of SOFTBANK Marketing Solutions, a global provider of Internet-based technology and services for major personal computer manufacturers. Before working at SOFTBANK, Doctor held the position of general manager and vice president at Information Access Center, a service company specializing in the development and hosting of online applications. Doctor has also held key positions at Lotus One Source, Datext, Inc., Ziff-Davis Publishing Company, and The Thomson Corporation. He graduated from the College of the Holy Cross with a bachelor of arts degree in mathematics, magna cum laude, Phi Beta Kappa.

Highwired.com Products

Johnson and Flaherty had identified five major areas of high school life: classrooms, guidance offices, newspapers, sports teams, and student activities. At launch, HighWired.com had created and offered a publishing product to meet the needs of each of these segments. Along with simplified publishing tools and unlimited server space for their articles, "My HighWired," which consisted of message boards and free e-mail, was also offered to students.

Gary Bergman, director of educational technology, school programs and support services for the New York City Board of Education, said, "Like all school districts, we're trying to integrate more technology into the curriculum. HighWired.com is perfect for us because it treats technology as a tool, not as a subject." To support this initiative, in early 1998, a cluster of New York City high schools were piloting the High-Wired.com system.

Growth and Venture Capital Financing

The growing network of high schools had achieved its 1,000th member by May 11, 1999, drawing schools from 50 states and 18 foreign countries. In addition, HighWired.com took the opportunity to announce that it had launched another suite of products, the "Student Activity Site Builder," and the "Classroom Site Builder" (website building tools). As well, the company announced sponsorship relationships with The New York Times Learning Network, Lycos, the Family Education Network, and The Learning Company. HighWired.com also began cosponsoring the Student Online Journalism Awards with the EdPress Association. Flaherty commented that "these top-tier partners know HighWired.com is the definitive channel to reach high school educators and students."

In late July 1999, HighWired.com announced that it had raised US$7 million in venture funding led equally by Charles River Ventures and North Bridge Venture Partners. By then, the network counted 1,900 high schools in all 50 states and 32 countries. Its 5,000th school was achieved in January 2000—two years after the company was founded. High-Wired.com raised a second round of US$30 million in March 2000, and concurrently launched "HighWired.com Sports," an online team management tool for high school coaches to help them track their team information, such as rosters, statistics, schedules and scores. By July 2000, HighWired.com had achieved over 12,000 member schools in its community.

History of Technology Decisions at Highwired.com

With an angel round of financing, HighWired.com initially chose Intel-based hardware running Windows NT[3] and used Microsoft's SQL Server (US$1,000) as a database. This was done to manage the initial costs, as other options were more costly by degrees of magnitude.

Costing HighWired.com in the low thousands of dollars to set up, the Intel-based hardware was used to run HighWired.com's main application, Vignette StoryServer.[4] Because HighWired.com aimed to provide content management tools and serve content to hundreds of thousands of people, a move was made within the first few months to switch to Sun Solaris hardware equipment.

A compelling reason was the fact that Vignette's software support personnel were more familiar with Sun equipment. HighWired then brought on board two Sun E250 servers, which were in the mid- to low-price range in the Sun family to run the web server and the StoryServer software, with communication links between both machines.

By doing this, HighWired.com chose what it believed was a stable platform that would match their software, although there were commercially available Intel, Dell or Compaq servers that were, on paper, faster and less expensive (e.g., recent Sun server chips were running at 450 MHz versus Intel's 700 MHz chips).

To minimize service disruption due to hardware damage, HighWired.com hosted all its hardware at Exodus Communications, which had built out huge data centers with Internet bandwidth, fire suppression, high security, redundant power, and air-conditioning. These fixed costs were paid on a per-square-footage basis. At the end of the day, it was just a storage space, but it would have been too costly for HighWired.com to build out a small data centre. Doctor noted, "You don't want people to know that you have the family jewels behind a thin wall at your office." There were many national and regional data centre services, and they offered different levels of service, type and cost. Since HighWired.com did not have the facilities or expertise in-house to run a "7 × 24" operation—providing bandwidth for itself, fire-

---

[3]Windows NT—operating system through which software is accessed and used. Think of the relationship between Microsoft Windows and the Microsoft Word software.

[4]Third-party software that HighWired.com chose to buy, instead of developing it themselves.

proofing, climate-control, power, redundant power, water protection, leak detection, security—it decided to outsource hardware hosting to Exodus.

Doctor continued,

> We have a Linux[5] "box" (US$5,000) that is a packet filter,[6] sits in front of our two servers (US$15,000 each), and communicates with our database machine (US$15,000), and three local disk storage devices[7] (US$5,000 each). We were originally storing our servers right in the office! In the beginning, there was a low traffic load (up to one-half million page views per day could be handled by the original system) on the product because our service was in the early days of being launched, and there was a level of tinkering that had to go on as a result of our learning process,[8] so unfortunately, things were not 100 per cent reliable or stable. We've since moved our hardware storage to Exodus' data center[9] in Waltham. That is because we don't want to keep our mission-critical servers in a low-security environment.

CURRENT HIGHWIRED.COM HARDWARE CONFIGURATION

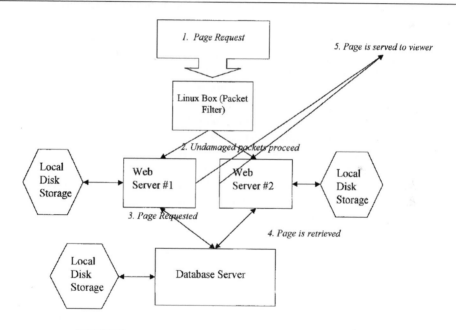

---

[5]Linux was an open-architecture operating system originally created by Linus Torvalds in the early 1990s. Linux's key feature was that it was designed to permit individual programmers to tinker with the operating system code.

[6]Packet filter—monitors "data packets" coming into the server and refuses access to deformed packets, acting much like a coffee filter.

[7]Local disk storage devices stored information much like a hard drive and were able to be accessed only by the machine to which they were attached.

[8]Engineers were able to increase server processing speed by reconfiguring the dials on the server.

[9]Data storage centers kept expensive hardware in a climate-controlled, secure environment.

Doctor noted that there were not any non-critical hardware components as they were all linked to one another. The only distinction that could be drawn from a service perspective was internal versus external requests. If it came down to a choice, it would be preferable for High-Wired.com to forgo internal e-mail for a couple of hours instead of affecting external traffic to the live, commercial HighWired.com site.

Bandwidth was the only variable cost. In HighWired.com's case, it was charged by Exodus for a one megabit per second threshold, sampled every 15 minutes. At a cost ranging in the hundreds of dollars, it was not significant relative to hardware costs.

Site Performance Metrics

There were two basic performance measures for websites: response time and down time. A site's response time indicated the time lapse between data request and data delivery, and down time indicated the amount of time a site was not responding to requests.

Response Time

HighWired.com used a third-party website performance measurement service called Keynote. (See Exhibit 1.) Keynote had servers around the world that measured performance at HighWired.com's URLs, noting the amount of time it took for their requests to be filled. Keynote thus played the role of an end user.

These results were benchmarked against a basket of companies called the Keynote 40, the largest Web companies including Yahoo!, ZD-Net and AOL. Thus, customers of Keynote could measure their site's performance against this index. However, customers had to account for the fact that their sites may not serve the same content as the static pages that Yahoo!, or ZDNet might serve; requests for dynamic, rich content would take more time to fill.

Doctor elaborated,

> We compare our response time relative to our brethren. Since I get the report nightly, it does give me a good representation of the prior day's activities. We've also written our own tool that goes out and measures load and response time on our servers. That tells me what the load is on our back-end database servers, and basic disk space utilization. (See Exhibit 2.)

Down Time

HighWired.com targeted its site to be up 99.8 per cent of the time. There were two types of down time: scheduled and unscheduled. Scheduled down time allowed engineers a window to perform systems infrastructure changes. A third-party service, Red Alert (see Exhibit 3), monitored HighWired.com's site from a service perspective. High-

EXHIBIT 1   Keynote—Daily Performance Report

[Keynote—The Internet Performance Authority]
DAILY PERFORMANCE REPORT—April 8th, 2000

Alias	www2.highwired.com/SchoolCentral/HomePage/0,3275,3,00
URL 1:	http://www2.highwired.com/SchoolCentral/HomePage/0,3275,3,00.html
Agent Group	US 10 NT02
Measurement Type	Full Page
Valid Measurements	734
Measurements with Errors	2
Trimmed Measurements	0
Total Measurements	736

PERFORMANCE   [*][*][*] AVAILABILITY   [*][*][*][*][*]

Your Page	8.78 seconds	Your Page	95.73%
Keynote Business 40	2.82 seconds	Keynote Business 40	98.33%

Download Time Distribution   Top 5 Errors

0–0.5 seconds	0.00%	1. Connection Timed
0.5–2 seconds	2.61%	1101 Out 2
2–8 seconds	57.84%	2. DNS Lookup Failure
8–30 seconds	25.41%	3. Content Error
30+ seconds	14.14%	4. Page Load Failure

Alias	www2.highwired.com
URL 2:	http://www2.highwired.com/SchoolCentral/HomePage/1,3275,3,00.html
Agent Group	S 10 NT02
Measurement Type	Full Page
Valid Measurements	11
Measurements with Errors	35
Trimmed Measurements	0
Total Measurements	36

PERFORMANCE   [*][*][*] AVAILABILITY   [*][*]

Your Page	3.10 seconds	Your Page	96.60%
Keynote Business 40 seconds	2.82	Keynote Business 40	98.33%

Download Time Distribution   Top 5 Errors

0–0.5 seconds	0.00%	9999	Content error	23
0.5–2 seconds	14.35%		Connection Timed	
2–8 seconds	84.25%	1101	Out	1
8–30 seconds	1.41%		Host/Net	
30+ seconds	0.00%	1103	Unreachable 1	

Source: HighWired.com, company records. Unabridged.

EXHIBIT 2   Production Status

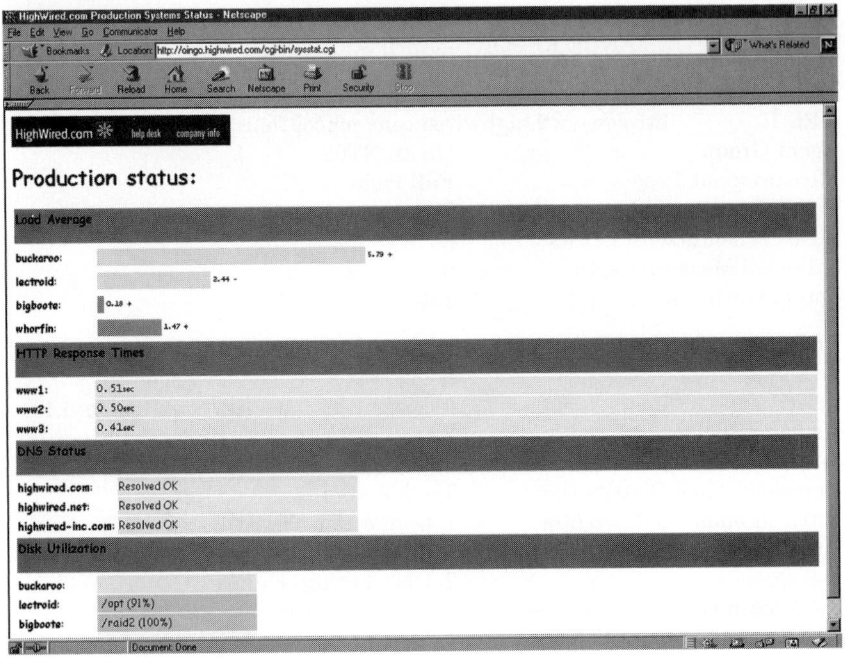

Source: HighWired.com, company records.

Wired.com could run as many Red Alert tests on its site as it wished to pay for. HighWired.com would create a test script and send it to Red Alert who would then execute the request multiple times per hour, day or week. For example, the test would see if a user could log in successfully; if the test failed, an e-mail would be sent to HighWired.com. There were 15 different tests that were run by Red Alert on HighWired.com's site, including dynamic page creation tests, authentication verification tests, primary domain server tests and secondary domain server tests. Thus, HighWired.com had access to the results of 96 checks per day, four per hour.

Server Configuration Options

Generally speaking, there were five ways to minimize response time and down time:

- Utilizing software to make the current complement of servers more efficient.
- Purchasing a "big box" server.
- Replicating data onto separate servers.

EXHIBIT 3　Red Alert Report

Monitoring Statistics for April 18th, 2000
HighWired.com
Overall Account Performance
- -
For YOUR account: 1344 checks, 4 errors ==> 99.7024% accessibility
Average for ALL Red Alert accounts: 98.7694% accessibility
Accessibility of Monitored Devices
- -
14 devices monitored on this day, listed from
lowest to highest accessibility:

CommTouch New Messages (URL)
96 checks, 4 errors ==> 95.8333% accessibility

Dynamic Page (www1) (URL)
96 checks, 0 errors ==> 100.0000% accessibility

Secondary DNS (2) (domain name server)
96 checks, 0 errors ==> 100.0000% accessibility

Secondary DNS (1) (domain name server)
96 checks, 0 errors ==> 100.0000% accessibility

Home Office DSL (unspecified TCP device)
96 checks, 0 errors ==> 100.0000% accessibility

www2 auth (URL)
96 checks, 0 errors ==> 100.0000% accessibility

www1 auth (URL)
96 checks, 4 errors ==> 95.833% accessibility

Dynamic Page (www2) (URL)
96 checks, 0 errors ==> 100.0000% accessibility

Primary DNS (domain name server)
96 checks, 0 errors ==> 100.0000% accessibility

Allstater Home (URL)
96 checks, 0 errors ==> 100.0000% accessibility

HighWired.com Internal Mail (SMTP email server)
96 checks, 0 errors ==> 100.0000% accessibility

CommTouch SMTP (2) (SMTP email server)
96 checks, 0 errors ==> 100.0000% accessibility

CommTouch SMTP (1) (SMTP email server)
96 checks, 0 errors ==> 100.0000% accessibility

Internal POP Mail (POP3 server)
96 checks, 0 errors ==> 100.0000% accessibility

END OF REPORT
Red Alert

Source: HighWired.com, company records.

- Dividing data between separate servers.
- Geographically locating replicated servers, allowing for regional handling of data requests.

Reviewing these options, Doctor concluded that there was not any better software option to consider, given HighWired.com's financial and technical commitment to Vignette and Oracle. Exchanging these packages for something else was not his recommendation. What he was doing, however, was optimizing existing code and performing more frequent code reviews before code was deployed into production. He had senior staff optimizing StoryServer templates, SQL queries, and delving into the nuances of the hardware and networks to determine if there remained the possibility for further optimization. During the period of time before site capacity limits were being tested, High-Wired.com had the luxury of not having to worry about, as Doctor noted, "squeezing every inch out of every line of code, SQL query and server."

Doctor was reluctant to recommend purchasing one large server to meet HighWired.com's needs.

> Buying one big one of anything puts you into a situation where you have put all your eggs into one basket. If that server goes down, your site is hosed. It's better to have a site performing in a slightly degraded manner with the absence of a single server out of a group of servers than to be off air 100 per cent. Also, consider that software licensing can get very costly if you just buy one big server with plenty of CPUs (e.g., Oracle licensing). Lastly, most web software I have seen and used recommends an environment in which the load is distributed over many servers, as opposed to hitting one big monolithic server. Since we do not rely on heavy computing—we don't crunch numbers—there really is no real need for a single, big, super powerful box serving out the content.

Data currently was not replicated over servers. Rather, Doctor had built redundant, network-attached disk storage on which High-Wired.com stored content to which all servers pointed. By definition, all servers saw the same data and were kept seamlessly in synchronization with each other. As long as disk storage was big and fast enough, this strategy would work for HighWired.com. As for the fourth option, Doctor felt that it was not possible because HighWired.com had one Oracle database from which all content was drawn.

Doctor, however, was interested in the fifth option.

> This type of geographic routing of requests is a service offered by companies like Akamai and Mirror Image. These companies offer a service through which your most frequently used content is stored on their server infrastructure at numerous geographic locations. Requests for this cached content are fulfilled from these "local" servers as opposed to being serviced from a single site. Additionally and separately, Cisco also makes a box that would

allow us to do the routing of requests to geographic disparate data centers. To do the latter, you are in the big leagues because you have now basically duplicated your website into two (or more) physical locations. Thus, you have doubled your hardware infrastructure, your variable costs, and added WAN-data-synchronization as a problem that must be solved. All these issues are not issues if you have a big enough budget. But, hey, I'm a guy with wine tastes on a beer budget right now. The Akamai solution requires changes to our content so that their servers can intercept the appropriate parts of our page and content requests. And, given that our site is so hugely dynamic from a content perspective, Akamai doesn't really offer us a viable solution at this time.

Additional Hardware Recommendation

To optimize his response time and down time, Doctor recommended that HighWired.com replace its Linux packet filter with two Arrow-point CS 150 Web Switches (US$25,000 each), add one new web server (US$14,000 each), replace the current database server and add a second machine for redundancy (US$33,000 each), and replace local disk storage with a primary and secondary network storage device (US$45,000 each) to eliminate all single points of failure.

All our content from the database and StoryServer pages is stored on Network Appliance F720 Filer network storage devices. If you stored your database locally on a database machine, if your database machine goes down, you've got downtime. But by extracting data out one level, not having it stored locally, we will have, from an availability standpoint, much higher throughput than if we had the data stored locally. In fact, we could have any amount of data we want on our network. This adds scalability and availability.

The Web switches were load balancers, pieces of hardware that are placed in front of their web servers, taking incoming traffic, and using an algorithm to route traffic to the most appropriate Web server box. There were, however, many different types of algorithms to choose from, depending on how the load balancers were installed. One option could be what was known as the "Round Robin Algorithm" where packets of "requests" were allocated in order: the first Web server gets the first request, the second Web server gets the second request, and so on. This was not all together advantageous because the algorithm would not balance the load. Each request could require different processing resources. A "Round Robin Algorithm" would not account for different "page sessions" being served. For example, a static page was less taxing than a sophisticated database query where the server had to answer the query, create the page, then serve it. The latter took more time to complete and demonstrated that not all requests were created equal.

With literally millions of user requests to allocate, there was a real chance that a single server could get bogged down with complex requests. "Along with the load balancers," Doctor offered, "the Arrowpoint, CS150—content-smart Web switches could also do some elementary packet filtering."

Doctor preferred to, in his words, overengineer components. Since no one was certain of users' usage patterns, and audience numbers could change based on the results of press releases or marketing campaigns, Doctor did not want to lose end users due to site performance failures. These changes were expected to cost many times what HighWired.com paid for its current hardware setup. In addition, upgraded software licenses for the new configuration were expected to cost US$350,000 in total.

Anticipated Changes

Doctor did not expect that Oracle or Vignette StoryServer, their primary pieces of software, would change all that drastically since both were considered to be stable and robust. Changes were expected to be more rapid on the hardware side because in general, costs were going down even as processing speed increased.

The upcoming school year promised to be challenging for High-Wired.com as it aimed to garner 30 million page views in the month of December 2000. With his recommendation to purchase two Web switches, an additional Web server, a faster and more powerful primary database machine, a secondary database machine, primary and secondary network boxes and load balancers, Doctor felt that High-Wired.com would be well prepared.

WaveRider Communications, Inc.: The Wireless Last Mile

By Professor Scott Schneberger and Ken Mark

Introduction

"Would it be advantageous for us to seek alliances with rival Internet access technology companies?" questioned Charles Brown, vice president (VP) marketing for Toronto-based WaveRider Communications, Inc. It was March 2, 2000, and WaveRider had brought to market its "Last Mile Solution," offering Internet service providers (ISPs) the opportunity to provide wireless Internet access at broadband speeds in the unlicensed 2.4 gigahertz (GHz) spectrum. The wireless Internet access industry was still relatively untapped, and Brown was wondering if it made sense to seek an alliance with a competing technology company as WaveRider started its growth phase.

WaveRider, still in the start-up phase, aimed to provide five to 10 per cent of the worldwide wireless Internet access with a viable, scalable alternative to wired access in the unlicensed spectrum. The United States government allocated various spectrums for various uses, and both the 900 megahertz (MHz) and the 2.4 GHz spectrum were unlicensed, meaning that signals could be broadcast within those frequencies without having to apply for a broadcast license.[1]

Charles Brown

With 17 years of experience in the telecommunications and cable communications industries, Brown joined WaveRider in February 1998 as the firm's VP of marketing. In this role, he was responsible for the development and execution of WaveRider's overall marketing and product strategy. Before joining WaveRider, Brown was VP and chief information officer (CIO) of Clearnet Communications, and had worked at other telecommunications firms in the past. In addition, Brown had obtained his MBA degree from the Richard Ivey School of Business.

WaveRider Communications

Founded in 1997, WaveRider's mission was to become the leader in the global wireless information technology by developing, selling and supporting products that enabled wireless Internet service providers. During its first two years as a development stage company, WaveRider had raised US$27.5 million to finance ongoing product research and development, acquired U.S. Federal Communications Commission approval for its new products, and signed agreements and installations in over 30 countries. Counting over 100 employees by early 2000, WaveRider had begun to develop sales momentum. A difficult challenge that WaveRider faced was mustering the necessary

IVEY Ken Mark and Professor Scott Schneberger prepared this case solely to provide material for class discussion. The authors do not intend to illustrate either effective or ineffective handling of a managerial situation. The authors may have disguised certain names and other identifying information to protect confidentiality.

Ivey Management Services prohibits any form of reproduction, storage or transmittal without its written permission. This material is not covered under authorization from CanCopy or any reproduction rights organization. To order copies or request permission to reproduce materials, contact Ivey Publishing, Ivey Management Services, c/o Richard Ivey School of Business, The University of Western Ontario, London, Ontario, Canada, N6A 3K7; phone (519) 661-3208; fax (519) 661-3882; e-mail cases@ivey.uwo.ca.

Copyright © 2001, Ivey Management Services   Version: (A) 2001-02-07

---

[1]For a list of the U.S. fixed wireless spectrum allocations, see Exhibit 1.

EXHIBIT 1   1999 U.S. Fixed Wireless Spectrum Allocations

Name	*Frequency (GHz)*	*Allocation*
ISM (Industrial Scientific & Medical)	900 MHz	Unspecified
PCS (Personal Communication Service)	1.85–1.99 (6 bands)	A block: 30 MHz B block: 30 MHz C block: 30MHz (split in two) D block: 10 MHz E block: 10 MHz F block: 10 MHz
MDS (Multipoint Distribution Service)	2.15–2.162	2 channels
WCS (Wireless Communications Systems)	2.305–2.32 2.345–2.36	30 MHz in two 15 MHz bands
ISM (Industrial Scientific & Medical)	2.4	Unspecified
ITFS & MMDS (Instructional Television Fixed Service) (Multichannel Multipoint Distribution Service)	2.5–2.68	31 channels
ISM/U-NII (Industrial Scientific & Medical) (Unlicensed National Information Infrastructure)	5.7	5.15–5.25 GHz indoors 5.25-5.25 GHz campus 5.725–5.825 GHz community
DEMS (Digital Electronic Message Service)	24.25–24.45 25.05–25.25	400MHz in five of 40MHz channels
LMDS (Local Multipoint Distribution Service)	27.50–28.35 29.1-29.25 31.075–31.225 31.0–31.075 31.225-31.3	*A block (1150 MHz):* 27.50–28.35 29.1–29.25 31.075–31.225 *B block (150 MHz):* 31.0–31.075 31.225–31.3
38/39 GHz	28.6–39GHz	14 100 MHz blocks of 50 MHz blocks

Source: First Security Van Kasper Research Report, 2000.

resources to develop business opportunities. To remedy that issue, it had embarked on a partnership drive with resellers and technology installers in early 2000.

Brown commented,

Only 5 per cent of the North America population has access to high-speed service. The rest of the 95 percent has to deal with 28.8 kbps to 56 kbps. Outside of North America, 80 percent of the world has never heard a dial tone and fully 75 per cent of the world has never dialed a phone. We're targeting these second- and third-tier markets that serve pockets of less than 50,000 users (500,000 users or less for the U.S. market). Our products can deliver high-speed access to these markets cost-effectively.

With a view to developing a family of fixed wireless Internet/intranet network access systems capable of providing high-speed access to businesses, organizations, and consumers, WaveRider had recently launched its two main product families (see Exhibit 2).

EXHIBIT 2   NCL and LMS Brochures

NCL135

WaveRider® NCL135 Bridge/Router

Take advantage of the wireless world – replace your fractional T1 or ISDN lines with WaveRider's wireless NCL135 bridge/router. The fully-featured NCL135 enables high-speed wireless connectivity for LAN-to-Internet and LAN-to-LAN applications and provides secure, reliable connections to corporate computer networks, outlying offices, and the Internet.

Using Frequency-Hopping Spread Spectrum modulation in the license-exempt 2.4GHz ISM band, the NCL135 can be deployed quickly and easily without applying for regulatory approvals, and without incurring licensing or monthly service charges. Compared to the cost of traditional leased lines, NCL135 wireless links typically deliver ROI payback in less than a year.

The NCL135 supports both point-to-point and point-to-multipoint communication, making it ideal for:

- Providing Internet access in areas without a suitable telecommunications infrastructure
- Linking remote offices to corporate offices without the recurring costs of leased lines
- Connecting academic or corporate campus buildings to each other and to the Internet
- Providing WAN or Internet services for temporary facilities, special events, etc.

NCL135 at a glance

- Operates in the 2.4GHz ISM band, license-exempt in the U.S., Canada, and many other countries
- Frequency-Hopping Spread Spectrum radio is highly resistant to interference and ensures secure communication
- Supports both point-to-point and point-to-multipoint applications
- Forwarding Modes: IP Routing and Bridging (default Learning Bridge Static Routing)
- Delivers over-the-air data rates of 1.6 Mbps and up to 800 Kbps of real world user data throughput
- Built-in SNMP functionality ensures trouble-free integration and management with existing networks
- Maintains optimal throughput up to 10 miles (16 kms)
- Routing features/protocols: RIP v2, Static IP

EXHIBIT 2   *(continued)*

NCL 135 TECHNICAL SPECIFICATIONS

	NCL135	NCL135CU
Models	NCL135	NCL135CU
Order Number (SKU)	100-0100	100-0101
Operating Frequency Range	2.400 to 2.4835GHz	2.450 to 2.4835 GHz
Radio Type	Frequency-Hopping Spread Spectrum	
Radio Modulation	Quadrature and Binary Frequency Shift Keying	
Over-the-Air Data Rate	Up to 1.6 Mbps	
User Data Rate	Up to 800 kbps	
Maximum Link Path Distance (typical)	Up to 10 Miles (16 km)	
Channels	15	
Bankwidth	1.0 MHz per channel	
RF Tx Output Power	+18 dBm at the antenna port	
RF Rx Treshold	−80 dBm	
Antenna Connector	Reverse polarity TNC	
Network Interface	Ethernet 10BaseT RJ-45	
Configuration/Setup Port	RS232 DB9 (Console port-DCE)	
Flash Memory	4 MB	
LED Indicators	Fault, Power, RF link status, Ethernet tx/rx	
Power Supply Input	100-240 VAC, 50-60 Hz, auto-sensing	
Power Supply Output	+5 VDC/3.0 A	
Operating Temperature	0° to 149° F (0° to 65° C)	
Humidity	5% to 95% relative humidity (non-condensing)	
Physical Size (LxWxH)	9.1″ × 8.7″ × 1.1″ (230mm × 220mm × 27mm)	
Product Weight/Shipping Weight	5.01 lbs. (2.24kg)	
Regulatory approvals		
NCL135	FCC Part 15, ETSI, CE	
NCL 135CU	Industry Canada RSS-139, FCC Part 15, ETSI, CE	
Warranty	1 year limited parts and labor	
	(see WaveRider Warranty Agreement)	

Note: WaveRider's Continuous Improvement Policy means that specifications are subject to change without notice.

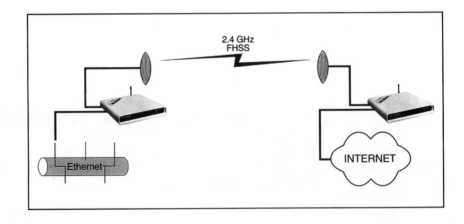

EXHIBIT 2 (*continued*)

Aimed at medium and large businesses and organizations requiring medium to high-speed throughput, combined with high availability, the LMS2000 provides the Wireless Internet Service Provider (WISP) with superior subscriber, equipment and network management, enhanced security, advanced billing support and a variety of maintenance features including real time alarms - all of which help to ensure that communication flows and profits soar - in a cost effective, easy to use, turnkey package.

LMS2000 at a glance

- *Is a complete system solution incorporating "best-in-class" components to maximize system capabilities and availability*
- *Provides sophisticated subscriber, network and equipment management for a cost effective solution which can be scaled to meet the long term needs of the WISP in a variety of environments*
- *Has superior maintenance features which allow operators to verify the configuration and operation of network modules on a scheduled or on-demand basis*
- *Generates real time alarms of failure of critical components*
- *Has automatic redundant fail over of key components to maximize system availability*
- *Provides environmentally hardened cabinets for key components to further enhance system availability and reduce maintenance costs*
- *Allows roll out of new system features from a central location in a controlled fashion*
- *Delivers IP communications links between a customer LAN and the Internet*
- *Operates in the 2.4 to 2.4835 GHz license exempt frequency band*
- *Has a raw data rate of 11 Mbps and provides access at speeds of up to 7.0 Mbps which is comparable to cable modems and xDSL*
- *Offers cost effective network infrastructure which can be easily scaled to meet the long term needs of the WISP*
- *Migrates easily to and from other LMS family products to ensure a long term solution and maximize return on investment*
- *Is a layer 3 end user modem to provide flexible, cost effective end user solutions*

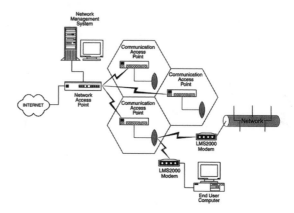

LMS2000 TECHNICAL SPECIFICATIONS

NAP Specifications

The following tables list the technical specifications for the LMS2000 NAP including the NMS Workstation.

CAP-NAP Backhaul Interface Specifications

Maximum Number of CAP-NAP Links	7
Physical Interface	10/100Base Tx auto-sense Ethernet

EXHIBIT 2   *(continued)*

NAP-Internet Interface Specifications

Maximum Number of NAP-Internet Links	1
Physical Interface	10/100Base Tx auto-sense Ethernet, full or half-duplex

The following tables list the technical specifications for the LMS2000 CAP, CCU & EUM configured for operation in the FCC/IC RF Regulatory Domain.

CAP Radio Specifications

Maximum Number of Operational CCUs and Orthogonal Channels	3
Maximum Number of Standby CCUs	1

Ethernet Backhaul Interface Specifications

Physical Interface	10/100BaseTx auto-sense, full or half-duplex

CCU and EUM Radio Specifications

Minimum Channel Center Frequency	2.412 GHz
Maximum Channel Center Frequency	2.462 GHz
Channel Bandwidth	22 MHz
Center Frequency Spacing Increment	5 MHz
Minimum Separation Between Orthogonal Channels	25 MHz
Maximum Orthogonal Channels	3
Orthogonal Channel Set	1, 6, 11
Orthogonal Channel Set Center Frequencies	2.412 GHz, 2.437 GHz, 2.462 GHz
Maximum Output Power	+15dBm
Modulation Scheme	CCK (Complementary Code Keying) DSSS (Direct Sequence Spread Spectrum)
Receiver Sensitivity for BER < 10-5	−72 dBm
Maximum Over-the-Air, Raw Data Rate	11 Mbps

Ethernet Interface Specifications

Physical Interface	10BaseTx half-duplex

Power Supply Specifications	**NAP**	**CAP & CCU**	**EUM**
AC Input	110/220 ±15% VAC single phase	110/220™15% VAC single phase	110/220 ±15% VAC single phase
AC Input Frequency	50/60 ±3 Hz	50/60±3 Hz	50/60 ±3 Hz
Maximum input power	1000 VA	1700 VA	1.5 A
Maximum UPS Operating time at full load	10 minutes	10 minutes	User defined

Environmental Specifications	**NAP**	**CAP & CCU**	**EUM**
Operating Temperature	10° to 40° C, indoor environment, 5%to 95%, RH non-condensing	10° to 40° C with integral fan cooling 10° to 55° C	10° to 55° C, indoor environment, 5% to 95%, RH non-condensing
Storage Temperature	−40° to 70° C	−40° to 70° C	−40° to 70° C

Source: Company records.

NCL

WaveRider's first product, the NCL 135, was a wireless high-speed router that provided secure, reliable connections to corporate computer networks, outlying offices and the Internet. It was designed to replace T1 or ISDN lines onsite. If a customer had two offices and one of the two had a local area network (LAN) with digital subscriber line (DSL) Internet access, then NCL 135 would allow both offices to share the Internet connection wirelessly. Even at this early development stage, WaveRider had already launched a second version, the NCL 1135, enabling broadband connections for LAN-to-Internet and LAN-to-LAN applications.

LMS

Designed to provide "last mile" wireless Internet access to a consumer. Targeted at wireless ISPs, this product included network access points that accessed fiber lines, communication access points that accessed a network within a 10-mile radius, and modems to end-user computers. LMS 2000 utilized license-free radio technology in the 2.4 GHz spread spectrum[2] frequency band.

Rémi Gaudet, a business analyst, commented,

> Our environment is changing every few months and, consequently, our needs change. Our LMS product was a shift from our NCL product, which was developed to get our feet wet. Instead of being a pure developer of wireless technology, we're now a software development and system administration company.

Jim Chapman, VP strategic alliances, continued,

> Clients now buy from us because we've built software around optimizing technology itself. We've given them technology, opportunities and tools to optimize the level of service to their clients. Our competition says we have 2.4 GHz equipment and technology but it is more than that. We have created the tools to enable this installation as well. At the beginning, we were just building this radio for Internet access, and as we got into product development and discussion with our customers, we saw that to distinguish ourselves, we needed to add network management to our product suite."

The Internet Access Industry

In 2000, competition in the market for data communications services was intensifying as a number of factors were combining to generate demand for broadband access technologies. Internet use was driving data

---

[2]Spread spectrum: an RF (radio frequency) term, indicating that the frequency that WaveRider utilized was spread over 2.4 to 2.4835 GHz, thereby minimizing the effect of isolated RF "noises" on certain specific frequencies.

traffic levels higher as Internet traffic doubled every six months and the number of businesses and individual users on the Net continued to climb at a staggering pace. In addition, the growing use of e-commerce and business productivity applications had made high-speed local access networks more valuable than ever to companies and their employees.

Although the penetration of broadband access among Internet users was still in the single-digit percentages, the Internet access industry realized that consumers and businesses would soon demand access at speeds higher than the 128 kilobits per second (kbps) rate (which was called ISDN) due to the constant worldwide development and deployment of newer, richer online software applications. Furthermore, the demand at the business level was higher as compared to the home access average of 56 kbps for cable modems.

Internet service providers (ISPs) had traditionally been providing Internet access to small businesses and consumers through phone lines. Technology industry analysis by WaveRider indicated that there was a large gap between the "wired services" infrastructure currently available and what the worldwide marketplace desired due to the reluctance of large telecommunications providers to rapidly upgrade their old networks. High-speed Internet access (one megabit per second or faster) was often unavailable outside dense metropolitan areas, and in fact, some underdeveloped regions of the world did not even have telecommunications infrastructure outside main cities. There were thought to be four major factors driving demand for telecommunications services and equipment:

1. Internet growth and increased data traffic;
2. An increase in demand for overall connectivity (especially in developing countries);
3. Upgrades to existing infrastructure as technology improved; and
4. Privatization and deregulation, which drove increased competition.

The convergence of telecommunications, network computing and broadcasting had increased the value of control over last-mile access to the end user. Although control of access was valuable, content delivery had become increasingly more important to service providers.

Thus, Internet bandwidth demand had spurred interest for all types of telecommunication products from ISPs. These products involved three currently available media: copper wire (including coaxial cable), fiberoptic cable, and wireless systems.[3] Although each of these transportation media had its own advantages and disadvantages, wireless

---

[3]A fourth medium, satellite delivery of Internet access, was much less prevalent in 2000.

required less infrastructure and therefore less installation. Implementation and cost recovery of a wireless-based system required less time than those that were dependent on hard-line connections.

WaveRider was focused on the terrestrial-fixed wireless market, which was affected by the same drivers as the overall telecommunications market as well as by some more specific influences:

- Demand resulting from Internet access for greater bandwidth at the local loop ("last mile");
- Competition by competitive local ISPs, driven by the Telecom Act of 1996 and FCC allocation of spectrum;
- Competitive local ISP desire to bypass the incumbent telephone company copper networks; and
- Technological improvements driving development of wireless broadband transmission equipment.

However, several factors had stymied wireless competition at the local ISP level:

- Equipment and ISPs had neglected the wireless space until mid-1998, when the FCC modified regulations regarding MMDS[4] spectrum (2.5 GHz) to permit two-way transmission.
- Point-to-multipoint wireless system development had not progressed rapidly until recently. Reliable equipment capable of allocating bandwidth had only recently (in 1999) started to enter the market.
- Wireless connections had a negative perception in the marketplace, which was the result of the high drop call rate of cellular phones.[5]

Given these factors, the U.S. fixed wireless market was expected to post a five-year compound annual growth rate of 65 per cent through 2003 to US$74 billion. The number of wireless data users in the United States alone was expected to increase from the current 2.9 million to 12.6 million by 2002, reported the Yankee Group in April 1999. And growth in underdeveloped regions would accelerate as well: Freedom-Forum reported in early 1999 that Haiti had less than one phone line for every 100 people, and in Africa, there were only 14 million telephone lines and 1.5 million users online for over 700 million people.

The Wireless Internet Access Competitive Environment

Worldwide, telephone companies, cable operators, wireless operators and Internet service providers were deploying various high-speed access solutions to meet the needs of their end users. These included access through fibreoptic lines, satellite, cable modem, DSL (digital subscriber

---

[4]Multichannel multipoint distribution service.
[5]IDC Research from First Security Van Kasper Research Report.

lines), and other wireless access technologies such as LMDS[6] and MMDS. Among these solutions, fixed wireless access[7] technology had emerged as a strong contender for solving the last-mile access bottleneck.

WaveRider had to contend with wireless products developed by competitors, including Adaptive Broadband, AirSpan, BreezeCOM, Cisco Systems, Lucent Technologies, Motorola, Nokia and Wi-Lan. Two of them are listed below:

- BreezeCOM—Headquartered in Tel Aviv, Israel, BreezeCOM was a manufacturer of broadband wireless access equipment. Counting over 300 employees, 30 per cent of whom were in research and development. Breeze-COM had offices in North and South America, Uruguay, Hong Kong, China, Russia and Romania. The company stated that it had a network of over 300 partners and distributors in more than 60 countries worldwide. Its BreezeACCESS solution delivered wireless connectivity in the licensed 3.5 GHz and MMDS 2.5 to 2.7 GHz frequency bands, as well as in the license-free 2.4 GHz ISM band. BreezeCOM also offered wireless network and modem solutions operating in the license-free 2.4 GHz ISM band.
- Wi-LAN—specialized in high-speed Internet access, LAN/WAN extension and fixed wireless access. In June, Wi-LAN broke industry barriers with the launch of the "I.WiLL Access Point," a high-speed 30 Mbps wireless networking product. Targeting the demand for fixed wireless access products, the I.WiLL Access Point used Wi-LAN's patented technology to meet the stringent, industrial-strength demands of large telecommunications providers including telcos, fibrecos, cablecos, major ISPs and integrators. The I.WiLL 300-24 Access Point operated in the 2.4 GHz band to achieve a peak data rate of 30 Mbps in 20 MHz of bandwidth. This wireless product held many advantages over copper wire landlines, including low-cost, rapid installation and scalability.

Creating a Template to Classify the Competition

In order to compare access technology alternatives, it was necessary to first establish what were the most important criteria, which determined a "good" technology for high-speed access. Gaudet created this list:

- **Cost to Deploy**—The cost to deploy broadband technologies was comprised of two components: the cost to prepare and upgrade the network, and the cost to connect each individual user. The first component was a fixed cost for the whole network, and did not vary based on how many subscribers were signed up. Upgrades to entire networks or launching of satellites, for example, were fixed costs. The second component was a variable capital cost, and was proportional to the user base.

---

[6]Local multipoint distribution service.

[7]The term "fixed wireless" denotes wireless service that was delivered to the end user using installed components.

- **Actual User Speed**—Aside from raw bandwidth, other important factors also dictated what speed of service the user would actually experience. Was the bandwidth dedicated to each user or was it shared among many? What was the level of system overhead and the quality of service functionality built into the technology?
- **Secure Connection**—Inherent network security was important, especially for businesses sending sensitive data. Any technology that used an insecure medium would have to pay additional costs for encryption to offer its users a secure service.
- **Coverage**—For realistic mass-deployment, a technology had to be available to a large percentage of homes and businesses.
- **Reliability**—The broadband access network had to be designed, built, and maintained for reliability.
- **Near-Term Deployment**—For a technology to capture a large share of the market, it had to be ready for deployment in the near-term.

See Exhibit 3 for a comparison of the technologies.

EXHIBIT 3   Competing Technologies

	Fixed Cost to Prepare Network	*Variable Cost to Deploy Network*	*Speed (Mbps)*	*Dedicated Bandwidth*	*Secure Connection*	*Coverage*	*Reliability*	*Time Frame for Deployment*
WaveRider LMS Family	$15–$30K per cell	$500–$1,500 per user	128 Kbps–11.0	Yes	Yes	Non-Line of Sight	High	Today
WaveRider NCL Family	$5–$10K per cell	$1,500–$4,000 per point	1.6–11.0	Yes	Yes	Line of Sight	High	Today
MMDS	$35K to $500K	$1,500 per user	10.0 down	Yes	Yes	Line of Sight	High	Today
DSL	$50K to $100K per CO	$350–$700 per user	0.5–50.0	No	Yes	70% of homes in U.S.	High	Today
Cable Modem	$300 per home passed	$250 per user	10.0–30.0 Shared	No	No	15% of homes in U.S.	Low	Today
LMDS	$500K to $1 Million per cell	$5,000 per user	10.0–50.0	Yes	No	Line of Sight	High	Today
Satellite	Billions	$3,500 per user	<1.0	No	Yes (up) No (down)	Global	Medium	6 months
Optical Fiber (Fiber to the Home)	Very high—$1K per home	$500–$1,000 per user	No real limit	Yes	Yes	Land Lines	High	>5 years

Current Shortcoming of Wireless Access

One of the key drawbacks of wireless access was its inability to provide non-line of sight (NLOS) access—access without direct line of sight to a provider's antennas. Without NLOS, current wireless technologies could not provide connectivity because any obstruction (trees or buildings) would interfere with data transmission. Adverse weather conditions including fog, heavy snow, or rain, however, were not an issue. But to get around large ground objects, WaveRider had to install "repeaters" on the top of a mountain, for example, sending an RF signal up one side and down the other to maintain the integrity of the signal. Without repeaters, tall buildings, foliage or rock formations in the way of LOS prevented wireless access. NLOS wireless access would also reduce what the Internet access industry termed as "truck roll"—the need to send a service employee out to install Internet access equipment onsite.

Some Customer Barriers to Overcome

In the fast-paced, nascent world of wireless access providers, there were several sales barriers to overcome, one of which was the long-term viability of WaveRider.

In an industry with giant companies such as Nortel, Lucent and Cisco beginning to eye the wireless Internet access space, WaveRider had to demonstrate that it had staying power. At the present time, it could not show thousands of installations or a large market capitalization. WaveRider management noted that there existed competitive "noise" in the marketplace, defined as unreachable promises made by competition, which served only to confuse the market and delay the sales cycle. This noise frequently led customers to delay their cycle because they wanted to wait another two quarters for the "next version."

Thus, the customer base demanded that WaveRider salespeople keep on top of competitors and allow access to information on the latest technologies. This meant that WaveRider salespeople had to work closely with product research and development to keep up to date with the latest news. WaveRider held a quarterly sales training seminar in Toronto to update its sales force on the latest developments. Brown stated, "When a customer casually mentions a competitive technology they're thinking of looking at, I want my salespeople to know about it."

Evaluation of Opportunity

The existence of various broadband access technologies coupled with rapidly growing demand for high-speed access gave rise to some interesting options for WaveRider to partner with rival technologies. Should WaveRider consider either a marketing or a technical alliance, or a combination of both? The company would need to be extremely wary of such an alliance, thought Brown. Combining WaveRider's sales efforts with another company's was certainly a tempting option. And if this turned out to be the chosen path, which technology should WaveRider form an alliance with?

Canadian Imperial Bank of Commerce Wireless Strategy

By Professor Michael Wade and David Hamilton

It was March 21, 2000, and Kevin Lasitz, director of business development in the electronic banking division of the Canadian Imperial Bank of Commerce (CIBC), was feeling both relief and apprehension. On the one hand, his division had just been given a "yellow" light by corporate management to develop and implement a wireless banking strategy. The light wasn't "green" because the project would have to be developed "out of plan," meaning that it wasn't incorporated in the annual budget. As such, it would have to be completed with as few resources as possible.

While Lasitz was excited at being given the opportunity to finally go forward with a wireless strategy (CIBC was initially enthusiastic about wireless banking, then shelved the idea), he felt a little apprehensive at the myriad of choices and decisions that lay ahead of him. For example, decisions had to made about which wireless devices to support—pagers, personal digital assistants (PDAs), mobile phones, and so on; whether or not to partner with one or more telecommunication carriers; and what wireless services to offer. In addition to customer focused applications, Lasitz wondered how wireless technology might be able to support internal operations.

Lasitz had only a couple of weeks to prepare and submit a wireless banking strategy to the bank. He knew that he would have to start making key decisions about the strategy very soon.

CIBC

Formed out of a 1961 merger between The Canadian Bank of Commerce and the Imperial Bank of Canada, CIBC was one of North America's leading financial institutions offering retail and wholesale products and services through its electronic banking network, branches and offices around the world. As of May 2000, CIBC had 45,000 employees worldwide serving six million individual customers, 350,000 small businesses, and 7,000 corporate and investment banking customers. The company managed assets of $250 billion, and had a net income of $1.029 billion in 1999. An organizational chart of the bank is shown in Exhibit 1.

CIBC's electronic banking division was part of the newly formed electronic commerce, technology and operations group. The mandate of the business development unit within the electronic banking division was to act as a "visionary" for the bank. The group's main objective was to monitor emerging technological trends and to gauge their impact on the bank. Results of the unit's work could impact the bank in three ways. First, new products or services, product or service line extensions, or entirely new businesses could be developed and offered externally to the bank's customers. Second, new technologies could be implemented internally within the bank, enhancing productivity. Third, investment opportunities for the bank could be identified.

EXHIBIT 1   Canadian Imperial Bank of Commerce: Organizational Chart

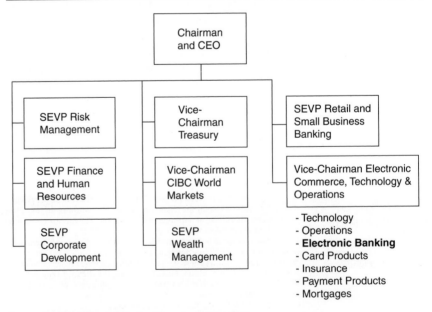

Source: Canadian Imperial Bank of Commerce, June 2000.

A History of Wireless at CIBC

Remote customers comprised 30 percent of all CIBC customers, one of the highest rates of all North American banks. These customers fulfilled most of their banking needs electronically and seldom visited the bank's branches. Remote customers tended to be highly mobile professionals who were more profitable, but less loyal than traditional customers. CIBC began thinking about a wireless strategy in December 1998, with the idea of providing anytime-anywhere banking to its customers. While management was convinced that the wireless Internet would play an important part in CIBC's future, at the time it appeared premature to develop a product. In late 1998, no Canadian mobile telephone carrier offered wireless Internet access. Hence, the idea was temporarily shelved.

The Wireless Market

In mid-1998, there were six million wireless subscribers in Canada, a penetration rate of 20 percent and 41 percent of the population claimed to have access to a mobile phone. By 2005, total penetration of mobile phones was expected to reach 40 percent of the Canadian population. Carriers showed a 40 percent increase in new subscribers between 1998 and 1999. Most subscribers were on first generation analogue technology phones. Digital subscriber growth had been slower than expected. Bell Mobility supported 17 percent of their clients on a digital network, while Telus had 10 percent of their subscribers on the digital network. Performance data for individual mobile telephone carriers is provided in Exhibit 2.

EXHIBIT 2   Carrier Performance—Second Quarter 1999 ($ million)

Cdn$	*Bell Mobility*	*Telus*	*Microcell*	*Cantel*	*Clearnet (PCS/Mike)*	*Trends/Outlooks*
ARPU	$53	$59	$48	$49	$56	Falling/leveling
Churn	1.4%	1.3%	1.9%	1.54%	1.61%	Intense pricing actions
COA	$479	N/A	$456	N/A	$592	Declining
Share Price	38%	(26%)	111%	75%	82%	Cost containment
Subs	1.6M	1.02M	0.40M	1.9M	0.44M	Solid growth
Rev(Q2)	249M	94.2M	53M	325M	69M	Drive for profitability

ARPU: Average revenue per user
Churn: Customer turnover
COA: Cost to acquire a customer
Subs: Subscribers

Source: Canadian Imperial Bank of Commerce, June 2000.

Canada had one of the lowest wireless prices in the world at approximately $0.10 per minute. Revenue per user was low, estimated at $15 to $20 per month. Utilization was also low, estimated at 50 to 64 minutes per month; however, that amount had been rising steadily.

In addition to increased penetration, carriers were eager to increase usage. One method to increase airtime was to offer additional services such as access to the Internet. In May 1999, Bell Mobility launched Mobile Browser, making it the first company in North America to put an Internet browser into a personal communications services (PCS) handset (see glossary for an explanation of wireless terminology). Mobile Browser users were able to access and view a number of Internet sites especially adapted for small display screens, including Amazon.com, Yahoo!, Charles Schwab, Sympatico.ca, i/money, TD Waterhouse, Veev (from competitor Bank of Montreal), Canada.com, canoe.ca, and Web 411.

"Today we deliver on George Gilder's prophecy that the most common PC of the next decade will be the digital cellular phone," said Randy Reynolds, president and CEO of Bell Mobility.

> We are dedicated to delivering to our customers the power and interactivity of the Internet from a range of wireless devices. Together with our partners, we have made the convergence of wireless communications and the Internet a reality.

In the year 2000, 4 percent of wireless users subscribed to the wireless Internet. By 2001, 24 percent of users claimed that they would subscribe to the wireless Internet. By 2001, wireless Internet devices were expected to outsell the personal computer. By 2003, the world was expected to have between 800 million and one billion wireless subscribers conducting 10 percent, ($38.1 billion) of all e-commerce with Wireless Application Protocol (WAP)-capable devices (see glossary for an explanation of WAP).

North American Telephone Carriers

In Europe, most mobile telephone carriers utilized one common technology, GSM. In North America, a variety of different network technologies were utilized; CDMA was the most common network platform, while GSM, TDMA, and iDEN were also utilized (see glossary for explanations). With no North American industry standard for network technology, a wireless solution compatible with all carriers was necessarily complex. Each carrier was at a different stage of readiness to provide access to the wireless Internet.

By the spring of 2000, Bell Mobility was the only Canadian mobile telephone carrier that offered wireless Internet access to subscribers. Rogers AT&T, Clearnet, Microcell and Telus were all expected to match

EXHIBIT 3   Expected Wireless Launch Dates

Data Capable Subscribers (K) *First Quarter*	*Technology and Protocol*	*Status*
925	CDMA (PCS) @ 1.9 HGz	Live
1.5	TDMA (PCS) @ 800 MHz	Third Quarter 2000
	Mobitex (Packet)	
	AMPS (analog)	
900	GSM (PCS) @ 800 MHz	July 2000
560	CDMA (PCS) @ 800 MHz	April 2000
100	CDMA (PCS) @ 800 MHz	Third Quarter 2000
50	CDMA (PCS) @ TBD	TBD
360	FLEX	Live

Source: Canadian Imperial Bank of Commerce, June 2000.

Bell Mobility's product offering before the end of the summer, 2000. Clearnet was expected to launch a wireless Internet service in April 2000. Aliant was uncertain if it would implement a wireless Internet solution for subscribers. Exhibit 3 identifies the network specifications and expected wireless Internet launch dates for each of the Canadian mobile telephone carriers.

In mid-2000, the technology for delivering wireless Internet access was still in the early stages of commercial development. Data services were limited by existing circuit switch connections operating at speeds of 9.6 to 14.4 kilobits per second (kbps)—a speed less than a quarter of the typical home dial-up modem. Some areas of the country had no access at all to a digital network. Existing speeds limited the number and complexity of services that could be offered to consumers. As current networking technologies were replaced with newer, more efficient systems, wireless devices would have an enhanced ability to provide integrated graphics and video, transaction processing, and so on. Once these levels of service were widely available, consumer acceptance and use of the wireless Internet was expected to grow rapidly. Exhibits 4 to 6 illustrate the evolution of bandwidth and the implications for wireless services.

The Future of Wireless in North America

By mid-2000, mobile telephone devices used numeric telephone keypads or very small alphanumeric keypads, both of which made data entry awkward and slow. Third-generation (3-G) mobile phones, which were

EXHIBIT 4 Transition of Wireless Data Speed and Technology

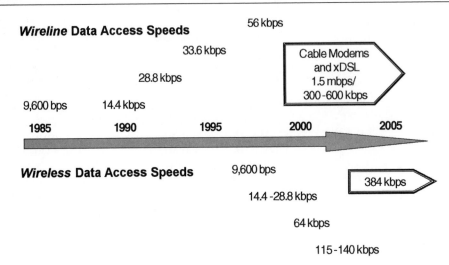

Source: Canadian Imperial Bank of Commerce, June 2000.

EXHIBIT 5 Online Commerce Evolution

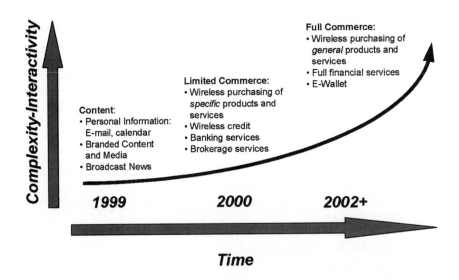

Source: Canadian Imperial Bank of Commerce, June 2000.

EXHIBIT 6   Wireless Applications and Services

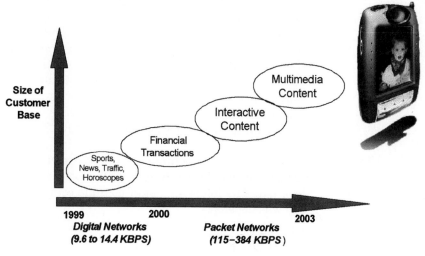

Source: Canadian Imperial Bank of Commerce, June 2000.

still a year or two away, would work globally, and be much more sophisticated, providing PC-like web access albeit in a much smaller format. 3-G phones would offer touch screen features, scroll through Internet text, voice recognition and voice conversion technology. This latter technology would "read" text message and web content to the user—useful for commuters. 3-G phones would also support digital signatures, making them valuable tools for e-commerce.

Europe, with extremely high cellular penetration rates, provided North America with a preview of how far the wireless Internet could go. For example, European companies were involved in pilot projects that allowed consumers to purchase items from vending machines using their cellular phones. Consumers paid for these and other items on their telephone bills.

Approval to Proceed

Lasitz knew that in order to receive senior management approval to proceed with a wireless strategy, a strong business case had to be developed. The bank had just completed a major restructuring with the goal of "increased profitability through rationalization." This had led to a climate of reduced spending, and the bank was reluctant to finance projects that did not focus on existing revenue-generating product or service lines, or on the bank's core areas of competence.

With this climate in mind, Lasitz was convinced that CIBC had to enter the wireless arena quickly. A crucial first step was to develop relationships with all potential partners and suppliers. The bank was eager to participate and influence the future landscape of wireless, especially the revenue model that its partners and suppliers would be utilizing. CIBC wanted to ensure that costs to develop, implement, run and maintain a wireless service would not be prohibitive for the bank or its customers.

Prior to requesting funding from the executive committee, Lasitz and his team decided to sketch out what a potential wireless strategy might look like. The following list of possible components of a wireless strategy was developed:

1. Internet devices
2. Mobile telephone carrier/wireless service provider (WSP)
3. Wireless portals
4. Application service provider (ASP)
5. Platform
6. Content/services

1. Internet Devices

Pagers, PDAs, PCS phones, Windows CE devices, in-car personal computers, and notebooks equipped with Wireless Application Protocol (WAP)-capable wireless cards, could all wirelessly access the Internet. Although any wireless infrastructure would support WAP, each device was uniquely engineered. For example, each device could use a different network technology, display ability (text, graphics, video), display size and micro-browser. Thus, support of all devices was necessarily complex. Exhibit 7 shows examples of WAP-capable devices.

The strategy of other financial institutions was to support only select devices. While cheaper and less complex, Lasitz knew that this strategy alienated some customers. He thought that to truly offer anytime-anywhere banking, he should investigate supporting all devices.

2. Mobile Telephone Carriers/WSP

In Canada, there were six major mobile telephone carriers: Bell Mobility, Telus, Microcell, Rogers AT&T, Clearnet and Aliant. In the United States, there were several wireless Internet service providers (WSPs) as well as mobile telephone carriers.

Lasitz knew that the more carriers CIBC partnered with, the more customers that would have access to the CIBC wireless website. On the other hand, selecting one carrier would use the least resources

---

EXHIBIT 7   WAP-Capable Devices

and entail the least complexity. The nation's largest carrier, Rogers AT&T, would not be ready to offer wireless Internet access until the third quarter of 2000. Bell Mobility's wireless Internet had been live since May of 1999 and Clearnet planned to launch a wireless Internet service in April 2000. Lasitz wondered how to balance maximum customer exposure with minimum investment. He also wondered if there was an advantage in differentiating CIBC's wireless strategy from the other banks, who had decided to work with only one carrier each.

EXHIBIT 7   *(continued)*

Source: Canadian Imperial Bank of Commerce, June 2000.

3. Wireless Portals

Wireless portals were growing in number each day. Carriers like Bell Mobility and Rogers AT&T had their own portals. Traditional Internet portals had also created wireless portals—Yahoo!, Microsoft Network (MSN), and America Online (AOL), to name a few. It was extremely desirable for a financial institution to have a direct link to a wired Internet portal, often purchased at a substantial premium. It was believed that with the limited data-entry capability of the mid-2000 WAP devices, and the infancy of voice recognition, partnerships with portals would be vital. Hyperlinks to popular portals would be necessary to maximize traffic on the wireless Internet. Alternatively, CIBC could develop its own wireless portal.

4. Application Service Provider (ASP)

Accessing the bank through the wireless Internet was foreign to most CIBC clients. To encourage adoption of the new channel, a user-friendly interface had to be created. Lasitz felt that wireless Internet would have to be as easy to use as an automated teller machine. CIBC could internally develop the necessary software, like most of its competitors, or it could outsource development tasks to solution providers like 7/24 Solutions, Hewlett Packard, or Wysdom. Lasitz thought that it would be difficult for the bank to quickly gain the knowledge that these wireless Web solution providers had developed. At the same time, he was concerned with outsourcing such an important aspect of the strategy.

5. Platform

The bank's existing information technology infrastructure was not designed to communicate with wireless devices. The bank used a metabase platform that accessed all bank systems. A wireless server would have to be created to access all pertinent information from the bank's middleware platform. This server would, in turn, communicate to carriers in a WAP compatible method by utilizing WML, HDML and HTML languages (see glossary for explanation of terms). Possible suppliers of CIBC's wireless platform included IBM, Hewlett Packard, Oracle and MobileQ.

A signal would be transmitted from the bank's servers through the Internet (128-bit encryption) to the transmitting tower of the mobile telephone carrier. From the tower, the signal would be transmitted to the subscriber's handset. Exhibits 8 and 9 illustrate how this flow of information would work. CIBC was confident with the level of security both on the Internet and on the carriers' network. Increased security could be achieved through the addition of a chip in the user's device; however, it was thought that this would present too much of a barrier to widespread adoption.

6. Content/Services

Lasitz felt that the wireless site should provide the same information and the same ability to transact that presently was available online, i.e., personal banking and brokerage services. Lasitz was uncertain how much further to take this new distribution channel. He was considering augmenting the services offered to include CIBC broadcasts, general information and location-based services.

EXHIBIT 8 Wireless Platforms

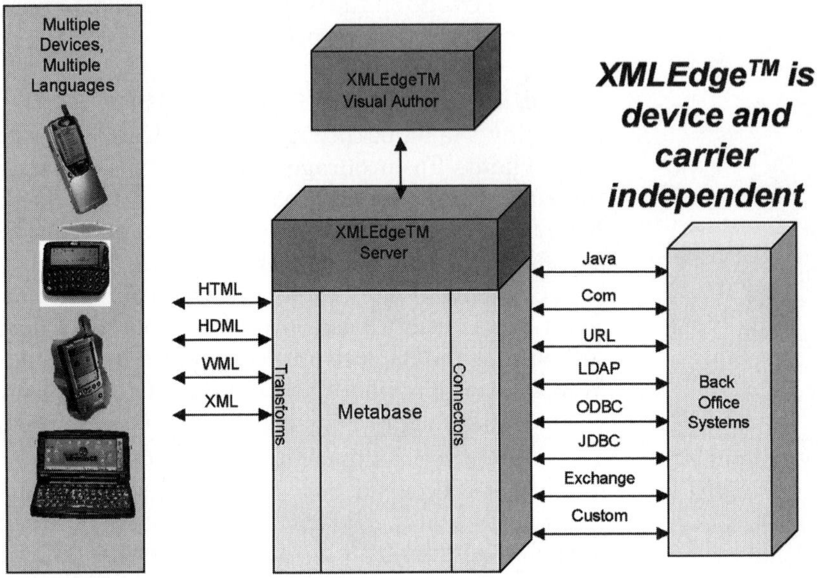

Source: Canadian Imperial Bank of Commerce, June 2000.

CIBC broadcasts would allow users to customize a user profile to receive specific product or service information as requested. If a particular client was shopping around for mortgages or renewing a mortgage, a CIBC broadcast message would make the client aware of any mortgage promotions. CIBC did not, at present, have an electronic channel through which to push this information on interested clients. It was thought that these services could be outsourced to an information aggregator.

CIBC could provide its clients with access to general information. Aggregators such as i3 Mobile, Mobeo, WEB2PCS and Smart Ray had formed partnerships with various information sources. CIBC could provide access to weather, sports and business news, health information, and TV listings if the bank desired to purchase services from one of these companies. The aggregator would also compile CIBC's promotional information and include this as content. It was unclear to Lasitz whether clients would find value in this service. Lasitz believed customer loyalty would increase if they went to the CIBC site for both banking and non-banking needs.

A number of companies were very close to perfecting the technique of triangulating the cellular signal to determine the location of every wireless device in the world. Lasitz envisioned the utilization of loca-

EXHIBIT 9 Wireless Transmission Infrastructure

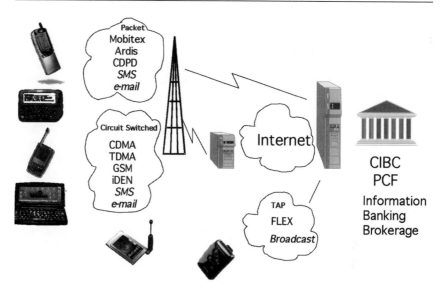

Source: Canadian Imperial Bank of Commerce, June 2000.

tion-based services to notify customers of special promotions in nearby CIBC branches. President's Choice Financial, CIBC's partnership with Loblaws (a large supermarket chain), could utilize location-based services to suggestively sell grocery items. Lasitz believed this was an important development but was uncertain how it would impact his wireless strategy.

Pilot Project

Lasitz and his team had investigated the above components plus some additional areas. In August 1999, the wireless team made a presentation to the executive committee and requested (and received) approval to immediately proceed with a wireless strategy. The presentation focused on:

- Wireless to become more popular than the personal computer (PC)
- Competitive response or parity before year 2000 freeze
- Learn complexities of new delivery channel
- Build organizational capability in wireless
- Maintain pace with customer and technology
- Establish strategic partnerships and alliances
- Low cost pilot leveraging existing infrastructure

The pilot project was severely time constrained. On November 1, 1999, the bank experienced a year 2000 freeze. From August to November, the wireless team had three months to complete the systems component of the wireless pilot. The team had to identify an experienced solutions provider and Bell Mobility was still the only carrier that offered wireless Internet service. Lasitz knew from conversations with Bell Mobility that MobileQ provided services for Bell.

An agreement was signed with MobileQ to develop CIBC's wireless infrastructure. The next two weeks were spent mapping out the requirements of the system. Six weeks were then spent coding, followed by two weeks of testing. The system was a wireless-capable back-end coupled to a wireless front-end that duplicated the existing online banking and brokerage services.

Year 2000 Freeze and Thaw

On November 1, 1999, Lasitz' application for a year 2000 freeze "exemption" was refused. Resources were scarce and the information technology group had other projects that were deemed of higher priority. Lasitz knew this hiatus in development would allow competitors an opportunity to gain ground in the race to launch wireless services. Exhibit 10 identifies the status of wireless projects at other financial institutions.

The wireless project was not the only project that had been put on hold. It was in a queue with other projects, many of which were competing for the same resources. To successfully launch the wireless service, resources from the call centre, marketing and information technology

EXHIBIT 10   Competitive Positioning for Wireless Services

Financial Institution	Carriers	Devices	Services	Expected Launch Dates
Bank of Montreal	Bell Mobility	PCS Phone Palm PDA	Info/e-mail Banking Brokerage	Spring 2000
Royal	Microcell (Fido)	PCS Phone	Info/e-mail Banking	Summer 2000
Scotiabank	Cantel	RIM Pager PCS Phone	Info/e-mail Banking Brokerage	Summer 2000
Schwab Canada	Bell Mobility	PCS Phone Palm PDA	Info/e-mail	Spring 2000
i/money	Bell Mobility	PCS Phone	Info/e-mail	Spring 2000
TD Waterhouse	Bell Mobility	PCS Phone	Brokerage	Spring 2000

Source: Canadian Imperial Bank of Commerce, June 2000.

groups would all be required. In early 2000, with tax and investment season in full motion, Lasitz was not sure the wireless project would ever get started again. It was not until March 21 that Lasitz gained management approval to again proceed with the bank's wireless strategy.

Final Thoughts

Lasitz had many decisions to make before rolling out a pilot to 500 select customers. Many of the technical decisions had been made, yet most of the business decisions were still unresolved. He knew he would have to make a decision whether to support all devices and all carriers or WSPs or limit the strategy to a select few—a tradeoff between customer coverage and operational complexity. In addition to completing the hardware infrastructure with MobileQ, Lasitz would have to select an application service provider to develop the applications that would operate on this hardware. A decision was required on whether to partner with one or more wireless portals, providing a direct link to CIBC's wireless website. Lasitz knew he wanted to include brokerage and banking services but was uncertain if he should also include non-banking information and location services. Lasitz was so focused on creating the consumer wireless strategy that he had not spent much time investigating the benefits of developing an internal wireless strategy. He wondered if he should simultaneously develop a sales force automation strategy or test the consumer wireless strategy first.

Lasitz felt a mix of excitement and nervousness. At last, he had been given the go-ahead to move forward with a wireless strategy for the bank. He felt strongly that wireless was the "way of the future" and looked forward to putting the necessary pieces of a strategy together. At the same time, he realized that many of the key decisions that could affect the success or failure of the venture still had to be made.

Glossary

WIRELESS TECHNICAL TERMS

AMPS   Advanced mobile phone service (AMPS) is a standard system for analog signal cellular telephone service in the United States and is also used in other countries. It is based on the initial frequency spectrum allocation for cellular service by the Federal Communications Commission (FCC) in 1970. Introduced by AT&T in 1983, AMPS became the most widely deployed cellular system in the United States by mid-2000.

bandwidth   Bandwidth is the capacity of the transmission medium stated in bits per second or as a frequency. The bandwidth of optical fiber is in the gigabit or billion bits per second range, while Ethernet coaxial cable is in the megabit or million bits per second range.

CDMA   Code division multiple access (CDMA) is one of the three wireless telephone transmission technologies; it takes an entirely different approach from GSM and the similar TDMA. CDMA, after digitizing data, spreads it out over the entire bandwidth it has available. Multiple calls are overlaid over each other on the channel, with each assigned a unique sequence code.

circuit-switch   Circuit-switched is a type of network such as the regular voice telephone network in which the communication circuit (path) for the call is set up and dedicated to the participants in that call. For the duration of the connection, all resources on that circuit are unavailable for other users. Voice calls using the Internet's packet-switched system are possible. Each end of the conversation is broken down into packets that are reassembled at the other end.

DSL   Digital subscriber lines (DSL)—this technology uses copper pair wiring that exists in almost every home and office. Special hardware attached to both the user and switch ends of line allows data transmission over the wires at far greater speed than the standard phone wiring.

digital   Digital refers to data or voltages consisting of discrete steps or levels, as opposed to continuously variable analog data.

fast packet   Fast packet is one that is transmitted without any error checking at points along the route. Assurance that the packet arrived without error is the responsibility of the receiver. Fast packet transmission is possible because of the extremely low incidence of error or data loss on high bandwidth transmission technologies.

flex   Flex refers to the chipset for modems that provides the capability to send and receive data over ordinary phone lines.

GSM   Global system for mobile communication (GSM) is a digital mobile telephone system that is widely used in Europe and other parts of the world. GSM uses a variation of time division multiple access (TDMA) and is the most widely used of the three digital wireless telephone technologies (TDMA, GSM, and CDMA). GSM digitizes and compresses data, then sends it down a channel with two other streams of user data, each in its own time slot. It operates at either the 900 MHz or 1800 MHz frequency band.

HDML   Handheld devices markup language (HDML)—now called the wireless markup language (WML)—is a language that allows the text portions of web pages to be presented on cellular phones and personal digital assistants (PDAs) via wireless access.

HTML   Hypertext markup language (HTML) is the set of markup symbols or codes inserted in a file intended for display on a World Wide Web browser. The markup tells the web browser how to display a web page's words and images for the user. The individual markup codes are referred to as elements (but many people also refer to them as tags).

iDEN Integrated digital enhanced network (iDEN)—Motorola enhanced mobile radio network technology that integrates two-way radio, telephone, text messaging and data transmission into a single network.

LEO Low earth orbit (LEO)—mobile communications satellite between 700 and 2,000 kilometers above the earth.

microbrowser Modified web browser that allows users to access Internet data from many digital cell phones, PDAs and Internet appliances.

PCS Personal communications services (PCS) is a wireless phone service somewhat similar to cellular telephone service but emphasizing personal service and extended mobility. It's sometimes referred to as digital cellular (although cellular systems can also be digital). The "personal" in PCS distinguishes this service from cellular by emphasizing that, unlike cellular, which was designed for car phone use with transmitters emphasizing coverage of highways and roads, PCS is designed for greater user mobility. It generally requires more cell transmitters for coverage, but has the advantage of fewer blind spots. Technically, cellular systems in the United States operate in the 824 to 849 megahertz bands; PCS operates in the 1,850 to 1,990 MHz bands.

packet A chunk of data. The Transmission Control Protocol/Internet Protocol (TCP/IP) breaks large data files into smaller "packets" for transmission. When the data reaches its destination, the protocol makes sure that all packets have arrived without error.

packet-switched Packet-switched describes the type of network in which relatively small units of data called packets are routed through a network based on the destination address contained within each packet. Breaking communication down into packets allows the same data path to be shared among many users in the network. This type of communication between sender and receiver is known as connectionless (rather than dedicated). Most traffic over the Internet uses packet switching and the Internet is basically a connectionless network.

open source software Open source software (OSS) refers to software that is developed, tested, or improved through public collaboration and distributed with the idea that the source code must be shared with others, ensuring an open future collaboration.

TAPI Telephony application program interface (TAPI) is a standard program interface that lets you and your computer "talk" over telephones or video phones to people or phone-connected resources elsewhere in the world.

TDMA Time division multiple access (TDMA) is a technology used in digital cellular telephone communication to divide each cellular channel into three time slots in order to increase the amount of data that can be carried. TDMA is used by Digital-American Mobile Phone Service (D-AMPS), Global System for Mobile communications (GSM), and Personal Digital Cellular (PDC). However, each of these systems implements TDMA in a somewhat different and incompatible way.

SMS Short message service (SMS)—electronic messages on a wireless network, such as those used in two-way paging.

tags   Tags are formatting codes used in HTML documents. These tags indicate how the parts of a document will appear when displayed by a web client program.

WAP   Wireless application protocol (WAP)—open global specifications that empowers mobile users with wireless devices to easily access and interact with information and services instantly.

The WAP Forum is an industry group dedicated to the goal of enabling sophisticated telephony and information services on hand-held wireless devices such as mobile telephones, pagers, personal digital assistants (PDAs) and other wireless terminals. Recognizing the value and utility of the World Wide Web architecture, the WAP Forum has chosen to align certain components of its technology very tightly with the Internet and the WWW. The WAP specifications extend and leverage mobile networking technologies (such as digital data networking standards) and Internet technologies (such as IP, HTTP, XML, URLs, scripting and other content formats).

The WAP specification initiative began in June 1997, and the WAP Forum was founded in December 1997. The WAP Forum has drafted a global wireless protocol specification for all wireless networks and will contribute it to appropriate industry and standards bodies. WAP will enable manufacturers, network operators, content providers and application developers to offer compatible products and secure services on all devices and networks, resulting in greater economies of scale and universal access to information. WAP Forum membership is open to all industry participants.

The objectives of the WAP Forum are:

- To bring Internet content and advanced data services to digital cellular phones and other wireless terminals.
- To create a global wireless protocol specification that will work across different wireless network technologies.
- To enable the creation of content and applications that scale across a very wide range of wireless bearer networks and wireless device types.
- To embrace and extend existing standards and technology wherever appropriate.

WSP   Wireless service provider (WSP) is a company that offers transmission services to users of wireless devices (hand-held computers and telephones) through radio frequency (RF) signals rather than through end-to-end wire communication. Generally, a WSP offers either cellular telephone service, personal communication service (PCS), or both.

WML   Wireless markup language (WML), formerly called HDML (hand-held devices markup language), is a language that allows the text portions of web pages to be presented on cellular phones and personal digital assistants via wireless access. WML is part of the wireless application protocol that is being proposed by several vendors to standards bodies. The wireless application protocol works on top of standard data link protocols, such as GSM, CDMA, and TDMA, and provides a complete set of network communication programs comparable to and supportive of the Internet set of protocols.

XML   Extensible markup language (XML) is a flexible way to create common information formats and share both the format and the data on the World Wide Web, intranets, and elsewhere. XML is similar to the language of today's web pages, HTML. Both XML and HTML contain markup symbols to describe the contents of a page or file. HTML, however, describes the content of a web page (mainly text and graphic images) only in terms of how it is to be displayed and interacted with. For example, a <P> starts a new paragraph. XML describes the content in terms of what data is being described. For example, a <PHONENUM> could indicate that the data that followed it was a phone number. This means that an XML file can be processed purely as data by a program or it can be stored with similar data on another computer or, like an HTML file, that it can be displayed. For example, depending on how the application in the receiving computer wanted to handle the phone number, it could be stored, displayed or dialed.

Windows CE   Windows CE is based on the Microsoft Windows operating system but is designed for including or embedding in mobile and other space-constrained devices. Although Microsoft does not explain the "CE," it is reported to have originally stood for "consumer electronics."

Source: whatis®.com and WAP Forum—W3C Cooperation White Paper, *W3C Note,* October 30, 1998.

Cisco Systems Inc.: Managing Corporate Growth Using an Intranet

By Professor Michael Parent and Debra Rankin

The 1997 fiscal year had closed and once again Cisco Systems Inc. had surpassed industry growth rates. Since 1993 the company had been following an aggressive growth strategy in order to expand into all data networking markets. A significant portion of that growth came through acquisitions, despite the high failure rate experienced by large-scale mergers. John Chambers, Chief Executive Officer and President of Cisco since 1995, looked at the networking market as operating "in Internet years, as opposed to calendar years. Things are changing so fast with regard to the Internet that each regular business calendar year equals seven Internet business years."[1] The frenzied pace of change in the networking industry required a dynamic and responsive organization. Cisco coped with organizational growth by using its technology to develop and deploy an extensive corporate intranet. The challenge remained to ensure that Information Systems (IS) and Information Technology (IT) continued to support the scaling of Cisco's organization as it continued to expand.

Company Overview and History

Headquartered in San Jose, California, Cisco was the world's largest supplier of data networking equipment and the leading global supplier of computer networking solutions.

A network has been defined as:

> ". . . a collection of individual [nodes], connected by intermediate . . . devices, that functions as a single large network."[2]

In the past, every department in an organization built its own network in order to facilitate communication among the department's staff. Because these LANs (local area networks) used different protocols and media access methods, the flow of information beyond the department was impeded. Cisco was the first company to come up with a device that enabled networks to communicate. In 1997, Cisco developed, manufactured, sold and supported the hardware and software that together distributed and translated data from one network to another, and connected individuals and remote locations to those networks. Cisco's vision was to link LANs and WANs (wide area networks) across geographically dispersed locations throughout the world via a single, seamless infrastructure.

---

[1]As quoted in the article by G. Rifkin, "Growth by Acquisition—The Case of Cisco Systems," *Strategy & Business* (Booz, Allen & Hamilton Inc. 1997).

[2]M. Ford, H. Kim Loo, S. Spanier, and T. Stephenson, *Internetworking Technologies Handbook.*

The Cisco story was the dream of every entrepreneur. Leonard Bosack and Sandy Lerner were a husband and wife team who worked in different departments at Stanford University: she in the business school and he in computer science. In order to be able to transfer information between their computer systems, they developed a device that translated the computer languages used by their respective department networks. This device was a router. It distributed the data, and had software that allowed the messages to be readable by different languages and operating systems. This was the beginning of the soon-to-be "Cisco." Bosack and Lerner left the academic world and in 1984 together with three other colleagues set up the company from their home in California.

Cisco sold its first network router in 1986. In late 1987, the company received its first, and only, venture funding, $2.5M (all dollars in US), which in fact was never spent. By 1988, Cisco started to target large corporations, not just universities and government departments. With sales growing from $1.5M in 1987 to $28M in 1989, Cisco went public in 1990. Later that year, the founders left.

By 1991, sales reached $183M. Increased competition from both start-ups and giants such as IBM and Digital Equipment began to confront Cisco. This competition was fuelled by the rapid growth of corporate networking. This growth was greatly attributed to the acceptance of the TCP/IP "Internet protocol" as the means by which to transmit data. This standard allowed individual networks to be linked by cheaper, faster and smarter devices. Also, there was a concurrent increase on the part of both end users to use their PCs for communication purposes on the Internet and for businesses to develop their own networks.

Cisco continued to grow through product enhancements and expansion of its product line, as well as through international sales. However, in 1993, management was convinced that although revenues were doubling and Cisco had 80 percent of the router market, switching was becoming a compelling, complementary technology that customers were asking for. Consequently, Cisco decided to shift its business philosophy and expand into all networking technology (both switches and routers) through a highly aggressive growth strategy. This was to be accomplished through strategic alliances, minority investments and acquisitions, together with internal development.

Cisco's first acquisition was in September 1993. The company bought Crescendo Communications Inc., which had annualized revenues of $10M, for $89M. Within 18 months of the purchase, the product originated by Crescendo, and enhanced by Cisco, was generating over $500M in revenues. Since then Cisco had acquired nearly 20 companies that spanned four networking technologies: LAN and WAN switches, remote dial-up access, and Internet software. Exhibit 1 illustrates and describes the rate and extent of these acquisitions.

EXHIBIT 1   CISCO Acquisitions

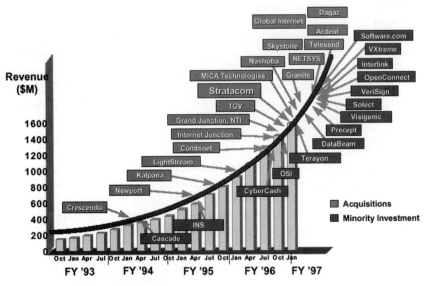

Source: Cisco documents (used with permission).

ACQUISITION	DATE	TECHNOLOGY
Crescendo Communications, Inc.	September 1993	High-speed switching solutions for the workgroup
Newport Systems Solutions, Inc.	August 1994	Software-based routers for remote network sites
Kalpana, Inc.	October 1994	LAN switching products
LightStream Corp.	December 1994	Enterprise and workgroup ATM switching, LAN switching and routing
Combinet, Inc.	August 1995	ISDN remote-access networking products
Internet Junction, Inc.	September 1995	Internet gateway software for central and remote office Internet access
Grand Junction, Inc.	September 1995	LAN switching and Fast Ethernet products
Network Translation, Inc.	October 1995	Network address translation and Internet firewall hardware and software

EXHIBIT 1 (*continued*)

ACQUISITION	DATE	TECHNOLOGY
TGV Software, Inc.	January 1996	Internet software products for connecting disparate computer systems over local area, enterprise-wide and global computing networks
StrataCom, Inc.	April 1996	ATM and Frame Relay high-speed WAN switching equipment
Telebit Corp's MICA Technologies	July 1996	High-density digital modem technology
Nahoba Networks, Inc.	August 1996	Token Ring LAN switching
Granite Systems, Inc.	September 1996	Multilayer Gigabit Ethernet switching
Netsys Technologies	October 1996	Network infrastructure management and performance analysis software
Telesend	March 1997	WAN access products
Skystone Systems Corp.	June 1997	High-speed Synchronous Optical Networking/ Synchronous Digital Hierarchy
Global Internet Software Group	June 1997	Windows NT network security
Ardent Communications Corp	June 1997	Communications support for compressed voice, LAN, data and video traffic across public and private Frame Relay and ATM networks
Dagaz (Integrated Network Corporation)	July 1997	High-speed information transmission over existing copper phone lines

Source: Internal Cisco documents.

By 1997, Cisco offered end-to-end connectivity solutions and product lines covering a wide range of routers, LAN and WAN switches, dial-up access servers and network management software. Virtually all of these products incorporated Cisco IOS software, which provided the intelligence that integrated Cisco products so that disparate groups, varied devices and multiple protocols could work together. Cisco IOS software was also licensed to many vendors, including some competitors, as an integral part of their products (e.g., Hewlett-Packard and Digital Equipment computers, Time Warner and Toshiba cable modems, Alcatel and Siemens telecommunications CO switches).

Cisco's workforce had grown from 94 employees in 1989 to 11,000 in 1997, of which about 2,000 were from acquisitions. None of Cisco's acquisitions resulted in layoffs, because the motivation behind an acquisition was product development and market expansion, not cost savings through consolidation. Compared to the industry, Cisco's overall attrition rate was low.

Cisco sold its products through 125 locations in 75 countries with international sales accounting for 47 percent of its revenues. The company had technical support centres in California, North Carolina, Australia, Belgium and Canada. Cisco's major equipment markets were low-end, mid-range, and high-end routers; workgroup and backbone LAN switches; WAN switches; and remote dial-up access. It was either number one or number two in all of these markets except remote access dial-up ports. Its revenues were made up of 49 percent routers, 22 percent LAN switches, 12 percent WAN switches, 6 percent remote dial-up access, 11 percent services and other. While the industry had been growing at 30 to 50 percent, for each of the fiscal years 1993 to 1996, Cisco's revenues grew in excess of 80 percent. In fiscal year 1997, Cisco's revenues were $6.4 billion.

Cisco was listed on the Fortune 500 for the first time in 1997 as one of the top five for both return on revenues and return on assets, a record matched only by Microsoft and Intel. Exhibit 2 provides financial highlights from 1994 to 1997. Cisco had no long-term debt and an unused line of credit of $100M. Cisco stock was traded over the counter on the NASDAQ National Market. It had a market capitalization of $55B, third in value on NASDAQ after Microsoft and Intel. The stock had split five times in six years and had increased over 14,000 percent since it went public. The stock's 1997 52-week high was $83¼.

EXHIBIT 2 Financial Highlights

Consolidated Statement of Operations Data
(in thousands, except per-share amounts)

Years Ended	7/26/97	7/28/96	7/30/95	7/31/94
Net Sales	$6,440,171	$4,096,007	$2,232,652	$1,334,436
Income before income taxes	1,888,872	1,464,825	737,977	522,500
Net Income	1,048,679	913,324	456,489	322,981
Net Income per common share	$1.52	$1.37	$0.72	$0.54
Shares used in per share calculation	689,319	666,586	630,711	596,639

Consolidated Balance Sheet
(in thousands)

	7/26/97	7/28/96	7/30/95	7/31/94
Total assets	$5,451,984	$3,630,232	$1,991,949	$1,129,034
Shareholders' equity	$4,289,622	$2,819,622	$1,562,276	$904,323

Industry/Market Trends/Competition

The rapid pace of change in the networking industry was attributed to a number of factors. While the market had expanded to include small, medium and large businesses as well as consumers, networks were typically doubling in size in less than a year. The 1997 data networking market was estimated at $27 billion and was forecast to reach $93 billion by 1999. Overall, IT expenditures were forecast by the U.S. government to be more than 40 percent of U.S. capital spending by the year 2000.

Since end users wanted to communicate with more people and send more data faster, networking technology was being driven to provide higher capacity and faster and more functional services. For example, organizations required global networks to conduct their businesses internally with the use of an intranet. Also, businesses were transacting through commercial networks directly with their customers. Fierce competition for these markets led to a shift from complementary to converging technologies and to a blurring of the line between "computing" and "communicating." As a result, there was increasing overlap in the businesses of the various players.

In 1996, the worldwide networking market share[3] was as follows: Cisco 21.9 percent, 3Com 12.8 percent, Bay Networks 11.6 percent, IBM 8.3 percent and Cabletron 6.0 percent. The rest of the market was highly fragmented, with no other player having more than a 3.3 percent share. However, the competitive field shifted frequently, and the increased number of consolidations and alliances in the industry were influencing the pace and degree of the shifts. As Chambers recently stated, "Our biggest competitor two years ago was 20 percent bigger than us. Today we are 300 percent bigger than them. Anyone who thinks that can't happen to them is wrong."[4]

Organizational Changes in Cisco From 1993 to 1997

In 1993, Cisco started to move beyond routers as it expanded its market. It recognized that the networking industry was shifting to a more complex environment in which a number of technologies would need to coexist. Cisco was concerned that if it became too strongly tied to any one technology it would not be in tune with market needs, and thus it would risk failure. Cisco started on the road to change by borrowing some of the best practices from other corporations. It decided

---

[3]Source: Strategic Networks Consulting, Inc. As reported in the article by S. Borthick, "Turning Point of the Router Market?" *Business Communications Review* (December 1996).

[4]Chambers as quoted in the article by J. Cooper Ramo, "Cisco Guards the Gates," *Time* (June 9, 1997).

to segment the market on the basis of end users, as Hewlett-Packard had done, and to move away from being organized around products. It also chose to follow GE's policy of being number one or two in every market it entered, or else exiting from that segment. Lastly, Cisco aimed to be THE one-stop vendor for networking solutions, much as IBM had been for mainframes.

In expanding its product lines, Cisco would have preferred to develop all its technology internally as it had done in the past. However, in a business where product cycles were less than 18 months, time to market was critical. Cisco decided it would have to look outside. It entered into scores of joint ventures, joint marketing and joint development agreements. In situations where the company could not develop technology to get to market within six months, it acquired. The company was, and remained, prepared to do as many as eight to 12 such deals per year.

In 1994, Cisco reorganized around decentralized business units that were responsible for product development and marketing in their respective markets, but which had different core technologies. Cisco's three decentralized lines of business were named for the markets they served: Enterprise, Service Providers, and Small/Medium Business. For the purposes of manufacturing, distribution and finance, Cisco maintained a centralized organization in order to take advantage of the synergy and economies of scale provided by a large company. One of the hallmarks of the organization was frequent reorganization in order to respond to rapidly changing markets.

Cisco underwent a significant increase in its workforce with more than half of its 11,000 employees hired within the last four years. Its hiring rate was as high as 350 employees per month, not including employees from acquisitions. Cisco also expanded its senior management. It added 25 vice presidents in 1996, and in 1997, had over 50 in total. In scaling up the business and the workforce, Cisco set up an extensive suite of electronic interactive services which it called the Cisco Connection for customers, partners, employees, shareholders and prospects.

In 1995, John Chambers became CEO. He joined Cisco in 1991 after having worked for IBM and then Wang. He viewed one of his worst professional experiences as having to lay off 4,000 employees at Wang. "I learned at both companies that in high tech, if you don't stay ahead of trends, they'll destroy everything you work for and tragically disrupt the lives of your employees. I don't ever want to go through that again."[5]

---

[5]J. Chambers as quoted in the article by B. Schlender, "Computing's Next Superpower," *Fortune* (May 12, 1997).

Acquisitions

In addition to its 15 minority investments, Cisco had acquired 19 companies since 1993. (See Exhibit 1 for a summary.) These acquisitions, which were primarily paid for with Cisco stock, cost in excess of $5.5B. The company estimated that about 30 per cent of its revenues came from acquired product lines, although the distinction between acquired products and internally developed products became blurred once a company had been part of Cisco for more than two years. Most of the acquired companies were privately held and ranged in size from 20 to 150 employees with the exception of StrataCom which was a public company with 1,200 employees. The acquisition of StrataCom at $4 billion was one of the largest in the industry. On average, Cisco has paid $500,000 to $2 million per employee. Cisco has retained more than half of the CEOs of the acquisitions for at least six months and many have stayed on in major roles. The attrition rate is actually lower for the acquired employees than for the new hires.

The "Art" of Acquisition

Cisco had a business development team of 50 to 60 employees who looked for businesses with technology in development that the market was seeking but that Cisco could not develop fast enough internally. Cisco expected its acquisitions to provide revenue equal to the purchase payment within three years. Based on its experience in joint ventures, Cisco elected to seek out similar cultures to avoid conflicts. Cisco developed a reproducible model for the acquisition process: target selection, approach, purchase and integration. The whole process took from three to six months. The target selection was key. In this type of acquisition the company was basically purchasing the employees and the technology they were developing. If the employees did not stay, then the value of the acquisition was lost. Therefore, in selecting the target company it was vital that it shared Cisco's vision of technology.

Generally, Cisco targeted small, privately held technology start-ups that were growing fast. The targets had to be culturally similar to Cisco, geographically close and entrepreneurial. The take-over had to be friendly and uncomplicated with a rapid integration. This supported two of Cisco's goals. First, in order to be first-to-market, the deal could not be tied up in lengthy negotiations and legalities. Second, there should be minimal inconvenience to both Cisco's and the acquired business's customers. The integration of the employees, products and technology in development had to be virtually transparent to the customer. An internal group made up of leaders from various parts of Cisco sponsored the acquisition and took ownership of merging it into Cisco. As soon as the purchase agreement was signed, a dedicated team of Cisco

IT staff worked on integrating the acquired company's IT systems into Cisco's, including electronic mail, web sites, product order systems and sales automation.

Cisco Employee Connection (CEC)

The Cisco Connection was a combination of Internet and CD-ROMs/intranet applications which were available to customers, partners, shareholders, prospects and employees. It provided online information and interactive services worldwide on a real-time basis, including software upgrades, technical assistance, order status, seminar registration, documentation and training. Cisco's employee intranet was known as the Cisco Employee Connection (CEC). It was designed to provide information and services to meet the needs of Cisco employees. Its access was restricted to employees only. Exhibit 3 illustrates the CEC's first-level menu. The CEC was designed to be employee-friendly and intuitive in order to minimize training time. The benefits, from Cisco's viewpoint, were instant global communications, enhanced productivity, consistent business systems, lower business costs, and scalability.

CEC was based on a secure and transparent architecture and used firewall network security. It provided information and interactive tools for facilities, travel arrangements, technical documentation, human resources, training, sales and marketing, and financial matters.

Once employees logged on to the CEC, they were presented with a main menu that allowed them to access a vast array of information through different feature selections. These selections included categorization by lines of business, business functions, company and employee-related information. There were also a number of repositories called "dashboards" which grouped links on particular topics. One dashboard was called "new hires." It facilitated an efficient integration of new employees into Cisco by providing links to information needed by new hires. For example, its opening screen provided a list of frequently asked questions (FAQs).

The other dashboards were used as job-specific tools to aid personnel in their daily operations relating to sales, engineering, managers and system engineers. For example, in the area of sales, since Cisco now offered end-to-end networking solutions and scores of products, CEC provided the employees with up-to-date information on new products and company developments. Since 1996, Cisco's sales force had been supplied with portable computers so that every sales representative could access CEC. This included a bank of sales presentations which could be customized on customer sites within minutes.

EXHIBIT 3   CEC Illustrated

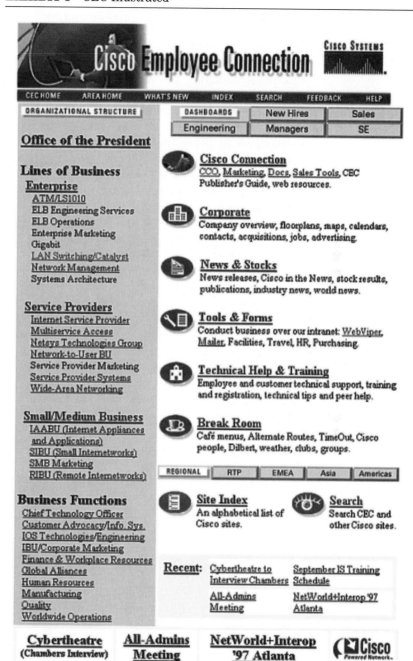

Source: Cisco Systems Inc.

John Chambers' Concern

The challenge for John Chambers was to ensure that IS and IT continued to support Cisco during its aggressive growth strategy. By all measures, the CEC had been tremendously successful in facilitating employee acculturation. It had also proved to be a powerful showcase for Cisco's technology.

As Cisco continued down the path of eight to 12 acquisitions a year, Chambers was concerned about the limitations of the intranet for managing growth. He was well aware that the company's growth rates provided considerable challenges that could not be overlooked. As he put it recently, "We're paranoid. A lot of companies are arrogant. They're on top and they believe they belong there. We've got almost the reverse attitude. We've got a tremendous fear of failing. We make Andy Grove at Intel look relaxed."![6]

---

[6]J. Chambers, as quoted in footnote 1.

Chapter 3

Sourcing of E-Commerce Capabilities

One of the most fundamental business choices is the "make or buy" decision—whether to produce something in-house or outsource it to a third party. This chapter explores the outsourcing decision for e-commerce and information systems services. Although outsourcing has been commonplace in many business areas and functions for decades, it is relatively recent in the area of information systems services.

There are a number of reasons for this. When computers filled rooms and were enormous capital investments, just having a computer may have been a competitive advantage. As a strategic resource, then, companies were reluctant to depend on someone else to fulfill that need. Furthermore, most programming was done in-house by full-time employee software analysts, programmers, and testers who typically developed one-of-a-kind programs tailored to each firm. As information systems became more important on an operational and strategic level, firms were reluctant to divest control over large computer and technical staff investments.

This situation changed significantly in the late 1980s as leading "top 100" companies started outsourcing their information systems needs wholesale. Some did it to lower costs, while others did it to defocus on what had become common commodity processing and refocus on areas of competence. Some have since retreated a bit in one way or another, but information system outsourcing is still expanding in scale and scope—including outsourcing key e-commerce services.

The first case, "OP4.com: Choosing a Website Design Agency," looks at the issues of outsourcing website design and development. In particular, OP4.com executives must decide between an inexpensive new, small, very informal, and "very cool" company and an older, much more expansive, larger, more established, and highly formalized company. Among the many dilemmas the company faced was that while the smaller firm may understand the target audience better and cost less, the larger firm may provide a more reliable product that would cost less in the long term. Many of the common issues in outsourcing surface in this case. It can also serve to highlight the more technical issues of web page design and development.

The second case, "Enerline Restorations Inc: Stay with an ASP?" introduces the concept of outsourcing over the Internet with application service providers, or ASPs. While more traditional information systems outsourcing is a one-to-one arrangement between the outsourcer and the hiring company, the Internet allows a one-to-many arrangement between one outsourcer and many customers sharing the same software on a pay-per-user basis. Furthermore, the users could take advantage of Internet benefits: a simple user interface (the browser) and worldwide access. Similarly, the outsourcer can take advantage of near zero marginal variable costs for additional Internet users; huge profits are possible with popular software packages and good outsourcing service. In this case, Enerline Restorations hired an outsourcer for all its data processing for economic reasons while it concentrated on corporate expansion. What happened to the outsourcer later in the case, however, gave them serious reasons to reconsider.

The third case is "SalesDriver: The Lorimer Request," which provides a counterpoint to Enerline Restorations. SalesDriver is an ASP facing many of the same online outsourcing issues from the "opposite" perspective. SalesDriver is trying to reach a critical mass of users to achieve high returns after making significant up-front fixed cost investments in equipment, personnel, and software. Along the way, Sales-Driver gets a request from Lorimer to tailor a software package specifically for them. SalesDriver wants Lorimer's business for many reasons, but has to wrestle with a request that goes counter to the very business model they're based on—one-to-many.

OP4.com: Choosing a Website Design Agency

By Professor Scott Schneberger and Ken Mark

Introduction

Tom Pressello, bCEO (business CEO) of OP4.com was getting frustrated. "I'm not sure our web agency, MillenPro, understands our youth space. Ray, Stuart and I just wanted a little teaser site and what they have put together for us is not what will appeal to this demographic." It was January 2000, and Vancouver-based OP4.com had just secured half a million dollars in private placement financing from a prominent West Coast venture capitalist contact. "In the meantime, I've got a proposal from another agency, BaseSync Inc., and we've got to decide which agency to pick. We're funded now and it's time for OP4.com to get developed."

The Concept of OP4.COM—"Our Place 4 Everything"

Stuart Saunders, a co-founder of OP4.com, described his vision for the concept: "To be honest, I started this to have a positive web community for kids. I had the vision but not the dollars and cents—I was thinking strictly of the kids." His fellow co-founders Ray Matthews, a successful direct sales entrepreneur, and Tom Pressello, a former strategic consultant and merchant banker in the technology arena, were aiding in bringing the concept to fruition.

OP4.com's objective was to build itself to be a "portal," an Internet site whose goal was to attract and retain a large percentage of its visitors by providing multiple features and site products wanted by its audience. Thus, OP4.com would allow teenagers to congregate, discuss topics with each other through chat rooms, e-mail, posting messages in reply and submitting articles. The OP4.com concept would immediately have to appeal to this demographic group in order for its business model to work. OP4.com wanted to position itself as the premier youth-oriented site, with proprietary content as a cornerstone.

All three co-founders were aware that in the increasing presence of Internet-savvy teenagers in the year 2000 and beyond lay a business opportunity. OP4.com's site advertising model would be unique from its competitors. OP4.com had a unique user aggregation model—Saunders owned a motivational speaking company that had a reported reach of 10 million North American high school students. Whereas other sites would rely on online and traditional media advertising, OP4.com intended to stand out from the crowd with its grassroots, viral marketing model.

IVEY Ken Mark prepared this case under the supervision of Professor Scott Schneberger solely to provide material for class discussion. The authors do not intend to illustrate either effective or ineffective handling of a managerial situation. The authors may have disguised certain names and other identifying information to protect confidentiality.

Web Design

Introduction to a New Medium

While people had been designing, publishing and reading printed material on paper and other hard-copy material for millennia, web page design was a very new field with comparatively few design experts. Moreover, the technology they designed for was constantly changing—as were the expectations of the web page users as they became more web-savvy.

Issues and Challenges in Web Design

Pressello understood that there were challenges to overcome in designing a web page:

Page Size

The size of an appropriate web page depended on a user's monitor resolution, monitor size and even the operating system of the computer the browser was running on. The result was that some web pages showed up oversized and users could not view the entire page—making the user frustratingly scroll back and forth to see everything.

Feature Viewing

Color fidelity depended on the brightness of a particular brand of monitor and its age and the brightness, contrast and gamma settings in effect. These characteristics meant that a graphic that looked bright and attractive to one user could look dull and pale to another. Some users may have their graphics display turned off. They wouldn't see charts or animation that others would. Type faces, line lengths, use of color and italics—designed for paper—may be counterproductive on a web page. Different user browsers treated rules (horizontal lines) differently.

Attention Span

Furthermore, screen readers tended to have a much shorter attention span than paper readers, and they could not as easily scan using their eyes or head (they had to scroll or click to another page). In short, the medium, the technology and the user were different and these differences had to be taken into account in good web design.

Web Advantages

Pressello also understood, however, some of the unique opportunities web page design offered. First and foremost, the content could be dynamic: what the user saw could be continuously updated to be current, it could be tailored to the user's unique needs and it could be responsive or interactive with a user. That would not be possible with the paper medium. Moreover, a web page was technically an infinite space; it could be scrolled down or sideways, or linked to other pages, indefinitely. A web page could also use video, sound and animation. It could provide links to databases for information, to other pages or even other related websites. Web pages could be accessed worldwide in seconds— or take 10s of minutes locally, depending on Internet connections, loading and the user's modem. Finally, a web page could conduct business: it could display information, collect information, make a sale, accept payment and (in the case of digitized products or services) distribute the merchandise.

Determining the Scope of a Web Site

Pressello had articulated OP4.com's goals to BaseSync over the course of several meetings. With the proliferation of web agencies and web advice sites, it was not difficult to locate a template that would aid business users in defining their web site goals:

Type of Site	Purpose	Typical Features
Brochure	Potential customers from around the world can learn about your company.	• Some graphics (logos or photos) • Description of your company • E-mail link or guestbook form
E-commerce	Customers from around the world can purchase your products or services via the Internet.	Features of a brochure site, plus: • Customer shopping cart • Credit card processing • Customer security functions
Marketing	You can increase consumer awareness of your company or your brand or services by strategically linking and affiliating your site with related sites.	Features of a brochure site, plus: • Advertising (e.g., banner ad exchange) • Marketing (e.g., affiliate programs)
Community	A portal site, you can create an attractive audience to sponsors by driving people from your disparate sites to your central community site.	Features of a brochure site, plus: • Advertising (banners) • Sponsor site integration • Features to support community site (e-mail, chat, message boards)
Database-driven	You can allow your customers to access their account data, search for documents that support your product, or learn more about products or services you sell offline.	Features of a brochure site, plus: • Custom database design • Search tools
Extranet	You can use your website to share sensitive or confidential information with your customers or suppliers in a secure fashion.	Similar to a database-driven site plus: • Password-protected access • Data security functions

Design Costs

When talking to his contacts, Pressello learned that designing a web site could be a very expensive process—if database and e-commerce services were included. A quick search on the web produced these data points:

- Sophisticated e-commerce sites could easily exceed Cdn$200,000;
- Typical costs were Cdn$300–500 per page (rough estimate);
- Cdn$50–150 per image/graphic (logo design was more costly);
- Cdn$2,500–5,000+ for e-commerce/database functionality, increasing significantly with the number of products sold.[1]

Teen Sites Competing in OP4.com's Space

The most prominent site was Bolt.com, touted as the leader in the teen site arena. It had become a popular hangout for high school students in North America, and its content leaned towards what OP4.com's founders considered "teen inappropriate." OP4.com wanted to project a positive teen image and was planning to solicit content from appropriate role models in the youth leadership world—successful students, student leaders, motivational speakers and politicians, to name a few examples. Other competitors included Alloy.com, iTurf.com and Snowball.com, each with its own cultural "feel."

Another factor that would differentiate OP4.com's concept from other teen sites, according to the founders, was the fact that their consumer aggregation model would be unique: it relied on Leadership Innovations' speakers (Saunder's current motivational speaking company) to market to its audience. Another key factor would be its proprietary written content. It would publish its own staff articles (entertainment pieces, expert opinions, articles on current teen-related topics like AIDS) and monitor the quality of solicited content on its site with the goal of developing a consistent, wholesome brand image.

Millenpro

Approached by OP4.com to do a mock-up site, MillenPro built an initial "landing" web page and developed a logo for OP4. A "flash" introduction was created along with the initial page and a short questionnaire collected pre-registration information (see Exhibit 1—OP4.com's MillenPro Flash Movie Screen Captures). A minor disagreement arose between OP4.com and MillenPro about ownership of pre-registration data that was being collected, stating that the data belonged to MillenPro as part of the reduced site building cost and specifications plan offered to OP4.com (Cdn$34,000). Request for changes to the initial mock-up site took a couple of days before responses were given, and OP4.com's management had to go over the new requirements an average of three times before MillenPro's project manager understood the nature of the changes to be made.

---

[1]Source: BizBuyer—Web Design. Accessed October 12, 2000.

EXHIBIT 1 OP4.Com's Millenpro Flash Movie Screen Captures

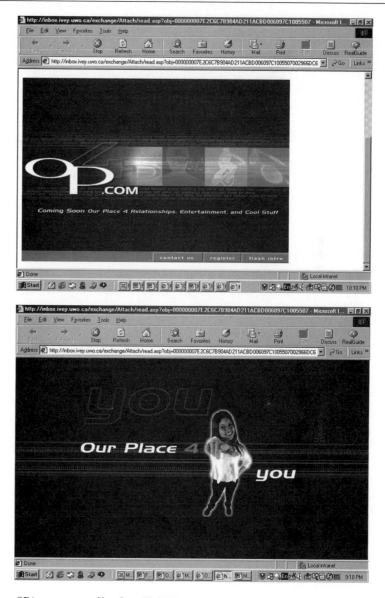

Source: OP4.com company files, June 25, 2000.

Approaching Basesync Communications Inc. For A New Bid

Although planning to use MillenPro for the larger project, because of the initial disagreements after the landing page, Pressello decided to hedge their bets and approach BaseSync to bid on the project.

BaseSync, considered a Vancouver "hot shop" for innovative interactive web design, was regularly featured in industry and consumer media reports and had won accolades and large accounts for its work.

Pressello remarked, "We needed someone who understood that space. Did BaseSync understand the youth space? I'm sure of it because they did work for Universal, Nike, Lego, Nintendo—entertainment space, youth demographics. This, however, is their first teen portal site." BaseSync had been swamped with projects, but had been finally convinced to provide a business requirements document (BRD), charging OP4.com Cdn$25,000. If OP4.com wanted to move to the next stage, a usability design document that laid out all the inner workings of the site would cost another Cdn$25,000. BaseSync had estimated the cost of building the site to be Cdn$450,000, with future user interface changes estimated at another Cdn$35,000. Pressello began to read the BDD that BaseSync had created after several meetings with OP4.com (see Exhibit 2—Business Development Document).

The Choice Facing OP4.com

Two barriers to hiring BaseSync were its proposed site price range (over half a million dollars at the middle point of the estimate) and the fact that BaseSync was extremely busy. Pressello commented, "It's hard to create a win-win situation when the company you're wanting to work with (BaseSync) turns away 95 per cent of their business. More importantly, are we satisfied with their vision of OP4.com?"

Pressello was conscious of the fact that OP4.com needed to make a decision rapidly and did not want to expend additional time researching lists of web design firms. Already, their major competition was acquiring thousands of new users on a weekly basis and getting press coverage. Not wanting to be left behind by his competitors, Pressello narrowed his options: proceed with the BaseSync recommendation or give MillenPro another chance.

EXHIBIT 2   BaseSync Business Development Document BaseSync Communications Inc.

Objectives

Primary
- To aggregate members by creating a dynamic virtual community where teens can communicate freely and contribute content.
- To be a protected society online, where students can speak, act and initiate their dreams, desires and ambitions.
- To be the authentic online voice of high school students in North America.
- To build loyalty and enthusiasm for the target demographic.

EXHIBIT 2   *(continued)*

Secondary

- Create lateral synergies with corporations and organizations, providing income streams through sponsorships, advertisements and e-commerce opportunities.

Branding

- Charged with creating a brand and online identity in the truest sense, OP4.com will start as an e-brand in which everything that follows will flow from the look, feel and overall experience of the site. It is crucial that branding remains consistent in terms of feel and navigation throughout the site.

Community

- A primary goal of OP4.com is to provide members with a sense of community while they access information that is relevant to their needs and interests. Essential to this sense of community are the issues of self-expression, absence of hate and dishonesty. Promote respect for each member and loyalty for the entire membership.

Freshness

- Freshness is an essential element to the success of OP4.com. New information such as stories, articles and features will be posted daily.

User Profiles

- Another essential element of OP4.com is to gather user profiles into a database, which can then be mined for future marketing, advertising purposes and site enhancement. Therefore, the site must include features that will reward the user for divulging the necessary personal information. This information must be easily accessed so that specific news and promotional information can be readily delivered to this audience.

Metrics For Success

The success of OP4.com will be measured by:

- The number of registered users and their profiles gathered.
- The amount of positive feedback from the target audience.
- The increase of visibility of OP4.com with the primary audience resulting from successful marketing strategy.
- The number of third-party web companies who will partner with OP4.com and/or sponsor OP4.com events.

EXHIBIT 2   *(continued)*

- Total sales created in the sponsor's website by successful advertising or exposures on the OP4.com site.

Target Audience and Three Key Interests

Community
- Audience expects OP4.com to create a community where its members can engage in a wide variety of activities, share ideas, check out new sites and explore the Internet. Members will use OP4.com to connect themselves with activities and content that reflect their specific needs and interests. Kids can find out about the hottest new brands, read or write reviews on their favorite movies or books.
- Other community-building features will include chat rooms, bulletin boards, instant messaging (OP4-notes) and e-mail capabilities.

Customization
- Members expect to make OP4.com their home online. In order to feel like home, it must look the way they want it to. The look and feel of OP4.com must be customizable and appealing to each member based on his/her preferences or mood.

Interactivity
- The OP4.com audience is looking for a site that provides more than information. Members must be able to interact with the site through games, trivia, polls and be involved providing content for the site.

Site Design and Requirements Analysis

General Look and Feel
- The site should look fun, funky, genuine and constantly be evolving.
- OP4.com should reflect its members' diversity, honesty, sincerity, and evolution.
- OP4.com must meet the demand for new information from its community of users.
- The main navigation interface must clearly communicate what OP4.com has to offer and the overall look and feel of what members can expect from the site. Users will immediately identify with the familiar colors, layout and site icons; however, return users will see and expect something new with each visit.
- The home page will be funky, interactive, exciting and fast loading. It will entice new members to sign on and instantly begin taking advantage of what OP4.com has to offer.

EXHIBIT 2 *(continued)*

- The design of OP4.com should be edgy, exciting and, above all, inviting. Things that appeal most to boys and girls age 13 to 17 will be a priority; therefore the site needs to be techno-savvy, quirky and armed with what this demographic is looking for and wants to be a part of. Although the site will be "flashy," pages should display information in a clear manner, remaining light, fast and architecturally consistent. The site design will be based on a series of unique templates, which will allow for a consistent look and feel throughout.

Content Requirements

- The intention of the site is to provide the user with fresh information in a creative and fun manner. Content will be provided by members, OP4.com and limited information from third-party providers. Content, such as contests, events, news and online community activities will be designed to enhance the overall experience of OP4.com and will continue to evolve based on user feedback. The site must be fun, interactive and engaging. New users will be encouraged to register as a member.

Navigational Requirements

- The site will be designed to be scalable to accommodate new content and functionality. BaseSync will also create administration tools, which will facilitate the updating of content, images and text.

Site Functionalities and Content Organization

This section will describe what kind of content will be populating the OP4.com website, and how this information is being organized logically.

All section names, sub-section names, feature names and link names should be finalized at this stage. All functionality should be described from a business perspective, while the actual functional design and technical specifications will be addressed in separate documents: The Functional Design Document (FDD) and the Technical Specifications Document (TSD), respectively, during the early stage of production.

Page Number	Function/Links	How Does It Work
Home Page	Content	Introduction text, teasers, bits, etc. (TBD)
	Special Requirements	This page should have a browser detect function built-in to determine whether or not the user is using a supported browser version. If not, the user should be re-directed to an error page with links to upgrade their browsers.

EXHIBIT 2 *(continued)*

Page Number	Function/Links	How Does It Work
Common Navigation Items	Registration	Link to a form page: Required Information: • User ID • Password • Retype password Optional Information • Cheater Questions/Answers (for retrieving password) • E-mail address (default: userid@op4.com) • Sex (radio button) • Age (exact birthday?) • Province/State (drop-down list—North America) • Country (drop-down list) • Postal Code/Zip • Where did you hear about us? • Each registration should give the member a Contest point. • Phase 2 will include more survey questions for the E-Pal feature. • This page should be secured.

Interactive Functions

Interactivity is one of the critical success factors of OP4.com. The section will describe what kind of interactive tools OP4.com would like to offer in Phase 1.

Off-the-shelf products are preferred to minimize development and integration time, but the following capabilities are required:

- The package needs to be "brandable" (i.e., front-end can be customized to reflect OP4.com's look and feel).
- The package has to be scalable to support large amounts of traffic and heavy usage (0.5 million users projected in the first six months, and growing to one million in one year).
- The package has to be compatible with all platform and browser versions OP4.com supports.
- The package has to be robust and reliable with minimal downtime.
- Prefer to have one integrated package that provides all required functionalities.

Business Process Requirements

The following sections describe some general business process guidelines for site preparation, site construction, and site performance.

EXHIBIT 2   *(continued)*

Data Conversion

There are two data-sources (registration information and school information) that need to be converted into the website database. They should be:

- Available digitally.
- Formatted consistently.
- Contained either in a RDBMS format (e.g., MS SQL Server) or file format that can be easily uploaded into a RDBMS (Relational Database Management System).
- Initial data conversion is part of Phase 1.
- Regular updates and synchronization will be implemented in Phase 2.

Initial Database and Template Population

The client provides all copies on the OP4.com site and they should be checked for spelling and grammatical mistakes before submission. BaseSync will store this information either in the database and/or include them in the HTML pages.

Three revisions/changes are allowed for logical batch of copies (e.g., copy on the same page or belong to the same table in the database). Additional changes will be treated as change requests.

BaseSync will provide all images, graphics and design elements used on the site.

Membership

Membership is one of the critical success factors of the OP4.com site. In order to attract most people, the registration process should be simple and fast. All member information should be stored in the database for future analysis. The login process must be secured, fast and reliable.

Phase 1 will support a single tier membership structure (i.e., one type of membership). A simple loyalty program will be included (point collection for the contest). Members will receive newsletter and special announcements.

In Phase 2 when e-commerce is available, members will enjoy discounts and coupons and other promotional privileges.

Security Requirements

- Sensitive content pages (e.g., registration, log-in, and update profile pages) must be done with secure connections.
- Passwords should be encrypted in the database when being stored.
- Usage of cookies is allowed but not relied on—the cookie should not store passwords and/or any other sensitive information.
- Security requirements will be further defined in Phase 2 when e-commerce is available.

EXHIBIT 2   *(continued)*

Performance and Compatibility Guidelines

- In the first six months, the site is expected to have 0.5 million viewers per day, and 2,500 concurrent viewers at peak times.
- Within 12 months, the site is expected to have 1 million viewers per day, and 5,000 concurrent viewers at peak times.
- Maximum size of each page (excluding Flash components): 100 KB (including text and images).
- Maximum number of individual images (all optimized for web use): 30.
- Maximum time for database access and server side preparation for each page: two seconds. Total turnaround time cannot be used to measure performance because it depends on the connection speed, but the goal should be less than six seconds on a 56k modem.
- Site design should be based on a minimum screen resolution of 800 × 600.
- Phase 1: The site should be compatible with current platform and browsers. Although all programming will be done with the goal to support most versions on most platforms, thorough testing will be done in Phase 1 to ensure compatibility to the above combinations. In Phase 2, we can broaden the support and conduct more testing for other environments.

QA and Testing Criteria

QA and testing will be done to ensure:

- All links are operational.
- All functions/features are working properly.
- All requirements specified in this document are met.
- Usability level is acceptable.
- General look and feel/layout/navigation are user-friendly and consistent.

Not in scope items are (but will report if error is noticed):

- Quality of articles and copies (e.g., spelling, grammar, writing style, etc.).

Third Party Software and/or Technical Specifications

- No specific technical constraints and/or development tools limitations have been required by OP4.com (BaseSync recommends using Java, JSP, XML, if applicable).
- Operating system and database specifications:
  - Operating System: UNIX (Sun Solaris recommended).
  - Database: Oracle 8i (recommended).
- Possible third-party software for integration:
  - iChat for interactive tools (TBD).

EXHIBIT 2 (*continued*)

- WebTrend for network traffic monitoring and reporting (TBD).
- Hosting Company Integration: (TBD)—requirements include support high bandwidth, upgradeable 7 × 24 technical support.
- Hardware requirements (client's responsibility):
  - Production site: Minimum two high-end servers (one web server and one database server). Might need another iChat server for load balancing.
  - Testing and Staging site: two lower-end servers (one web/iChat server, and one database server).
  - BaseSync will develop the site using our in-house development servers.

Site Administration

The maintenance of this site is a key consideration in its design.

The objective is to store as much of the site in a database as possible, and separate data from business logic and interface.

OP4.com personnel will be able to add polls, surveys, content, images and files to existing content categories and content areas through a simple web-based interface. Information can be added or deleted from existing categories with minimum manual procedures.

These tools will be designed to save time and money and help keep the site fresh and dynamic with new content being added regularly.

The site design will build flexibility into all sections that need to receive regular or periodic updates by using templates that designate "locked" areas of a page, which remain constant version-to-version, and "editable" areas that accommodate regular changes.

The Richard Ivey School of Business gratefully acknowledges the generous support of the MBA '89 class in the development of these learning materials.

Enerline Restorations Inc.: Stay With an ASP?

By Professor Scott Schneberger and Jane Movold

On April 1, 2000, Ron Hozjan, chief financial officer (CFO) of Enerline Restorations Inc. (Enerline) in Calgary, Alberta, Canada, had a decision to make. Enerline had more than doubled in size since Hozjan signed the initial contract with the company's application service provider (ASP), FutureLink, in February 1999, and the existing arrangement was no longer adequate. Hozjan needed to determine if the ASP model was still appropriate for Enerline, given the continued rapid growth and change the company was experiencing, or whether it was time to invest in building an internal information technology infrastructure.

Enerline Restorations Inc. Background

Enerline was Canada's leader in both pipeline liner systems for corrosion, and production tubing liner systems for progressive cavity pumping, rod pumping, injection and disposal well applications. Enerline opened for business in May 1996, with a staff of three employees. By the year 2000, the company's technologies were field-proven with several hundred pipeline liner systems in service, as well as over a thousand lined tubing strings in producing oil wells. Enerline was a 100 percent Canadian, privately owned business that had grown to 30 employees. The company had more than doubled its annual revenues to approximately $3.5 million, with projected revenues of $7.4 million for the year 2000.

The original division within the organization was the Ener-Liner division which offered pipeline liner systems. The subsequently formed Ener-Core Tubing Liner division offered the pumping and disposal well applications, and was still considered to be in its infancy in 1999. The head office in Calgary was the base for a small manufacturing shop and for the liner crews. The construction of a larger manufacturing plant in Stettler, Alberta, for the growing Ener-Core product line had been completed by January 2000, and was operating at full production capacity by June of that year. Additional locations were likely to be acquired or constructed in the near future, as this rate of rapid growth due to increasing product demand was expected to continue. However, as Hozjan explains,

> Capital was definitely tight during this time due to plant construction combined with the development of a new product line. Therefore, this constrained economic environment weighed heavily in my decision-making process for acquiring all new operational items, including a much-needed information system.

Ener-Core was the company's product solution designed to increase runtime to their customers' producing, injection and disposal wells. Ener-Core was a high-density, polyethylene-lined production tubing that guaranteed reduced friction and rod torques, elimination of tubing wear, power savings, and corrosion protection, while it also resolved wax and paraffin problems. The Ener-Core tubing liner was used in heavy oil-producing areas in Alberta and Saskatchewan, and Enerline was rapidly expanding to other areas of Canada and the United States.

C. E. Franklin was the company's distributor for the Ener-Core product, with 40 locations in Western Canada. Said Edwin Quinn, Enerline's sales manager,

> We formed a strong relationship with C. E. Franklin early before commencing production at our Stettler facility. C. E. Franklin is convinced that our liner system will greatly impact the way producers operate wells in the future. Even when oil prices dipped below $11 a barrel, C. E. Franklin was still willing to commit a generous amount of new tubing to be lined with Ener-Core liner.

The increased demand for this product was evidence of the ongoing cost savings realized by its customers.

Ron Hozjan, CFO

Ron Hozjan joined Enerline as chief financial officer in June 1998. In this position, he was responsible for the overall management and control of the operations and financial areas of the business. All Enerline employees reported to Hozjan; Hozjan reported directly to the president, Graham Illingworth, and also had a dotted-line reporting relationship to the five-member board of directors. The Enerline organizational chart is attached in Appendix B. Hozjan would periodically meet with the board of directors to keep them informed of his decisions and actions toward improvement within the organization. The board of directors empowered him to make decisions and implement the solutions for improvement within the organization.

This responsibility for the overall operations within the organization included the area of computerization and information systems. Hozjan was well aware that much effort would be required in this area to transform Enerline's operations into an efficient and competitive business environment. He also knew that he would need to make some key decisions regarding the company's systems and operations in a timely manner to be successful. At this time, Enerline had only one stand-alone personal computer which was running Simply Accounting, online banking, and Microsoft Office. Hozjan explained that "Enerline was operating at least 10 years behind the times when I joined the company, and it was obvious that its operations and information systems infrastructure needed to be upgraded if the company was going to succeed." Over the ensuing five months, Hozjan familiarized himself with the Enerline business and the potential ramifications of the projected areas of business growth. Hozjan had previous experience within a similar industry; therefore, he had already gained a solid understanding of the general operational requirements for conducting business successfully within this marketplace.

Search for a Financial Information System Solution

In November 1998, Hozjan launched an organized and focused search for a complete information system solution to meet Enerline's needs. Several alternative solutions were evaluated in detail. Hozjan decided that the selected solution would be one that was either at one end of the spectrum, where absolutely every part of the system was hosted at a provider's site, or would be a solution that was entirely resident in-house. He had ultimately determined that building a partial information system infrastructure within the organization would not be a valid option, based on his evaluation of existing hybrid solutions. He reached this decision because he realized that a hybrid solution would require him to allocate internal resources or hire information systems staff to maintain this partial infrastructure, while also allocating monetary resources to the external solution provider.

Hozjan's evaluation of the aspects involved in this all-or-nothing scenario (such as in-house staffing, training, his management time and constrained monetary issues) clearly led him to the criteria by which he would select the optimum solution. He was searching for an online ASP that would meet every one of his information system and infrastructure needs. Ideally, he wanted an ASP that would supply his hardware, software, communications, consulting, ongoing maintenance, support and system backup functions. As Hozjan explained, "One-stop shopping that resulted in a reliable solution was exactly what I was looking for." He was well aware that Internet connectivity between Enerline and the ASP in this one-stop-shopping scenario would be a key element of the overall solution, as well as the ASP's ability to host the financial software of his choice.

If Hozjan found such an organization, he planned to compare the financial and operational aspects of the ASP model to the conventional in-house information system infrastructure setup to which he was accustomed. In a conventional IS shop, hired in-house specialists, trained and experienced in information technology, would design, develop, test, implement and maintain information system components. The decision to move forward with the online ASP model and enter a business relationship with FutureLink was made prior to the selection of the specific financial software to be used. Hozjan felt confident at this point that the financial software package selected could be hosted in this flexible ASP environment. Hozjan's 1998 comparison of the ASP model versus the in-house setup is attached in Appendix A. It was this comparison that led him to establish the business relationship between Enerline and FutureLink.

Futurelink ASP

The online ASP industry was still in its infancy in 1998 when Hozjan launched his search for the ideal provider. In fact, Hozjan explained that FutureLink was really the only ASP based in Canada at the time, and there were no more than five ASPs in North America. FutureLink was the Canadian pioneer in this industry at that time, with 50 to 60 employees offering a variety of IS services. The ASP model was so new at this point that there were not even any FutureLink pricing models in existence when Enerline joined FutureLink as its first customer in February 1999.

Hozjan was introduced to FutureLink via a former employee of Sysgold, a company that had successfully set up an internal network of approximately 10 personal computers and an Internet solution for him at a previous place of employment. He had developed a positive business relationship with Sysgold as their work had been reliable, and the network they implemented was easily maintained.

Hozjan interacted primarily with FutureLink's founder and president at the time, Cameron Shell, to establish the initial contract and parameters for their ongoing business relationship. Throughout the negotiations, Hozjan found FutureLink a flexible organization and claimed that they were open to hosting any software application if they were given approximately four weeks to successfully test the new software in their environment. This ongoing flexibility and openness to explore new solutions was critical in the positive development of the business relationship between the two organizations. Hozjan reported that,

> I do not feel bound or constrained to consider only specific information systems solutions, as my ASP has not established a rigid scope of applications which they are prepared to host. This freedom of choice is very important to me as I am responsible for the operations of a rapidly growing organization with changing and expanding needs.

Alternative Financial Software Solutions Evaluated

Several specific financial software solutions were considered to determine which was best suited for the Enerline operations.

The Great Plains accounting software solution was evaluated. This solution would cost Enerline approximately US$30,000 to US$40,000 to purchase and implement for a five-user license, plus additional maintenance fees—a sizable sum for Enerline at the time. Great Plains was located in Seattle, and the fact that Great Plains did not have a local Canadian presence or close relationship with other local IS-related vendors that Enerline dealt with was a disadvantage. Software customizations would also be required with this solution.

The PeachTree software solution was evaluated and was a much less costly solution for Enerline—Cdn$1,500 to purchase and implement for a five-user license. This software package was more prevalent in the local community and was already hosted by FutureLink for other customers. However, Hozjan determined that this software package was not sufficiently sophisticated to meet Enerline's financial reporting requirements.

QByte was an industry-specific financial software package that in-cluded general ledger, accounts payable and accounts receivable mod-ules, as well as some reporting functionality. It was developed by the PriceWaterhouseCoopers accounting firm with input from various oil and gas producers, and was already offered on a time-share basis for smaller organizations. The monthly access cost of the QByte software was $900 plus $145 per month for dedicated connectivity. Hozjan was in-timately familiar with QByte's application offerings as he had imple-mented this software for a previous employer and was quite satisfied, from a functionality perspective, with its capabilities. Microsoft Access and Excel were already utilized for generating Enerline internal finan-cial statements by using exported data from the existing Simply Ac-counting system; this existing financial reporting process was intended to be continued. This same process of utilizing the importing and export-ing functionality within the QByte software for ease of financial data ma-nipulation was also previously utilized successfully by Hozjan. This was a solution he was certain would meet Enerline's existing information re-quirements. Many large corporations in the industry, such as Canadian Natural Resource, used the QByte software, as well as many smaller companies similar in size to Enerline. This software was offered on a time-share basis; therefore, any ASP could connect to the QByte host and, in turn, could provide the link to their customers if they so desired.

Ultimately, Hozjan chose the QByte software solution for Enerline.

The Enerline—Futurelink Existing Business Arrangement

The three-year contract between Enerline and FutureLink was signed in February 1999. Hozjan decided to enter the three-year contract with FutureLink at $1,800 per month, rather than a one-year commitment at $3,000 per month to reduce the company's overall cash outflow.

The contract included five thin client workstations (monitor, key-board, box to run the Citrix software), five dedicated connections to the FutureLink ServerFarm, five licenses to run MS Office Pro suite, QByte software implementation and system access for two users, a laser printer, firewall security, Internet access, consulting, maintenance and system backup activities and 24-hour support. All of the hardware and software was owned by FutureLink.

The FutureLink contract stipulated that their organization guaran-teed 99.9 percent uptime for their customers during normal business hours of operation between 8 A.M. to 5 P.M. If this quality of service was not delivered, the customer was allowed to exit the contract agreement with no penalty fee, or to receive one month of FutureLink services free of charge. The penalty for exiting the contract without cause was equal to six months of service fees ($6 \times \$1,800 = \$10,800$).

FutureLink established a help-desk department with four priorities of service calls. Hozjan indicated that he had used the help-desk serv-ices several times, even on the weekends, and they were successful in meeting their service objectives. Hozjan explained, "The help-desk can even 'shadow' your screen and take control of your system to further assist in resolving the problem in a timely manner. It's great!" Hozjan also added, "I am working with my third monitor and second keyboard. However, the parts were replaced at no charge, on the same or next day, by FutureLink, depending upon the urgency of the situation, which resulted in little interruption of service."

By mid-March 1999, FutureLink had the hardware and communications setup completed, and the five users from Enerline were connected to FutureLink for their work in Outlook E-mail and MS Office Pro. All Enerline company files were stored at the FutureLink location.

In late-March 1999, it was actually the FutureLink ASP organization that assisted Hozjan in evaluating financial packages. Hozjan communicated the particular Enerline business information requirements to FutureLink, and FutureLink responded with their evaluation, based on his criteria, for him to review. Ultimately, Hozjan decided on the recommended QByte solution, and FutureLink successfully implemented this solution for Enerline's two key users within the next 60 days. Although QByte remained the host for this application, FutureLink established a dedicated line between their own server and the QByte location. Therefore, Enerline received easy access to the QByte software because of their existing connection to FutureLink. This stable, direct communications connection was key to Enerline users as they were constantly importing or exporting data between MS Excel or Access, which was hosted on the FutureLink ServerFarm and the QByte software.

Enerline also had remote users who relied on their information systems to conduct business, and these sales personnel regularly dialed up to FutureLink through the Internet. Two members of Enerline's sales staff were on the road 60 percent to 70 percent of the time.

The Enerline Stettler production facility relied heavily on a Microsoft Access-based system, developed by FutureLink programmers, which was the driving force for their daily production activity. The Stettler production site had a dedicated Telus Planet phone line to the FutureLink server farm site where the Access database resided.

Challenges Introduced

In September 1999, Hozjan was informed by FutureLink's founder and president, Cameron Shell, that FutureLink was experiencing serious financial difficulty. This information was a complete and unpleasant surprise to Hozjan. There had been no previous mention of FutureLink's financial difficulties when Hozjan signed the business contract, or subsequently. Now, seven months into a three-year contract, Hozjan discovered that the ASP hosting all of his applications was in financial trouble. Although receiving this information was unsettling and did not contribute toward further development of a strong business relationship, Hozjan reported that Enerline had not experienced any evident degradation of service due to FutureLink's financial difficulties.

In November 1999, FutureLink merged with a California-based organization. The head office for FutureLink was subsequently moved to California, and significant turnover within all levels of the existing FutureLink organization began to occur. Hozjan commented,

> It was very difficult as everyone I had dealt with at FutureLink left the organization. There was significant turnover from the top on down, including FutureLink's founder and president, Cameron Shell. Even all of the original technical staff had left since November of last year. The California-based management team had taken over.

Hozjan added that, "Although things were different and 1999 was a bad year for FutureLink, Enerline was still receiving reliable service, and the new management was still agreeable to changes that were requested in their business agreement."

In November 1999, when the merger took place, the stock price of the new FutureLink Corporation skyrocketed from $10 per share to between $30 to $40 per share for almost a five-month period. However, by late March 2000, and early April, the stock price had plummeted back to below $10 per share. Certainly, from the perspective of a growing customer base, the development of key industry partnerships, and tremendous growth in annual revenues due to acquisitions, prospects appeared to be very bright for the new FutureLink Corporation. However, their overall financial picture was not a bright one, and large losses were growing. The new California-based FutureLink organization reported that their higher losses reflected the expansion of the ASP business. By this time, the ASP marketplace was an environment with increased competition.

Changes in the Information System Industry

During the previous two years, there had been several major changes in the information system industry that directly affected the ASP marketplace. A critical element of the ASP model was the communications infrastructure between the customer and the provider. The ongoing communications cost and the cost of initial setup for communications within the previous two years had decreased significantly as technology improved and competition increased. Also, this decrease in communications cost was combined with further advances in technology that allowed improvements in the standard communication speeds offered to customers. This evolution in the communications area ultimately resulted in speedier access for users at less cost, and also played a major role in making the ASP model much more attractive and competitive, especially when compared to in-house or hybrid solutions.

Another change within the information systems industry revolved around the Internet. A dramatically increasing number of popular enterprise resource planning (ERP) packages and other software applications had been redesigned and developed for Internet-based deployment. This Internet-based phenomenon made the hosting of popular applications much easier and less costly for ASPs. Therefore, the cost-savings in providing these services could be passed on to customers, which further assisted in making the ASP model more competitive.

E-business and e-commerce business models were major evolutions within the information systems industry over the past two years. Implementing these business models combined well with an ASP solution for many customers launching into this new arena.

Going Forward

As the available options were analysed and system implementation decisions were being made, Enerline was rapidly growing. Hozjan said,

> It was like trying to hit a moving target! The business needs were growing as we were trying to make the appropriate decisions. The key to making appropriate decisions is to allow for growth. But when your organization doubles in size and expects the same rate of growth for the near future, this decision-making process is a difficult task.

Hozjan indicated,

> Since I joined the company in 1998, it was in a serious growth period where we were building a new large production plant, and new product lines were being developed. The economic environment within the organization was a key factor in selecting the ASP model to meet our immediate information needs. I knew roughly what the equipment and infrastructure would cost the company to purchase and set up, so the monthly cost of the ASP fees was merely that lump-sum amount distributed over a three-year period. It was a no-lose situation from an economic perspective, as most of the equipment has a three-year life span at most anyway. The only real concern at the time was whether the ASP would be reliable enough to provide ongoing, stable service to Enerline for a sustained period of time. I had faith in the people and in the technology, so with the economic analysis making sense due to the monthly cash outlay—I said "Let's do it!" Internal staff and capital resources were scarce, so it was basically a "no-brainer" at the time.

Two years later, Enerline had grown substantially and had developed a solid market presence with the continued success of their established product lines. The world of information systems had also changed during that two-year period. Enerline needed additional communications infrastructure, as their business operations in new locations were actually being driven by production-oriented applications that were hosted at the FutureLink location. Enerline was also purchasing companies in the United States that had to be brought online with their systems. Enerline was becoming increasingly dependent on their information systems for actual daily production activity and business transactions, making the nature of their information systems much more mission-critical. Hozjan needed to determine whether renegotiations to upgrade the information system services with FutureLink would be of benefit to Enerline, or whether it was time, based on the considerable growth and expected rapid pace of change, for Enerline to provide for themselves from an information systems perspective. Given FutureLink's financial problems, should he seek a different ASP to replace FutureLink? And while an ASP had seemed perfect for Enerline's needs two years earlier, would it meet the company's current needs, or its needs two years in the future?

Appendix A: 1998 Internal Infrastructure Setup Versus ASP Model Comparison

1. **Internal Infrastructure Setup** $80,000 in Year 1
   (Then increasing due to further staff resources and training required in this area as Enerline grows and the IS infrastructure demands full-time management.)

   - Microsoft NT Server & Software
   - 5 personal computers
   - 5 MS Office Pro licenses
   - 5 QByte licenses
   - Internet Access
   - Firewall router and security software
   - Backup software and tape drive equipment
   - Staff training and resource allocation to this area
   - Consulting, implementation, and setup fees
   - Support
   - Communications

2. **ASP Model** $1,800 per month for Year 1 of the contract = $21,600 of sunk cost.

   $1,600 per month was renegotiated for the remaining 2 years of the contract = $38,400.

Includes all of the above.

Note: The $1,800 per month fee in Year 1 included a five-user setup. The $1,600 per month fee for Years 2 and 3 was negotiated for a seven-user setup.

Appendix B: Organizational Chart   (As of April 1, 2000)

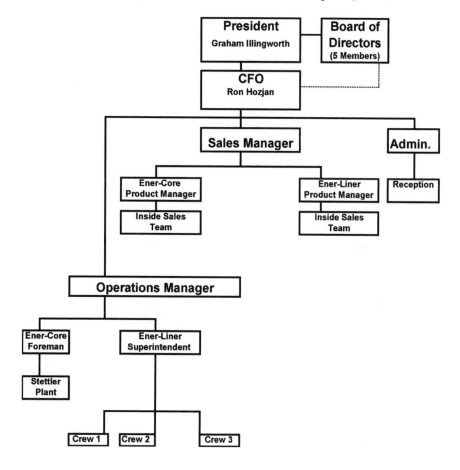

Salesdriver: The Lorimer Request

By Professor Scott Schneberger and Ken Mark

Introduction

"Should we provide a customized solution to meet the data collection request from Lorimer?" Keith McSpurren, general manager of Sales-Driver.com (SalesDriver), had just finished speaking with his vice president (VP) of sales. It was May 1, 2000, and SalesDriver, a Boston-based e-commerce start-up had just achieved its 1,000th user mark and the opportunity to snag software giant Lorimer Development Corp as a new client could not be ignored. "However, this solution that Lorimer has requested will alter our current product offering by adding functionality that our other users might not need."

Background

In December 1998, Webguru Inc., the predecessor of SalesDriver, was started with seed financing of US$250,000. Focused on reducing redundant tasks for sales and marketing managers, the company began with a broad business plan. In April 1999, the company was renamed SalesDriver and rewrote its business to create a "self-serve, online software package for building and running sales incentive contests." This allowed sales managers to build, run and reward an internal sales contest entirely online.

Co-founded by Joel Silver and Keith McSpurren in 1998, SalesDriver was based in Boston, Mass., with a development office in Toronto. Sales-Driver provided a turn-key solution for sales managers to manage their sales contests online. Sales contests were used by sales managers to motivate their staff, but were often accompanied by the time-consuming details of contest creation, management, and prize fulfillment. As an application service provider (ASP), SalesDriver provided these time-starved managers free access and use of its turn-key sales contest management software in return for a 12 per cent commission on the fulfillment of prizes. The SalesDriver concept was also designed to develop loyalty among users by rewarding sales productivity with its proprietary currency, "Driver Dollars." "Driver Dollars" could be used by contest participants to pay for selected prizes provided by SalesDriver's e-tailer partners. Since the e-tailers handled all prize-fulfillment processing and shipping, SalesDriver could focus its efforts on site development and marketing.

Richard McCann joined SalesDriver in May 1999 as the company's third co-founder. As site architect, McCann began building prototypes and tested them with feedback from salespeople, leading to three major rebuilds of the site. In September 1999, SalesDriver launched its first live sales contest with Bayer Pharmaceuticals. SalesDriver secured US$3.3 million in first round venture capital on December 24, 1999, from key investors including Vengrowth, CastleHill, and several angel investors.

The Application Service Provider (ASP) Industry

An ASP managed and delivered software application capabilities to multiple entities through the Internet. The one-to-many service offering differentiated ASPs from the typical Value-Added Reseller (VAR) or IT outsourcer. ASP applications were packaged as a standardized offering and included minimal customization, other than writing interfaces to a customer's in-house application. Online ASPs required less on the part of the client since IT integration was achieved via the Internet, with Internet browsing the only requirement for access. ASPs combined the expertise of systems integrators with the functionality of complex business applications.

An ASP sold an application, not a business process. Popular enterprise applications included e-commerce and productivity applications such as sales force automation, accounting and human resources management. Here is an overview from Merrill Lynch Global Securities Research & Economics Group's "Internet Infrastructure 2000" report:

- ASPs = Fully Outsourced Enterprise Applications.   ASPs enable both small and large enterprises to access IT solutions on a fully outsourced basis. This entails the deployment, hosting, ongoing management, and network access to remotely hosted enterprise applications such as e-commerce, CRM and ERP. In many ways, ASPs represent a return to the old time-sharing model of computer services: customers traded the headache of purchasing software and hardware, managing software implementation risk, staffing, and managing an internal IT department, and suffering from unpredictable budgets. In return, ASP solutions deliver a single contract, a single point of responsibility, and a flat monthly fee.

- Why It Will Happen.   Software industry leaders such as Larry Ellison of Oracle have predicted that within three years, as much as two-thirds of applications will be sold on an ASP basis instead of the typical in-house implementation today. We find this statement intriguing. We agree that the traditional software implementation route is fundamentally inefficient—it often requires significant installation efforts and leaves the deployment onus on the customer. This situation has also somewhat "warped" the software industry—with software vendors focusing instinctively on the "next upgrade" as opposed to driving customer utility.

- Supply and Demand Drivers Coming into Focus.   The levers appear to be coming into place for the ASP model. These include a rapidly improving network infrastructure, the deployment of broadband access, and a multitude of companies working to optimize applications for an

ASP environment. Advantages of the ASP model are significant, and include faster time to market and more consistent upgrades. In addition the ASP model rides the powerful waves of e-commerce—which should be the largest ASP application—and the IT outsourcing trend, which continues to be strengthened by IT talent shortages.

- The ASP Landscape Is Expanding. On the provider side, the ASP landscape is rapidly developing, with application vendors and traditional IT service providers joining pure play ASPs. This has dramatically expanded the landscape. Over time, we believe all software vendors will craft an ASP strategy, leveraging it (either directly or indirectly) as an added distribution channel.

    Large operational and market-related challenges clearly remain. The ASP market is very young and continues to wrestle with infrastructure issues (data center and network consistency), customer support responsibilities, and the implementation of various software applications in an ASP environment. Moreover, most ASPs are just beginning to market and sell their services, and are still very much in the position of educating their customers on the basic ASP value proposition.

Forrester Research estimated that companies would outsource US$21 billion to ASPs in 2001. ASP services, provided by companies such as SalesDriver, had the potential to become an extremely attractive solution for companies who did not wish to develop, purchase or maintain costly software. Through ASPs, businesses were able to afford software needed to streamline their operations, up to the most complex enterprise-wide software applications on the market.

International Data Corp. estimated that corporate spending on high-end outsourced applications, such as ERP and e-commerce, would grow from an estimated US$150.4 million in 2000 to US$2 billion by 2003, a compound annual growth rate of 91 percent. This figure was a conservative estimation, as it did not take into account the majority of software applications currently used by most businesses.

The Development of ASPs

In its January 2000 report, *Packaged Software Rental: The Net's Killer App,* ASPnews.com outlined the origins, shape and directions of application services, and identified three separate trends from which ASPs were emerging.

- From the IT services industry—a trend towards *selective outsourcing.* Instead of handing over their complete IT infrastructure to an outside provider, organisations have selectively outsourced specific parts of IT. The ASP model added fixed, per-user pricing, often levied in the form of a monthly subscription. Early ASP start-ups such as USinternetworking, Corio, and Futurelink fell into the selective outsourcing category, where they found themselves joined by established IT and professional services organisations such as EDS, IBM Global Services and KPMG (in its joint venture with Qwest).

- Among ISPs (Internet service providers) the relevant trend had been towards application hosting. Internet service providers had always been ASPs to the extent that the provision of hosted mail and web servers had been an application service. Over time, the ISP industry had split between those who provided access and connectivity services, and those who offered hosting services. The latter, particularly as they moved into sophisticated e-commerce, messaging and other complex web hosting services, were effectively ASPs. Managed hosting providers included examples such as Concentric Networks, Digex and Navisite. Vendors who acted as e-business or infrastructure service providers include Akamai, CyberSource, eGain and LivePerson.com.

- Finally, Internet-based enterprises had begun to offer online applications as part of a phenomenon the report called "portal computing." Websites started out as Internet destinations that offered only static content, mainly words and images. Today, information sites had became portals and, seeking the "stickiness" that kept users returning to their site, they added applications to create dynamic, interactive experiences. Meanwhile, a new generation of software vendors were bringing their applications to market as web-based services, accessed directly over the Internet. Hundreds of enterprises, most of them recent start-ups, fell under the fast-expanding portal computing umbrella. They included net-based application vendors such as Agillion, NetLedger and Upshot.com; Internet business services such as ELetter and Employease; and a wide range of vertical industry portals, online trading exchanges and enterprise extranets.

Convergence

Although each of these separate strands emerged from different historic roots, each took advantage of the same technology enablers to deliver applications from an online data centre to a community of users. They were all converging on the same ASP model. As they did so, more and more of them became identified as ASPs, even though they might not originally have seen themselves in this light.

This convergence was evident in subcategories such as application outsourcing and application server hosting, or hosted e-business services and net-based application vendors, who developed significant overlaps.

The Sales Incentives Market, Target Customers, Competitors

Sales Incentives

Often, in order to motivate their sales force, companies would hold sales contests offering prizes and/or cash if targets were met. There existed hundreds of possible contest goals, including inter-team competition, intra-team competition, numeric sales targets, numeric customer acquisition targets, etc. Usually, the responsibility for these sales contests fell upon the sales manager, who would have to come up with a theme, create and print materials, and coordinate the contest with other team members. He or she would also have to monitor the contest and keep track of changes. Finally, the manager would have to manage the logistics of prize allotment, fulfillment, and bill payment, a full-time endeavor. As a result, sales managers often turned to firms that offered to administer these services, although many of these firms were expensive.

The Competition

According to a 1999 incentive survey performed by Ralph Head & Associates, the total revenues of the incentives industry were US$23 billion. Incentives spending was spread out among four areas—consumer programs, sales programs, dealer programs, and non-sales programs. There were several objectives to offering these incentives to these groups—increasing or maintaining sales, building morale, building customer loyalty/trust, and improving customer service. Some of these incentives offered included group or individual travel rewards, cash, apparel, plaques and trophies, sporting goods and electronics. Thus, the incentives industry included consumer products revenues of US$6.5 billion and group travel revenues of US$3.1 billion. The remaining revenues of US$13.3 billion came from the management and prize fulfillment of sales contests.

Although there were no other online sales contest management companies, SalesDriver indirectly competed with several online start-ups in the incentives market. SalesDriver had categorized its competitors on two dimensions. The first dimension ranged from competitors who did not charge setup fees and did not require IT integration into the customer's software to competitors that charged setup fees and required some degree of IT integration. The second dimension ranged from competitors that provided sales results and allowed competition between participants to those competitors that did not provide sales results and did not allow competition. When SalesDriver launched its first online contest with Bayer Inc. in September 1999, SalesDriver was the only company that provided sales results, administered participant competition, did not have setup fees, and did not require software integration into the organization's software base.

The Dilemma of Being an ASP—Offering One Standard Product
Silver explained,

> From an Internet standpoint, several ASP companies have proven that they can target small companies as well as large ones. But from a marketing standpoint, customers represent different things for start-ups. If we want to acquire customers fast, we would go after small customers because they generally move faster. From a public relations and reputation standpoint, large

customers give you a lot more clout—but because of their processes, they act a lot slower. Conventional behavior would lead us to choose to service either large or small customers, but in our case, we want to set up our service so that we don't have to choose—we'll service both segments.

Dealing with clients of different sizes also raised a functionality issue for SalesDriver. In general, large clients were used to customized software solutions and were known to demand extra functionality from a site. Smaller clients, on the other hand, did not necessarily need the extra "functionality" and often found a feature-rich site too unwieldy for their needs.

McSpurren continued,

It boils down to an interface issue. Can you have the Boston Red Sox and a minor league baseball team play in the same field? There are issues when you build in functionality for larger customers—do you stand the risk of confusing the smaller ones? Would we lose the simplicity of our SalesDriver concept—to make the site as simple as possible? We always run the risk of "featuring" the site to death.

Even though Silver and McSpurren were worried about the complexity of their site, they noticed that since their application was not part of their target customer's software core (Enterprise Resource Planning or payroll, for example), sales managers were more likely to use the SalesDriver site without the input of their IT department. This led SalesDriver to believe that marketing to the sales manager would overcome some of the perceived barriers to acceptance.

SalesDriver IT Challenges

One IT challenge was to develop a product in a short amount of time. McSpurren explained,

What happens often is that our internal managers will say: "That's great, now add this feature and add that feature." We've then got the option of getting it 70 to 80 percent right in order to deliver it on-time, then going back a while later to re-build it correctly the second time around. We've got to be able to let the VP sales offer this or the next feature before we have it; then we'll pull together a solution that works. Being first to market is the key to our success and to us staying one step ahead of the competition. Thus, there is always friction between product development and sales. But we know that if we've got no customers, we've got no future. We can move fast to get customer reaction and then give ourselves time to shore it up.

Another challenge that SalesDriver faced was managing the number of times its web site had to be overhauled. The SalesDriver site had been revamped six times since May 1999 as feature upon feature was added. "The guys who plan it thoroughly and try to do it right at all costs will lose because others will do it faster," concluded McSpurren.

The Request

SalesDriver counted 1,000 cumulative users as of May 1, 2000. VP Sales Mark Sullivan had just met with Lorimer Development Corporation and was very excited about closing this important client. Sullivan contacted McSpurren and suggested that SalesDriver make the following change to its site to meet the needs of Lorimer, who were used to customized solutions built specifically for them.

Here was their request,

> When we submit results for sales contests, we have a series of questions (customer profiling questions) we'd like to pose to our members, and keep it in our Lorimer database—we call this a "claim form." We'd like SalesDriver's data fields to match our data fields so that we can migrate your data to ours.

Sullivan asked McSpurren if he could have this feature to offer to Lorimer.

- SalesDriver would prompt the Lorimer reps to provide lead profiles as they updated their scores.
- The lead profile survey had to be accessed, filled in and transmitted between SalesDriver's site and Lorimer's database.

As Lorimer was a client with world-wide reach, the Lorimer account would be a big win for SalesDriver—immediately, it would have access to 70 consumers, with the potential for thousands more. In addition, Lorimer was a brand-name customer SalesDriver wanted to have in its sales and PR efforts. Currently, SalesDriver's site did not provide any vehicle to ask for customer information. More importantly, the SalesDriver site did not integrate with any third-party software because SalesDriver was an ASP. But did SalesDriver's other customers want or need this extra feature?

Developing this option as a one-off for Lorimer would cost SalesDriver a week's worth of part-time development time. However, if it decided to offer this service to all customers, it would take 30 to 60 days, or US$40,000 to US$50,000 to come up with an integrated "claim form" solution. "What should we do?" McSpurren thought to himself. "By keeping one product for all users, we gain huge economies of scale. By tailoring our product for Lorimer, or others, we can gain economies of scope." McSpurren paused, then said to himself aloud, "And which is best in the long run?"

EXHIBIT 1 OP4.Com's Millenpro Flash Movie Screen Captures

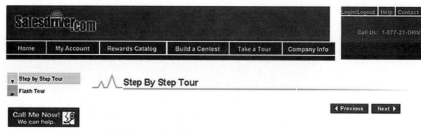

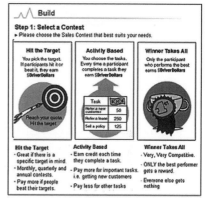

Build Your Contest On-Line

We know salespeople, and we know every situation they face is different. Our on-line tools let you build a contest—to suit your sales goals—in 20 minutes or less!

You create the rewards plan: you give any amount for any task or target you choose. If you need help building your contest, just give us a call. Our Customer Care team is ready to answer your questions.

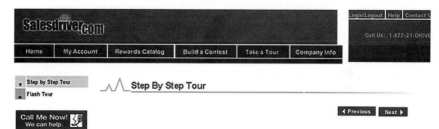

Communicate with DriverMail

DriverMail is Salesdriver.com's proprietary e-mail system. It works behind the scenes of your contest, and keeps everyone involved informed of the latest contest developments.

When the manager of a Sales Contest updates results, or makes changes, DriverMail automatically notifies participants. Do you need to tell 1500 resellers that their contest target has changed? DriverMail does it for you, so you can get back to more important things.

EXHIBIT 1   (*continued*)

Source: www.salesdriver.com, June 2000.

Chapter 4

Financial Systems and Choices

How e-commerce is financed is a critical management issue from a variety of perspectives. Ventures seeking financing need to understand the costs and benefits of the available alternatives. Lenders need to understand the risks and rewards of investing in e-commerce firms. Established financial institutions need to understand how e-commerce might affect their businesses. This chapter explores these issues.

The first case is written from the position of a growing e-commerce venture seeking to evaluate the financing alternatives. The executives of CYBERplex, an Internet design and development company, are anxious to raise additional funds and to take their rapidly growing company public. A wide range of alternatives are being considered, including an initial public offering, a reverse takeover of a NASDAQ listed firm, and sale to a junior capital pool. The principals of the firm must evaluate each alternative and come up with an optimal solution.

The second case is written from the perspective of a lender deciding whether or not to invest in a growing e-commerce venture. A partner in a venture capital company is assessing the relative merits of Grocery Gateway, an Internet grocery retailer. In order to decide, he must evaluate the strengths, weaknesses, and risks involved. The venture capitalist must conduct a valuation of the company and then structure a deal that is attractive to the existing owners.

A number of firms have developed systems that facilitate online payments without directly exposing credit card numbers online. One of the first online systems was developed by First Virtual Holdings Inc., a company based in San Diego. What made the system unique was that users didn't have to divulge their credit card numbers to merchants or anyone else. Instead, to make purchases, buyers used an alias provided by the company. The advantage of the system was that buyers could make secure online transactions using only an Internet browser and e-mail. No additional software was required. However, First Virtual was beginning to see competition from much larger and better financed competitors. The case examines online payment schemes and provides a discussion of the information systems infrastructure required to operate an online payment scheme.

The chapter's final case discusses the launch of Advance Bank, a branchless bank in Germany offering a full range of banking services and investment advice. A decision was made early on to build Advance Bank from scratch without relying on the products and banking infrastructure of its parent company, a large bricks and mortar bank. Advance Bank's strategy was to source its products and services from different financial providers spread all over Germany and integrate them through a seamless interface with the customer. The case discusses how a bank manages the offering of its services through a variety of distribution channels (telephone, PC, and Internet). For highly personalized and complex products, financial advice was offered by integrating telephone and Internet capabilities, thus allowing simultaneous voice and data communication with the customer. The case concludes by highlighting the future challenges facing Advance Bank in its efforts to become profitable in 2001.

CYBERplex Interactive Media

By Professor James E. Hatch and David Pennington

Marc Lavine jumped up and grabbed his coat. With his plane leaving at 5 P.M. on this mid-October day, he barely had time to get home and pack an overnight bag. He hadn't noticed the time flying by as he had sat working with his partner, and CYBERplex's president, Dean Hopkins. As he strode out of CYBERplex's offices in the theater district of Toronto, Lavine thought again about the myriad of financing options that faced them. As CYBERplex's vice president, he had taken responsibility for managing the process of meeting the two-year-old firm's financial needs and planning for future acquisitions. The financing option the partners had originally decided on was to obtain a public listing through a reverse takeover of Newpath, a Junior Capital Pool (JCP) listed on the Alberta Stock Exchange (ASE). The JCP (a publicly listed shell company whose only asset was cash) would exchange new shares from treasury for all of CYBERplex's outstanding shares and, since CYBERplex was larger than Newpath, the owners of CYBERplex would have controlling interest in the new company and access to Newpath's pool of cash.

Unfortunately, the JCP option appeared to be unravelling at a critical stage. Newpath's underwriters had shown an unwillingness to allow the JCP to consolidate its shares before purchasing CYBERplex, and CYBERplex considered the deal to be unfair if the JCP did not complete the consolidation. With this problem facing them, Lavine and Hopkins would probably have to quickly reconsider one of their other options. As the chill air streamed in the window of the taxi, Lavine worried that, with the late October 1996 deadline to sign the lock-up agreement for the JCP rapidly approaching, they would need to make their decision soon.

The Internet

The Market

The Internet
CYBERplex provided services for companies interested in having a presence on the Internet, a worldwide network of computers sharing a common set of protocols that permitted them to readily share information. The Internet had been growing at an annual rate of more than 90 percentage points for the previous three years and it was generally considered that this growth rate would continue in the near future. The Internet had reached a critical mass of users and was quickly becoming as fundamental to communication as telephones and televisions. Companies which could exploit the expansion and rapidly changing nature of the medium would have possibilities for growth that simply hadn't existed for decades.

The World Wide Web and the Browser
The impetus behind the dramatic growth in the Internet was the introduction of the browser (a program originally called Mosaic, and more recently, Netscape and Explorer). The browser allowed easy navigation

IVEY David Pennington prepared this case under the supervision of Professor James E. Hatch solely to provide material for class discussion. The authors do not intend to illustrate either effective or ineffective handling of a managerial situation. The authors may have disguised certain names and other identifying information to protect confidentiality.

of the World Wide Web through a simple graphical interface. Although the Web had existed for a number of years, the introduction of the browser allowed unsophisticated users easy access to a medium where elaborate keystrokes and commands had formerly been required. The basis for the Web was documents (or computer files) that were based on a standardized format that could be read by any computer. A browser loading one of these documents would output a formatted page (to a computer screen) that closely resembled a printed page. But it differed from a printed page in that this computer-based page could easily be updated, take input from a computer user or allow a user to jump to a new page with a simple mouse click.

The Website

A collection of these web pages on a single computer (or server) was called a website. Originally, a web page contained printed text and links to other pages with more printed text. With the explosion in the use of the Internet these pages had increased dramatically in numbers and sophistication, with the result that they now contained graphics, animation, carefully designed formatting and search engines. In addition, their connection to databases and computer applications had changed their role from passive to interactive. Although designing and posting a web page was relatively easy (in fact, the growth in the World Wide Web had been partly driven by this ability to become your own publisher) posting a sophisticated web page required considerable time and expertise. A good comparison to this process is that anybody can write and photocopy a newsletter, but only a person with considerable expertise, artistic skill and capital can publish a magazine. What CYBERplex did was assist a client corporation in publishing its own Internet "magazine."

Corporate Internet Customers

Unlike a magazine, however, the World Wide Web offered an enormous number of other opportunities that a passive paper-based medium did not provide. As a result, many corporations were interested in formulating and implementing a strategy to use the Internet. For many, the main use would initially be to advertise their goods and services and to provide investor relations material. In addition to this basic material, many corporations were developing lifestyle or entertainment sites that would attract potential customers. Entertainment and information companies were also flocking to the Internet and providing services to users for a fee or financing them through the sale of advertising. Because many of these companies did not have the in-house expertise to develop a sophisticated website, they required outside assistance to bring their ideas to fruition.

Company Operations

For clients, CYBERplex designed, developed and executed Internet-based business strategies. CYBERplex's services included analysing the client's industry and business to highlight potential areas where it could use the Internet to create value, and by defining the objectives and approaches to capture this value, designing the solution, implementing the solution, and maintaining and managing the resulting website. These Internet strategy services included consulting on organization redesign, training, technology implementation and communication strategy. To augment its future growth, CYBERplex was also developing websites whose purpose was to generate revenues by selling products or services. These Internet based businesses (IBB) were often developed in conjunction with a corporate partner.

CYBERplex had 16 full-time employees, including the two partners (Lavine and Hopkins), three account executives, two artists, three programmers, four developers, one product development manager and one administrator.

CYBERplex derived revenue from two activities. It received development fees on either a fixed bid or a cost-per-hour basis for the strategic analysis of the client's market and the subsequent creation of the website. It also received support fees to maintain the hardware and software resources that underlie the website. CYBERplex negotiated these contracts with its clients on a time and materials basis.

Capabilities

Over the previous two years, CYBERplex's sales had grown on the strength of its strategic and business problem-solving skills, drawing on Hopkins' and Lavine's background as management consultants, and the employees' creative and technological capabilities.

CYBERplex had recruited an outstanding creative and technical team which was continuously researching emerging technologies and techniques. Their expertise spanned multimedia authoring, databases, programming languages, interface design, and the integration of content, software and hardware. Hopkins, Lavine and Lobo had experience in providing strategic management consulting advice (with McKinsey & Company) and Hopkins also had a background in systems design.

CYBERplex provided its customers with a skill set and a depth of experience that any competitor entering the field would have difficulty matching. The company's programmers and designers had been working on website projects longer than most people in the industry. As a result, the team had the ability to complete difficult projects more effectively and in a shorter time than would otherwise be possible. The size of CYBERplex's in-house staff also allowed the company to handle large projects for major corporations with the assurance that it could meet the client's needs within the allotted time frame, a guarantee that was of particular importance in an industry where the underlying structure and technology was changing daily. CYBERplex's focus on cutting-edge technology and website development and the opportunity to work on sophisticated and challenging projects had allowed the company to continue to attract the people it needed in order to expand.

As it built new websites, the company often developed software tools that increased the effectiveness and the speed of this construction. Because CYBERplex could apply many of these tools to new projects, this "construction equipment" provided an advantage over its competitors, which often had to do the same tasks "by hand." Examples of these tools are seen in Exhibit 1.

EXHIBIT 1   Portfolio of "Construction" Software

CYBERplex had developed several software solutions, including:

Product	Function	Description	Clients
TextLink	To permit the searching of large databases of full-text documents	Using a highly customized version of the WAIS[*] searching protocol, this adaptable solution permits users to search through large amounts of text. Site managers can quickly tailor the solution to their own text and site appearance.	Maclean Hunter Nabisco Where Bernardin
NewsLink	A full featured multi-news feed processing and presentation system	This software and process allow a site maintainer to manage a variety of news feeds. The tool facilitates filtering of the news feed, the selection of stories, and the formatting of those stories directly into HTML.[**]	Mutual Group Reuters Daily Smile
F'Link	An Internet publishing tool which automates the publishing of web pages from FoxPro	This system accepts a FoxPro database as input and produces as output a fully searchable set of HTML documents. F'Link works in concert with TextLink to produce a fully interactive website.	Where
PageLink	A site management system which publishes websites directly from a relational database using templates and remote user input	This system permits the central control of a site that is contributed to by many remote participants. Using templates and an HTML publishing interface, users create their own pages which are stored in a relational database. The pages are published on the fly as they are requested by Internet users.	Mutual Group

EXHIBIT 1 (*continued*)

Product	Function	Description	Clients
SiteAnalyser	A diagnostic tool which permits site maintainers to analyse their sites for errors, dead-links, and improper HTML coding	This tool analyses a specified Internet site and generates an HTML and e-mail report documenting all of the errors of HTML style problems encountered. It canbe run at various levels of scrutiny. This permits a high degree of quality control over a website.	All CYBERplex clients
SitePublisher	An administrative tool which manages the interface between a development environment and a production environment	SitePublisher solves the problems that many site developers encounter when moving a site from a development environment into production. This tool ensures that the entire site or selected sections of the site are properly moved from the development machine to the production machine. The tool also restricts this publishing process to specific users. For audit purposes it maintains a log file of the files moved and the ID of the user which authorized the publishing.	Mutual Group

*WAIS is an acronym for Wide Area Information Server—a system that allows users to search an Internet database with a single interface.
**HTML is an acronym for Hypertext Markup Language—the formatting code that is used to build standardized web pages.
Source: Company documents.

CYBERplex's impressive list of clients provided many opportunities to market its services. Potential clients, which would see the company's existing work on the Internet, would invite it to bid on new projects they were developing. In addition, many corporate clients which were concerned about the relative newness of the industry were much more comfortable hiring a company that had proven itself capable of completing the required work.

Success for CYBERplex in the future would be based on the ability to stay one step ahead of its competition. The entire industry was developing in sophistication and technical abilities and any constraints on the growth and development of the company would allow its competitors to catch up. Thus, it was imperative that CYBERplex should have the money it required to grow and develop its capabilities, and the continuing delays in financing had started to concern Hopkins and Lavine.

Competition

The information the company had supplied to investors indicated that the Internet had become more competitive since CYBERplex started in 1994. However, CYBERplex had continued to differentiate itself from the market with its ability to develop and execute strategic Internet solutions as opposed to simply building web pages.

CYBERplex faced competition from a number of sources, including Internet access providers, in-house information technology departments, advertising agencies, multimedia production companies, independent freelancers, and integrated marketing communication firms. In addition, several companies had positioned themselves as direct competition, including Quadravision, ICE, Mackerel and Webworks.

The key weaknesses of its competitors stemmed from their lack of experience or focus on Internet technologies. Advertising agencies frequently did not have the technical expertise to implement their Internet advertising strategies and were therefore unable to provide an integrated service to their clients. On the other hand, many of the smaller Internet players had the technical background but were unable to provide the strategic insight that many corporations were looking for.

CYBERplex believed that the principal competitive factors in the Internet strategy sector were the ability to: understand the client's business and develop sound strategic Internet solutions, communicate and inspire confidence in the client's senior management, develop strong client relationships, manage projects efficiently, demonstrate broad and deep technical expertise, design creative and innovative concepts, and produce high-quality products. CYBERplex believed that it competed effectively with respect to each of these factors.

Internet-based Businesses

CYBERplex's plan for the future was to grow the business from a time and services model where it was paid for the design and construction of websites, to a product-oriented model. The company believed that it could combine its expertise acquired from providing advice to others with its strategic objective to identify business niches for products that were Internet based. Lavine and Hopkins thought this part of their business would become an important source of revenue in the future and had hired Jon Erlich, an experienced marketing person, to investigate and study these opportunities. These IBBs would target specific consumer groups and provide them with products and services that were not being provided on other parts of the Internet. An example of

EXHIBIT 2 Company Client Case Studies Illustrating the Breadth of CYBERplex's Services

Client	Strategic Challenge	CYBERplex Solution
Labatt Breweries	To utilize the Internet to extend the relationship with Labatt consumers	An interactive website that is fully integrated throughout all marketing, promotional, customer service, and corporate communications efforts. CYBERplex manages this site and continues to develop new strategies for Labatt's use of the Internet.
Maclean Hunter MD Link	To develop a new profit centre for Maclean Hunter Medical Publishing	An Internet-based community restricted to health care professionals that offers exclusive access to Medical Publishing content, research and services. This site offered one of the only legal locations for Canadian pharmaceutical product advertising on the Internet and includes the ability for doctors to order patient drug samples directly. CYBERplex is responsible for maintaining and updating the site, and has developed a proprietary approach to extracting and publishing the magazine content each week.
Where Magazines	To develop a profitable new business targeting pre-travel visitors with existing Where content	After reengineering the magazine publishing process, and installing a CYBERplex developed publishing system, CYBERplex developed and manages a fully searchable website that includes over 15 cities of content that are updated monthly. The site is supported by advertising, and the ads are produced using CYBERplex developed ad production software.

Source: Company documents.

this was MD Link (Exhibit 2), which was an Internet extension of Maclean Hunter's physicians' magazine. CYBERplex would collect revenues from a combination of advertising fees, sponsorships, listing fees, subscriptions and pay-per-view features.

Capital Needs

As they planned for the future, the partners identified several areas that would need additional outside capital. First, an increased presence in the United States, Europe and Asia through strategic acquisitions would require either cash or the issuance of shares. Secondly, maintaining the company's high level of service to an expanding customer base would require additional PCs, software and web servers. Finally, CYBERplex would probably enter into joint ventures with IBBs, predominately providing time and services, but occasionally providing necessary capital.

The Growth of CYBERplex

An Early History/First Stage Financing

The company first took shape in June 1994. Hopkins resigned from his job at McKinsey, and along with Vernon Lobo, who was also at McKinsey, provided the initial $30,000 financing to pay for Hopkins' living and business expenses as he tried to grow the operation. By the fall of 1994 Hopkins had managed to secure a few small projects, but the business was not growing at the rate they had expected and Hopkins and Lobo were starting to have second thoughts. By its first Christmas of operation the company had produced revenues of $6,000. When Lavine, who also had worked for McKinsey, joined the team at this time, he doubled the computing power of the operation by providing his own Powerbook computer. By early 1995 they had gained a few more small clients, including the Shaw Festival and an auto dealership, with most of their success based on the concept of providing strategic advice along with their technical help. When the cash ran out late in the spring of 1995, Lavine and Hopkins were working with no salary. Lobo invested another $2,500 into the business, but insisted that would be the last cash infusion. About this time the company presented the IBB idea to Maclean Hunter; proposing to set up an Internet site for its medical-based specialty magazines. When the publisher agreed to the idea, CYBERplex had its first big account and its fortunes started to turn. By the fall of 1995 the company had initiated projects for Novotel, Domtar and Labatt, and by Christmas of 1995 it had six-month revenues of $375,000.

The Cachet Deal/Second Stage Financing

As business increased significantly in the fall of 1995 and winter of 1996, the partners saw that they were going to need additional cash to expand. The company required capital for a number of purposes including moving into an office that could support a web server and paying for the additional staff (graphics designers and programmers) and computer equipment that it would require as its corporate contracts increased.

Debt financing was not an option for CYBERplex because of its limited operating history. However, a major advantage resulted from its Internet involvement at a time when the Internet had become the buzz word of the year and companies involved with the giant network were going public at incredible valuations. For example, iSTAR Internet had gone public on the Toronto Stock Exchange (TSE) in November, 1995, at a multiple of about 10 times the year ended May's revenue. More recently the issue had been trading at about three times revenue (see the Comparable Company summary in Exhibit 3), and

EXHIBIT 3   Selected Data from Comparable Companies

Comparable Companies

Industry	Company	Ticker	P/E	P/Sales	P/Book
U.S. Advertising Services					
	Creative Programming	CPTV	negative	8.0	0.7
	Dimensional Visions	DVGL	negative	4.8	N/A
	Eagle River Interactive	ERIV	negative	16.2	1.5
	Harmony Holdings	HAHO	negative	0.2	1.4
	National Media	NM	9.9	0.5	1.8
	Northwest Teleproductions	NWTL	negative	0.5	1.5
	Outdoor Systems	OSIA	1940.6	16.1	3.6
U.S. Internet Companies					
	Netscape	NSCP	negative	43.2	20.8
	America Online	AOL	89.7	2.1	4.5
	Netcom On-Line Communications	NETC	negative	2.5	1.2
Canadian Internet Companies					
	Hookup Communications	HU	negative	3.2	1.2
	iSTAR Internet	WWW	negative	3.5	2.7

Source: Bloomberg LP/Company Documents, October 17, 1996.

the market in the United States was equally excited with companies such as Netscape Communications, whose shares were issued at an incredible 30 times revenue. Because many potential investors continued to see these issues as very attractive, they might view an investment in CYBERplex at this point in its development as having the potential to provide significant returns. The problem for CYBERplex in tapping the public equity markets was that, at its present size and stage of development, it was not big enough and was considered too risky to merit a major public market listing or valuation. However, CYBERplex was very attractive to private company investors looking for a large potential return when it did reach a significant enough size (to be taken public), and to other Internet companies which were looking to reach a critical mass through acquisitions before they did their first major public issue.

CYBERplex could raise money from private company investors either through a direct investment by a single venture capitalist or through a private placement to multiple institutional investors. After talking to a number of firms, the partners found that although the private investors were just as excited about the Internet as the public market, they were unwilling to pay the high valuations that were seen in the public market. This left the CYBERplex partners with lower valuation than they thought their company was worth. The lower valuation also meant that the private investors would likely have majority voting control of their company. Even if the venture capital companies didn't gain simple voting control, the partners found that their proposals were structured to maintain control in other ways.

The other alternative for CYBERplex was to be acquired by another Internet company and receive a higher valuation due to the additional value a strategic merger would provide. The problem that arose from this option was that the company's strategic concept would be diluted. The opportunity to provide strategic Internet advice had still not been thoroughly marketed to potential clients and a merger would make CYBERplex more of a publisher of Internet web pages than a provider of strategic Internet advice to corporations. Unfortunately, as the company negotiated with other partners it always seemed to end up as the publishing part of another organization. The main reason why the partners eventually discarded the idea of merging with a similar entity was that, although they received a higher valuation than with a private investor, they would not be maximizing the value of the company. They determined that selling at this time would be too early and, given more time to develop the company, they could achieve a significantly higher valuation.

The option the three shareholders finally decided upon was to sell 50 percent of their shares to Cachet Communications in return for $2.5 million composed of cash and Cachet shares. This $5 million valuation of the CYBERplex equity, negotiated by the partners, was confirmed to be fair by an analysis by Wise, Blackman Independent Business Valuators. The Cachet investment balanced the partners' need for an attractive valuation with a corporate partner which would not interfere with their strategy for CYBERplex's growth.

Cachet was a Toronto-based, growth-oriented communications and marketing company that provided a broad range of consulting, production and manufacturing services to its corporate customers. Cachet wanted to become "the preferred communications out-sourcing choice for the leaner corporation of today." In this sense, CYBERplex's focus on corporate Internet communications was a good match with Cachet's strategy, but Cachet had no desire or understanding to manage or set strategic direction for CYBERplex. The company was publicly listed on the ASE. As part of the deal, Cachet promised to assist CYBERplex in taking itself public in the fall of 1996. Because Cachet had gone through a public issue process in the past, CYBERplex thought it could benefit from that experience when it pursued the third stage of its financing. The partners started talking to Cachet in the fall of 1995 and had an agreement in principle by the end of the year, but it took three months and $30,000 in legal costs to negotiate a share purchase agreement. The deal officially closed in June 1996.

The terms of the deal were as follows:

- Cachet would pay $415,000 in cash and the balance in Cachet shares (valued at $0.68 for a total of 3,066,176 Cachet shares) for half of the original shareholders' existing shares.
- Cachet would also provide a working capital loan of $300,000 to CYBERplex and, as an indication of its good faith, it would provide $100,000 of this loan during the negotiation period. The length of the unsecured loan was one year (from the June close date) or an initial public offering (IPO), whichever came first.
- Cachet would also pay $70,000 in management bonuses to CYBERplex managers and, in turn, the two principals would sign three-year management contracts.

Four months into this relationship, the partners remained happy with the participation of Cachet, which had kept its promise to assist them in locating financing (it had been instrumental in identifying the JCP alternative the partners were now having difficulties with), had allowed CYBERplex to continue its own course of business in Internet strategy, and had been helpful in client referrals. Cachet's primary interest was still to take the company public as soon as possible. Cachet figured that since its present shares would be escrowed[1] for three years following an IPO, the sooner CYBERplex went public the sooner it would be able to realize the return on its investment. Looking back, the original shareholders realized that their only concern about their Cachet deal was that the Cachet shares had performed poorly. These shares were now trading at $0.40 (see Exhibit 4 for a graph of Cachet's price/volume trading on the ASE). As a result, Lavine, Hopkins and Lobo had resolved that in order to minimize this risk in the future, they would try to obtain cash from or shares in a company over which they had an influence.

---

[1]To protect the new public shareholders of an IPO'd firm, the pre-IPO owners of the company are prevented from selling their shares (i.e., their shares are escrowed) for a period of time. This limitation on sales prevents the original shareholders (often the management shareholders) from driving the price down as they sell out and their continuing investment in the business aligns their interests with those of the new shareholders. A JCP financing carried a mandatory three-year escrow, with shares being released from escrow at a rate of one-third per year. A straight IPO held similar restrictions which were imposed at the discretion of the securities commission.

EXHIBIT 4   Cachet Share Price and Volume of Trading

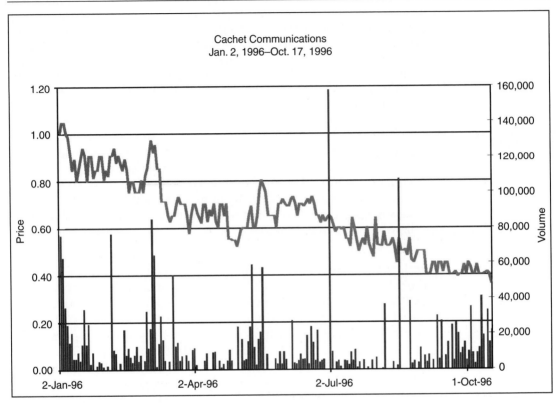

Cachet Communications
Jan. 2, 1996–Oct. 17, 1996

Source: ASE.

Plans for the Future/Third Stage Financing

As the partners looked to the future of the company, they decided that their objective would be to increase the focus of its Internet marketing business on projects that required (high added value) strategic planning skills and to steer away from the simple implementation of the web page designs of others. They also wanted to increase the IBB projects to make them a higher percentage of overall revenue. They would provide more opportunity for growth, but the Internet marketing business provided better margins. To reach these goals the company needed the financial flexibility to grow its IBB concepts and a way of motivating the existing and potential managers to take a view as business owners.

The partners saw a successful public financing as a key part of this growth strategy. The availability of a freely tradable stock that they could use as a currency for acquisitions, IBB joint ventures and the compensation of new managers would be of primary importance. A freely tradable share would allow them to attract and motivate the managers and staff needed to run the business after they had completed its incubation period and moved on to other ventures. As the partners attempted to raise money for this next stage of their development, their calculations of the value of their business at about $9 million were based on their expectations of further growth being driven from internal cash flow (outlined in the projections in Exhibit 5). The existing projections did not include any projects that would be financed from any additional money raised.

EXHIBIT 5 CYBERplex Projections (includes Cachet financing)

Income Statement	*1995 A*	*1996*	*1997*	*1998*	*1999*	*2000*
Revenues						
Corporate Internet Marketing	369	1,224	2,253	3,358	4,501	5,408
Internet-based Businesses	—	35	704	1,896	3,412	4,862
	369	1,259	2,957	5,254	7,913	10,270
COGS						
Corporate Internet Marketing		462	992	1,411	1,844	2,191
Internet-based Businesses	—	81	646	1,421	2,319	3,086
		543	1,638	2,832	4,163	5,277
SG&A	232	506	794	1,031	1,293	1,499
	232	1,049	2,432	3,863	5,456	6,776
EBITDA		210	524	1,391	2,457	3,494
Depreciation & Amortization	—	40	121	170	165	161
EBIT		170	403	1,221	2,292	3,333
Interest		17	18	(5)	(104)	(274)
Taxes	—	38	173	551	1,078	1,623
Net Income	137	115	212	675	1,318	1,984

Firm Valuation						
		115	212	675	1,318	19,835
NPV @ 20%	9,239					
Exit Multiple						10X
NPV as Multiple of '97 Earnings	43.7					
NPV as Multiple of '97 Revenue	3.1					

Selected Ratios						
EBITDA Margin		16.7%	17.7%	26.5%	31.1%	34.0%
EBIT Margin		13.5%	13.6%	23.2%	29.0%	32.5%
Net Income Margin	37.2%	9.4%	9.4%	20.1%	29.3%	36.7%
Sales Growth		231%	84%	49%	34%	20%
EBITDA Growth			149%	166%	77%	42%
Net Income Growth			84%	219%	96%	50%

Note: These numbers have been disguised.

EXHIBIT 5   *(continued)*

Income Statement	1995 A	1996	1997	1998	1999	2000
		Selected Ratios				
Revenue % Marketing		97%	76%	64%	57%	53%
Revenue % IBB		3%	24%	36%	43%	47%
Gross Margin Marketing		62%	56%	58%	59%	59%
Gross Margin IBB		−133%	8%	25%	32%	37%

Balance Sheet

	1995 A	1996	1997	1998	1999	2000
Assets						
Current Assets						
Cash	38	106	0	51	1,044	2,740
A/R	80	301	435	773	1,164	1,510
Prepaids	4	4	4	4	4	4
	122	411	439	828	2,212	4,254
PP&E	86	189	371	470	469	465
Total Assets	208	600	810	1,298	2,681	4,719
Liabilities & Equity						
Current Liabilities						
Additional Financing Required	0	0	246	0	0	0
A/P	58	50	101	161	227	282
GST Payable	15	0	0	0	0	0
Loan Debt Due	0	0	0	0	0	0
	73	50	347	161	227	282
Long Term Debt	0	0	0	0	0	0
	73	50	347	161	227	282
Shareholder Loans	30	330	30	30	30	30
Share Capital	0	0	0	0	0	0
Retained Earnings	105	220	432	1,106	2,424	4,407
	135	550	462	1,136	2,454	4,437
Total Liabilities & Equity	208	600	809	1,297	2,681	4,719
	(0)	(0)	(0)	(0)	(0)	(0)
ROE	101%	21%	46%	59%	54%	45%
ROA	66%	19%	26%	52%	49%	42%
ROCE		31%	57%	107%	93%	75%

Note: These numbers have been disguised.

EXHIBIT 5　*(continued)*

Cash Flow Statement	1995 A	1996	1997	1998	1999	2000
Operating Activities						
Net Income		115	211	674	1,318	1,983
Non Cash Items:						
D&A		40	121	170	165	161
Changes in Working Capital		(244)	(82)	(278)	(325)	(292)
Capitalized Software	—	(103)	(206)	(206)	(103)	(103)
		(192)	44	360	1,055	1,749
Investing Activities						
Capital Expenditure		(40)	(97)	(63)	(62)	(54)
Proceeds from Sale of Assets		0	0	0	0	0
Investments	—	0	0	0	0	0
		(40)	(97)	(63)	(62)	(54)
Financing Activities						
Shareholder Loans		300	(300)	0	0	0
Long-term Debt		0	0	0	0	0
Equity Issues		0	0	0	0	0
Dividend Payments	—	0	0	0	0	0
		300	(300)	0	0	0
Net Change in Cash	68	(352)	297	994	1,696	
Beginning Cash	—	38	106	(246)	51	1,044
Ending Cash	38	106	(246)	51	1,045	2,740

Note: These numbers have been disguised.

Source: Company documents.

Hopkins and Lavine thought that the stock issue they were contemplating during the fall of 1996 could easily be done at a higher valuation than the Cachet deal, which they had accepted when they had only two employees and unproved projections on which to base their negotiations. Now the company had money in the bank and more than a dozen employees, and was meeting projections set a year earlier. This time the owners wanted to give up a maximum of 20 percent of the company ownership to any new investor in return for cash to finance the new projects they had planned.

The partners saw their investment and employment horizon as the five to seven years required to make CYBERplex independently viable. Once they had achieved the company's public listing on a smaller exchange, they wanted to work towards increasing it to a size where a TSE listing would be possible. If a TSE listing weren't possible in five years, then the partners had decided they would work toward getting the company far enough along to sell it at a good valuation to a company that had achieved the critical mass to list on the TSE.

By the year 2000 the partners saw revenues going to a 50 percent mix between corporate Internet marketing and IBBs, with total revenues of $10.3 million and net income of about $2.0 million.

Factors Influencing the Decision

As Lavine sat on the plane with his files arrayed before him, he knew that if this JCP deal fell through, within a few days he and Hopkins would need to pursue the next available option.

The next choice they made would have to meet their overwhelming desire for an IPO at as high a valuation as possible, given their other constraints. It would also have to take into account certain escrow and tax consequences. Being public wouldn't be useful if Cachet couldn't sell its existing shares or if the process was going to trigger a large cash liability that the three original shareholders could not pay. Hopkins, Lavine and Lobo had a combined adjusted cost base of only $139 (the rest of their investment had been in shareholder loans), so they were concerned about a potential tax liability whenever they sold their shares. In addition, the IPO needed to be a good spring board for future equity issues. Because CYBERplex would likely continue to require growth capital, a successful IPO marketing program, good after-market support and a wide investor base would all provide fertile ground for follow-up issues. Investors that were not happy with the performance of the company would probably not reinvest in future development plans.

The partners had learned from their previous financing experiences that no financing was guaranteed but that both their financial and legal advisors often wanted up-front fees or non-contingent compensation. Thus, an unsuccessful financing would actually put them in a worse cash position than they had been in before. An IPO was expensive because of a combination of investment banker's fees and the cost of preparing a prospectus. The accounting and legal costs for a variety of options being considered are included in Exhibit 6. As a result the partners must carefully take into account the value they were receiving for their shares, as well as the likelihood of the deal's being completed. Since they had a number of time-sensitive projects ready to go, the speed at which they could raise the money and then apply it to projects would be of considerable interest.

Another minor consideration was the partners' preference that the shares of CYBERplex not trade below $1: they wanted their stock price to reflect the professional nature of their business and not to appear as speculative and high-risk.

EXHIBIT 6   Estimated Costs to Complete the Available Financing Options

	IPO	Special Warrants	Private Placement	JCP	RTO	Acquired
Accounting & Legal Costs Incurred before the Issue	$150,000	$50,000	$5,000	CYBERplex: $20,000 Newpath: $80,000	$20,000 for each side	$10,000
Accounting & Legal Costs Incurred after the Issue		$150,000				
Underwriting Commission	8.75%	8.75%	0%	Not Applicable	Not Applicable	Not Applicable

The Options

The partners' options fell into two broad categories. They could either sell treasury shares, or they could sell their personal shares to another company (in whole or in part) and have that company raise additional cash. Their two treasury options were to sell shares in an IPO onto a public exchange (either a simple IPO or by special warrants) or to do a private placement. The personal stock sale strategies they were discussing included a reverse takeover by a small NASDAQ-listed firm, sale to a JCP (where the JCP bought the company), and a straight takeover by a U.S. firm.

1. Sell Treasury Shares

a. Initial Public Offering

The most financially attractive option for the partners was to do an IPO straight away and realize the value of the company in an attractive market for Internet stocks. Numerous Internet companies had gone public in the United States in the previous year at valuations that many considered excessive. There was a widespread feeling, which had been outlined to the principals by their investment bankers, that investors were looking to invest in Internet stocks and were willing to pay a premium for companies that would benefit from the explosive growth potential of the Internet. Even with this great potential, the problem still existed that CYBERplex was unable to work with one of the larger underwriting firms and list on the TSE because of its small size and limited operating history. Typically, a deal with a larger investment firm could be arranged at a four to six percent commission, which was significantly less than that offered by one of the smaller investment banks. An IPO managed by one of the large underwriters would also impress investors and customers.

CYBERplex's most recent potential IPO had been suggested by Westcoast Securities, a Vancouver-based investment bank that specialized in small capitalization financing. Westcoast Securities had shown strong interest in underwriting an issue on a "best efforts" basis. As Lavine understood the process, this was the weakest form of underwriting and had the greatest risk for the issuer and the lowest risk for the underwriter; the latter would not at any time risk owning the deal, but would only commit to acting as an agent to put buyer and seller together.

Westcoast Securities had indicated that the fastest an IPO could be completed would be three months, taking into account the time required to write the draft prospectus, have it approved by the securities commission, market the issue to investors, get the final prospectus approved and then close the deal. Westcoast Securities had indicated that CYBERplex should price its securities to achieve $8 million to $10 million valuation, of which Westcoast Securities believed it could raise $2 million to $3 million on the ASE. From what others had told him and the fact that Westcoast Securities was not legally required to reach these levels, Lavine had calculated that the valuation and the amount raised would likely be smaller, and possibly half. If this were the case, CYBERplex would have to accept the lower amount or the deal would fail. The issue would also probably be sold only to investors in Alberta and Ontario.

In return for underwriting the deal Westcoast Securities had outlined a variety of conditions and fees that Cyberplex must meet. Many of these fees were not conditional on the successful completion of a deal and might seriously affect the company's cash flow. The fees and rights that Westcoast Securities would require in return for structuring and marketing the deal are listed in Exhibit 7. In addition to these expenses, there was the likelihood that CYBERplex would have to cover the costs of the proposed marketing campaign, as well as accounting and legal fees of $150,000.

b. Special Warrants

When the partners had raised the issue of the IPO's timing, Westcoast Securities had suggested the alternative of special warrants: a process by which a public equity issue was split into two steps in order to expedite the cash raising portion of the process. In the first step, special warrants were sold to institutional investors and high-net-worth individuals on a private placement basis (using an inexpensive offering memorandum); and in the next step, the prospectus was cleared and the warrants converted into common shares. Because the investors typically paid the full value of the underlying share for the warrant, there was no option value or leverage involved. The key advantage with special warrants was that

EXHIBIT 7   Proposed Westcoast Securities IPO

Terms & Conditions	Description	Contingent on Success?
Initial Work Fee	$35,000 was payable upon signing.	N
Closing Work Fee	$15,000 was payable on the deal closing.	Y
Placement Fee	8.75% of the Gross Deal value was payable on closing.	Y
Out of Pocket Expenses	The company was responsible for reimbursing Westcoast Securities for any reasonable out-of-pocket expenses. After discussions with Westcoast Securities Lavine had estimated these at $2,000.	N
Fiscal Agency Costs	After closing CYBERplex was to pay a $5,000 a month retainer to Westcoast Securities for three years. In return Westcoast Securities would provide capital markets advice and guidance.	Y
Greenshoe	To aid in its market stabilization activities after the issue, Westcoast Securities would require an option to purchase additional shares up to 15% of the issue for 60 days, at the offering price.	Y
Option to Purchase	As additional compensation Westcoast Securities also required an option to purchase shares, for the issue price, equivalent to 10% of the issue for two years following the closing.	Y
Limit on Options	After the issue the company is limited in the number of options it can issue.	Y
Right to Lead	Westcoast Securities would have the right to lead this deal.	Y
Right to Participate	Westcoast Securities would have the right to participate in any subsequent transaction for the next three years.	N
Deal "Out" Provisions	Westcoast Securities would have the right to not fulfill its portion of the contract if: • the market experienced unreasonable fluctuations (a "Market Out"); • due diligence or material fact was withheld from it; • the action of the financial markets made the transaction unprofitable to it; • a change in the law affected the value of the company; • a lawsuit was launched which impaired the value of the company; • a cease trading order was levelled against the company; and • if the company breached any term of the agreement.	Y
Right to Appoint	Westcoast Securities would have the right to appoint a CYBERplex board member.	Y
Right of Access	The company will provide access to any people or documents that are required by Westcoast Securities during the process.	N

Source: Company documents.

writing and clearing the prospectus was done after the warrant issue had been sold, so it was possible to complete a deal very quickly to take advantage of optimal market conditions. The costs of prospectus level disclosure were delayed until after the issue had been sold. In effect, it was the "high speed" issue that was available to non-POP[2] issuers in Canada. One other advantage of special warrants was that, if the issue wasn't successful, CYBERplex would not be burdened with the costs of writing a prospectus. Once the company had signed an underwriting agreement, the deal could be marketed to investors and would close two weeks later. Once the subscription forms had been received and the warrants paid for and distributed, the shares were released into escrow. The preliminary prospectus was issued 30 days later. During the 90 to 120 days following the issue of the preliminary prospectus, the final prospectus was filed and approved by the securities commission and the warrants were converted into freely tradable common shares.

Because special warrants were technically a private placement, there were usually a number of large institutional investors involved in the process. For CYBERplex this presented both advantages and disadvantages. One concern was that listing on many exchanges required a minimum number (usually 400) shareholders. If it had only a few large shareholders, then CYBERplex would not be able to move to a larger exchange such as the TSE in the future unless it followed up with a new public issue. Another concern arose from having only a few investors: when the time came to raise funds for future expansion, the more investors the company had, the greater its chance of obtaining the required financing from its existing shareholders. This would be of particular importance if CYBERplex did its next issue by the cheaper method of a rights issue.[3] Another problem was that, although the money had been raised at a particular price, CYBERplex would be unable to access it until the final prospectus had been filed and the warrants converted.

c. Private Placement

The other option to raise money via a private placement—had the advantage of a quick completion, which would allow the partners to have more time for detailed consideration of the other options. The partners figured they could probably raise $500,000 by way of a private placement and achieve at least the $5 million valuation that they had agreed

---

[2]Prompt Offering Prospectus—A legal status whereby a company has enough operating history and has filed detailed enough documents that the securities commission allows it to issue securities with a less detailed prospectus.

[3]A rights issue is a process whereby a company gives all its exiting shareholders the right to buy new shares at a fixed price based on their present ownership. For example, for every share you own you get the right to buy one additional share for $10.

on with Cachet. This option would also allow them to dilute Cachet's investment (and its potential for control) in the business. The cash issuing costs for a private placement were also less than an IPO.

A private placement to finance a particular project was also possible. In this case, CYBERplex would not raise cash for the whole company but would finance a particular IBB with the returns to investors depending on the performance of the new venture. The basic structure of this option, assuming a $150,000 investment, would be to set up a separate company and have the investors provide $120,000 in cash. CYBERplex would provide $30,000 in time and services for 20 percent of the business. Once the business started to produce cash flows, the profits would be split between the new investors and CYBERplex according to their respective ownership.

The key problem with either type of private placement was that it wouldn't advance the partners any closer towards their IPO goal and the beginning of the process to realize their gain on their investment. Cachet might also be concerned that CYBERplex was diluting its holdings without gaining access to an opportunity to divest.

2. Sell Personal Shares

a. Reverse Takeover—Netco

One of the options involving the sale of personal shares was to achieve a public listing through the process of a reverse takeover (RTO). In particular, a company called Netco, based out of Halifax but listed on the NASDAQ, and a U.S. corporation had suggested this option to CYBERplex as an opportunity for the owners of Netco to grow their own company and realize some value. In an RTO, the smaller company buys the larger company and the large issue of shares used to buy the larger company gives the larger company's shareholders a controlling interest in the combined company. Because of tax issues, this takeover would have Netco issuing shares to take over CYBERplex and somehow structuring the transaction so Canadian rollover[4] rules could be used to avoid triggering a taxable event for the Canadian shareholders. As of October 1996, the partners still didn't have a workable solution to the problem, but thought that with additional legal and tax advice a workable solution would be possible. There was some chance that the U.S. shareholders would be taxable, but there was the potential to use a tax treaty to mitigate these circumstances as well. Any dividends subsequently paid by CYBERplex to its shareholders would not

---

[4]Revenue Canada allows a shareholder of a taxable Canadian corporation to defer a capital gain in a situation where two companies are amalgamated in a share for share swap.

be as valuable as the same amount of Canadian dividends.[5] It was expected that for the exchange CYBERplex's shares would be valued based on a $6-million company value in order to give CYBERplex's shareholders a 70 percent ownership in the new combined business. Once negotiations had been completed, the takeover bid would likely stay open for the mandatory 28 days.

Netco's primary business was also in the area of Internet marketing. In particular, the company created sophisticated website designs and marketing plans for its clients. It was also involved in Internet software development and Internet product marketing, and was pursuing a number of Internet joint ventures in a Soviet republic.

Netco had a relatively clean balance sheet, with the only major obligations being a fibre optic lease and an office lease. In addition, the company had no employment contracts and some non-binding business agreements, so that any changes that CYBERplex would need to make after the merger would be quite easy. Also, Netco had several executives who would go a long way toward meeting CYBERplex's growing management needs.

There were also a number of unquantifiable benefits that would come with an association with Netco. The company had done a lot of the preliminary public relations work that was so important to maintaining the financial attractiveness of a newly listed company. It also had a number of press releases ready to keep up investor interest and had set up a number of contracts that were almost ready to be announced. Finally, Netco had arranged for market makers in the United States and Canada to maintain the liquidity of its stock and keep it trading at as high a price as possible.

b. Junior Capital Pool—The Newpath Option

An interesting variation on the RTO alternative, and the option that Lavine was pursuing in Calgary, was the RTO of an ASE-listed Junior Capital Pool (JCP). Investors in a JCP would give the "founders" cash because of the assumption that this cash would be used to buy an asset that would convert the company from an investment vehicle into an operating corporation. Traditionally these assets had been oil and gas wells or mines, but there was no limitation on the nature of the asset. Every JCP had two steps in its life cycle: the initial IPO in which the seed capital was raised, and the major transaction in which the company bought a Canadian-held asset worth at least $400,000 or an existing public company. (A complete list of the steps is included in Exhibit 8.) Lavine had learned of the benefits of JCPs from the relationship with Cachet, which had gone public in this way a few years earlier.

---

[5]Dividends from U.S. corporations to Canadian shareholders are not eligible for the dividend tax credit.

EXHIBIT 8   List of the Steps a JCP Completes to Close Its Major Transaction

---

1. A Lock Up letter is signed (Intent Letter).
2. A Lock Up agreement is signed (Contract).
3. A press release is issued and a Material Change Report is submitted to the ASE.
4. An Information Circular is put together and submitted to the ASE.
5. The ASE makes its response, which includes comments and changes made to the Circular.
6. Changes are made based on the ASE response. (Steps 5 and 6 can take up to two months.)
7. In the case of the Newpath/CYBERplex deal, a private placement is made before the transaction takes place.
8. The Final Information Circular is submitted to the ASE.
9. After the Circular has been received there is a 30-day period during which the Circular is distributed and a special shareholders' meeting of the JCP is held.
10. If approved by the majority of the minority of Newpath, a take-over bid for CYBERplex is launched and is open for 28 days.
11. The deal is closed and CYBERplex is now publicly listed on the ASE and has access to the JCP's cash.

Source: Company documents.

In the case of the Newpath JCP, the promoters had indicated to investors that their JCP would invest in companies in the "new economy." JCPs were required to complete a major transaction within 18 months of their listing date or be subject to delisting by the ASE. The Newpath JCP had done its initial issue in August 1996 and had offered to CYBERplex the opportunity to be its major transaction, to be announced concurrently with the issue starting trading on the ASE. Once the major transaction had been agreed to, the JCP shareholders seldom rejected it.

Lavine understood from his company's financial advisors that, traditionally, JCPs are financed on a 1:2:5 proportion (the 1:2 proportion is the limit for JCPs set by the Alberta Securities Commission). For example, the founders invest at $0.10 a share, the public shareholders invest at $0.20 a share, and the shares are used to buy a major asset at $0.50 a share. In the case of Newpath, the founders invested $100,000 and received one million shares, and the next stage public investors received 1.5 million shares for $300,000. The partners had negotiated with the JCP's shareholders to have Newpath consolidate its shares by a factor of 1.5 (2.5 million shares to 1.67 million shares) before the acquisition took place. These calculations are summarized in Exhibit 9. The problem was that Newpath's underwriters thought

---

EXHIBIT 9   JCP Calculations—with Consolidation

	Share Price	*Shares*	*Cash In*	*Ownership*
Current JCP				
JCP Founders—Escrowed	0.15	666,667	$100,000	40.0%
Public	0.30	1,000,000	$300,000	60.0%
		1,666,667	$400,000	100.0%
After Vend In				
HLL Group	0.75	4,000,000		41.4%
Cachet	0.75	4,000,000		41.4%
HLL* Purchase of Founders Shares	0.36	300,000		3.1%
Cachet Purchase of Founders Shares	0.36	300,000		3.1%
JCP Founders—Escrowed	0.15	66,667	$100,000	0.7%
Newpath Public Float	0.30	1,000,000	$300,000	10.3%
Total		9,666,667	$400,000	100.0%
Float After Vend In				
Free Trading Float		1,000,000		10.3%
Control Block		8,666,667		89.7%
		9,666,667		100.0%
Acquisition Price Ratios				
Founders Shares	0.15	1.0 x		
Public Shares	0.30	2.0 x		
Major Transaction Shares (CYBERplex)	0.75	5.0 x		

These calculations ignore the effect of a concurrent private placement, the underwriter's option for 150,000 shares @ $.20, and management's option for 250,000 shares @ $.20.

*Hopkins, Lavine, Lobo.

Source: Company documents.

---

that the consolidation would confuse the JCP's investors and produce too few shares to create a stock that was liquid in the secondary market. Unfortunately, the underwriters had expressed these concerns on the eve of the transaction's lock-up agreement signing. The problem for the CYBERplex shareholders was that, without the consolidation, the Newpath shareholders would buy their company for eight million shares valued at $0.75 each. Although the CYBERplex partners would receive an attractive $6 million valuation for its company, they would receive a smaller proportion of the new company than they thought was fair. The ownership calculations are done on a non-consolidated basis in Exhibit 10.

EXHIBIT 10   JCP Calculations—without Consolidation

	Share Price	Shares	Cash In	Ownership
Current JCP				
JCP Founders—Escrowed	0.10	1,000,000	$100,000	40.0%
Public	0.20	1,500,000	$300,000	60.0%
		2,500,000	$400,000	
After Vend In				
HLL* Group	0.75	4,000,000		38.1%
Cachet	0.75	4,000,000		38.1%
HLL Purchase of Founders Shares	0.24	450,000		4.3%
Cachet Purchase of Founders Shares	0.24	450,000		4.3%
JCP Founders—Escrowed	0.10	100,000	$100,000	1.0%
Newpath Public Float	0.20	1,500,000	$300,000	14.3%
Total		10,500,000	$400,000	100.1%
Float After Vend In				
Free Trading Float		1,500,000		14.3%
Control Block		9,000,000		85.7%
		10,500,000		100.0%
Acquisition Price Ratios				
Founders Shares	0.10	1.0 x		
Public Shares	0.20	2.0 x		
Major Transaction Shares (CYBERplex)	0.75	7.5 x		

These calculations ignore: the effect of a concurrent private placement, the underwriter's option for 150,000 shares @ $.20, and management's option for 250,000 shares @ $.20.

*Hopkins, Lavine, Lobo.

Source: Company documents.

There was one additional wrinkle. The people who were initially involved with the JCP had their founders' shares escrowed for three years, due to strict ASE regulations. As part of the deal, they wanted to recapture their capital by having CYBERplex shareholders pay $216,000 for 900,000 of their (pre-consolidated) shares.

If they could negotiate a resolution of the consolidation issue, the CYBERplex partners would find this option particularly attractive. The deal would be completed quickly, fit many of Cachet's requirements for an IPO, and risked very few fees in the event of cancellation. In addition, the shell had $400,000 (less any expenses) available to finance any projects that CYBERplex had in the short term. There was also the potential to do a private placement concurrent with the major transaction in order to raise additional financing.

Lavine and Hopkins also wondered if they were overly concerned. Although the transaction didn't follow industry practice (of 1:2:5), maybe it was still attractive. Lavine wondered what the ownership structure would look like after the deal, whether consolidated or unconsolidated. Also, with the timing so critical, should they be more concerned with other areas such as the $6 million valuation? One thing the partners knew they should look at was what the returns would be for the various investors if this deal were completed.

c. Get Acquired—Interco Marketing

Another realization option was to sell the company in its entirety to another party. One option was to sell to Interco Marketing, a NASDAQ-listed Internet marketing firm. As Lavine was quickly starting to realize, firms in the U.S. market had a much easier time finding financing at very attractive valuations and with very little in operations other than an impressive business plan. After glancing through the firm's prospectus summary (Exhibit 11) to refresh his memory, he remembered that the problem with Interco Marketing was that it lacked any revenue-generating Internet projects. Although the company billed itself as a creator of interactive marketing solutions, it generated 75 percent of its revenues from advertising on ski lift poles. CYBERplex was also faced with the same problem it had faced in previous acquisition discussions. Interco Marketing wanted CYBERplex to become more of a publisher of Internet web pages and had little interest in the company's focus on the development of Internet strategies for corporate clients.

EXHIBIT 11   Selected Information Taken from Interco Marketing's Prospectus
Prospectus Summary

The following summary is qualified in its entirety by the more detailed information and the Company's Consolidated Financial Statements and Notes thereto appearing elsewhere in this Prospectus. Investors should carefully consider the information set forth under the heading "Risk Factors." Unless otherwise indicated, all information in this Prospectus (i) assumes no exercise of the Underwriters' over-allotment option, (ii) reflects the three-for-one stock split of the Common Stock that will occur on the effective date (the "Effective Date") or the Registration Statement files in connection with this Offering (the "Stock Split"), and (iii) reflects the issuance of 4,026,000 shares of Common Stock upon the conversion of the outstanding shares of the Company's Series A Preferred Stock that will occur on the Effective Date (the "Preferred Stock Conversion").

The Company

Interco Marketing (together with its subsidiaries, the "Company") creates, develops and deploys interactive marketing solutions that assist companies in communicating effectively with their targeted audiences. The Company develops interactive marketing solutions that include World Wide websites, information and transaction kiosks, CD-ROMs, computer-based multimedia presentations and proprietary online service offerings.

EXHIBIT 11 (*continued*)

The Company seeks to become the leading worldwide developer of interactive marketing solutions for Fortune 1000 companies. The Company also offers traditional outdoor media advertising at ski resorts in the United States. Outdoor media advertising, which appears on lift towers and other locations at ski resorts, generated approximately 75 percent of the Company's revenue in 1995. Although the Company did not generate significant revenue from interactive marketing services until the second half of 1995, the Company expects its revenue mix to continue to shift significantly during 1996.

Interco Marketing competes in the rapidly evolving interactive segment of the marketing communications industry. Interactive marketing is designed to enhance a company's sales and marketing efforts by offering the opportunity to: (i) provide in-depth information that is not easily available or accessible through traditional marketing methods, (ii) capture a consumer's attention with engaging and entertaining content, (iii) reduce costs and shorten sales cycles by decreasing dependence on salespersons, and (iv) open new distribution channels.

The Company believes that the following strengths distinguish it from its competitors:

* *Technology Expertise.* The Company's technical team assesses and ranks the most promising existing and emerging technologies for incorporation into its interactive marketing solutions. This technology expertise spans multimedia authoring software tools, databases, programming languages and the integration of content, software and hardware.
* *Creative Excellence.* The Company believes it has recruited an outstanding creative development team. In developing creative interactive marketing solutions, the Company emphasizes easy-to-use and intuitive interfaces, seamlessly integrated technologies and an engaging look and feel.
* *Strategic Marketing Experience.* The Company's management team and sales and marketing staff are experienced in understanding customers' business challenges and in developing strategic marketing plans to address those challenges. The Company often works with its customers' senior management to determine how best to integrate interactive marketing into the customers' business plans.

The Company targets Fortune 1000 companies in industries that can take full advantage of interactive marketing. In 1995, the Company's customers included American Express Travel Related Services, Sony Development, Sprint, PageNet and Saatchi & Saatchi Pacific (on behalf of Toyota Motor Sales USA). With the exception of Sony Development and American Express Travel Related Services, which generated approximately eight percent and five percent of the Company's revenue during 1995, respectively, none of these customers generated more than 1.25 percent of the Company's revenue during the period. In 1996, Hewlett-Packard, Sun Microsystems and Electronic Data Systems, Inc. became customers of the Company.

Common Stock Offered ....3,650,000 shares
Common Stock Outstanding after the Offering............10,813,448 shares (1)
Use of Proceeds..The Company expects to use the net proceeds from the Offering, which are estimated to be approximately $36,589,500, for the repayment of debt, working capital and general corporate purposes, including possible acquisitions. See "Use of Proceeds."
NASDAQ National Market Symbol...............................

EXHIBIT 11   (*continued*)

(1) Excludes 3,000,000 shares of Common Stock reserved for issuance to executive employees and directors under the Company's 1995 Executive Stock Option Plan (the "Executive Option Plan") (or which options to purchase 1,913,700 shares have been granted) and 600,000 shares of Common Stock reserved for issuance to employees under the Company's 1995 Employee Stock Option Plan (the "Employee Option Plan") (of which options to purchase 357,210 shares have been granted). It is expected that options to purchase approximately 987,600 shares of Common Stock will become exercisable approximately 15 trading days after the completion of the Offering. In addition, the Company has reserved 150,000 shares for issuance under the Company's Employee Stock Purchase Plan (the "Employee Stock Purchase Plan"), none of which shares have been issued. See "Management—Stock Option Plans" and "—Employee Stock Purchase Plan."

Summary Financial Data

	Predecessor Business (1) (in thousands)		_____ Inc. (in thousands, except per share amounts)	
	Year Ended April 30, 1994	Eight Months Ended December 31, 1994	Period from Inception (May 25, 1994) to December 31, 1994	Year Ended December 31, 1995
Statement of Operations Data:				
Revenue	$2,811	$ 987	$ 128	$5,273
Operating income (loss)	(226)	(813)	(339)	(2,617)
Income (loss) from continuing operations and before extraordinary items (2)	(798)	(1,275)	(362)	(3,225)
Unaudited pro forma data:				
Unaudited pro forma net loss from continuing operations per common and common equivalent share (3)				(.60)
Shares used in computing unaudited pro forma net loss per common and equivalent share (3)				5,360

	April 30, 1994	December 31, 1994	December 31, 1994	December 31, 1995	Pro Forma (5) December 31, 1995	Pro Forma As Adjusted (5) December 31, 1995
Balance Sheet Data:						
Cash and cash equivalents	$ 387	$ 54	$267	$1,123	$1,123	$34,712
Working capital	570	(271)	193	(105)	(105)	34,084
Total assets	2,366	3,745	371	9,700	9,700	43,289

EXHIBIT 11 *(continued)*

	April 30, 1994	December 31, 1994	December 31, 1994	December 31, 1995	Pro Forma (5) December 31, 1995	Pro Forma As Adjusted (5) December 31, 1995
Total long-term obligations (current and non-current portions)	8,775	8,747	650	3,161	3,161	161
Mandatorily redeemable convertible preferred stock (4)	—	—	—	6,898	—	—
Total stockholders' equity (deficit) (4)	(6,522)	(6,891)	($362)	(3,947)	2,951	39,540

(1) Effective January 1, 1995, the Company acquired the assets and assumed certain liabilities of a predecessor entity (the "Predecessor Business") that had operated the outdoor media advertising business currently operated by SkiView, Inc. Due to the significance of the outdoor media advertising business to the Company's operations, the financial statements of the Predecessor Business have been included in this Prospectus.

(2) Prior to September 30, 1995, the Company was an S Corporation, and all taxable income or loss was reported by the stockholders. Effective on that date, the Company became a C Corporation. The Company incurred net operating losses for tax purposes subsequent to that date, which have been fully reserved for by a valuation allowance.

(3) Calculated on the basis described in Note 1 of Notes to the Company's Consolidated Financial Statements.

(4) Accrued preferred stock dividends of $187,654 have been recorded on the mandatorily redeemable convertible preferred stock. As discussed in Note 1 of Notes to the Company's Consolidated Financial Statements, such dividends will not be paid if the Offering results in a common share price of $5.00 or more, at which time the mandatorily redeemable convertible preferred stock will convert into Common Stock.

(5) Unaudited pro forma December 31, 1995, amounts reflect the conversion of 1,342,000 shares of preferred stock into 4,026,000 shares of Common Stock at $1.67 per share of Common Stock and the restoration of $187,654 of accrued dividends on preferred stock to additional paid in capital; unaudited pro forma as adjusted December 31, 1995, amounts also reflect the issuance of 3,650,000 shares of the Common Stock as contemplated by this Prospectus at an assumed price of $11.00 per share, net of $3,560,500 of offering costs and underwriting discounts, and the repayment of the $3,000,000 principal amount of the Term Note (as defined below) with the proceeds of such issuance.

Source: Interco Marketing's Prospectus (disguised).

In the initial discussions Interco Marketing had offered the partners 10 to 12 times trailing sales for the company, all to be paid in Interco Marketing shares, which were themselves trading at over 14 times trailing sales. Lavine and Hopkins were concerned that the market in the long term would be unlikely to continue to value stocks such as Interco Marketing with few operating assets at such a high multiple. This expected multiple compression could significantly reduce the value of the consideration received. This was of particular concern, because one condition Interco Marketing had set was that there would be a one to two year restriction on the sale of the shares CYBERplex received in the transaction. Interco's recent share performance is included in Exhibit 12. Another concern for Lavine and Hopkins was what the tax consequences would be in accepting such a deal. Receiving U.S.-listed shares for their Canadian shares might not allow them to use the tax-free rollover rules. One of the other problems that arose during the negotiation was that, as the partners negotiated with progressively more senior people at Interco Marketing, the worse the deal became with the most recent offer being five to six times trailing sales for all of CYBERplex, to be paid in Interco Marketing shares, as well as a much longer escrow period.

EXHIBIT 12   Interco Marketing Share Price and Volume of Trading

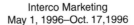

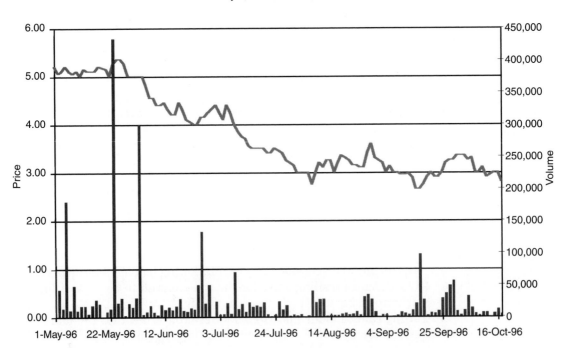

Source: NASDAQ data.

The Decision

With the plane circling to land, Lavine knew he would have to present the next opportunity to all of the shareholders tomorrow afternoon if his negotiations with the Newpath promoters fell through in the morning.

Grocery Gateway.com

Professor James E. Hatch and Amanda Clark

Introduction

It was a hot, sunny day in August 1998 as Stuart Lombard, a partner of J.L. Albright, sat at his desk, considering what his next steps would be in determining whether his firm would be interested in investing in Grocery Gateway, an Internet grocery retailer. He had received the company's business plan a few days prior and had also done some background analysis on the industry and the management team. The company was still at a very early stage, as it had opened for business only four months before. It currently had only approximately 20 customers. Lombard knew that this was to be the company's second round of financing, and that it was looking to raise up to $5 million to fund the ramp-up of the business. He wanted to make a decision quickly, because if it was a good opportunity, he did not want to miss it by delaying. If all the partners of J.L. Albright agreed that it would be a good investment opportunity, Lombard would need to value the company and structure a deal to propose to Grocery Gateway.

J.L. Albright

J.L. Albright was a venture capital firm that had been set up in 1996 to focus on investing in technology opportunities. The firm had approximately $60 million in available capital that it used to invest in early-stage companies. The companies were generally at a stage where they had a product or prototype that could be evaluated. Initial investments in companies were typically between $3 million and $5 million, while follow-on rounds of financing would bring the total investment up to approximately $9 million.

J.L. Albright had a number of competitive advantages. The partnership had a balance of operational and financial experience. Two of the partners had founded multiple successful technology start-ups and the other two partners had extensive experience in venture capital, investment banking and corporate law. The firm's focus on technology allowed it to stand out from other venture capitalists who weren't as familiar with how to evaluate technology opportunities. Each partner would have two or three investments to manage, and would often take an interim management role in the company, thus increasing their influence on the company's operations. A successful investment history, and an annual return on the fund of over 100 percent over the past three years increased the ability for J.L. Albright to raise additional money for the fund.

J.L. Albright had seven employees, including four partners. The four partners would generally make the investment decisions based on consensus; however, for each investment, one partner was typically responsible. Therefore, Lombard knew that if he decided that Grocery Gateway was an attractive opportunity, he would need to convince the other partners as well.

The partners of J.L. Albright focused on a number of areas when evaluating investments. Depending on the deal, some of the aspects would be more important than others. The main focus was generally on the viability of the business concept. They looked for businesses in large, fast-growing markets, where the company would have an opportunity to dominate that market. The management team was also a key factor, along with the business strategy and the quality of the product or service. Their concern was with the ability of the company to execute its business plan. The partners also reviewed the financial projections to determine their reasonableness and whether the company could make a profit in the long run. They considered an annual internal rate of return of 50 percent acceptable, although they did look for opportunities where they could make 10 times their money over the investment horizon. They preferred a two-to-three year investment time horizon, but would go out to five years if necessary.

Company Overview

Grocery Gateway provided Internet grocery shopping and delivery to consumers located in the Toronto area. The company considered itself to be the solution for customers who were looking for time-savings and convenience. Its goal was to be the premier Internet shopping and delivery company, providing a range of products and services in Canada.

Grocery Gateway consisted of an Internet website that allowed consumers to log on, order groceries and a limited range of health and beauty aids and have them delivered to their home within 24 hours. Grocery Gateway had a corporate office, but no stores and no warehouses. When an order was received, a confirmation e-mail was sent to the customer and the order was forwarded to a database server that processed the order and generated (1) pick lists, (2) a consumer tracking field, and (3) a consumer invoice. The invoice and pick lists were then forwarded to the retail outlet (Longo's, a Toronto-based supermarket chain). Company pickers downloaded the orders each morning to a computer at Longo's, and then picked and packed the items directly into the delivery case. Next, they put the items through the regular check-out process and company drivers delivered the order within a three-hour window chosen by the customer. Customers paid for the order at the door with cash, check, Visa or Interac, eliminating the worry for people about using their credit cards online. In order for the delivery process to be economical, a minimum order size of $45 was required and a delivery charge of $6 was charged on all orders, regardless of size.

The website, at www.grocerygateway.com was easy to use and customizable by the user. It was set up with a number of categories that the customer could click on to find the products that they were looking for, or they could use the search function to find a specific item. Each customer could also customize the site, by creating shopping lists that could be used over and over again, and which could be modified to make the shopping experience that much faster. The website also showed weekly specials with pictures of the items.

Internet Use

According to the International Data Corporation, world Internet use was expected to increase from approximately 88 million users in 1998 to almost 550 million users by the year 2000. The speed of adoption of the Internet was phenomenal, with thousands of businesses having sold their products online. In 1997, Internet sales totaled US$10.65 billion in the United States and US$707 million in Canada. Canadian sales were estimated to grow significantly to US$9.57 billion by 2000.

Approximately 8.1 million people, or 27 percent of the Canadian population, were regular users of the Internet; 12 percent of this group bought products or services online. In the United States, 29 percent of the Internet users used it for shopping.

One reason that electronic commerce was increasing in popularity was that it allowed a number of improvements to the way businesses traditionally operated. Virtual stores meant that companies could save costs by reducing warehouse space, locating in less expensive areas and eliminating store fixtures. Additional costs could be saved through eliminating intermediaries by going direct to the customer and improving efficiencies through automation. Marketing could be improved by using sophisticated databases to develop new levels of understanding the customers. This would involve using Internet technology to determine user preferences, based on their browsing patterns. The information generated would allow marketers to target segments as small as one person. The Internet also enabled companies to be exposed to new markets at a minimal cost. On the consumer side, the technology enabled the creation of a new shopping experience, thereby attracting new customers. It also significantly improved the information flow to the consumers, increasing their education about the products and services offered and enabling them to comparison shop.

Grocery Retailing

The revenues of the retail grocery industry in the United States and Canada totalled approximately US$413 billion[1] and Cdn$52 billion,[2] respectively. The industry was highly competitive as it was a very mature industry, with sales growth only slightly exceeding inflation. As competitors focused on price, prepared products and increased expenditures on infrastructure to improve in-store atmosphere, already slim margins narrowed further.

Estimates varied significantly on the size of the online grocery market. Jupiter Communications, a media research company, expected consumers to spend $3.5 billion on online grocery shopping by 2002, which represented less than one percent of the total U.S. grocery market. On the other hand, Andersen Consulting believed that the amount would be much higher; its forecast indicated that by 2007, the amount spent in the United States on groceries online would reach $85 billion.

---

[1] Progressive Grocer, 1995 total U.S. grocery sales.
[2] 1995 Canadian Grocer.

Competition

The Internet grocery shopping and delivery industry was expanding rapidly in the United States. At the time Grocery Gateway was getting into the business in Canada, there were more than six major companies with over 200,000 customers in total in the United States generating sales of approximately US$150 million.[3] In Canada, Grocery Gateway faced very little competition since there were only a few companies who were concentrating on niche market strategies, such as neighbourhood delivery and orders by fax and phone. These companies had not used technology to gain advantages, nor had they allocated resources to build a brand name, consumer confidence or a critical mass.

Potential new entrants to the Internet grocery and delivery industry included major grocery chains and other Internet retailers. Grocery chains were a threat because they were established with a well-recognized brand name, were well financed, had an existing customer base and had low cost product suppliers. Other Internet retailers were very successful in other products and could use their expertise to move into the grocery industry.

U.S. Internet Grocery Companies

U.S. Internet grocery companies differed widely in their business models, as each tried to find the model that would be the most successful. The distribution part of the business was very expensive, which resulted in companies choosing different methods, hoping that they could find the best solution. Some companies, such as Peapod and Streamline, limited the geographic area that they serviced, while other companies, such as NetGrocer, provided national distribution. Generally, the national companies used the services of already existing distribution systems, such as Federal Express, while the local companies used their own distribution systems. The distribution method chosen also had an impact on the company's product offerings. NetGrocer offered only non-perishable items, while Peapod and Streamline offered both perishables and non-perishables. Another difference was that some companies (Peapod, for example) aligned themselves with an existing grocery chain, while others built their own warehouses to source the products. Companies also differed in whether they charged a flat fee per month for delivery or charged per delivery, and whether they required someone to be at home for delivery (attended delivery) or whether they would leave the items if no one was home (unattended delivery). See Exhibit 1 for an overview of the strategies of the major U.S. Internet grocery companies.

---

[3]Estimates based on 1997 reported sales.

EXHIBIT 1 Overview of Internet Grocery Retailers

Company	Location	Products	Supply	Software	Delivery Method	Delivery Charge	Minimum Order Size	Delivery Window
HomeRuns.com	Boston	Perishables & nonperishables	Company-owned warehouse	N/A	Company-owned fleet of vans	Free if order > US$60 US$10 if order < US$60 $5 service charge if order by phone/fax	Minimum US$30	2-hour window, Mon. to Sat. 8A.M. to 10P.M.
NetGrocer.com	Continental U.S. and Alaska	Non-perishable items only including drug and general merchandise	N/A	N/A	FedEx	Delivery charges based on location and value of order—ranges from $5.99 to $73.99	None	2–4 business days
Peapod.com	Austin, Boston, Chicago, Columbus, Dallas / Fort Worth / Houston, Long Island, San Francisco / San Jose	Perishables & nonperishables	Products offered through partnerships with retail grocers; beginning to warehouse dry goods	Proprietary software; must be downloaded by the customer before it can be used	Company trucks Attended delivery	US$5 membership fee + US$5 per delivery	N/A	2-hour window
Shoplink.com	Massachusetts	Perishables & nonperishables, health & beauty, general merchandise, flowers	Company-owned warehouse	CD-ROM based ordering	Unattended delivery in patented chilled containers	Flat fee of US$25 per month (four deliveries)	N/A	1 day per week
Streamline.com	Boston, Washington, Chicago	Perishables & nonperishables, home video, dry cleaning, shoe repair	Company-owned warehouse	Proprietary software	Company trucks Installs free refrigerator for unattended delivery	Flat fee of US$30 per month (four deliveries)	None	1 day per week
YourGrocer.com	New York City area	Perishables & nonperishables	N/A	N/A	Attended delivery	US$5 per delivery	US$50 minimum order	2-hour evening window

N/A—Information not available.

Source: Company websites.

Canadian Internet Grocery Companies

There were no Internet grocery companies in Canada; however, three companies provided grocery delivery service.

IGA

Located in Quebec, some of the franchisees accepted grocery orders for delivery by phone, fax, and the Internet. However, this was not central to their business strategy.

Peachtree

A software vendor that partnered with grocery companies to provide a grocery delivery service. It had 4,000 customers and less than $3 million in revenue. Part of its customer base was acquired through a partnership with Food for You, a Toronto-based grocery delivery company with 1,500 customers. Peachtree charged a premium for its groceries. It was beginning to expand in Western Canada by partnering with Quality Foods as its supplier.

Grocery Network

A Toronto-based grocery catalogue delivery service with sales of less than $1.5 million. Orders were taken by phone, fax and over Bell's Vista phones. The company's website was not completed yet. Products were bought from other retailers; however, the company did not have any formal alliances.

Technology

Since technology was an integral part of the business model, Grocery Gateway had realized the importance of having a proprietary computer system, which could present the customer with an engaging shopping experience and would provide the research customer with immediate knowledge. The basic premise was to use technology to build an electronic commerce model where all the different computer systems would communicate seamlessly. Therefore, all the transaction systems were to be automated and homogeneous. These included the Enterprise Resource Planning components (inventory, financial, warehousing, distribution, order processing), web interfaces, supply side EDI partners, and fulfillment side secure electronic payment. The goal was to create a barrier to entry that would keep traditional grocery stores out of the online delivery business. Grocery Gateway was developing its proprietary system internally and believed it would be the best system in Canada once it was completed. However, Lombard also knew that Grocery Gateway had only the web interface and database support in place at the current time.

Lombard knew that some of the U.S. competitors, such as Peapod and Streamline, had developed proprietary systems.

Start-up

Bill Di Nardo, president and chief executive officer of Grocery Gateway, had come up with the idea to start an Internet grocery and delivery company in 1996. After graduating with an Honours Business Administration degree from the Richard Ivey School of Business at the University of Western Ontario, Di Nardo worked for seven years in brand and category management at Warner-Lambert Company of Canada and Clorox Company. In that capacity, he introduced and branded new products to the Canadian market through channels that included most major grocery chains. Over the years, he purchased a considerable amount of consumer research on behalf of his employers. Finding it lacking in many areas, Di Nardo started thinking about the Internet as a research tool to gather consumer information. However, in order to gather research, he needed a business that would provide the consumers. He turned to groceries as an ideal starting point for a number of reasons. There was a latent demand for the service (people generally did not like grocery shopping), national brands made it easier for customers to make a purchase decision, there would be significant repeated purchases and, thus, an opportunity to create a habit.

Grocery Gateway was incorporated in October 1997, with Di Nardo as the only owner and employee. By January 1998, the company had a prototype of its website, a rough business plan and one more employee. In order to make customers and investors comfortable with the company, Di Nardo brought on well-respected corporate partners whose names would bring instant credibility to the business. For example, he partnered with Longo's, a local grocery chain well known for its quality produce, in order to take advantage of its grocery and retail experience, and he partnered with Digital Equipment for its web server expertise. IBM provided software and data warehouse expertise and Royal Bank provided the hand-held point of sale terminals. As Di Nardo continued to develop the business, these corporate partners, among others, made significant commitments to support the development of the company and most provided some sweat equity.

Di Nardo opened Grocery Gateway for business in April 1998, with the objective of becoming the premier Internet shopping and delivery company in Canada. By the end of April, Grocery Gateway had 10 customers. In June of 1998, Di Nardo approached his friends and family to raise seed capital for the business. The founders and advisors also put in some money for a total of $100,000. Grocery Gateway was also able to get a $10,000 line of credit from the bank. The money was used to further develop the proprietary system and business model to ensure that the company would be able to handle a much larger customer base. As a result of the focus on systems rather than on marketing, the customer base had grown to only 20 people by August 1998.

Growth Strategy

The company's growth strategy was very clear. Grocery Gateway intended to build its brand identity by aggressively promoting convenience, product quality and value of its services on a very targeted basis. By growing the primary customer base and creating satisfied customers, Grocery Gateway would also be able to generate additional revenue from the sale of advertising and research on customer trends.

The company intended to improve website technology by further customizing the interface, and adding intelligent shopping and online video demonstrations. New services would also be added, such as nutritional information and more recipes. Grocery Gateway had a number of partners offering various forms of expertise, and would continue to target others, such as wine and beer retailers. Di Nardo believed that in order to generate enough margin to make the business viable, Grocery Gateway would need to increase the items per delivery. In order to make this possible, the company planned to increase the products and services offered to include items such as dry cleaning, health and beauty aids, gift ideas, flowers, nonprescription pharmaceuticals, books and CDs, film development, loyalty points, movie rentals and alcohol. Di Nardo believed that what happened at the customer's door was one of the keys to success, and therefore wanted to have unprecedented delivery service quality. In addition, Grocery Gateway would collect anonymous information on its consumers and their buying habits; this information could, in turn, be sold to consumer packaged goods companies. This market research was expected to command a premium price per potential customer because of its targeted nature and the fact that it would have the potential to induce purchase at the time of viewing.

Di Nardo planned to expand Grocery Gateway into other markets once it had reached a critical mass in the Toronto area. As the company grew, Di Nardo wanted to use proprietary warehouses rather than continue with the retail stores. He believed that the retail store-based business model would not support a large company. His vision was to develop a warehouse that would utilize modern picking techniques to reduce the time required to pack the groceries.

Grocery Gateway was planning to target consumer groups that would benefit the most from the convenience of its service. These would include families with young children, busy professionals, disabled people who found it difficult to travel, single parents and people without cars.

Grocery Gateway believed that the best way to market to these groups would be through five different channels: direct marketing, limited mass media, public relations, print material and salespeople. Direct marketing would be based on customer profiles gathered online, while limited mass media advertising would be used to build brand awareness and establish credibility. Public relations was expected to involve mall demonstrations of the service to induce trial. Print material (flyers) would allow Grocery Gateway to maximize densities in target neighbourhoods before expanding geographically. Salespeople would be used to facilitate trials of the service.

Grocery Gateway was also planning to target research customers such as packaged goods companies, electronic research centres and demographic research companies. Grocery Gateway would be able to provide these groups with detailed information on customer trends and buyer behavior, all of which had been gathered from Grocery Gateway customers as they used the website. Grocery Gateway believed that it would have an advantage over other information service providers because of the low setup cost for each piece of research, compared to the high fixed costs for other providers that would need to find a target audience, interview them and follow up with them. A further advantage stemmed from the fact that Grocery Gateway's information would be based on actual consumer behavior, not on stated intentions.

Forecast Financial Performance

Grocery Gateway expected its strategy to result in significant growth in revenues and profits, as shown in the forecast financial statements. See Exhibits 2 and 3 for the projected income statement and balance sheet provided by Di Nardo. Although the company did not expect to become profitable until 2001, it expected to be very profitable thereafter. The company assumed that it could retain 6,000 customers in 1999, resulting in revenues of $14.2 million. This would grow significantly in 2000, as 18,000 customers would generate revenues of $47.1 million. As the company expanded into Edmonton, Calgary, Montreal, and Ottawa, the customer base was expected to reach approximately 117,000 by 2003. Di Nardo thought that as the business grew, he would be able to increase the gross margin from an expected 3.5 percent in 1999 to 12.4 percent in 2003, as a result of economies of scale and a higher margin product mix. He expected to be able to offer all services starting in 1999, with the exception of merchandise, which he thought he would start selling in 2000.

Management

Five of the six current major investors were in management positions at Grocery Gateway. Di Nardo, president and chief executive officer, was the largest shareholder at 47.6 percent. He had created his management team to consist of four other individuals with significant technology expertise. Although Di Nardo's team was currently working part-time with the company, its members had committed to joining full-time when the required financing was secured. Stephen Tallevi was the founder and principal of a full-service interactive agency that developed new media solutions for packaged goods manufacturers. At

EXHIBIT 2 Projected Income Statement (Cdn$)

	Year ended October 30,				
	1999	*2000*	*2001*	*2002*	*2003*
Revenue					
Grocery	12,240,000	36,720,000	87,924,000	152,640,960	239,612,280
Pharmaceuticals	720,000	2,160,000	5,172,000	8,978,880	14,094,840
Merchandise	0	2,700,000	6,465,000	11,223,600	17,618,550
Services	540,000	1,620,000	3,879,000	6,734,160	10,571,130
Delivery	720,000	2,160,000	5,172,000	8,978,880	14,094,840
Research	0	100,000	200,000	300,000	400,000
Advertising	0	1,619,692	5,440,600	9,442,824	14,819,582
Total Revenue	14,220,000	47,079,692	114,252,600	198,299,304	311,211,222
Cost of Goods Sold	13,725,893	42,367,806	100,509,576	173,591,837	272,499,741
Gross Profit	494,107	4,711,886	13,743,024	24,707,467	38,711,481
Operating Expenses					
Technology	433,859	497,830	550,100	651,150	644,150
Research	43,553	287,722	200,000	200,000	200,000
Salaries	515,375	611,408	1,755,000	1,855,000	1,854,999
Administration	202,956	232,191	166,800	172,200	172,200
Marketing	1,803,113	2,825,089	3,824,651	5,200,873	7,264,706
Containers	43,553	129,475	215,500	374,120	587,285
Miscellaneous	394,491	481,446	513,053	602,217	715,716
Total Operating Expenses	3,436,901	5,065,160	7,225,104	9,055,560	11,439,054
EBITDA	(2,942,794)	(353,275)	6,517,920	15,651,907	27,272,426
Depreciation	98,798	91,613	64,129	44,890	31,423
EBIT	(3,041,592)	(444,888)	6,453,791	15,607,017	27,241,003
Operating line	0	0	0	0	0
Convertible debt	0	0	0	0	0
Total net interest expense	0	0	0	0	0
EBT	(3,041,592)	(444,888)	6,453,791	15,607,017	27,241,003
Taxes	0	0	1,186,925	6,242,807	10,896,401
Net Income	**(3,041,592)**	**(444,888)**	**5,266,866**	**9,364,210**	**16,344,602**
Preferred Dividends	0	0	0	0	0

Miscellaneous includes: directors, travel & entertainment, training, HR development, and other.

Source: Grocery Gateway.

EXHIBIT 3   Projected Balance Sheet

	As at October 30,				
	1999	*2000*	*2001*	*2002*	*2003*
ASSETS					
Cash & Marketable Securities	**0**	**0**	**0**	**0**	**0**
Total Current Assets	0	0	0	0	0
Management Loan*	440,000	990,000	0	0	0
Capital Assets	305,377	213,764	149,634	104,744	73,321
TOTAL ASSETS	**745,377**	**1,203,764**	**149,634**	**104,744**	**73,321**
LIABILITIES & SHAREHOLDERS' EQUITY					
Operating Line	**0**	**0**	**0**	**0**	**0**
Income Taxes Payable	0	0	2,581,516	6,242,807	10,896,401
Total Current Liabilities	0	0	2,581,516	6,242,807	10,896,401
New Debt	**0**	0	0	0	0
Total Liabilities	0	0	2,581,516	6,242,807	10,896,401
Preferred Shares	**0**	0	0	0	0
Shares Issued on Exercise of Warrants	0	0	0	0	0
New Common Shares	**0**	0	0	0	0
Common Shares	108,670	108,670	108,670	108,670	108,670
Retained Earnings	(3,145,778)	(3,590,665)	281,609	9,645,819	25,990,422
Total Shareholders' Equity	(3,037,108)	(3,481,995)	390,279	9,754,489	26,099,092
Required Financing	3,782,485	4,685,759	(2,822,162)	(15,892,552)	(36,922,172)
TOTAL LIABILITIES & SHAREHOLDERS' EQUITY	**745,377**	**1,203,764**	**149,634**	**104,744**	**73,321**

*Management and employee loans in lieu of salaries. Shareholder equity will be used as collateral.

Source: Grocery Gateway.

Grocery Gateway, he was in charge of project integration and strategic technology and was responsible for a holistic approach in using technology to meet consumer needs. Ben Jones, with significant experience in systems integration, was responsible for the design and deployment of the enterprise management system which connected the user interface, database and corporate systems to automate daily operations. Tomas Berinstein was a professional web developer for four years; he

EXHIBIT 4   Beneficial Ownership before Private Placement

| Shareholder | Ownership | |
	# of Shares	%
Bill Di Nardo	1,143,427	47.6%
Scott Bryan	558,047	23.3%
Ben Jones	137,200	5.7%
Stephen Tallevi	137,200	5.7%
Tomas Berinstein	160,066	6.7%
Alan Lamb	144,060	6.0%
Minor Investors (2)	120,000	5.0%
TOTAL	**2,400,000**	**100.0%**

Source: Grocery Gateway.

joined Grocery Gateway to develop the web interface and proprietary web applications to integrate it with the database to allow extensive data mining. Alan Lamb had 20 years of experience in designing, maintaining and mining databases and statistics. He was responsible for the design and maintenance of the company's database. See Exhibit 4 for ownership information.

Di Nardo set up the board of advisors beginning in October 1997 as a first step to bring credibility to the company and provide access to strategic advice. It took him a number of months; however, he succeeded in building a board of eight individuals who would provide the management team with expertise in a number of different areas. Di Nardo had paid the board with equity since the company had limited cash available.

Scott Bryan, the second largest shareholder, at 23.3 percent, was on the board of advisors. He was a technology lawyer at Miller Thomson, a Toronto-based law firm. His role was to advise the company on corporate strategy and legal affairs. He also had an HBA from the Richard Ivey School of Business and a Bachelor of Laws degree from the University of Toronto.

The board of advisors consisted of seven additional people with a wide range of experiences. Members of the board included the former president and chief executive officer of the Canadian Council of Grocery Distributors, the executive vice president of Environics Research Group, the chief operating officer and vice president of Marketing at Hopewell Logistics, a former senior executive of Dominion Food Stores, the president of Nordinia Packaging, the president of Supply Chain Solutions, and the category manager at Warner-Lambert.

Financing Alternatives

Stuart Lombard identified three investment alternatives: debt, preferred shares and common shares. He wanted to structure the deal so that Albright would receive its required return and the management of Grocery Gateway would be willing to proceed.

Debt had one main advantage: it would rank senior to any equity holders. However, J.L. Albright had never financed a company with debt for two reasons: straight debt did not provide the returns they looked for, and the partners believed that debt limited the ability of the company to grow as it was too onerous. Therefore, if debt were employed, Lombard would need to propose some sort of equity kicker, such as warrants or making the debt convertible at some future date. He would also need to draft covenants. See Exhibit 5 for interest rate information.

If Lombard chose preferred shares, he needed to determine which preferential rights would be required. He could also include a dividend. However, he would probably need to add an equity kicker to the shares, such as warrants or making them convertible after some future date, such as in the year 2003, to increase the returns to a desired level.

EXHIBIT 5   Interest Rate Information

	As at July 31, 1998
Prime	6.500%
3-month T-Bills	4.970%
1-year Government of Canada bonds	5.290%
2-year Government of Canada bonds	5.297%
5-year Government of Canada bonds	5.418%
10-year Government of Canada bonds	5.464%
30-year Government of Canada bonds	5.575%
AA/AAA spread over 5-year Government of Canada bonds	44 bps

Source: Bloomberg.

Canadian Equity Market Risk Premiums
(January 1950 to December 1997)

Estimated Short-Term Canadian Market Risk Premium, Arithmetic Mean	4.831%
Estimated Short-Term Canadian Market Risk Premium, Geometric Mean	4.102%
Estimated Medium-Term Canadian Market Risk Premium, Arithmetic Mean	4.443%
Estimated Medium-Term Canadian Market Risk Premium, Geometric Mean	4.015%
Estimated Long-Term Canadian Market Risk Premium, Arithmetic Mean	5.945%
Estimated Long-Term Canadian Market Risk Premium, Geometric Mean	4.793%

Source: TSE Common Equities CD-ROM Product, 1998.

EXHIBIT 6　Comparable Public Company Trading Multiples

Comparable Companies	Price/Sales	Price/Cash Flow	Estimated Growth
Peapod Inc.	1.67x	na	50%
Egghead.com Inc.	1.76x	na	negative
CDNow Inc.	12.88x	na	175%
America Online Inc.	10.39x	67.77x	125%
Amazon.com Inc.	25.18x	533.26x	1500%
K-Tel International Inc.	0.95x	49.77x	negative
Average	**8.8x**	**216.9x**	

Company Descriptions

Peapod Inc.: an Internet supermarket, providing consumers with broad product choices and local delivery services. The company provides such services in various metropolitan markets in the United States. Peapod also provides targeted media and research services to consumer goods companies, offering its medium for targeting promotions and advertising at the point of purchase.

Egghead.com Inc.: an Internet retailer of new and surplus computer products, consumer electronics, sporting goods, and vacation packages. The company, through its auction site, offers bargains on excess and closeout goods and services.

CDNow Inc.: an online retailer of CDs and other music-related products.

America Online Inc.: provides interactive communications and services through its America Online and CompuServe worldwide Internet online services.

Amazon.com Inc.: an online retailer, selling books, music, videotapes, audiotapes and other products.

K-Tel International Inc.: markets and distributes entertainment and consumer products. The company sells recorded music from both its own music master catalog and under license from third-party record companies.

Source: Grocery Gateway and Bloomberg.

Common shares would rank behind any other securities outstanding, increasing the risk of this form of investment.

Lombard was concerned with the exit strategy. One possibility was to do a future initial public offering, and sell off some of the shares to the public. He wondered what the selling price would be, as he looked at comparable public companies' price-to-sales multiples that were hugely variable, from 0.95x for K-Tel International to 25.18x for Amazon.com. These companies were also typically valued on a price-to-cash flow multiple (using EBITDA as a proxy for cash flow). However, these multiples also had a huge range. The comparables were trading at ratios of between 49.77x and 533.26x. Another valuation method that was used in the industry was price per user. A recent transaction in the United States had valued a grocery customer at $12,000. See Exhibit 6 for multiples of other comparable publicly traded companies.

As Lombard thought about how he would like to structure the deal, his mind turned to Grocery Gateway. He knew that they were unwilling to give up control; however, he also suspected that they were in desperate need of this financing and had limited alternatives.

Conclusion

Lombard leaned back in his chair and gazed out the window. He didn't want to get too far ahead of himself in his thoughts. He needed to evaluate the strengths and weaknesses of Grocery Gateway, and consider the key risks that the company faced. If he believed in the concept, his next step was to convince the other partners of the viability of the investment. If they agreed, he then needed to value the company and structure a deal. He wanted to get his partners' consent, and have an indicative term sheet ready to present to Grocery Gateway next week.

First Virtual Holdings Incorporated (A)

By Professor Sid Huff and Mike Wade

First Virtual Holdings Incorporated (FVHI, www.firstvirtual.com) Chairman and CEO Lee Stein was driving along the San Diego Freeway thinking over the last 36 months. He felt satisfied that what was so recently just an idea was now a reality. He knew that he was riding the crest of a wave, one which was about to change the face of commerce. It had become accepted wisdom that commerce on the Internet would blossom and flourish. The only real questions were when—and, after the dust settled—who would be left on the playing field? By any standard, the progress made by the company he co-founded had been spectacular. First Virtual had become one of the most recognized names in the nascent world of online commerce. The First Virtual Internet Payment System (FVIPS) had proven itself to be secure and efficient. Nothing, however, was guaranteed in this business, and Stein worried whether his company had the backing and the resources to make it through the inevitable industry shakeup.

Lee Stein and First Virtual Holdings Incorporated

Stein had not always been in the information technology business. In fact, by trade he was an accountant and lawyer. While Stein was attending the Villanova University School of Law in Pennsylvania he saw an episode of the Merv Griffin show between classes. The guest was Hollywood producer Allan Carr, who talked about his business manager. A career as a business manager sounded "pretty cool," recalls Stein, who began knocking on doors in Hollywood after working for Coopers and Lybrand. "I was pretty highly trained," he said. "And there was no downside. All somebody could say was no."

Before long, Stein created his own company and signed his first client, Bo Goldman, an Academy Award-winning screenwriter for "One Flew Over the Cuckoo's Nest" and later a Golden Globe winner for "Scent of a Woman." Other well-known clients followed, including Gene Hackman, Matthew Broderick, Rod Stewart, Journey, and Men at Work.

Stein was developing his entertainment practice in Beverly Hills when his wife, a CPA and then just 24, developed a degenerative inflammatory disease of the spine. The couple was devastated, but refused to accept the prognosis and began exploring alternative remedies, including practices from the Far East. Some remedies were just "kooky California" ideas, but primarily through yoga, she was able to conquer the disease. Eventually, the two studied meditation in Kathmandu with a Tibetan lama, as the experience with the illness led them to re-order their priorities to health and family.

By the mid-1980s, the couple sold their entertainment business and moved to San Diego. Stein became involved in a number of real estate ventures. He also acted as chairman of the San Diego Stadium Authority, home to the Padres and Chargers. A self-described "techno-junkie," Stein was travelling to New York City when he began asking questions of a fellow traveller who was using a wireless device to communicate with the Internet. The other traveller was Einar Stefferud, a computer-savvy Internet veteran, MBA and expert on global messaging systems, who later jointly founded First Virtual with Stein. "He came out of a whole different world. And worlds collide. So we had to invest some serious effort in understanding each other, but we've always worked as a team," says Stefferud.

Along with Stein and Stefferud, the other founding members of First Virtual were Nathaniel S. Borenstein, Ph.D., the primary author of MIME, the Internet standard for multimedia and multilingual mail messages, and Marshall T. Rose, Ph.D., a leader in the development and implementation of key global Internet standards. For a biography of the four founders, see Exhibit 1.

Despite Stein's non-technical background, Stefferud credits Stein with the leadership role in bringing forth ideas during the founding group's initial meetings in early 1994, and then in developing First Virtual's business plan. "Lee became the hub of all the spokes to carry it forward," as Stefferud put it.

Stein recalled those early discussions:

> I was told that what we wanted to do was impossible. I was reminded that a lot of people had tried to build Internet commerce concepts before, and none had ever really worked. But I kept asking a series of questions, until somebody turned around and said, "Yeah, that could work." And then they turned my broad, goofy, upside-down concepts into reality.

EXHIBIT 1   First Virtual's Founders

Nathaniel S. Borenstein, Ph.D. Primary author of MIME, the Internet standard for multimedia and multilingual mail messages, Borenstein has served as an advisor to national and international agencies. He is a member of the Electronic Frontier Foundation, holds a Ph.D. in computer science from Carnegie-Mellon University and is the author of two books on multimedia and software.

Marshall T. Rose, Ph.D. Dr. Rose is a leader in the development and implementation of key global standards for electronic messaging and network management. He is the author of seven highly regarded books on Internet technology. Dr. Rose holds a Ph.D. in information and computer science from the University of California, Irvine, and is the former area director for network management on the Internet Engineering Steering Group, one of a dozen people responsible for overseeing the global Internet standardization process.

Einar A. Stefferud, M.B.A. A key contributor to the development of the global Internet since 1975, he is considered to be one of the leading experts on global messaging systems. He has been active in international standards activities through the American National Standards Institute (ANSI) and the International Federation of Information Processing. Named by *Communications Week* as one of the top 10 visionaries in the computer-communications industry, he is an adjunct professor of Information and computer science at University of California, Irvine, and holds an M.B.A. from UCLA.

Lee H. Stein, J.D. An attorney and accountant, he also serves as chairman of Stein & Stein Incorporated, a California-based firm which provided management services to luminaries in the entertainment and music industries. He has been a successful investor in West Coast real estate. He has served as chairman of the Jack Murphy Stadium Authority, San Diego, California and a director of the Scripps Foundation for Medicine and Science, La Jolla, California.

Source: First Virtual web pages: www.firstvirtual.com.

Initiated by Dr. Borenstein, the original idea was simple: sell jokes by electronic mail on the Internet. "Every time you turned on your machine, there would be a joke waiting for you. If you liked it, you'd pay a penny. If you didn't like it, you'd pay nothing," Stein explains. A penny a day collected from millions of Internet users could add up to significant numbers, the team realized. But the hang-up was the lack of a payment system. All four recognized the need for a secure, simple and widespread payment system for goods and services over the Internet, which led them into the business of electronic payment systems.

The company was built from the ground up to be a true virtual business. Its founders were based in San Diego, Orange County, Silicon Valley, New Jersey, and Michigan. The company had no physical offices for its first 15 months of operation. In fact, for awhile no two members of the company had the same zip codes or area codes. Their business cards contained only e-mail addresses and phone numbers. The servers were set up in a high security EDS facility near Cleveland; work-at-home customer service representatives were hired to answer customer service requests by e-mail while the data lines were routed to an MCI facility in Atlanta; marketing was handled from Washington, D.C.; public relations was based in San Diego. The company itself was registered in Cheyenne, Wyoming. Certainly not your typical organization.

Although the arrangement was flexible and allowed the founders to remain in their physical locations, the initial employees decided to consolidate most of the company's day-to-day operations in San Diego in late 1995. They found that the more mundane aspects of the organization were hampered by physical distances. It was more difficult, for example, to maintain employee morale, schedule meetings, keep people up to date and so on. Stein noted,

> There wasn't a big problem when individuals or small groups worked remotely; they would check in regularly so there would be a constant dialogue. The problem was when clusters of people worked together at a remote site. We would miss all the hallway and water cooler talk.

President Keith Kendrick added, "E-mail is no substitute for face to face meetings in any company, even one as 'virtual' as us." By the summer of 1997, the company employed 96 people organized into five functional groups under CEO Stein and new President Keith Kendrick, and ran all of its day-to-day operations from San Diego. Images of Lee Stein and First Virtual's San Diego offices are provided in Exhibit 2.

FVHI launched its first major product, the First Virtual Internet Payment System (FVIPS) in October 1994. By September 1996, the FVIPS was being used by 2,650 merchants and 180,000 consumers in 166 countries.

EXHIBIT 2   First Virtual Offices in San Diego: First Virtual CEO Lee Stein

The First Virtual Internet Payment System (FVIPS)

The FVIPS is based on the principle that no method of data security is truly secure, and that only non-sensitive information should be sent over the Internet. Using the FVIPS, buyers can make purchases using their credit cards, yet never send their credit card numbers over the Internet.

The first step for those who want to use the FVIPS is to send credit card information to First Virtual by traditional means, namely, telephone, fax or mail. They are then assigned a "VirtualPIN," which is a series of alphanumeric characters. They use the VirtualPIN as an alias for their credit card numbers to make purchases on the Internet.

The system works as follows. When making a purchase, the buyer sends his or her VirtualPIN to a participating online vendor. The vendor then forwards the buyer's VirtualPIN along with the amount and a brief description of the purchase to FVHI. FVHI uses the buyer's VirtualPIN and its internal network to look up the buyer's e-mail address.

First Virtual then sends an e-mail to the buyer confirming the amount of the purchase. The buyer returns the e-mail to FVHI either confirming the sale, "Yes," or not, "No." If the sale is confirmed by the buyer, FVHI charges the buyer's credit card for the amount of the transaction (via a network not directly connected to the Internet) and sends a confirmation number to the vendor. The vendor then closes the transaction and provides the service, or in the case of goods, ships the merchandise to the buyer.

The buyer also has the option of replying with the word, "Fraud." If a buyer replies to a confirmation request with the word, "Fraud," the sale is automatically cancelled and the matter is turned over to FVHI for investigation.

At no time during this process is the buyer's credit card information typed into a computer connected to the Internet. Nor does any sensitive information pass through the vendor, further reducing the chance of fraud.

Unlike competing systems, the FVIPS does not rely on encryption of data, nor does it require the buyer to use special software or hardware to function. First Virtual's founders envisioned credit card companies having the ability to automatically create and distribute VirtualPINs, thereby creating mass distribution and eliminating the need for the consumer to take any action.

Merchants who wish to become sellers using the FVIPS can sign up at the company's website. First Virtual has two categories of merchants: Express Merchants and Pioneer Merchants. Express Merchants are typically larger and more established with existing credit card merchant accounts; Express Merchants also have to pass First Virtual's credit approval process. Pioneer Merchants, on the other hand, are typically smaller merchants that might not otherwise qualify for a credit card merchant account.

Merchants pay First Virtual 29 cents per transaction plus two percent of the transaction price for each sale. Express Merchants receive payment from First Virtual after three to four days. Pioneer Merchants are paid after 90 days (the legal limit in the U.S. for reversing credit card charges).

As of September 30, 1997, the company had processed over 430,000 FVIPS transactions and had registered more than 3,800 merchants and 240,000 consumers in over 160 countries.

Security

Lee Stein commented on security concerns:

> We may be subject to a one-off attack. In such an attack, a person would have to eavesdrop on a consumer's electronic mail to intercept his or her VirtualPIN. But since the VirtualPIN can be used only with the First Virtual system, the attacker would have to be able to intercept the user's electronic mail, read the confirmation message from First Virtual's computers, and send out a fraudulent reply. A single user can be targeted, but a large scale attack would be very difficult . . . there are too many packets moving . . . to too many different machines.

Director of Development Winn Rindfleisch described the FVIPS as procedural security, not technical security. "Many people think we're anti-encryption, which isn't true at all. In fact, we use encryption and digital signatures when we send messages to our merchants so they know the message is coming from First Virtual." Director of Strategic Business Initiatives Chris Wand added, "If we thought we needed encryption, or that buyers would be comfortable using it, we'd have it. Our challenge in this area is to create a system, which combines convenience for the user, along with a sufficient number of built in 'levels of inconvenience' to deter hackers and minimize the risk of wide spread, automated fraud."

Furthermore, Stein pointed out, "If somebody's account is compromised, the worst thing that happens is that the consumer notices the fraudulent transaction on his or her credit card bill and declines the charge. Put it this way: Our charge-back ratio, which is usually tied to fraud, is extremely low." Stein added,

> The biggest misconception is that the words "security" and "encryption" are identical, or even closely related. A more balanced perspective on discussions of Internet commerce can often be obtained by replacing "computer" and "encryption" with "automobile" and "door lock." The mere existence of a door lock does not imply that the ignition keys (or a wallet) should be left inside the car. In general, it is safest to lock your car *and* remove your valuables. Similarly, while encryption can provide a modicum of additional security on the Internet, it is far more important to consider what is being encrypted, and not to encrypt anything that is better kept off the Internet in the first place. In the system we developed, the worst case would be that a single user's account is compromised; in encryption-based systems, however, if a criminal cracks the code, the consequences would be widespread and catastrophic.

FVHI is so confident that its system is safe that it has published the means by which a hacker could break in, though none has yet been able to do so. To prove that sensitive data is susceptible to being intercepted before it is encrypted, First Virtual wrote and distributed a program that simulates how a hacker could circumvent most encryption systems by monitoring keystrokes and checking for input that resembles credit card information. On security concerns, Stein concluded,

> We have two advantages over our competition. First of all, technically, we have the right stuff. Our scientists have come up with a significant number of patches to deal with the difficulties of achieving reliable, automated e-mail communications across a myriad e-mail client programs, hundreds of ISPs and loosely implemented e-mail standards in over 160 countries. Our technicians can answer virtually any questions users might have. Fortunately, we don't get many, which brings me to my second point. Unlike other systems out there, ours is simple to understand and simple to use. If you know how to send and receive e-mail, you can buy and sell on the Internet using First Virtual. Other companies have a heck of a time explaining complex encryption mechanisms, public/private keys, key lifetimes and so on to their customers, most of whom are Internet novices.

"Their electronic mail protocol is a pretty low-tech solution to doing Internet commerce, but it has the advantage that it's pretty easy to understand exactly what the likely risks are—unlike some crypto-gizmo protocols," said Alan Bawden, a computer researcher in Cambridge, Massachusetts. "There are risks, the biggest probably being that you have to trust them (First Virtual) with your credit card number. But I probably take a bigger risk when I hand my credit card to the teen-age clerk at the local hardware store."

Stein put it more bluntly: "There has been so much noise out there about this coming software encryption stuff. We believe in encryption and use it here at First Virtual—all of our employees use public key encryption on a daily basis. But the truth is that many users can't even figure out how to use web browsers, let alone turn on and use sophisticated features like encryption."

Strategic Alliances

From the beginning, FVHI's founders recognized that making good strategic alliances with established industry players was critical to its success. They realized that the winners in the race for the Internet commerce market would not necessarily be the companies with the best products, but those who had the largest share of the market. With this in mind, they strove to develop relationships with the biggest and the best in the business.

Strategic Investors:

First USA Paymentech, Inc.
- The third largest processor of bank card transactions in the U.S., processing US$30.9 billion in sales volume and 574 million transactions during 1996.

- Agreed to offer a free 90-day trial VirtualPIN to its credit card customers.
- A First Virtual investor.

Next Century Communications Corporation
- Marketing and lobbying firm specializing in direct response marketing, promotional and fund-raising campaigns.
- A First Virtual investor.

Sybase, Incorporated
- Sixth largest independent software company in the world. Developer of database, middleware and tools products for four major client/server market segments: new media, online transaction processing, mass deployment and data warehousing.
- A First Virtual investor.

GE Capital Corporation
- Diversified financial services company with assets of over US$185 billion. Provides mid-market and specialized financing, specialty insurance and a variety of consumer services such as car loans, home mortgages and credit cards.
- A First Virtual investor.

First Data Corporation
- Provides credit card and other information processing services to financial institutions, government agencies, insurance companies, merchants and consumers through its network in 120 countries around the world.
- 5.9 billion credit and debit card transactions processed and revenue of US$4.9 billion in 1996.
- A First Virtual investor.

Online Commerce Providers:

Microsoft Corporation
- Microsoft Corp. chose the FVIPS as one of the payment methods for its new Merchant Server software. The Merchant Server software offers easy-to-use templates and other tools to minimize the development costs associated with Internet storefront development. It allows merchants of any size to build an online presence.

Sun Microsystems, Inc.
- The FVIPS will be a "Java cassette" included in the latest version of the Java Commerce Toolkit. The toolkit is a set of software tools used by

Java developers to create Java language-based commercial projects, such as online shopping malls, home banking and electronic brokerage.

The Vision Factory
- The Vision Factory's most well known product is Cat@log, a software package used by professional developers to design and operate web-based storefronts.
- The Vision Factory will integrate the FVIPS as a payment method in the latest version of Cat@log.

First Virtual Customers:

InterNIC
- The FVIPS was chosen to provide online payment for InterNIC domain name registration services.

The Electronic Frontier Foundation (EFF)
- The EFF represents and protects civil liberties of Internet users. The organization has been at the forefront of legal and policy battles to ensure that individual rights are protected online.
- The EFF chose the FVIPS to process online donations.

Saatchi and Saatchi
- Saatchi and Saatchi teamed up with FVHI to create the VirtualTAG, an interactive point-of-sale banner. The VirtualTAG is a multilevel banner that allows potential buyers to purchase products and services without leaving the web page on which they found the banner.

Other Internet Commerce Payment Systems

By the beginning of 1996, there were dozens of payment systems vying for a place in the Internet commerce spectrum. Some specialized in very small transactions, called micropayments, typically a few cents or even fractions of a cent. These systems were primarily designed to pay for small amounts of information, generally one-time access to a particular web page or site. Other payment systems incorporated traditional payment means such as credit card or check but provided strong security features to allow safe passage of sensitive information. Still others were proprietary systems that required users to open accounts with special online banks.

Micropayment Systems
Millicent, NetBank and Digicash are three companies that have designed systems to sponsor micropayments. These payments might be made to purchase up-to-the-minute financial data, download a daily

joke, picture, newspaper or magazine article or other online information, much of which is currently free.

Millicent was developed by Digital Equipment Corporation to facilitate anonymous microcommerce online. (Digital defines microcommerce as purchases of less than one cent). Millicents come in "scrips," which are basically small, transitory, prepaid accounts that can be purchased from participating "brokers." A scrip worth, say, $5 is sent to a vendor, who returns a new scrip worth $4.995 in return for allowing the user to view the contents of the vendor's web page. Since the dollar amount of each transaction is small, no elaborate security features are built into the Millicent system.

NetBank offers a similar system where users trade Netcash certificates anonymously online to purchase low value goods and services. The Netcash certificates can be purchased and redeemed from NetBank, a Maryland-based company.

Digicash, based in the Netherlands offers "ecash" and "cyberbucks" to pay for online goods and services. Unlike Millicent and Netbank, Digicash uses complex encryption algorithms to encode its ecash and cyberbucks when travelling over the Internet. As a consequence, larger anonymous transactions are possible. Digicash is also a leader in card security technology and is working with Visa and MasterCard on a smart card design.

Cybercash

Cybercash uses encryption technology to allow real-time secure credit card transactions, electronic checks and microtransactions on the Internet. The company has support from the Internet Architecture Board, the World Wide Web Consortium, CommerceNet, the Electronic Funds Transfer Association, Netscape, First Data Corp., and the National Automated Clearing House Association.

The system is based on the "Cybercash Wallet," a browser plug-in, through which users can make purchases using their credit cards, electronic checks (see below for a description of the PayNow electronic check system) or electronic cash for small purchases. Credit card purchases are made using data encryption and digital signatures compatible with the emerging Secure Electronic Transaction (SET) standard. Cybercash and Netscape have collaborated closely to develop a secure payment system for Netscape's new line of SuiteSpot servers and Communicator browsers. Cybercash embarked on a widespread television advertising campaign in the summer of 1997.

PayNow

The PayNow Secure Electronic Check Service is a system that allows Internet users to pay for goods and services online using their bank checking accounts. Bank account numbers are encrypted, then sent across the Internet to vendors who, in turn, pass them along to a clearing house that debits the user's bank account for the value of the purchase. In early 1997, the system was being used to allow utility company customers to pay for recurring monthly expenses online. By the end of 1997, the system is expected to be able to handle the purchase of services and hard goods, as well as peer-to-peer and business-to-business transfers.

Smart Cards and Mondex

Smart cards look like regular credit or debit cards except that they include a tiny computer chip imbedded in the card itself. This chip can be used to store and process information of various kinds. On the Mondex smart card, the chip stores a binary representation of actual cash, along with the user's digital signature. Hence, this type of smart card is often called a "stored value" card. When inserted into a special reader device connected to the user's computer, the card can be used to download funds from the user's bank account. These funds can then be spent online or offline in regular stores, or transferred from card to card using a small transfer unit. The idea behind smart cards is to create a system as convenient as cash, but far more secure. While the use of digital signatures makes the cash stored on such a card more secure than conventional cash, nonetheless, if a person loses their stored value card they have lost the cash that was stored on it.

The leader in the stored value cash cards is Mondex. Mondex is 51 percent owned by MasterCard and 49 percent owned by a consortium of British and International corporations, including: National Westminster Bank, Ulster Bank, and Midland Bank, Scotiabank, Credit Union Central of Canada, The National Bank of Canada, Bank of Montreal, Canada Trust, Le Mouvement des caisses Desjardins, Toronto-Dominion Bank, Royal Bank of Canada, Canadian Imperial Bank of Commerce, The Hongkong and Shanghai Banking Corporation, Wells Fargo, AT&T, Chase Manhattan, First Chicago NBD, Australia and New Zealand Banking Group, Commonwealth Bank of Australia, National Australia Bank, Westpac Banking Corporation (Australia), ANZ Banking Group (New Zealand), Bank of New Zealand, Countrywide Banking Corporation, The National Bank of New Zealand, ASB Bank and Westpac Banking Corporation (New Zealand).

The key components of a Mondex chip are an 8-bit CPU, a 16K ROM, 512 bytes of RAM (and 8K EEPROM for data storage). The Mondex chip has a clock speed of up to 10 MHz and is about 20 mm square.

The first Mondex product specification was issued in April 1994. Currently more than 450 companies in over 40 countries are working with these specifications to develop cards and compatible products such as point-of-sale readers, bank cash machines, desktop readers and wallet-size balance readers.

Mondex cards have sophisticated security features built into the design to help prevent unauthorized use or duplication. Cardholders have unique "digital signatures" and have the ability to "lock" their cards when they are not being used.

Mondex cards are currently in the advanced trial stage. One such trial is going on in Guelph, Ontario. At the end of July 1997, there were over 7,500 cardholders in Guelph, or one in 20 residents. To date, about $1,000,000 of electronic value has been issued to the cardholders. In March 1997, the first full month following the launch of Mondex, the average amount of electronic cash issued on a daily basis was $15,339.

Smart Cards are not expected to be in widespread circulation until mid- to late 1998.

Proprietary Systems

Many servers and Internet Service Providers (ISPS) such as Prodigy, Compuserve and America Online (AOL) operate their own proprietary online payment systems.

Traditional Payment Methods

Many users mistrust information sent across open networks such as the Internet. There will continue to be a large percentage of Internet users who will avoid purchases on the Internet entirely, preferring to stick to more traditional methods of payment such as telephone, fax, mail or face-to-face.

There are also users that are comfortable sending payment information over the Internet either using security features integrated into popular web browsers such as Netscape Communicator and Microsoft Internet Explorer or with no security at all.

The Secure Electronic Transaction (SET) Standard

The SET standard is a technical specification for securing credit card transactions over the Internet. The SET specification is jointly being developed by Visa and MasterCard with input and support from IBM, Microsoft, Netscape, Oracle, GTE and VeriSign. The system is based on advanced encryption technology to encode credit card information, and uses digital signatures or certificates to identify credit card holders (See Exhibit 3 for a description of public key encryption and digital certificates). The integrity of the system is designed to equal a traditional point-of-sale purchase in which the buyer, merchant and credit card are physically present. Most suppliers of electronic commerce software have made a commitment to build in support for SET-based transactions.

EXHIBIT 3   Public Key Encryption and Digital Certificates

In a public key system a key pair is mathematically generated, consisting of a public key and a private key. The key pair is generated so that a message may be encrypted with one key and decrypted with the other (either key can be used for encryption). The message *cannot* be decrypted using the same key that was used to encrypt it. Each user's public key is usually made widely available to anyone wishing to send an encrypted message while the user's private key is kept secret.

For example, if Frank wishes to send an encrypted message to Tony, he would encrypt his message using Tony's public key. After the message has been encrypted using Tony's public key, it can only be decrypted using Tony's private key. Not even Frank could get his message back.

The great advantage of this kind of cryptography is that, unlike conventional cryptosystems, it is not necessary to find a secure means of transmitting the encryption key to the intended recipient of the message. Another useful feature of such cryptosystems is the ability to "sign" messages by encrypting them with the sender's private key. Anyone can then decrypt the message with the sender's public key, and can be sure that only the owner of that public key could have encrypted the message (with the corresponding private key). This is referred to as providing a digital signature.

For example, not only does Frank want to send an encrypted message to Tony, but he wants to assure Tony that it is really he who is sending the message. So Frank encrypts the message using Tony's public key, then re-encrypts it using his own private key. When Tony receives the message, he first decrypts it using Frank's public key, thus proving that it could only have come from Frank, then he decrypts the message itself using his own private key.

In practice, it is not usually necessary to encrypt an entire message in order to insure a digital signature—rather, a small portion of "signed" data attached to the full message is sufficient. This approach is often termed a "digital certificate."

Once widely released, the SET standard is expected to be popular with merchants since traditional credit card processing fees will be reduced, perhaps by as much as one percent.

Constant delays in the final end-user introduction of the SET system have caused tensions to emerge between the co-sponsors. MasterCard is using a prerelease version of the SET standard in certain markets, while Visa recommends its credit card holders not to use the system until the final product is released. Technical problems have delayed SET's debut, which was originally slated for late 1996. SET is now not expected to be rolled out until mid-1998.

Marketing

First Virtual had a three-fold strategy for marketing the FVIPS to buyers and merchants. First, through press releases and traditional PR channels, FVHI hoped to attract the attention of journalists who would then publicize the company in the press. So far, articles concerning First Virtual and CEO Lee Stein have appeared in *Business Week, Newsweek, Fortune,* the *Economist,* the *New York Times,* the *San Jose*

Mercury News and more. Second, the marketing department targeted large transaction processors who might be interested in extending their business online. Third, they targeted third-party integrators such as AOL, and large ISPs.

However, it should be noted that for much of its history, First Virtual lacked a formal marketing and sales effort. Part of the reason for this was that First Virtual believed it was essential to have a stable, scalable infrastructure in place before significant marketing was undertaken. First Virtual did not want to be in a position of not being able to meet demand.

Financial Information

For the year ended December 31, 1996, FVHI revenues increased over 250 percent to $696,000 from $198,000 for the year ended December 31, 1995. Revenues for the year ended December 31, 1996, include $150,000 in consulting revenues received from a strategic partner. Net loss for 1996 was $10.7 million as compared to a net loss of $2.3 million for 1995. Net loss per share was $1.25 based on weighted average shares outstanding of 8,524,068, as compared to a net loss of $0.30 per share for 1995 based on weighted average shares outstanding of 7,599,106. See Exhibit 4 for FVHI's Statements of Operations and Exhibit 5 for FVHI's Condensed Balance Sheets.

Commenting on the results, Chairman Stein said, "We are at an exciting stage in the development of our company. First Virtual sees a market opportunity in providing solutions for Internet commerce. We are using a portion of the Initial Public Offering (IPO) proceeds to develop both the technology and the organizational infrastructure necessary to take advantage of this opportunity."

First Virtual received its major initial financing from several strategic investors including First USA Paymentech, GE Capital and First Data Corporation, who together invested $12.5 million between December 1994 and August 1996. First Virtual Holdings Inc. went public on the NASDAQ exchange on December 13, 1996. The offering was for 2 million shares at $9.00 a share. The gross amount raised by the offering was $18 million ($15 million net), and the stock price closed at $9.00 after the day. Exhibit 6 charts First Virtual's stock price from December 1996 to October 1997.

Even though IPO Network ranks First Virtual among the bottom 10 percent of offerings in 1996 and 1997, CFO John Stachowiak notes that bad timing was mostly to blame.

The final months of 1996 were a bad time for technology stock offerings. The euphoria generated over a number of high profile IPOs earlier in the year had fizzled. Investors were becoming more cautious about investing in new technologies. Besides that, while we were on the road promoting the offering

EXHIBIT 4 First Virtual Holdings Incorporated Statements of Operations

	Three months ended December 31,		Year ended December 31,	
	1996	*1995*	*1996*	*1995*
Revenues	$197,604	$110,672	$695,866	$197,902
Operating expenses:				
— Marketing and sales	1,091,539	104,314	1,836,545	346,400
— R&D	1,747,770	339,951	3,248,958	530,809
— G&A	2,126,807	263,007	6,431,286	1,522,784
Total op. expenses	4,966,116	707,272	11,516,789	2,399,993
Loss from operations	(4,768,512)	(596,600)	(10,820,923)	(2,202,091)
Int. income (expense)	58,886	(15,833)	130,983	(67,890)
Net loss	(4,709,626)	(612,433)	(10,689,940)	(2,269,981)
Net loss per share	(0.54)	(0.07)	(1.25)	(0.30)
Shares used in				
per share computation	8,769,491	8,668,046	8,524,068	7,599,106

about a week before the IPO, Allen Greenspan came forward and issued a warning about unsustainably high stock prices. This sent the market reeling. Two other companies about to go public dropped out, but we hung in there. Against the odds, our placement was completed.

Current Issues and Plans for the Future

FVHI had achieved remarkable growth since its inception. The FVHI user base and transaction volume had doubled about every six weeks. As part of a continuing development program, the company planned to internationalize the FVIPS to include multiple language and currency support, to develop better support for microtransactions, better support for the sale of hard goods, add additional mechanisms for buyers to pay into and sellers to receive payment from the FVIPS system. They also planned to open the system to participation by multiple processors and acquirers in the banking world.

The company was also exploring future products which were complementary to the FVIPS model. One area where the company had invested a significant amount of R&D was the VirtualTAG (www.virtualtag.com, www.virtualadz.com). The VirtualTAG was an interactive, multi-level Internet banner advertisement. Because it was multi-layered, a buyer could make purchases through a VirtualTAG without leaving the page on which they found it.

Despite the growth and the new product ideas, First Virtual's future was certainly not guaranteed. The company was still a long way from

EXHIBIT 5   First Virtual Holdings Incorporated Condensed Balance Sheets

	For the year ended December 31,	
	1996	*1995*
Assets		
Current assets:		
— Cash and cash equivalents	$17,127,971	$2,091,651
— Short-term investment, available-for-sale	200,000	—
— Accounts receivable	88,278	—
— Prepaid expenses and other	83,840	10,953
Total current assets	17,500,089	2,102,604
Furniture and equipment, net	1,964,635	304,320
Information technology, net	59,226	113,333
Organization and other costs, net	105,798	50,569
Deposits and other	62,809	4,000
Total assets	$19,692,557	$2,574,826
Liabilities and stockholders' equity		
Current liabilities:		
— Accounts payable	$1,626,198	$513,893
— Accrued compensation and related liabilities	372,739	8,170
— Accrued interest	196,340	100,340
— Deferred revenue	64,683	—
— Current portion, amount due to stockholders	400,000	—
Other accrued liabilities	576,077	—
Total current liabilities	3,236,037	622,403
Amount due to stockholders	312,500	—
Notes payable to stockholders	1,200,000	1,200,000
Total stockholders' equity	14,944,020	752,423
Total liabilities and stockholders' equity	$19,692,557	$2,574,826

EXHIBIT 6   Share Price in US$ Per Share

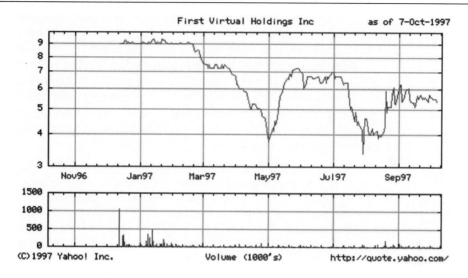

profitability. Widespread acceptance of the FVIPS would be necessary to guarantee its success, and the market was crowded with alternate payment schemes and players. It was still to be determined whether the FVIPS was the payment system most suitable to the Internet of the future. Questions remained about the tradeoff between security and convenience. How much convenience would consumers be willing to sacrifice for security? Despite FVHI's successes, retail electronic commerce on the Internet had been below most analysts' expectations.

As he exited the freeway and approached First Virtual's offices, Lee Stein wondered briefly where the company would be next year at this time. Stein knew that in an Internet-based business such as his, one year was equivalent to five to 10 years in a "real" business—so trying to think a year ahead was long-range planning indeed.

Banking on the Internet: The Advance Bank in Germany

By Professor Tawfik Jelassi and Albrecht Enders

Walking through the bank's call center in Munich on March 28, 1998, the two-year anniversary day of the bank, Volker Visser was wondering what suggestions he could make to the other members of the Executive

Board of Advance Bank at their next business strategy meeting. As he observed some agents answering customer calls, he wondered how to better manage customer relationships and whether new technological capabilities could be effectively used to create value in an electronic world. He knew that with the intensifying competition in the branchless banking sector 'his' direct bank needed to further customize the financial advice it offered, especially if it wanted to achieve its goal of 250,000 customers by the year 2001. While recognizing the tasks that lay ahead in order to achieve that goal, he thought that the uniqueness of the Advance Bank concept would still be a strong competitive weapon in the market place.

> Marketing and winning over customers who fit our target profile is our key challenge. We are not afraid of current competitors or new entrants because we believe [that] we have a niche and a differentiated quality service. . . . Brick-and-Mortar branches don't have a future. Why should the customer keep paying for their fancy branches in prime locations and for their large staff payroll, while dealing with restricted opening hours and lousy service quality?

1 The Banking Industry in Germany

The banking industry in Germany is dominated by large universal banks that offer comprehensive banking services to both private and corporate customers. Unlike in other financial systems such as in the U.S., German universal banks are allowed to offer both commercial and investment banking services. In order to exploit economies of scale and synergies and to build global scale, many German banks have merged with one another. The largest bank merger in Germany took place in 1997 when the two Bavarian banks Vereinsbank and Bayerische Hypotheken and Wechselbank (Hypo-Bank) decided to join forces and create a single bank. Today, there are four major universal banks operating in Germany: Deutsche Bank, Vereinsbank/Hypo-Bank, Dresdner Bank, and Commerzbank.

IVEY This case was written by **Professor Tawfik Jelassi,** Dean of Academic Affairs, Euro-Arab Management School, Granada, and **Albrecht Enders,** Research Assistant from the Leipzig Graduate School of Business, Germany, while the latter spent a research term at the Euro-Arab Management School. It is intended to be used as the basis for class discussion rather than to illustrate either effective or ineffective handling of a management situation. For feedback and comments, please contact the authors at: Enders.96@alumni.dartmout.org and Jelassi@eams.fundea.es.

The case was made possible by the co-operation of Advance Bank (Germany).

© 1999 T. Jelassi, Euro-Arab Management School, Granada, Spain.

Distributed by The European Case Clearing House, Cranfield University, Wharley End, Bedford MK43 0JR, England.

To order copies, phone: +44(0)1234 750903, fax: +44(0)1234 751125, e-mail:ECCH@canfield.ac.uk.

All rights reserved. Printed in UK.

A central feature of the German banking industry is the strong link between banks and companies from other industries. For example, Deutsche Bank owns over 20 percent of Daimler Benz (valued at DM15 billion) and 10 percent of the insurance company Allianz (valued at DM10 billion). Allianz, on the other hand, owns 22 percent of Dresdner Bank.

Two important events have marked recent developments in the German banking industry. The first event, which took place on July 1, 1990, was the federal monetary union which integrated the states of the former German Democratic Republic into the West German monetary system. The inclusion of the five new *Bundeslaender* (states) opened up new market opportunities and motivated almost all banks to open branches in these states. The second important event is the launch of the European Monetary Union (EMU) which will establish, on January 1, 1999, the EURO as the single currency within the 11 European Union member states that have so far been admitted in the EMU.[1]

A second major trend in the banking industry in Germany is the rationalization of bank branches and the staff reduction that often results from it. Deutsche Bank, for instance, intends to cut the number of employees by 4,100 by the year 2001 and to close 200 to 300 of its current 1,600 branches. The German Employees Union foresees that overall staff reductions might amount to a loss between 100,000 and 140,000 positions during the coming years. To a large extent, this trend results from an increasing use of technology in banking, which is illustrated by the widespread use of automatic teller machines (ATM), money transfer terminals, and direct banking institutions.

2   The Competitive Environment in Direct Banking

In 1996, the direct banking market in Germany was divided into two categories. First, traditional banks offered telephone banking delivery channels, built as extensions to their branch network which provided increased availability for the customer beyond traditional business hours. Already in 1989, Citibank had launched a telephone banking service, and other banks (such as Postbank and Vereinsbank) had followed with a similar service. In 1994, the Direkt Anlage Bank started a discount brokerage, offering cheap transactions with only limited advice to the knowledgeable investor. The discount brokerage service was also appealing to other banks with a branch network since the risk of cannibalization was considered to be low, thus allowing the branch network to coexist with the new direct banking channel. Therefore, many

---

[1]These member states are Austria, Belgium, Finland, France, Germany, Ireland, Italy, Luxembourg, the Netherlands, Portugal and Spain.

traditional German retail banks, such as Commerzbank (with Comdirect), Berliner Bank (with Bank Girotel), and Deutsche Bank (with Bank 24), started a direct banking service limited to discount brokerage services. In order to get a full range of banking services, customers still had to go to a traditional branch-based bank.

The strategic intent of Vereinsbank's new direct bank (called Advance Bank) was to go beyond the above-mentioned categories. It aimed instead at offering a full range of banking services and extensive investment advice, through the telephone and later through the Internet.

In early 1998, direct banks in Germany have cumulatively 1.8 million customers. Market studies suggest that out of the current 63 million customers of German banks, 10 million of them are interested in direct banking; however, only 3 million customers intend to switch to direct banking in the near future. Commenting on this competitive environment, Hans Jürgen Raab, Member of the Executive Board at Advance Bank said:

> The direct banking market is growing quickly, but not as fast as there are new competitors entering the market. In the spring of 1996, there were eight direct banks; today [in January 1998] there are already 39. About one-third of them won't survive.

3   Vereinsbank's Direct Banking Strategy

Vereinsbank is a large, regional bank in Germany with 22,000 employees and 770 branches nationwide. The branches are mainly located in Bavaria (the southern part of the country) and in the Hamburg area (in the northern part), and a few scattered branches in the rest of the country. In 1993, the Vereinsbank Board decided that, in order to stay competitive and attract a larger customer base, it was necessary to expand the scope of the bank's operations to other parts of Germany. One possible option to achieve this goal was to physically expand the branch network to the central part of Germany; however, this option was discarded because of the high costs associated with it (a single branch would have cost DM1–3 million annually). The additional branch network of 100–200 branches needed to reach enough customers would have been too expensive. A second problem that needed to be addressed was the "over-age" customer base of Vereinsbank with a disproportionately large number of customers aged 50 years and above (see Exhibit 1).

In order to address these issues, Vereinsbank decided to launch a direct (branch-less) bank to offer ubiquitous access throughout Germany (via the telephone, letter, fax, PC and Internet) and to attract a younger customer base. In 1994, a feasibility study for the direct bank project was conducted, and it was agreed that the design and implementation of the new bank should be completed in just two years. Andersen Consulting was then selected to provide the required know-how

EXHIBIT 1   Vereinsbank's Customer Base

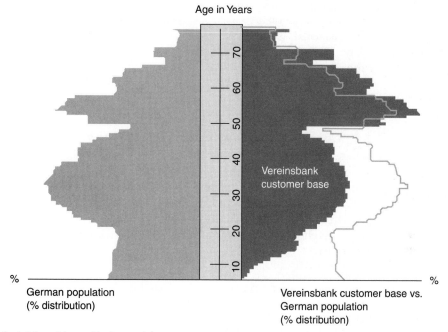

Age in Years

Vereinsbank customer base

%
German population
(% distribution)

%
Vereinsbank customer base vs.
German population
(% distribution)

Source: Adapted from Advance Bank material.

and personnel. The three main challenges were: (1) to build from scratch a completely new banking system, (2) to align this system with the newly defined business processes, and (3) to implement this system within a completely new organization. Tasks allocated to Andersen Consulting included conducting a pre-study, designing the system, acting as general contractor for the system implementation, and training the personnel. Because of the new banking concept, Andersen consultants had to design by themselves large parts of the required software and hardware. During peak periods in the development process, over 100 Andersen consultants worked on the direct bank project at a total cost of over DM50 million.

In December 1996, the new direct bank employed 269 people,[2] 40 percent of which had an academic degree and 55 percent a banking or business educational background. In 1997, after the merger of the parent company Vereinsbank and Hypobank, Advance Bank was sold to Dresdner Bank, which is now the sole owner of Advance Bank.

---

[2]This number includes part-time workers.

4   The Advent of a Virtual Bank

We wanted to be the first direct bank in Germany that offers value-added service in terms of price-performance, [customer advice] objectivity, and convenience.

Frank Spreier
Manager, Organization and IT
Advance Bank

4.1   Choosing a Name for the Virtual Bank

When looking for a name for the new bank, many possibilities were considered; including "First Choice" and "Bank High 3." However, they had to be discarded later because the name was either already patented, not accepted outside Germany, or there were some laws against using a particular name. Eventually, the bank's marketing group was left with only two choices: "Quantum" and "Advance Bank". Volker Visser commented:

> During the first two years of the project, we thought it would be easy to find the right name for the bank, so we didn't think too much about it. That was a mistake.

Finally, the name selected was "Advance Bank" because the word Advance (which was an artificially created word since it is missing the "d" at the end), was thought to best convey the new bank's philosophy of being future-oriented and forward looking. Another important advantage was that the first two letters of the name (i.e., "A" followed by a "d") put the name at the beginning of almost any alphabetically ordered list. This characteristic will become more important as the Internet expands since the WWW browsers typically sort their hits alphabetically.

The name for the new bank was then protected worldwide to keep open the possibility for an eventual international expansion of the business.

4.2   Key Features of Advance Bank

An important feature distinguishing Advance Bank from other direct banks is that it was designed and built from scratch without relying on the banking infrastructure and products of the parent company. This independence, combined with advanced information technology, enabled Advance Bank to create a virtual bank that could source its services and products from different financial services providers spread out all over Germany. When choosing a partner, Advance Bank looks throughout Germany for the best provider of a given financial service or product. Applying this best-of-breed strategy has resulted in having the individual parts of Advance Bank service assembled by different companies spread out all over the country. The bank's headquarters and main call center are located in Munich; another call center is in Wilhelmshaven (in northern Germany), an area where the unemployment rate is at 16 percent.[3] Furthermore, the accent which is spoken in that area of Germany is easy to understand, which facilitates the search for well-suited call agents. Regarding the selection of Wilhelmshaven, Volker Visser said:

> There is no reason to have all the call centers in Munich. Because of the high unemployment rate in Wilhelmshaven, the call agent salary is on average 29 percent lower than in Munich. This makes a big difference when we talk about costs.

IBB, a subsidiary of IBM, in Schweinfurt maintains the mainframe computer data[4] Eurocom Printing (in Frankfurt) prints all letters and statements and distributes them together with brochures and leaflets. GZS (also located in Frankfurt) processes all incoming Euro-card statements, while the Hamburgische Landesbank (HaLaBa) in Hamburg processes securities and payments.

In order to integrate all the above listed services provided by the different companies, a custom-designed front-end of Advance Bank was necessary. A highly integrated seamless interface with the customer has therefore been created, which gives him/her the impression of dealing with just one institution.

4.3 Security System

In order to ensure that customer information is kept confidential and secure at all times, Advance Bank relies on a complex security system. Upon opening an account with the bank, the customer receives a personal identification number (PIN) and a computer generated six-digit secret code. Every time the customer accesses his account by telephone or Internet, he is first requested to provide his PIN; then, the bank's computer system randomly asks for three numbers from the customer's secret six-digit code (e.g., the first, the fourth and the fifth digits). Marc Hemmerling, an Advance Bank customer, explained:

> I am more concerned about security when I leave my credit card number with the waiter in a restaurant or with the cashier at the gas station. I believe that the Advance Bank security system is reasonably safe.

---

[3] Before choosing Wilhelmshaven, Advance Bank considered for its second call center 29 possible locations which were assessed based on 220 quantitative and qualitative criteria including: availability of qualified personnel, wages, government subsidies, and real estate prices.

[4] Initially, Advance Bank considered using the data center of its parent company Vereinsbank. However, since this center could not provide the required 24-hour accessibility, Advance Bank looked for another provider.

This security system is used for two reasons. First, to ensure that even if someone were to intercept the customer message to the bank, he/she wouldn't have all the required information allowing him to access the account. Second, this system ensures also that even the call center agent handling the customer's call cannot know the complete customer's authorization code. An illustrative phone conversation between a call center agent and a customer, with the relevant identification procedure, is shown below:

Claudia (Advance Bank agent): *Advance Bank. Good evening. How may I help you?*

Hr. Schmitt (customer): *Hello. This is Herr Schmitt. I would like to make a transaction.*

Claudia: *Would you please tell me your personal number, Herr Schmitt?*

Hr. Schmitt: *My [personal] number is 92466503.*

Claudia: *Thank you. Then I also need the first, second and fourth digit of your authorization code.*

Hr. Schmitt: *9, 4, and 2.*

Claudia: *Thank you. Your account information is now being loaded into my PC; this will take a second. [. . .] How much money would you like to transfer?*

Hr. Schmitt: *200 Marks.*

Claudia: *200 Marks. Which account do you want to transfer this money to?*

Hr. Schmitt: *Account number: 1800 252191.*

Claudia: *And the number of the corresponding bank?*

Hr. Schmitt: *860 555 92.*

Claudia: *Who is the recipient?*

Hr. Schmitt: *Thomas Schmitz.*

Claudia: *Thank you. 200 Marks will be credited to account number 1800 252191 at the Stadt und Kreissparkasse Leipzig. The recipient is Thomas Schmitz.*

Hr. Schmitt: *Excellent. Thank you very much.*

Claudia: *Is this all you need?*

Hr. Schmitt: *Actually, I also need 1,000 U.S. dollars in traveller checks.*

Claudia: *No problem. Shall I send the [traveller] checks to your home address?*

Hr. Schmitt: *Yes, provided that I get them before my trip to New York which will be at the end of next week.*

Claudia: *You should receive them in 3–4 days. Do you need something else, Herr Schmitt?*

Hr. Schmitt: *No, thank you.*

Claudia: *You're welcome. Good bye!*

A few weeks later, Herr Schmitt called back Advance Bank. After being greeted by the Call Center agent and being authenticated through the identification procedure (explained above), the following dialogue took place:

Peter (Advance Bank agent): *I hope that your visit to the U.S. went well, Herr Schmitt. I heard that there was lately a major snow storm on the East Coast [of the United States].*

Hr. Schmitt: *Yes, indeed. However, I was quite lucky since I left New York before the start of that storm.*

Peter : I am glad you did! How can I help you this morning?

Within the bank, there are also various security systems to ensure that only authorized personnel can obtain and manipulate customer data. Depending on his/her user class, every call center agent works at a desktop with access to specific software applications. Every time he wants to use one of these applications, he has to enter his user ID number and his personal password. When a call center agent wants to contact a customer, he must first provide a word code (already specified by the customer) to prove his identity to the customer.[5]

The above-mentioned security system seems to work well, since two years after its launch, Advance Bank has had no security-related incident in carrying out its operations. However, in case a customer authorization code falls into wrong hands, Advance Bank is liable for 100 percent of all damages, provided the customer informs the bank about it as soon as it happened. In case the customer does not find out about the misuse nor notifies the bank on-time, his/her maximum liability is only 10 percent of the caused damage; thus personal risk is minimized.

5 Advance Bank's Marketing Strategy

5.1 Market Positioning

> *We need to differentiate our bank from our competitors. Eventually, we will only be able to capture our target customer group if we can establish a well-known brand with a differentiated appearance and a clear profile.*
>
> Hans Jürgen Raab

---

[5]Upon dialing the customer's telephone number, the call center agent can access on his PC that customer's password if and only if the customer picks up the phone. The call agent then asks whether he has the customer him/herself on the phone; only then, he identifies himself as an Advance Bank employee and gives the customer the word code.

An important marketing issue was to define the customer group that Advance Bank should target. The options were either to offer products that do not require financial advice (such as discount brokerage) or those that necessitate the bank's expertise. A marketing study showed that only 500,000 potential customers would be able to do their personal banking without any advice. Furthermore, the discount brokerage market was already crowded with players such as Bank24 and Comdirect bank. Advance Bank has thus carved a niche for itself by offering investment advice, hence targeting customers who are interested in joining a direct bank and who want to receive personalized advice.

Advance Bank targets the so-called "individual customer" (IK) who typically earns more than DM5,000 per month, owns or rents a house, lives in an urban area, enjoys sports and culture, and is either self-employed, a freelancer or an executive (see Exhibit 2). Although this group represents only 17 percent of the potential customers population, it generates for the bank an average annual profit of DM2,400 per customer. The other two groups consist of "universal customers" (UK) who represent 80 percent of potential customers but only generate an average profit of DM650 annually, and "private investors" (PI) who generate an annual average profit of DM5,000 but represent a mere 2 percent of the potential customers population. Additional information on the profiles of Advance Bank customers (in terms of age as well as employment status and sector) is provided in Exhibit 3.

5.2   Promotion and Advertisement Campaigns

In order to attract its target customer group, Advance Bank first started a direct mailing campaign to potential customers informing them in detail about the bank's product line. Besides being very expensive (due to the printed material and postage), these campaigns did not

---

EXHIBIT 2   Profile of the "Typical" Advance Bank Customer

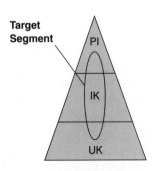

Age:	25–49 years
Education:	high school graduate and higher qualifications
Profession:	self-employed, freelancer, executive
Income:	>5,000 DM net/month
Resident:	urban areas (>200,000 population)
Housing conditions:	tenant/owner of a house
Hobbies:	sports, culture
Other characteristics:	high mobility (frequent traveler, etc.)

Source: Adapted from Advance Bank material.

EXHIBIT 3   Advance Bank Customer Profiles (as of January 1997)

Average Account Balances
Cash-Management Account: US$ 52,000
Portfolio: US$ 63,000

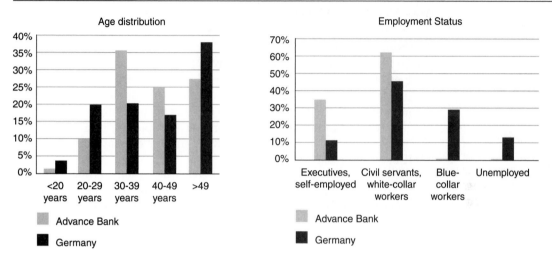

Source: Advance Bank.

achieve much impact since the "Advance Bank" brand name was not yet known to the public yet. In the fall of 1996, the bank had to stop all advertisement campaigns due to budgetary constraints. This action did not help strengthen the brand name, especially at a time when the public had just started to take notice of the bank. In total, DM44 million were spent on marketing in 1996, out of which DM22 million went into traditional advertising.

Having learned from the above mistakes, Advance Bank devised a new marketing strategy along two dimensions. First, a brand image campaign was launched to make the name more known to the public. Part of this campaign was based on the sponsoring of the weather forecast during the nightly news program "Heute" on ZDF,[6] one of the most popular news broadcasts in Germany. The advertisement consisted of a short cartoon only focusing on the Advance Bank brand name; including more information would have been too expensive for the bank. Similar advertisements also appeared in other programs (such as N-TV) which are popular among the above-mentioned target group. Second, a

---

[6]ZDF is one of the two public television networks in Germany.

content advertisement campaign was launched through several high quality German newspapers and newsmagazines aiming at conveying the benefits customers can accrue through Advance Bank.

5.3 *Acquiring New Customers at Advance Bank*

As of May 1998, Advance Bank had a customer base of 79,000 people. This relatively small number of customers partly results from the difficulty of pitching promotion campaigns at the desired target group and the high advertising costs involved.[7] To overcome these problems, Advance Bank has considered new ways of reaching potential customers such as offering special rates to companies whose employees match the profile of the Advance Bank target customer. Companies that were first considered included those that were already cooperating with Advance Bank such as Andersen Consulting and CompuNet.[8] This offer was later extended to other companies with similar employee profiles like McKinsey, Microsoft, and Oracle.

Another approach has consisted of cooperating with other non-bank companies that offer products complementary to Advance Bank's financial products; this included the technology retailer TELIS and the Internet Service Provider AOL.[9] Through this cooperation, customers are offered a low-priced package solution (containing an ISDN[10] card, a modem, and the Internet service) for online banking. This package is subsidized by Advance Bank as to make online banking more attractive and accessible.

6 Opening an Account at Advance Bank

In order to open an account at Advance Bank, prospective customers go through a screening process that assesses their creditworthiness. Personal data (such as the income tax form, information from the SCHUFA,[11] marital status, and employment) are used to rate them. This rating is necessary to reduce the loan default risk of new customers who, upon joining the bank, instantly receive a credit line of DM30,000.[12] 94 percent of all applicants pass the screening process; of the remaining 6 percent, half of them typically choose to make the required time deposit of DM30,000 and become customers of the bank.

Upon requesting the application material (either through the Internet, phone, fax or postal mail), prospective clients receive a package including information about Advance Bank's products and services as

---

[7]Each newly acquired customer costs on average DM600.

[8]CompuNet delivers computer hardware equipment to Advance Bank.

[9]AOL stands for America Online.

[10]ISDN (Integrated Services Digital Network) is capable of handling data, voice, text and image transmission over the same communication line.

[11]SCHUFA, which stands for "Schutzgemeinschaft für allgemeines Kreditwesen", records the credit history of bank customers and provides this information to banks when customers want to open up a new account.

[12]DM10,000 for each account, the VISA card and the Euro-Check card.

well as the application form. Walter Klein, a new customer at Advance Bank, commented:

> Before choosing my direct bank, I requested information packages from both Advance Bank and Bank 24. In the end, I found the Advance Bank offer more convincing.

They then fill out the application form, attach the income tax file as proof of income and put these documents into a blue envelope (included in the package) and seal it. This envelope is then given to the post office where the prospective customer presents his/her passport to a clerk (as a proof of identity). The post office forwards this envelope to Advance Bank.[13] Upon passing the above-mentioned screening, the customer receives from Advance Bank a confirmation letter containing the six-digit secret code (mentioned above).

7 Advance Bank Product Portfolio and Price/Performance

Advance Bank's product line consists of two main products: the cash management account and the investment-fund service. In addition to these products, Advance Bank also offers insurance and retirement funds.

7.1 The Cash Management Account

The cash management account is the central piece of the Advance Bank service. This account provides the combined features of a current (checking) account and those of a savings account; i.e., the availability of the customer funds at all times and an interest-bearing account.[14] The customer can subdivide his/her main account into up to nine sub-accounts used for different purposes (e.g.; household, car, rent, etc.). For interest payments, these accounts are automatically totaled and the customer receives (or pays) interest on the cumulative balance of both accounts. During the first quarter of 1998, the interest that the bank applied was 3.3 percent on deposits and 8.75 percent on loans. Philip Torsten, who has been a customer at Advance Bank since its creation, explained:

> Advance Bank charges more but also offers more service than other direct banks. I don't want to be checking the balance of my current account every two weeks to make sure that I don't have money sitting idle there that should better be put into an interest-bearing account. At the same time, I don't lose any interest whatsoever, and I don't end up paying interest for overdrawing one of my sub-accounts. This [service] is very important for me.

Customers can choose between the standard cash management account (which allows up to 50 free transactions per quarter) and the cash management account plus (which allows up to 150 free transactions per

---

[13]The German law requires every bank to confirm the customer's identity before opening an account.

[14]In January 1997, the average account balance was the equivalent of US$52,000.

quarter). A Eurocard Gold or a VISA Gold credit card (offering withdrawals of up to DM6,000 per week) and a Euro-Check card (with withdrawals of up to DM5,000 per week) are given free of charge once the account is opened.

Following an agreement with a group of German private banks (including Deutsche Bank and Commerzbank), Advance Bank allows its customers to use all the automatic teller machines (which total 6,000 in Germany) of these banks free of charge. In addition, Advance Bank customers have free access to all the ATMs of Vereinsbank, Hypo-Bank and Dresdner Bank. Furthermore, customers can also withdraw cash at any ATM in Germany (in total, there are 38,000 ATMs in the country), and Advance Bank will reimburse each customer up to DM30 of ATM fees per quarter.

At the end of each month, each Advance Bank customer receives by postal mail a financial report (DIN A4 format) containing detailed information on all transactions as well as changes in his/her main account and sub-accounts. Additionally, the customer is immediately informed when an incoming transfer (that exceeds DM20,000) or an outgoing transfer (of more than DM10,000) is made.

Every month, Advance Bank charges its customers a flat fee of DM16 if they hold a cash management account and DM28 if they have a cash management plus account. However, if a customer has a cumulative annual charge to his credit card of over DM8,000, the monthly fee is reduced to respectively DM13.50 and DM25. If this cumulative annual charge exceeds DM25,000, then the fee is waived for the cash management account holder while it is lowered to DM12 for the cash management plus account holder.

7.2   *Investment Fund Service*

Through its investment fund selection service, Advance Bank offers "objective" advice for selecting investment funds. In contrast with most other banks, which primarily sell their own funds to their customers, Advance Bank uses the expertise and experience of the "Feri Trust" investment specialists. Based on the information they receive, Advance Bank's financial consultants first select the 50 best-performing funds out of a group of 2,700. They then recommend to the customer an individual portfolio strategy that takes into account personal investment goals, return and risk preferences as well as the customer's tax situation, as to maximize after-tax returns. Customers can choose from five different strategies:

- DM conservative
- Germany conservative
- International growth
- International chance
- Europe growth

In addition to sending its customers a monthly market assessment and a personalized analysis of their portfolio, Advance Bank also sends up-to-date buying and selling recommendations. The fee the bank charges for managing the customer's asset portfolio is DM79 per year, regardless of the portfolio size. In January 1997, the average balance of a customer portfolio was the equivalent of US$63,000. Volker Visser commented on the average balances of the portfolio and of the cash management account:

> When you look at these average balances, you see that we are doing fine quality-wise. But we are not doing so well quantity-wise, and we need to increase the number of [Advance Bank] customers.

7.3   *Advance Bank Price/Performance*

To compensate for the fees it charges, which are higher than those of other direct banks, Advance Bank aims at offering a uniquely differentiated value through its all-inclusive banking services as well as its high customer service satisfaction. For example, prior to a trip abroad, a customer may deposit at the bank copies of important personal documents (such as his/her passport). In case that one of these documents was lost or stolen, Advance Bank would fax the customer a copy of it and also provide money within 24 hours. If a customer gets ill while abroad, he can contact the Bank's medical consultation service where multilingual doctors are on call around the clock to give advice over the phone and, if necessary, to arrange for transportation back to Germany. Furthermore, to cover emergencies while abroad, customers receive up to 62 days of free insurance coverage, which fully covers treatment and medication costs and allows the customer to consult the doctor of his choice. All of the above-listed services are free for customers with a cash management account at the Advance Bank.

Advance Bank also decided to give the same benefits, including a free Euro-Check card, to heterosexual as well as homosexual couples when they open a joint current account.[15] The bank's service quality is constantly monitored and each customer complaint is answered within 24 hours. If the latter is not met, then the bank sends the customer a compensation gift (e.g., a Jazz compact disc). In order to enhance service quality further, complaints are tracked for each customer and aggregated under six categories: service, bank's appearance, competence, reliability, customer treatment, and product range. These complaint records are also analyzed when designing new applications and processes or training call center agents.

Volker Visser elaborated on the price/performance issue at Advance Bank:

> We offer quality to our customers. We have to pay for quality and our customers are willing to pay us for this quality because in the end they profit

---

[15]The bank does not require from homosexual couples to provide a proof of their relationship.

from it. Our customers are willing to pay us for this quality because in the end they profit from it. Our customers are not so much interested in low fees. They want the best information they can get to help them make money [by] investing into the funds we recommend to them. They don't care about the extra three marks that we charge for our services. If they did, they would do discount brokerage with another bank.

8   The Call Center: The Heart of Advance Bank

Since the call center agent is the only Advance Bank employee who has direct contact with the customer, special attention was given to the setup of the call center during the bank's design and implementation stages. The goal was to reach a high level of service quality by combining well-trained call center agents and sophisticated information technology to make the customer's banking experience as convenient, pleasant and efficient as possible.[16] This was done in order to remedy problems of traditional brick-and-mortar branches such as the ones described below by Susanne Meier, another Advance Bank customer:

> When I still was customer of a brick-and-mortar bank, I had to deal with lots of incompetent people who weren't able to help me out. In order to get a hold of competent bank agents, I was often sent from one branch to the next before I got the service I wanted. Restricted opening hours also really got to me, especially during weekends when I would have had the time to sit down and do my banking. Now, every time I call up Advance Bank, on the other hand, I receive good and qualified service quickly.

Key features of the call center architecture include:

- **Availability:** supports operations 24 hours a day, seven days a week (actual availability is at 99.91 percent of the time);
- **High service level:** 85 percent of all calls answered within 15 seconds;
- **Personalized service:** human contact offered at all times;
- **Assured security:** all customer calls are recorded, secure customer verification;
- **Open architecture:** use of standard hardware and software components;
- **Scalability of the system:** supports up to 250,000 customers and beyond;
- **Interconnected call centers:** incoming calls are routed automatically to available call center agents independent of location;
- **Adequate technical support:** on-site service within four hours for critical components;
- **Outbound dialing;**
- **Management reports.**

---

[16]Advance Bank was awarded the Grand Prix Customer Service Award for being the best call center in Germany in 1997.

8.1   IT Support for the Call Center

We spend about 20 to 30 percent of the bank's budget on IT. This may sound exaggerated but it is not.

Frank Spreier

Advance Bank call centers, located in Munich and in Wilhelmshaven (with a staff of respectively 100 and 150 call agents), receive all incoming calls from current and prospective customers from 7 A.M. to 10 P.M., seven days a week.[17] Depending on availability, the Automatic Call Distributor (ACD) routes the incoming call to the least occupied call center. In order to optimize the call centers' utilization while reducing the wait time for incoming calls, Advance Bank designed a support system for the call centers that provides information on typical call frequencies (e.g., the breakdown of calls per day, week or month). The system also forecasts changes in call frequencies caused by special promotions, TV advertisements, mailings or newspaper/magazine articles, thus allowing the human resources manager to efficiently schedule personnel and to foresee possible bottlenecks.

Call center agents work in teams of five to six members, with each agent using a multi-task workstation (with a large display screen) to access all relevant data while talking to the customer. The workstation integrates the functions of a PC and those of a telephone through a UNIX-based CTI[18] platform. It allows the call center agent to receive calls without having to pick up the receiver and to simultaneously transfer calls and call-related information to other agents in the call center. Furthermore, the agent can place calls without having to dial but just by clicking on the customer name on his screen. He can then talk to him through a head-phone-speaker set which is connected to the computer workstation.[19]

8.2   Customer Information

Upon receiving a call, the call center agent first enters the customer's personal identification number and the three digits (provided by the customer) from his/her security code. A pop-up menu is then displayed on the screen which allows the agent to access and, if need be, modify the customer's personal account information. The information includes:

- *Customer contact information* such as home/office and e-mail addresses, phone and fax numbers, as well as his/her preferred contact times.

---

[17]Calls coming in during night hours are rerouted to an overflow call center located in Duisburg.

[18]Through CTI (Computer Technology Integration), databases are linked to the incoming call, allowing the call center agent to quickly access the file of the customer at hand.

[19]For security reasons, all customer calls are automatically recorded.

- **Customer credit rating** that Advance Bank assigns to each customer in order to determine his/her credit line and the interest rate at which he/she can borrow money. This rating is first given to the customer when he/she opens an account; it is then monthly updated based on the customer's transactions and other account activities.
- **Record of previous contacts:** When talking to the customer, the call agent can also view a detailed list of the past contacts the customer had with the bank. This list shows the time and date of each contact, the name of the call center agent who handled the call, the issue discussed, and any other relevant comments that the agent deemed important to record.
- **Customer lifestyle:** The call center agent may also record customer lifestyle information. For instance, if a customer tells the agent that he needs to withdraw 3,000 DM for a vacation in the U.S., the call center agent notes (in the lifestyle information column) that this customer likes traveling. Similarly, there are columns for musical taste, other cultural preferences, etc. Another column informs the call agent about individual customer characteristics (e.g., a hearing problem), so that each agent can take these characteristics into account when dealing with that customer the next time.
- **Customer likes and dislikes:** At the end of the first three months with the bank, every new customer receives the "honeymoon" questionnaire asking him to rate his satisfaction with the bank, its call center agents, the account opening procedure and the intelligibility of the information material sent to him. Another survey is sent annually to the bank's customers aiming at tracking their satisfaction level and finding new ways to improve the service quality and offerings. All surveys are scanned into the customer database and thus added to the already recorded customer information. When next talking to a customer, the call center agent can, from his workstation, instantly access this scanned information. Furthermore, to avoid "annoying" a given customer by repeatedly offering him/her a certain product or service, the call center agent has the option to block certain capabilities. For instance, if he finds out from a phone conversation that a given customer would rather not receive direct mailings from Advance Bank, he can block this permanently by crossing out this function in the customer database record. Likewise, if a customer turns down a call agent's offer (over the phone) to open a cash management account, the agent makes a note of this refusal in the corresponding database record to take into account future contacts with that customer.

8.3 Maintaining the Human Touch

We can also talk about non-banking matters during our conversation with the customer. In fact, we are even encouraged to ask one question aside from banking to make things more human. By doing so, I create a positive atmosphere, where the customer gets the feeling that I am there to help him make a decision and not to push him over. Once I establish this atmosphere, the customer usually opens up and tells me more personal information which then makes it easier to suggest the right product to him.

Klaus Eutin
Call Center Agent
Advance Bank

Making the customer feel comfortable and at ease while banking over the phone is one of the crucial challenges faced by a direct bank. Advance Bank tries to meet this challenge by authorizing its call center agents to also talk to customers about topics that are not banking-related. Klaus Eutin further elaborated on this matter:

> Some customers also ask personal questions, about your age, for example, or your hobbies. There are some call agents here in the office who met their future spouses while working.

Furthermore, call center agents were trained to keep the customer's best interest in mind. They are advised to make the decision with the customer instead of trying to "push him/her over" and make the sale at any cost. The guiding principle of Advance Bank is to pull the customer and not to push him to buy a product. Marc Hemmerling elaborated on this point:

> It is important to build up a personal trusting relationship with a call [center] agent; this can only happen over time. When you think that you've really received excellent service and advice from a call agent, you'd like to come back to him and build on this good initial understanding. It's very much a psychological thing. I want an excellent product, but I also need to have the trust that the call agent is not trying to sell me something [that] I don't need.

8.4 The Call Center Agent

Initially, we thought that we needed to hire [for the bank's call center] tele-marketeers and give them banking training. That turned out to be a mistake. Now we hire first-rate bankers and we give them a tele-marketing training.

Volker Visser

Since call center agents are the crucial interface between customers and a direct bank, Advance Bank carefully selects then trains and motivates its call agents. Before getting invited to an assessment center, applicants for call agent positions are first interviewed over the phone. During this interview, the recruiter has the opportunity to test the applicant's telephone "appearance," which is the call agent's most important qualification. Besides having a warm and welcoming voice, a call agent must be able to communicate clearly and intelligibly over the telephone. Regional dialects are irrelevant as long as the call agent can make himself well understood to the customer. Although call agents have varying educational backgrounds, they must have a service mentality when joining Advance Bank. Many of them have completed a banking apprenticeship, but there are also university students, former restaurant employees, and housewives. After passing the telephone interview, applicants are invited to an assessment center where they have to demonstrate, over two days, that they are stress-resistant and also somewhat persistent, especially with regard to sales conversations.

Before starting their work, new call center agents undergo a six to seven week, full-time training program during which they first get to know Advance Bank's philosophy, computer system and product portfolio. Call agents are then trained as to how to handle a phone conversation with a customer and how to talk to him/her. For example, instead of saying "no problem" which might suggest to the customer that he is a problem, call agents are trained to say, "I will gladly do so" or similar non-judgmental sentences. During the final part of the initial training which focuses on sales, call agents learn how to sell the bank's products to the customers using the following steps. First the agent needs to establish a personal contact with the customer and create a rapport of trust with him/her. Second, the call agent needs to inquire about the customer's needs and then make the appropriate offer. The final step is closing the deal.

In order to improve the training quality, experienced call agents model the "optimal call process" with its most frequently recurring parts such as needs analysis, necessary explanations and possible customer objections. They then develop a script for the new call agents which they can refer to. After the call agent starts his/her work, a team trainer provides coaching on the job, listens to customer conversations and gives instant feedback afterwards.

9   What Next?

9.1   Internet-Based Banking

I switched to Advance Bank because I want to be able to do my banking anytime and anywhere, as long as there is a phone or an Internet connection available.

Rudolf Pfitzer
Advance Bank customer

From the start, Advance Bank recognized the importance of the Internet as an additional information, communication, marketing and sales channel as well as customers' willingness to use it to perform financial operations (see survey results in Exhibit 4). The bank strategy stipulated the use of this technology-driven media to offer banking services. An Internet website was set up to inform prospective customers about the bank's products and services. Since summer 1997, customers have been able to also access their main- and sub-accounts through Advance Bank's Internet website (without having to purchase any additional banking software) and perform all banking operations online (e.g., transactions, standing orders and funds management) from any computer with Internet access. As of April 1998, 42 percent of all money transfers were conducted through Advance Bank's website. Susanne Meier added:

> With many other Internet banks, you need to install specialized software packages on your PC to access your banking account online. This limits the usage [of Internet-banking] to your home PC. With Advance Bank, I have universal access to my account as long as I can get a hold of a PC with Internet access. I could conceivably check my account in the U.S. during vacation and make a transaction in case I have forgotten to pay my rent, for example.

However, for security reasons, the bank put a DM10,000 ceiling on transactions and transfers done through the Internet. Volker Visser explained:

> Our Internet transactions are very secure. For each transaction, we provide the customer with a transaction authentication number and a confirmation receipt. However, if something goes wrong, for example a customer transfer does not reach its destination, we bear the cost and pay for it.

9.2   Towards a Two-Channel Distribution System: Integrating Telephone and Internet Banking

Banking through the Internet, without any human interaction, works well for selling standardized or simple financial products. However, for highly customized or complex products (such as a mortgage or a life insurance policy), the provision of customer advice is highly desirable, if not even required, by the client. For the latter case and in order to meet customer demands and expectations, Advance Bank intends to integrate the telephone into its Internet banking service as to offer simultaneous voice and data communication between its call center agents and the bank customers.

For example, when choosing a real-estate mortgage, the customer first provides through the Advance Bank Internet website some personal data (e.g., duration, amount, rate, etc.). This data is then used to instantaneously produce some "what-if" analyses and scenarios. If the customer wishes to receive some personal advice, he/she then clicks on a specific icon on the screen. Subsequently, an Advance Bank call agent calls up that customer and discusses the matter with him/her: both parties have the possibility to look at the same document while talking and, if need be, modify the mortgage data the customer has entered on the Advance Bank Internet website. The resulting communication is very similar to the traditional form of communication at a bank branch; for instance, the call agent can suggest over the phone changing parts of the mortgage (e.g., the duration or the deposit) to obtain a better offer. Simultaneously, the

EXHIBIT 4 Survey of Internet Users

What kind of financial information would you like to access through the Internet?

based on 8,435 responses from Internet users:	Total	Women	Men	age (in years):				
				<19	20–29	30–39	40–49	>50
Information about stocks and investment opportunities	52.1%	41.3%	53.4%	46.7%	53.7%	52.9%	48.6%	52.7%
Information about insurance (prices, premiums, services)	36.1%	33.7%	36.5%	16.7%	36.5%	39.9%	36.7%	34.0%
Information about mortgages and real estate financing	19.6%	17.6%	19.8%	9.7%	18.2%	23.8%	21.3%	14.5%
Databases with general financial information	38.1%	32.7%	38.8%	22.2%	37.9%	41.2%	38.4%	38.0%
Articles about general financial topics	32.0%	27.4%	32.6%	25.9%	32.5%	33.9%	30.2%	29.6%
Statistical tables and graphical displays	332.2%	22.0%	34.6%	32.5%	35.6%	33.0%	29.7%	30.1%
Stock quotations	48.1%	38.1%	49.3%	48.6%	51.1%	47.8%	44.4%	42.6%

based on 8,435 responses from Internet users:	employment status:			High school students apprentices	University students
	civil servants	self-employed	other employees		
Information about stocks and investment opportunities	44.9%	55.4%	52.9%	46.5%	53.9%
Information about insurance (prices, premiums, services)	38.4%	38.8%	40.7%	18.5%	30.1%
Information about mortgages and real estate financing	20.5%	22.3%	22.9%	11.9%	14.2%
Databases with general financial information	30.5%	44.0%	40.5%	25.1%	34.5%
Articles about general financial topics	30.2%	35.0%	32.5%	26.8%	32.8%
Statistical tables and graphical displays	26.7%	36.7%	32.7%	32.7%	37.5%
Stock quotations	37.0%	49.5%	47.9%	47.3%	52.1%

Would you perform the following financial tasks through the Internet?

based on 6,292 responses from Internet users:	Total	Women	Men	age (in years):				
				<19	20–29	30–39	40–49	>50
Online Banking (account management)	95.4%	93.2%	95.6%	96.5%	95.8%	94.8%	95.7%	95.8%
Purchasing shares	56.1%	39.3%	57.7%	50.7%	58.4%	55.6%	53.0%	56.1%
Purchasing real-estate mortgage	14.9%	13.0%	15.0%	10.0%	13.7%	16.6%	23.8%	13.5%
Purchasing car insurance	39.8%	29.5%	40.9%	16.1%	35.3%	44.9%	41.2%	43.9%
Purchasing liability insurance	34.6%	28.8%	35.3%	12.0%	29.9%	40.0%	33.9%	36.1%
Purchasing home insurance	33.3%	29.5%	33.7%	11.1%	28.3%	38.7%	33.0%	37.1%
Purchasing accident insurance	28.4%	23.2%	28.9%	10.9%	24.5%	32.8%	47.8%	30.4%
Purchasing life insurance	20.2%	17.0%	20.5%	10.0%	17.3%	22.9%	47.8%	19.8%

based on 6,292 responses from Internet users:	employment status:			High school students apprentices	University students
	civil servants	self-employed	other employees		
Online Banking (account management)	96.5%	95.1%	95.7%	95.7%	95.1%
Purchasing shares	50.2%	59.5%	56.0%	50.7%	58.1%
Purchasing real-estate mortgage	17.1%	15.3%	16.8%	9.4%	10.4%
Purchasing car insurance	42.0%	46.2%	44.2%	17.1%	29.0%
Purchasing liability insurance	38.1%	39.7%	39.2%	12.8%	23.2%
Purchasing home insurance	35.8%	37.3%	38.2%	11.1%	21.7%
Purchasing accident insurance	29.2%	32.5%	32.0%	12.0%	18.8%
Purchasing life insurance	23.3%	23.3%	22.0%	9.4%	13.2%

(*Source:* Fittkau & Maaß, 1997)

agent can show on the web document what impact the change will have on the mortgage. Compared to traditional phone conversations, such an integrated telephone-Internet sales channel allows a reduction of call time since the customer now enters the request parameters by himself, hence also reducing the number of possible entry errors.

In order to further enhance its customer relationship, Advance Bank plans to install video cameras on top of the call agents' workstations thus allowing the customer to see the call agent on his/her PC screen while talking to him/her. In order to provide these complex services, transmission speed of the Internet will have to increase greatly. Already today, customers are complaining about slow Internet connections to the Advance Bank website, as illustrated by Marc Hemmerling's comment below:

> The main problem of Internet banking is that it takes too long to download the website. The initialization process [i.e.; the online identification of the customer] also takes too long. When I think about the online fees, it is almost cheaper to do my banking over the phone or even to fill out a form and send it in by mail.

9.3   Internationalization

Having gained good experience and expertise in offering direct banking services through its business operations in Germany, Advance Bank plans to expand its geographical presence by penetrating other European countries. This ambition to go international is not new at the bank as stated by Volker Visser:

> Advance Bank is not a German bank. If we had wanted to be a German bank, we wouldn't have called ourselves "Advance Bank" because Advance is not a German word. We would have called ourselves Hermann or Schmidt Bank. We chose an English name because we expect to expand throughout Europe.

9.4   Challenges Ahead

Preparing for his next Board meeting, Volker Visser was pondering the evolution of direct banking in Germany and in Europe, and the future of Advance Bank in the increasingly global and competitive business environment. What should Advance Bank do next in order to further attract new customers and build loyalty among existing ones? Should the bank broaden its business scope and extend its product portfolio? Should it go ahead at this stage with its plans to enlarge the geographical scale of its operations by launching its direct banking concept in other European countries?

Volker Visser is well aware that embarking on such ambitious projects is at the same time an opportunity and a threat for the survival and growth of Advance Bank. However, since the bank needs to achieve its goal of 250,000 customers by the year 2001 in order to break even, can it afford not picking up the opportunity and taking the risk that comes with it?

Chapter 5

Business-to-Consumer E-Commerce

In the beginning, there was B2B—that is, business-to-business electronic commerce. The early B2B activities of the 1970s and 1980s typically took the form of EDI-based interconnections between large business organizations using private networks. However, there is little doubt that the electronic commerce story of the past few years, at least so far as the popular and trade press is concerned, has been the Internet B2C (business-to-consumer) story. Most people today have heard of Amazon.com and E-trade. For companies less than a decade old to be so widely known is quite amazing.

B2C e-commerce is about individual consumers—you and me—searching for, researching, acquiring, and maintaining goods and services via the Internet. Normally included within the B2C "space" are topics such as Internet-based advertising, consumer-oriented electronic payment mechanisms, electronic promotion, and customer care systems based on the Internet, as well as conventional goods and services acquisition.

The cases in this section all center on various aspects of B2C e-commerce. The first case, "HomeGrocer.com," focuses on a type of physical product that practically everyone has shopped for on many occasions: groceries. The case describes a new company, HomeGrocer, and the business model this company developed to compete with both virtual and traditional grocery stores. Internet-based grocery stores have existed for some time, predating the advent of the World Wide Web by a number of years. Two of the best-known existing Internet grocery operations are Peapod and Netgrocer. Peapod's approach is to partner with existing real grocery chains, offering an electronic picking service that piggybacks on its partner's existing bricks-and-mortar facilities. In contrast, Netgrocer handles only nonperishable items and ships continentwide via Fedex, out of a huge central warehouse. Both companies have had considerable difficulty building their businesses and turning profits, for various reasons. HomeGrocer, in contrast, has developed a new approach, in which it is attempting to outflank both Peapod and Netgrocer by following a "best of both worlds" strategy. HomeGrocer handles a full line of groceries, but avoids the extra costs associated with the overhead of a physical grocery chain. By operating out of a warehouse in a low-rent district, HomeGrocer is able to maintain a considerably higher gross margin than its real-world competitors. In addition, the company made the interesting decision to restrict delivery to 30 miles around its warehouse, despite the fact that demand, at least in theory, could come from much further afield. HomeGrocer's key challenge is building its customer base. This entails changing people's mindsets, since shopping for groceries in a real grocery store—as opposed to an online store—is a practice that many people find hard to break.

The second case, "Autobytel and General Motors: David and Goliath," considers the metamorphosis that the automotive retailing industry has undergone since the birth of online automobile retailing outlets such as Autobytel. The case provides a vehicle for examining numerous issues, including: (1) the implications of the Internet on industry structures and processes; (2) the evolving role of intermediaries given ongoing developments in cyberspace; (3) restructuring of industry processes and management of change in automotive retailing; and (4) improved service in the retail sector, using creative and innovative applications of information technology.

The third case in this section, "Looks.com (A): Building Asia's First Health, Beauty, and Fashion E-tailer," focuses on an Asian e-commerce site for brand name cosmetics, fragrances, skin care products, and fashions. It had been well received among investors; the site had a viable business strategy and a solid first-mover advantage. The founder and managing director was ready to launch Looks.com within weeks to capitalize on the upcoming Christmas shopping rush and the intense "dot.com" fever that caught Hong Kong in late 1999. The biggest challenge the company now faces is persuading brand name cosmetic manufacturers to list their products for sale on the site. Look.com's managing director and buyer are finding that manufacturers' concerns about cannibalizing their existing sales channels and antagonizing their licensed distributors are dampening their enthusiasm for dealing with Looks.com. The company must develop strategies to convince manufacturers that using this alternative distribution channel can increase their revenue and the profile of their brands in Asia, with little impact on their current distribution network.

The final case in this section is "Blinds To Go: Evaluating the Blinds ToGo.com Retail E-Commerce Venture." Blinds To Go (BTG) is a retailer of window coverings. The case deals with how to evaluate performance for e-commerce ventures (through various metrics), as well as how an online division may affect an offline division and vice versa. When BTG was first proposed in mid-1999, its board of directors was lukewarm to the idea. However, after six months of operation and seeing other retailers start to go online and the tremendous valuation being given to dot.coms, the board encouraged BTG to devote more resources to the project. BlindsToGo.com was launched shortly thereafter. Senior management at BTG had received sales, spending, and survey results from BlindsToGo.com that indicated that the people who visited the site were the same people who visited the stores. The vice chairman of BTG wanted to evaluate the results of BlindsToGo.com by examining the fit of the e-commerce project within the overall business strategy to determine where resources should be focused.

Homegrocer.com

By Professor Sid L. Huff and David Beckow

"We're using only three trucks, we own 10, and we have yet another 10 on order. We had better be right about this thing." Mike Donald had reason to be concerned. Having spent three years and four million private investor and venture capital dollars (including over $100,000 of his own money) to build the Pacific Northwest's first online, Internet-based grocery store, he was finding that new customers were signing on more slowly than expected. "We're learning that Homegrocer is a deep sell," noted Donald as he bit his lip and glanced across his desk. He was referring to the fact that winning new ongoing customers was proving to be a lot more difficult than simply letting people know that Homegrocer was open for business.

IVEY David Beckow and Professor Sid L. Huff prepared this case solely to provide material for class discussion. The authors do not intend to illustrate either effective or ineffective handling of a managerial situation. The authors may have disguised certain names and other identifying information to protect confidentiality.

A New Business Model

"What makes Homegrocer unique is that it turns the traditional e-commerce business model on its head," exclaimed Terry Drayton as he headed to yet another meeting with investors. "Whereas the traditional Internet business model promises massive economies of scale and efficiency gains through its access to a worldwide market, Homegrocer is trying to make the model work while focusing on only a few square miles of territory."

Located in Bellevue, Washington, Homegrocer consisted of a warehouse facility plus an Internet website that allowed wired consumers to log on, purchase groceries via credit card, and have them delivered to their door within 24 hours. Customers could not actually walk into the Homegrocer building, but instead had to order everything over the Web. Corporate offices and the sole distribution center were built into a warehouse the size of a Boeing 727 hanger (see Exhibit 1A). Every morning trucks pulled into the loading bay of the warehouse, where each was loaded with the groceries of approximately 30 to 40 customers. Trucks were filled by pickers who wore a Borg-like prosthetic that stretched from their forearm down to the end of their fingers. The LCD screens on their wrists instructed them where to go in the warehouse and what to pick. Upon picking the item, they scanned it with the laser mounted onto the end of their index finger. This approach allowed the company to keep a real-time inventory of every item in the warehouse that, in turn, enabled a very efficient just-in-time replenishment strategy.

As the trucks were being loaded with their day's worth of deliveries, a sophisticated routing computer was determining the most efficient route for each truck. This route plan was provided to the driver, who then left to make his deliveries. The routing system was a third-party purchased system, essentially the same system currently used by UPS. Homegrocer had plans to enhance the system by adding a global positioning component that would continuously update the location of trucks to the routing system. That would allow the routing system to make adjustments for local traffic conditions as well as current vehicle locations. Effectiveness of the routing system was important because customers could choose any 45-minute window in which their groceries were delivered. To date the company had delivered groceries within its requested envelope approximately 98 percent of the time.

Mike Donald elaborated,

> Orders from customers come right into our server. They are then transferred to our software supplier in Vancouver. He then takes the orders off the server at midnight, converts them, and sends them back down to us. Once we get an order, it's put into the routing system, the routes are developed, items are sent out to the picking system and the orders are picked in a certain sequence and are put on a truck. The actual charge for the order is calculated after the order is picked and scanned, so that customers are

EXHIBIT 1 (A and B)   HomeGrocer's Warehouse and a HomeGrocer
Delivery Truck

only billed for what they receive. Trucks go out at about 1 P.M., and continue
delivering up until 9 o'clock at night. You get a copy of the order when it's
delivered. The customer has to be home to accept delivery. However, customers can schedule delivery times, in 45-minute windows, when they place
an order.

EXHIBIT 2A   Netgrocer's WebSite—Opening Page

Source: http://www.netgrocer.com, November 1998.

Competition

Homegrocer was not the first Internet-based grocery delivery service to begin operation. Several other players, including Netgrocer and Peapod, had been operating for some time. Netgrocer (see Exhibit 2A) offered national service, but only sold shelf-stable products. Orders took four to five days to be delivered via courier. Netgrocer offered low prices on many products.

The Peapod approach was somewhat different (see Exhibit 2B). They focused more on building their expertise in the software and logistics surrounding Internet grocery home delivery. They contracted their ex-

EXHIBIT 2B Peapod's WebSite—Opening Page

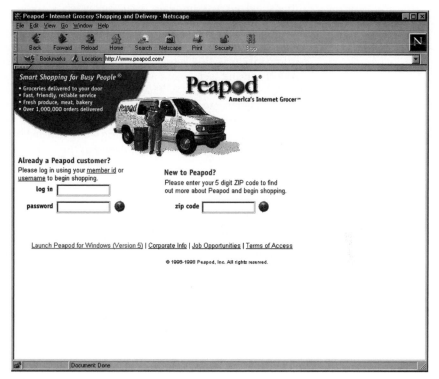

Source: http://www.peapod.com, November 1998.

pertise to existing grocery operations, such as Safeway, who wished to enter the Internet home delivery market. An existing grocery chain entering the Internet delivery business benefited from two key competitive advantages. First, since the existing grocery outlet already served traditional customers, further utilizing the facility to serve the home shopper produced little additional operating cost. Second, existing grocery chains such as Safeway had both a recognizable name and brand equity which new start-ups such as Homegrocer lacked. Nonetheless, differences between the traditional grocery business and this new business model remained vast.

Donald commented,

> Building a grocery store on the Internet is a very different business from running a traditional grocery business. There is a tremendous amount of integration work to be done in order for the software components to function together properly. Also, the labor component must be minimized. Without automated ordering and automated routing, you need too many people to perform basic clerical operations. Delivery and picking accuracy fail if you have

people on phones and by the fax machine, and the whole labor component gets out of hand very quickly. So it's really critical that you get the right systems and software in place from the outset.

People ask me, what are the barriers to entry? They try to tell me that everybody's going to be in this business in the course of a year. Well, the most likely competition is the regular grocery chains, but they're so busy doing what they're trying to do to maintain market share they don't have the time or the people to think about it. They're all grocery people. They don't have the technical expertise to understand this new type of business. Companies that are out there running grocery businesses are nowhere near ready to jump into the Internet on their own. One thing we've learned is that the biggest barrier to entry is just the overall complexity of the task.

Homegrocer Advantages

Homegrocer was unique because it eliminated many of the costs associated with the traditional retail setting. For example, a traditional grocery store would normally be located in a desirable retail district in close proximity to customers. It therefore bore the high costs associated with its location (premium rents both for the store and for sufficient parking, high property taxes, etc). Homegrocer, on the other hand, was located in a much less expensive industrial district; hence it was not subject to the same high costs as would be mandated by an appropriate retail setting.

Homegrocer also benefited from not having to position stock for retail display. In a conventional grocery store, large displays of produce had to be kept cool by refrigerators that pumped cold air straight through the produce and into the store. Because Homegrocer customers only saw an online display of groceries they were buying—not the real thing—there was no need to store inventory in this fashion. Produce was stored in a large walk-in refrigerator, which was much more efficient than conventional store storage, and resulted in substantial power savings. Also, because large amounts of inventory were necessary to make an attractive display, greater inventory levels—with correspondingly higher carrying costs—were required by traditional grocery stores. Further, regular stores incurred more spoilage (which must be written off) than did Homegrocer with its JIT system.

Finally, Homegrocer was able to deliver a superior product to the consumer. Donald elaborated, "We don't order the perishable products until our customers have ordered them from us. As a result, we have the freshest product available. The produce is better, the fish is fresher, and the meat is restaurant quality."

The savings possible through the kind of system Homegrocer had established were substantial. Traditional grocery store chains operated with a 28 percent gross margin, but carried just 1 percent or less to the bottom line. While Homegrocer achieved the same 28 percent gross margins as its rivals (its groceries were priced to sell neither at a premium nor a discount), Mike Donald anticipated that its efficiencies should allow it to carry almost 7 percent to the bottom line. Hence, in theory, Homegrocer should be about six times as profitable as a conventional grocery store.

While the potential savings and efficiency gains inherent in Homegrocer's system were enticing, up-front costs were substantial. Design of the Homegrocer website alone cost the firm over US$750,000. Considering most successful electronic commerce sites redesigned their websites from the ground up every few years, this was a rather significant cost that a conventional grocery store would not incur. As well, Homegrocer's fleet of refrigerated delivery trucks represented another cost most "bricks-and-mortar" grocery stores did not face.

The Technology

Because of management's lack of IT expertise, Homegrocer outsourced all software and back office system development efforts. Back office and administrative software was purchased largely off the shelf and then modified. Design and maintenance had, to date, been outsourced as well. However, this was beginning to change. Management had begun to realize that, to gain some control over its future development potential, the firm had to take closer control over its IT. According to Donald, effective integration of various technologies formed a substantial barrier to entry, which served to keep traditional grocery stores out of the online delivery business. To that end, the company had begun to hire in-house developers to reduce its reliance on external IT consulting and development firms. While this practice was adding to overhead in the short term, management felt that development of this capability "in house" would help the firm develop a sustainable competitive advantage.

Management

Homegrocer was the brainchild of Mike Donald's forum group in the Young Entrepreneurs Organization. The group met occasionally to discuss business opportunities and challenges. Initial discussions about the viability of an Internet-based grocery store took place at Bridge's Pub in downtown Vancouver, following YEO Forum Group meetings.

Mike Donald was also President of Concord Sales, one of the largest food brokers in British Columbia, and had worked much of his life in the grocery trade. Over the years he had developed a deep understanding of the grocery business.

Donald was joined in the venture by Terry Drayton, another YPO member. Drayton had been working with Loblaws in Ontario to develop home delivery of groceries (without the use of the Internet). Drayton had recently divested himself of Crystal Springs Water Co., a company he had founded ten years before, and was looking to move his career in a new direction. The water business had given him a solid understanding of distribution and home delivery. An MBA with a penchant for academia, he had recently enrolled in UBC's Business Ph.D. Program. However, after he had rediscovered the idea, four more years in school gave way to the excitement of a new business start-up.

Mike Donald also asked a friend of the family with a history of high tech experience, Ken Deering, to come in and help create the system structure. Drayton came on board as President of Homegrocer, Donald as Executive Vice President. Donald and Drayton became equal partners; Deering, not having the financing of the others, remained on as an employee.

Financing Issues

Homegrocer began on a shoestring, with Mike Donald, Terry Drayton and seed investors funding the first $300,000. As the company business plan began to take shape, James Wilson approached private investors and VC firms in hopes of raising the approximately four million dollars the project required.

One impediment to financing the start-up was the initial choice of geographic location. Because the principals all resided in BC, Vancouver seemed a natural location for the company. However, potential investors disagreed. Donald explained,

> We went to San Francisco to a big trade show and we talked to some investment companies who said, "Yeah, that's a really good idea; where are you starting out?" We said, "Vancouver," and they said, "Why there?" We said, "Well, that's where we live." They would say, "Okay, whatever," and then off they would go, and we'd never see them again.

At one point, a potential institutional investor suggested that the same deal in a "techno-sexy" town, such as Seattle or Santa Barbara, would make the deal significantly more attractive. In addition, the favorable tax environment offered to firms (and resident employees) in the U.S. further enhanced the financial appeal of the deal. Donald observed,

> As soon as we changed it to Seattle, everybody perked up and loved the idea. We figured the U.S. was the place to be anyway, because in Canada there may be a handful of cities you can do well in, while in the U.S. there are hundreds.

Furthermore, Mike Donald was of the opinion that if they couldn't make the Homegrocer business work in the Seattle area, with its high proportion of Internet-adept, high tech-oriented workaholics, it seemed unlikely it would work anywhere.

Some of the initial financing was secured very creatively—by finding people who were willing to work for free initially. According to Donald,

> In October 1996, we brought in a few people who were out of work at the time. We were lucky to find a delivery guy who would work for nothing and accrue

his salary. There were software programmers who worked for nothing with the understanding that once we started to bring in some money, they would start getting paid. The project is so exciting and has so much potential that people wanted to volunteer. The consultant who came in to be our project manager we have now hired on permanently.

On more than one occasion, the firm was technically insolvent, and relied on small injections of equity from the principals, as well as services in kind from employees. However, the firm managed to stay afloat and the principals continued searching for a more permanent source of growth financing.

Drayton was able to arrange meetings with a number of VCs. The jewel was Kleiner Perkins, a highly respected high-technology venture capital firm. The merits of a "Kleiner" underwriting went well beyond the funding provided per se. The prestige and respect within the e-commerce and investment banking community that accrued from a Kleiner deal, often exceeded the actual financing provided, severalfold.

Kleiner did not come quickly, however. "These folks take the due diligence process pretty damn seriously," remarked Donald with a wry grin. In fact, the entire first round of financing was obtained through local "angel" investors, plus a major contribution from an Australian friend of Terry's, whom Terry had earlier helped with a business venture in Australia. The need for a major VC like Kleiner still existed, however. Eventually, Kliener completed its due diligence process and was satisfied Homegrocer would be a good investment. A special secondary round of financing was opened to accommodate them. As a result, more than twice the projected financing needs were raised. As it turned out, that was fortuitous, because the company experienced major cost overruns on its software development, and other parts of the business plan needed to be accelerated. As well, with Kleiner on board, Homegrocer's ability to raise more funds inexpensively in the future was greatly enhanced.

Start-up and Growth

Homegrocer was located near Seattle in Washington State partly because the local market contained one of the densest "wired" populations anywhere. Home to a host of high-tech firms led by Microsoft and Boeing, the Bellevue area provided an ideal testing ground to prove the new business model. Homegrocer opened for business in May 1998. Within a month it had acquired approximately 300 customers. A customer was defined as someone who ordered groceries online three times per month, and purchased at least $75 per order (orders under $75 were subject to a $10 delivery fee).

To break even, Mike Donald estimated that the company needed 4,000 such customers. Significant profitability would be achieved when the firm attained between 5,000 and 7,000 customers. Growth projections

EXHIBIT 3A Homegrocer's WebSite—Opening Page

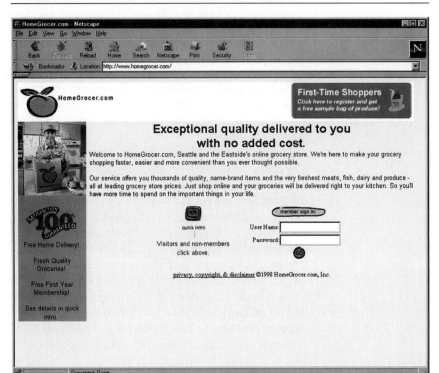

Source: http://www.homegrocer.com, November 1998.

were based on the current numbers drawn from the wired community as well as projected Internet usage growth over the next several years.

Homegrocer's five-year plan included opening 30 outlets across the U.S. Expansion was to begin up and down the West Coast, and then spread eastward. Donald expected that the expertise they developed in the initial Bellevue site would reduce both the start-up costs and the learning curve associated with each new location. Further, the proprietary back-end computer technology, as well as the firm's website, could be duplicated at very little cost, making additional location start-up costs dependent almost entirely on building and improvements.

Donald believed the greatest challenge to getting the necessary customer base was that each new customer acquisition required a very "deep sell." When asked to explain he responded,

Because it (ordering groceries online) is such a drastic change in behavior, it demands that you completely change a certain aspect of your way of life. Grocery shopping is not only enjoyable to some people but it's also pretty systemic. People go to the store not knowing what they want. They rely on

EXHIBIT 3B   Homegrocer's WebSite—Typical Grocery Shopping Page

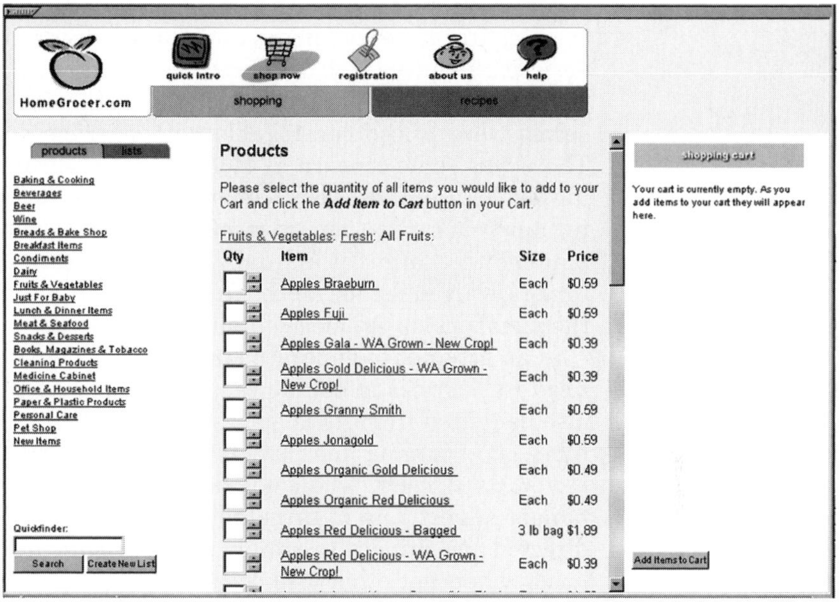

Source: http://www.homegrocer.com, November 1998.

the trip to the store to trigger whole patterns of behavior. A lot of people today would argue that couples with both people working would rather just sit at their terminal at work during their coffee break and click on your site . . . For sure, those people are easy to get. But if you're just a couple, you're not buying enough groceries to make it worthwhile. We need couples with families. Some of the findings that are coming out of other projects across the country are that people on the Internet shop three or four times and then they start to long for the grocery store experience, they miss it. You've got to be able to make the shopping experience fun and be able to bring new items out to people. The goal is to get three shops a month. If we can do that, we're successful.

The Homegrocer opening web page, at http://www.homegrocer.com, was quite simple. There was a dialogue box requesting a username and password for current customers, and there were hyperlinks directing prospective customers to both a signup page and a quick tour of the website. The rest of the site was designed as one might expect, with category hyperlinks, which, when clicked on, brought up individual category items. Some individual products were accompanied by a picture, while others were not. Exhibits 3A and 3B illustrate pages from the company's website.

The ideal customer for Homegrocer was a family of four. Such families were most likely to place individual grocery orders in excess of the $75 minimum. To encourage new customers to try out Homegrocer's service, first-time customers could order any quantity of groceries they desired and have them delivered free of charge. After that, Homegrocer charged a $10 delivery fee for orders less than $75. The groceries themselves were priced comparably with average walk-in grocery stores. There was some concern at Homegrocer regarding the effect of charging a substantial delivery fee for smaller deliveries, and the firm's pricing approach was a matter of continuing debate. Homegrocer also planned to charge an annual $35 membership fee, but to entice customers, waived the fee for the first year. Whether they would implement the membership fee idea remained to be seen.

In an attempt to generate traffic to the website, Homegrocer advertised its services in the newspaper as well as through direct mail. It also benefited from its large, easily identified delivery trucks (see Exhibit 1B) roaming the streets delivering groceries. Homegrocer directed its drivers, when not delivering groceries, to distribute door hanger advertising in targeted neighborhoods. They also occasionally directed the drivers to simply drive around the Belleview neighborhoods when not otherwise occupied, so people would see their trucks and become familiar with the logo and name. A smattering of other advertising options had been proposed, but none had been implemented yet, as management was unclear about which promotional options made sense for them.

Homegrocer also looked for ways to utilize the informational aspects of the Internet to better serve its customers. One idea they had implemented was the online recipe. A customer could create a personal recipe and save it on the Homegrocer site. Later, clicking on the recipe would automatically load all the necessary ingredients into the customer's shopping cart. Homegrocer also offered its own recipes that customers could try out.

Despite all these efforts, drawing in new customers had proven to be difficult. Consumers seemed reticent to try the service for the first time. There were several possible reasons for this. The first was that customers might be reluctant to transmit credit card information over the net. Second, there might be a general perception that groceries purchased online were not as fresh as groceries picked up at a store. A third reason was that customers might actually crave the shopping experience, and that a virtual shop precluded the enjoyable, impulsive, inspirational purchases made at a conventional grocery store.

It appeared to Donald that potential new customers had to visit the site several times before making the decision to sign up and try out the service.

EXHIBIT 4   Recent Forecasts About the Internet Grocery Business

---

Online Grocery Shopping Projections*
September 21, 1998

Analysts are predicting that online grocery shopping could be worth as much as US$1 billion by the year 2000. Andersen Consulting reckon that the market for groceries and retail items such as stamps and photographic services could reach US$85 billion by the year 2000.

Meanwhile in another case of disparate projections, Jupiter Communications predict that online grocery revenue will reach US$2.2 billion by 2000 while The Yankee Group put that figure at over US$6 billion.

Netsmart recently conducted research which showed that the primary reason people would shop online was for convenience (68 percent). Sixty-six percent were attracted by the idea of 24-hour access; 60 percent said it would save time; 57 percent said it would save money; and 47 percent were attracted by the idea of comparing prices from the comfort of a PC/web application.

---

*Excerpted from The Industry Standard: newsmagazine of The Internet Economy, *http://www.thestandard.com.*

Online Grocery Market Will Remain Tiny*
October 2, 1998

The sale of groceries online is predicted to generate US$10.8 billion by 2003 but the fledgling industry still has a long way to go before making an impact on the overall grocery market, according to Forrester Research.

While the amount of money that will be spent buying groceries online will increase dramatically on a year-to-year basis, by 2003 this will still only account for two percent of the whole grocery market.

Forrester noted that geographic location, lack of significant demand, delivery fees and a lack of stability in the market were factors impeding the growth of online grocery shopping. The market is expected to remain "tiny" for the next five years despite a projected 92 percent growth rate.

Convenience is the main attraction of online shopping and consumers will not be prepared to surf the Net for each brand item on their weekly shopping list.

Forrester predicts that sale of specialty goods online will overtake general grocery sales. As the majority of online consumers are in a high-income bracket, there is a healthy market for online luxury items. To realise profitable growth, online supermarkets will need to expand on their basic service and anticipate the consumer's every need.

---

*Excerpted from Forrester Research, *http://www.forrester.com.*

The Road Ahead

Recent studies by Forrester Research, Andersen Consulting, Jupiter Communications and The Yankee Capital group all pointed to rapid growth in the Internet grocery business (see Exhibit 4). Unfortunately, these studies did not indicate which approach would win the day. Were firms like Peapod, which piggybacked on existing conventional grocery stores, going to be the big winners? Or would firms like Netgrocer, dealing only in nonperishable goods but offering a wide range of products and servicing the entire country by shipping long distances, be the winners? Or was Homegrocer's approach, providing a full line of groceries via a lower-cost warehouse, the right solution? Or perhaps all three?

As July turned into August, Mike Donald wondered what lay ahead for the firm. Did their assumptions under this new business model still hold? Was the pricing model the right one? Would senior management's lack of IT experience, and the decision to outsource software development, prove to be a constraint down the road? Would financing for expansion continue to be as readily available in the future as it had been in the past? Finally, what would it take to get new customers to try the service in sufficient numbers, and subsequently become permanent customers? And these were only the obvious questions. Several more subtle issues lay just beneath the surface.

Auto-By-Tel and General Motors: David and Goliath

By Professor Soumitra Dutta, Professor Arnoud De Meyer, and Sudha Kunduri

Introduction

> *On the business side, we are looking at new ways to use information technology to sell and service our products. The World Wide Web certainly offers great promise as a "vehicle" for personalized relationship marketing to individual customers. And someday we may also be able to diagnose on-vehicle software problems and fix them via the Internet![1]*

Ken R. Baker, Vice President, GM Research and Development Center, Oct. 97[2]

In the early 90s the possibility of buying cars online was still in the realm of fiction. Most auto manufacturers considered it a futuristic retailing channel. Today, within just a span of a few years, customers are attracted to the numerous online engines which permit them to

---

[1] http://www.gm.com/about/info/overview/RD_center/websiter/intro/9710Kb_EdUM.html.

[2] Leadership for Technical Education and Training Conference, at the University of Michigan, on 9th October 1997.

buy the car of their choice, from the comfort of their homes at prices up to 10 percent lower than they would have got after tiring and lengthy negotiations with a traditional car salesman. In 1997, the Web accounted for approximately more than a fifth of all the car sales in America. These customers visited the dealerships only to pick up their cars after having completed the deal online. The Internet bug has really caught on and this percentage of online sales is only expected to rise each year to be around 50 percent by the turn of the century.[3]

General Motors, like its major manufacturing counterparts, is a recent convert to online retailing of automobiles. In October 1997, General Motor (GM) became the first auto manufacturer to create a consumer focused online service, called GM BuyPower. This initiative came, however, two years after Auto-By-Tel invented online automotive purchasing, in 1995. By 1998, Auto-By-Tel had helped well in excess of one million car buyers, through its free purchase request program and services, to obtain quotes from around 3,000 accredited dealers in America for new as well as used cars. The acknowledged industry leader, Auto-By-Tel is larger than the two other popular players, Car-Point and autoweb.com, combined.

The explosive growth of the Internet, the accelerating pace of new inventions and increased customer power are starting a potential revolution within the automobile industry. Internet intermediaries of the likes of Auto-By-Tel are posing a significant challenge to the existing model of distribution and retailing of automobiles. General Motors and other automobile manufacturers are only beginning to respond to the emerging dynamics of online automobile retailing. However, the initial feedback from consumers has been disappointing. Only about 200 GM vehicles were sold directly under GM BuyPower in the program's first 45 days.[4] The burning question for GM (and other automobile manufacturers) now is how to demonstrate appropriate leadership in Cyberspace and seize the initiative from dynamic Internet start-ups such as Auto-By-Tel.

IVEY This case was prepared by Sudha Kunduri, Visiting Research Associate at INSEAD under the supervision of Soumitra Dutta and Arnoud De Meyer, Professors of Technology Management at INSEAD. The case is intended to be used as a basis for class discussion, rather than to illustrate either effective or ineffective handling of an administrative situation.

Copyright © 1998 INSEAD, Fontainebleau, France.

Distributed by The European Case Clearing House, England and USA.

North America, phone: +1 781 239 5884, fax: +1 781 239 5885, e-mail: ECCHBabson@aol.com.

Rest of the World, phone: +44 (0) 1234 750903, fax: +44 (0) 1234 751125, e-mail: ECCI@cranfield.ac.uk.

All rights reserved. Printed in UK and USA. Web Site: http://www.ecch.cranfield.ac.uk.

---

[3]"Who Will Deal in Dealerships?" *Economist,* 14th Feb. 1997: http://www.economist.com.

[4]http://www.jrnl.com/news/98/Jan/jrn61090198.html.

General Motors: Company Background

While a major portion of GM's operations are derived from the automotive industry, GM also has financing and insurance operations, and produces products and provides services in other industries as well. GM participates in the automotive industry through the activities of its automotive business segments: GM-North American Operations (GM-NAO); Delphi Automotive Systems (Delphi); and GM International Operations (GMIO). GM-NAO designs, manufactures and markets vehicles primarily in North America under the following makes: Chevrolet, Pontiac, GMC, Oldsmobile, Buick, Cadillac and Saturn. GMIO meets the demands of the customers outside North America with vehicles designed, manufactured, and marketed under the following nameplates: Opel, Vauxhall, Holden, Isuzu, Saab, Chevrolet, GMC and Cadillac.

GM's principal competitors in passenger cars and trucks in the United States and Canada include Ford Motor Company, Chrysler Corporation, Toyota Corporation, Nissan Motor Corporation Ltd., Honda Motor Company Ltd., Mazda Motor Corporation, Mitsubishi Motor Corporation, Fuji Heavy Industries Ltd. (Subaru), Volkswagen A.G., Hyundai Motor Company Ltd., Daimler Benz A.G. (Mercedes), Bayerische Motoren Werke A.G. (BMW), and Volvo AB. All but Volkswagen and Hyundai currently operate vehicle manufacturing facilities in the US or Canada. Toyota and GM operate the New United Motor Manufacturing, Inc. facility in Fremont, California as a joint venture which currently builds passenger cars and light duty trucks.[5]

The Economist magazine recently commented on the challenges facing GM (in the late 1990s).[6]

> All empires contain the seeds of their own destruction. The ideas on which they were founded cannot adapt to changing times . . . Nowadays, General Motors' sole claim to imperial status is size: its 608,000 employees and $166 billion in sales . . . Today, GM pops up in management books only as an example of what not to do—blamed for not introducing products quickly enough, for poor labor relations and so on . . . the suspicion remains that the firm's leaders—all GM men practically since birth—still think that the firm is too big ever to lose its dominance.

Against this background, many experts cast reasonable doubt on the success of GM's attempts to forge a leadership position in Cyberspace.

---

[5]General Motors Corporation Annual Report on Form 10-K for the year ended December 31, 1997.

[6]"The Decline and Fall of General Motors," *The Economist,* October 10, 1998.

Auto Retailing: The Pot of Gold

Rampant competition in the automobile industry has driven all automobile manufacturers to launch numerous cost cutting measures, both in design and in operations. The literature [7] reports how Ford is even now redesigning its ashtrays yielding a paltry saving of *25 cents a vehicle.* What they are not seeing is that the Eldorado lies in fact, on the retail side of the business. Reported to be of the order of $600 billion a year, amounting to 25 percent of the average $22,000 price of every new car in the United States, this *$5,500* is clearly the car industry's *"pot of gold."*[8]

Car sales in the United States as well as in the rest of the world take place through retail dealers and distributors. The United States alone has more than 20,000 dealers. Substantially all of GM's automotive-related products are marketed through retail dealers and distributors. By December 31, 1997, there were approximately 8,500 GM vehicle dealers in the United States, 900 in Canada and Mexico, and 5,500 outlets in the rest of the world. Wholesale unit sales of GM passenger cars and trucks during the three years ended December 31, 1997 are summarized in Exhibit 1.

The industry's inefficient sales and distribution model is also an aggravating factor that amplifies the antagonism between auto buyers and sellers. There are many causes for the discord—from the sharp competition between dealers to the high costs of financing inventory, supporting commissioned salespeople, and paying for advertising. This has resulted in several attempts to reconfigure the auto retailing business:

Consolidators: Financial consortiums from outside the auto industry (and in some cases, groups of local dealers) have tried to accrue economies of scale by integrating dealerships and getting them to operate together. For example, United Auto Group controls US$3.6 billion sales per year and Republic Industries records US$12 billion in sales per year.[9]

Car superstores: Used-car mega-stores like Huizenga's AutoNation and Circuit City's CarMax have made a big impact on car retailing. Price tags are equitable and customers have a vast choice of vehicles without the overhead of haggling with the salesman. These superstores typically pay salaries proportional to customers' satisfaction with their service, instead of commissions.[10]

---

[7]"Who Will Deal in Dealerships?" *Economist,* 14th Feb. 1997: http://www.economist.com.
[8]"Who Will Deal in Dealerships?" *Economist,* 14th Feb. 1997: http://www.economist.com.
[9]"Who Will Deal in Dealerships?" *Economist,* 14th Feb. 1997: http://www.economist.com.
[10]http://www.arktimes.com/022098coverstory.htm.

EXHIBIT 1   Wholesale Unit/Sales of GM Passenger Cars and Trucks

Vehicle Unit Deliveries of Cars and Trucks (units in thousands)

	1997			1996			1995		
	Industry	GM	GM as % of Industry	Industry	GM	GM as % of Industry	Industry	GM	GM as % of Industry
United States									
Cars	8,289	2,689	32.4%	8,528	2,786	32.7%	8,636	2,956	34.2%
Trucks	7,210	2,077	28.8%	6,931	2,007	29.0%	6,484	1,939	29.9%
Total US	15,499	4,766	30.8%	15,459	4,793	31.0%	15,120	4,895	32.4%
Canada	1,424	451	31.7%	1,203	381	31.7%	1,165	385	33.0%
Mexico	496	143	28.8%	332	89	26.8%	232	48	20.7%
Total North America	**17,419**	**5,360**	**30.8%**	**16,994**	**5,263**	**31.0%**	**16,517**	**5,238**	**32.3%**
International									
Europe									
Germany	3,790	565	14.9%	3,746	581	15.5%	3,575	581	16.3%
United Kingdom	2,445	339	13.9%	2,282	328	14.4%	2,195	334	15.2%
Other West Europe	8,937	807	9.0%	8,444	780	9.2%	7,847	751	9.6%
Total West Europe									
Central/East Europe	2,979	133	4.5%	2,405	100	4.2%	2,102	58	2.8%
Total Europe	**18,151**	**1,844**	**10.2%**	**16,877**	**1,789**	**10.6%**	**15,719**	**1,724**	**11.0%**
Latin America, Africa and Middle East (LAAME)									
Brazil	1,942	410	21.1%	1,731	384	22.2%	1,728	348	20.1%
Venezuela	173	48	27.7%	68	16	23.5%	89	28	31.5%
Other Latin America	1,155	165	14.3%	1,036	143	13.8%	999	127	12.7%
Total Latin America	**3,270**	**623**	**19.1%**	**2,835**	**543**	**19.2%**	**2,816**	**503**	**17.9%**
Africa	663	101	15.2%	681	81	11.9%	633	86	13.6%
Middle East	691	52	7.5%	664	66	9.9%	560	58	10.4%
Total LAAME	**4,624**	**776**	**16.8%**	**4,180**	**690**	**16.5%**	**4,009**	**647**	**16.1%**
Asia and Pacific									
Australia	726	127	17.5%	651	131	20.1%	642	129	20.1%
Other Asia and Pacific	12,624	458	3.6%	13,081	494	3.8%	12,554	490	3.9%
Total Asia and Pacific	**13,350**	**585**	**4.4%**	**13,732**	**625**	**4.6%**	**13,196**	**619**	**4.7%**
Total International	36,125	3,205	8.9%	34,789	3,104	8.9%	32,924	2,990	9.1%
TOTAL WORLD	**54,276**	**5,049**	**9.3%**	**51,666**	**4,893**	**9.5%**	**48,043**	**4,714**	**9.7%**

Source: General Motors Corporation Annual Report on Form 10-K, year ended Dec. 1997.

Manufacturer initiatives: Automobile manufacturers are also selectively consolidating their dealerships. However, they fear that these consolidated superstores could become more powerful and demand price cuts and other concessions and perhaps even begin selling cars from other manufacturers. For example, Ford in partnerships with local dealers is consolidating (in some states) existing showrooms into a smaller number of superstores, with separate local service centers close to where people work or live. The dealers keep majority ownership, and licensed salespeople continue to sell cars.

Auto Dealerships: A Changing Business

Almost all over the world, dealerships are generally small businesses which have been started with a small capital and with minimal experience (and interest) in new technologies. In order to protect their businesses, these entrepreneurs have used local political influence to create legal barriers: for example, laws inhibiting manufacturers from setting up competing outlets and preventing them from selling direct to customers. These laws are a blocking factor in the transformation of the auto retailing industry.

Dealers' profits fell in 1997, to an all-time low of 1.5 percent of the total sales (the net profit per new vehicle sold in America being down to around US$300). New cars, which used to account for a bulk of the profits in yesteryears now account for less than 10 percent.[11] The focus of the retail business has now shifted to selling used cars,[12] servicing and financing.

It is becoming harder for dealers to make money and they are losing market share to Internet start-ups and used car selling giants like AutoNation and CarMax. Free Internet pricing sites listing dealer cost and Manufacturer Suggested Retail Price (MSRP) are increasingly shielding customers from dealers' tactics. Dealers are facing more informed consumers. An educated consumer "helps" the dealer shorten the negotiation process at the cost of reduced margins. Ron Claudon Jr., general manager and co-owner of Valley Pontiac-Buick-GMC in Auburn, Wash., and a participant in GM's BuyPower notes:[13]

> If the Internet dominates, the salesperson will become the automotive liaison and juggle the service needs for the consumer.

Though almost every auto dealer in America has ventured into Cyberspace with his own home page, the lion's share of the online retailing business has been captured by Internet middlemen such as

---

[11]"Who Will Deal in Dealerships?" *Economist,* 14th Feb. 1997: http://www.economist.com.

[12]Used car sales exceed new car sales by about a factor of 3.

[13]http://adage.com/interactive/articles/19970915/article2.html.

Auto-By-Tel. This phenomenon is paradoxical since most believed that the Internet with its freely available information would foster direct contact between seller and buyer. However, smart new intermediaries such as Auto-By-Tel are discovering new ways to add value to customers. Auto-By-Tel customer, Brad Saviello, of Atlanta, Georgia notes:

> I had been bargaining for a car with a local dealer for two days and was within US$800 of the invoice price listed in the "Net." Before I committed to the deal, I decided to try Auto-By-Tel after reading an article in *Inc.* or *Success*. To my surprise, I was contacted within two hours of submitting my request and was offered the same car I had been negotiating for US$100 over invoice by another local dealer. In addition, the financing rate was 0.4 percent better than either of the banks I normally use. The whole process took all of one day. Amazing! The total savings between the sale price reduction and the interest savings over the life of the car are almost US$1260. Thanks![14]

Auto-By-Tel

> *We're going to give the customer a proficient purchase process that will deliver the lowest price and the least amount of stress they've ever had purchasing an automobile.*

> Auto-By-Tel Co-founder and Chief Executive Officer Peter Ellis[15]

Pete Ellis' radical concept of online automotive buying and selling has won acclaim from both analysts and journalists as having completely redefined car retailing. Within two years of its inception, in June 1997, Auto-By-Tel was nominated the 4th Fastest Growing New Small Business in America by Dun & Bradstreet and Entrepreneur Magazine.[16] Before establishing Auto-By-Tel, Ellis himself owned and operated 16 dealerships and other automotive businesses, credentials that he has in common with many of Auto-By-Tel's top executives. This gives the company's leadership a unique understanding of both the dealer's and the customer's requirements.

ABT's Strategy to Success: Innovative Expansion
An October 1996 J.D. Power study of new vehicle buyers in the United States found that 68 percent had and used computers. The same study revealed that high-income households accounted for 55 percent of new vehicle sales, a number that's expected to reach 66 percent in the year

---

[14]http://www.autobytel.com/index.cfm.

[15]http://www.popularmechanics.com/popmech/auto2/98CBG/98CBGFBM.html.

[16]http://www.autobytel.com/index.cfm.

EXHIBIT 2 Auto-By-Tel's Phenomenal Growth

	Q2, 1996	Q3, 1996	Q4, 1996	Q1, 1997	Q2, 1997	Q3, 1997	Q4, 1997	Feb., 1998
New Vehicle Purchase Requests Filed	100,000	200,000	350,000	650,000	870,000	1,000,000	1,000,000	1,500,000
Auto-By-Tel Accredited Dealer Franchises	1,400	1,400	1,400	1,600	1,900	2,600	2,700	2,700

Source: Auto-By-Tel's website.

2000. Since high-income households typically own computers, Power concluded that "Auto-By-Tel dealers had the tiger by the tail."[17]

Ellis launched Auto-By-Tel on the Web in 1995, with only four employees, from a small office in Corona-del-Mar. After about a week, the upstart firm had around 2,000 new car purchase requests.[18] Purchase requests increased dramatically in 1996 and 1997, and Auto-By-Tel has today become a serious force to contend with in the US$600 billion per year new/used car retailing industry (see Exhibit 2).

Auto-By-Tel has revolutionized the way cars are bought and sold. The company is using technology, via the Internet, to change the way the automotive industry works. Exhibit 3 illustrates the process used at Auto-By-Tel to carry out a sale. All that the consumer needs is a connection to the Internet and to provide some basic information about himself and the vehicle of his choice. Access to Auto-By-Tel web site is without charge to the consumer and comes without any attached strings, no obligations, no hidden fees and no clubs to join. Auto-By-Tel eliminates the intimidation often found at dealerships, including unpleasant negotiations with multiple layers of salespeople and managers. Links from the Auto-By-Tel site provide easy access to the top automotive information sources such as AutoSite, Kelley Blue Book, Edmund's and IntelliChoice. Known to provide comprehensive unbiased automotive information, these third-party resources allow the client to query and obtain information on the vehicle of his interest. In addition, Auto-By-Tel puts out a Weekly AutoMarket Report, which contains advertisements, incentives and rebates announced by manufacturers as well as articles from top automotive journalists.

---

[17]http://www.theautochannel.com:8080/news/date/19961101/news02420.html.
[18]Auto-By-Tel press release, Irvine, CA, December 16, 1996, http://www.autobytel.com/dec16.cfm.

EXHIBIT 3   ABT's Car Purchase Process

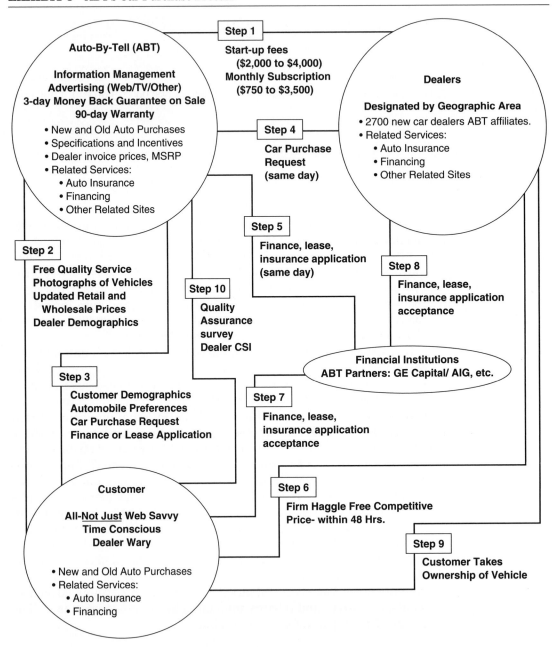

Once the buyer is in agreement with the offer or quote made by ABT's dealer, and consents to its financing options, all the paperwork and other formalities are already completed upon his arrival at the dealership and he can drive away with his chosen car in less than an hour! Notes Auto-By-Tel customer, Michelle V. Goldstein:[19]

> I can't believe this! Yesterday afternoon at 4:15 I found out about Auto-By-Tel—by 7:00 p.m. I received a call from the dealer and at 11:00 a.m. this morning I picked up the car I really wanted and paid a great price—I don't think I have ever been this satisfied, in the many years that I have been purchasing cars.

Ever since its inception, ABT has grown through the introduction of new and innovative services made possible by strategic alliances with partners on and off the Web in the auto industry, achieving a growth rate extraordinary even by the Internet's standards:

Auto-By-Tel rolled out its Certified Used Car CyberStore in March 1997. A sophisticated CyberStore search function enables consumers to find and purchase high-quality used cars by employing geographical area, make, model, price, class, and year of vehicle as search criteria. The CyberStore only stocks used vehicles that have been put through a severe 135-point dealer Certification Program designed to protect consumers. Auto-By-Tel's confidence in the Used Car CyberStore vehicles is backed with a 72-hour 100 percent Money-Back Return Policy and a 3 Month/3,000 Mile Home-and-Away Warranty from its Accredited CyberStore dealers. A travel repair service is available throughout the United States and Canada via the Auto-By-Tel Accredited Dealer Network.[20]

In December 1997, ABT, introduced FasTrakSM, a innovative tool through which buyers could initiate their search directly from the ABT home page. If users went out of the Auto-By-Tel site using any of the connected links, a framed version of FasTrakSM appeared on the screen. This allowed users to use the facility while exploring ABT's associate sites. This leveraged ABT's strength of numerous strategic partnerships with many of the top visited sites including Infoseek, CNN, Excite, GeoCities, AT&T WorldNet Services and NBC Interactive.[21]

ABT continued to innovate when it launched, in April 1998, Mobalist Rewards. This program is similar to a frequent-flyer program, but

---

[19]http://www.autobytel.com/backgrounder.cfm.

[20]Auto-By-Tel press release, Washington, DC, April 28, 1997, http://www.autobytel.com/april28.cfm.

[21]Auto-By-Tel press release, IRVINE, CA, December 9, 1997, http://www.autobytel.com/971209.cfm.

instead of earning frequent-flyer miles, cardholders earn points that can be used as an additional rebate toward their next vehicle.[22]

Auto-By-Tel is the only online automotive purchasing program that has made traditional advertising a key element of its overall marketing plan. Auto-By-Tel made history in 1997 as the first Internet commerce company to advertise on the Super Bowl. Within minutes of the commercial's airing, Auto-By-Tel's web traffic increased dramatically. Pete Ellis, President and CEO of Auto-By-Tel noted:[23]

> The numbers are incredible. Within minutes after the commercial aired, we were tracking a 1,700 percent increase in website traffic and an amazing 93 percent increase in Purchase Requests for new and used cars.

Auto-By-Tel's Auxiliary Services

Auto-By-Tel also provides supplementary services such as options for vehicle financing and insurance, making it a truly one-stop shopping site for total vehicle purchase solutions. It was joined by the American International Group (AIG), the leading U.S.-based international insurance in August 1996 for providing low-cost car buying and auto insurance. Auto-By-Tel's financing and leasing division, ABTAC (Auto-By-Tel Acceptance Corporation) opened for business in February 1997. By April 1997, ABTAC enabled consumers to apply for low-cost financing through Chase Auto Finance, Key Corporation, and Triad Financial. ABT added the low-cost leasing feature through GE Capital, in August the same year. Randy Ellspermann, Chief Operating Officer of Auto-By-Tel Acceptance Corporation added:[24]

> Car shoppers tend to comparison shop the price of a new car, but rarely do they think to do the same with financing. We want consumers to be aware that the cost of financing can greatly impact the cost of the car. At Auto-By-Tel's website, car buyers can shop and compare ABTAC's financing using independent sources to determine the lowest rates.

Once again, by emphasizing the ease of use of their feature, ABT made purchasing and financing simple and secure. After researching their vehicle of choice and comparing financing rates with the Bank Rate Monitor, car buyers can submit an optional credit application along with their Purchase Request. The application is then transmitted to the lender whose approval is sent back to both the customer and the

---

[22]Auto-By-Tel press release, New York, NY, April 8, 1998, http://www.autobytel.com/MobalistApril98.cfm.

[23]Auto-By-Tel press release, IRVINE, CA, January 27, 1998, http://www.autobytel.com/980127.cfm.

[24]Auto-By-Tel press release, Irvine, CA, June 9, 1997, http://www.autobytel.com/june9.cfm.

Auto-By-Tel Accredited Dealer (see Exhibit 3). A double firewall and state-of-the-art encryption technology ensures system security as well as the privacy of the customer's personal financial information. ABT claims that the pre-approved financing through ABTAC and vehicle delivery at an Auto-By-Tel Accredited Dealer takes less than an hour. Peter Ellis describes it as:[25]

> What better complement to no-hassle car buying than no-hassle financing. Car buyers want to avoid any frustrations and delays at the dealership level; no one likes to sit around while their credit is being scrutinized. With ABTAC Online Financing, approvals can come within minutes after the credit application is submitted. It's free, it's easy and the rates are great.

Transforming Dealership Rules

Auto-By-Tel builds and works continuously with its Accredited Dealer Network to transform the traditional sales model. Dealers accredited by ABT establish an Auto-By-Tel Department where an ABT Manager, not a traditional salesperson, receives the client. According to Mark Lorimer, Auto-By-Tel's Chief Operating Officer, the no-haggle policy among its dealers attracts customers to their web site. ABT dealers subscribe to the program (to access what is essentially a customer referral service) by paying US$2,000 to US$4,000 in start-up fees in addition to US$750 to US$3,500 a month. To ensure quality service and top attention to the information-empowered Internet consumer, Auto-By-Tel pre-qualifies its Accredited Dealers and provides them with extensive training, including coaching at its exclusive Auto-By-Tel University! Ellis believes much of Auto-By-Tel's dealers' satisfaction is owed to its extensive dealer training programs (21 regional sessions each month) which are designed to specifically educate dealers on reducing costs and passing that reduction on to Internet consumers.[26]

Using a Microsoft SQL Server database Auto-By-Tel has implemented a customized user interface that allows clients to access an ABT dealer's inventory. Accredited Dealers are connected on the back end through a proprietary Dealer Real Time Communications System, launched in February 1997, enabling instantaneous communication. In addition, Auto-By-Tel employs a quality assurance application that monitors dealerships for response time and consumer satisfaction. All dealers are required to maintain high CSIs (customer satisfaction index). The moment the customer makes a Purchase/Lease Request, it is

---

[25]Auto-By-Tel press release, Irvine, CA, June 9, 1997, http://www.autobytel.com/june9.cfm.

[26]Software Magazine, Dec. 1997, Electronic Commerce, http://www.sentrytech.com/97issues/Dec97/sml27f6.htm.

transmitted automatically to the dealers who subscribe to the Real Time system. This results in prompt customer service and an increase in sales productivity. Each dealer is also guaranteed exclusive access to a geographic region by assuring a limited number of affiliated dealerships.

All this has made Auto-By-Tel the leader among online buying services, according to the "J.D. Power and Associates 1998 Dealer Satisfaction With Online Buying Services Study". The Power study also shows dealers marketing through online buying services report lower advertising costs per unit than with traditional advertising. Auto-By-Tel estimates that its service cuts dealer overhead US$900–US$1,100 per car in advertising, staff salaries and sales commissions. Average new car dealers typically make US$1,800 to US$2,500 gross profit per car, while Auto-By-Tel dealers make just a few percentage points because of their focus on low sale prices.[27] Nevertheless, even though Auto-By-Tel's dealer revenue is assessed to lie only between US$300 and US$500 per car, it implies far more significant profits when lower costs and larger sales volumes of about 12–25 cars a month are taken into consideration.

Capturing the After-Market Segment

In February 1998, AT&T completed the Internet car buying equation by adding to its repertoire an after-market sales service and an extended warranty program: Auto-By-Tel Platinum Plus Service Agreements. With this announcement ABT filled a gap in easy accessible information about after market products including accessories like roof racks, custom wheels, and security systems. ABT research suggested that customers wary of the traditional sales channels for these type of products would be attracted to their new service. Even dealers stood to gain by saving on the sales personnel overheads for keeping these accessories in their product range. Third-party vendors were undercutting dealer prices, thus cannibalizing dealer sales in this segment. With Auto-By-Tel's after-market program, Accredited Dealers would be able to reduce overheads, because the customer is now buying financing and after-market products online without the traditional sales pressure, and thus re-capture that customer's business. The Auto-By-Tel Platinum Plus Service Agreements allow consumers to build an extended warranty product in accordance with their individual coverage and pricing needs—before going to the dealership. In accordance with other ABT services, the consumer is in complete control of the car-buying process.

---

[27]Auto-By-Tel press release, Corona del Mar, CA, January 15, 1996, http://www.-autobytel.com/jan15.cfm.

Sustaining Growth and Globalization

After three successful years in the United States and Canada, ABT is now moving into Europe. In February 1998 it announced the formation of Auto-By-Tel International and the launch of Auto-By-Tel U.K. Scheduled to launch by the end of 1998, Auto-By-Tel U.K. is in the process of finalizing its business model for the U.K. market.

Given the high penetration rate of the Internet in Nordic countries, Auto-By-Tel has entered into an investment agreement with Sweden-based Bilia AB which will have majority ownership in Auto-By-Tel Nordic. Bilia will have the rights to market Auto-By-Tel's businessconcept and technology in the four Nordic markets (Sweden, Norway, Denmark and Finland) and have access to its base of experience from the United States and other countries. Auto-By-Tel International has also identified France, Germany, Japan and Brazil as potential markets.[28]

GM's Response to Auto-By-Tel's Challenge

Unwilling to give away its business to independent third-party sources like Auto-By-Tel who promote loyalty to the hassle free process, not to a particular automotive brand, General Motors went online, unveiling its "GM BuyPower"[29] program in October 1997. This made them the first auto manufacturer to provide integrated consumer-focused online services. GM's BuyPower has been initially made available in California, Idaho, Oregon and Washington.

GM BuyPower users can easily compare features on more than a 100 of GM's current models. In addition the GM BuyPower location also provides numerous customer-oriented services. The site is intended to help GM target its brand, to draw traffic and encourage repeat visits through creative and impressive design that communicates memorable messages.

GM BuyPower attempts to put the consumer in the drivers' seat (see Exhibit 4). The car purchase process consists of a few simple steps.[30]

Step 1: The opening page clearly illustrates what the prospective buyer can do at the site and the steps, literally, required to search the General Motors product line for cars and light trucks. One can easily find the GM vehicles that match the buyer's criteria by using the search function.

---

[28]Auto-By-Tel press release, Irvine, CA, May 11, 1998, http://www.autobytel.com/980128.cfm.

[29]http://www.eds.com/97annual/fcs/fcs_gm_buypower.shtml.

[30]http://www.gmbuypower.com/cgi_bin/setframe.pl?about.

EXHIBIT 4   GM BuyPower website html page

Welcome to GM BuyPower

The new and truly remarkable way to shop for and ultimately purchase a new car. Put simply there's no quicker or easier way to acquire the vehicle of your choice. GM BuyPower will guide you through every step.

Step 1. **Find a Car**
Over 130 different models of cars and trucks

Step 2. **Compare to the Competition**
Save hours of research with 3rd party price and feature comparisons

Step 3. **Search Dealer Inventory**
Locate the vehicle you want at the dealer of your choice

Step 4. **Make an Online Request**
Schedule a test drive, hold a vehicle, and get the single best price with easy online message forms

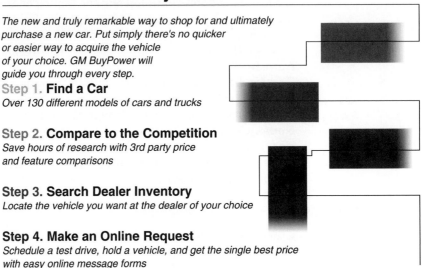

Step 2: The purchaser can make his own feature-for-feature comparisons between any GM car and comparable models from other companies. This bench-marking by an independent third party adds a lot of credibility to the information at the site and helps create trust.

Step 3: From any vehicle detail page, the customer has the ability to locate a Certified GM BuyPower dealer and search their inventory to determine the availability of the specific model. Customers have the option of selecting a specific dealer or can allow the system to select the three closest dealers.

Step 4: The final step in the GM BuyPower buying process facilitates the face to face interaction to actually complete a transaction and deliver a car. Buyers can take a test drive once they have the confidence that they are truly interested in the product. Dealers can focus on providing the best service they can because the "price haggling" factor has been removed from the sales equation.

GM's dealer subscription and franchising policies are constructed differently than those of ABT. GM proposed to include dealers on the system free of charge for the first six months and subsequently charge a periodic fee. GM produces and maintains the web site, and also monitors the operation. More than half (about 59 percent) of GM dealers in the four test states have signed up for GM BuyPower. When a dealer signs up, GM provides electronic links to their websites. The auto-maker also provides free Internet training for dealers. Ron Clauden, Jr., of Valley Pontiac-GMC-Buick in Auburn, Wash., was one of the dealers GM consulted in creating the program. He notes:[31]

> If providing information this way frees up one of our salespeople to focus on selling a car, then it's worth the effort.

The Reaction from Other Manufacturers

Following GM's pioneering venture to attract customers through its presence on the Web, other automobile manufacturers rapidly entered the Cyberspace arena. In early 1997, Chrysler inaugurated its Get a Quote web site, accessible initially only to buyers in California and Maryland. Through Ford's pilot Virtual Shopping Service launched in June the same year, factory price quotes and credit approval are available to customers online. George Hanley, Chevrolet's strategic manager for online projects notes:[32]

> We're looking at the Internet as more than just an advertising tool. It allows us to talk directly with consumers.

Toyota's in-house web guru, Jim Pisz adds:[33]

> The Internet has become our second-largest source of leads, right behind inbound telemarketing.

In spite of the race to embrace the Net, most auto-makers' e-commerce sites fail to provide web-savvy customers with the information they need and have come to expect. For example, they do not link web shoppers to the Kelley Blue Book or other resources where they could conduct price comparisons. Nor do they supply information on dealer invoice prices, manufacturer discounts, or other sales incentives. Instead, they merely post the suggested retail price (MSRP).

In fact, this may stem off from the fact that the intent of car makers behind putting their sites online, is distinct with respect to independent third-party retailers like ABT. Chrysler spokesman McKesson notes:[34]

> We see the Internet at this point as a channel that allows us to make contact with customers we might not have access to otherwise and put them in contact with our sales channels. But we do not see the Internet as a direct sales tool. Buying a car is not like buying a stereo or television. It's much more

---

[31]http://adage.com/interactive/articles/19970915/article2.html.

[32]http://www.popularmechanics.com/popmech/auto2/98CBG/98CBGFBM.html.

[33]http://www.popularmechanics.com/popmech/auto2/98CBG/98CBGFBM.html.

[34]http://hpcc940.external.hp.com/Ebusiness/october/index_auto.html.

emotional. It would be very difficult to dispose of a trade-in vehicle online. Or, for that matter, to test-drive a new vehicle.

Larry Dale, a Ford Motor Co. online marketing specialist and web-master says:[35]

> Not many people will spend US$20,000 or US$30,000 without looking, touching and feeling. Can you work out the mechanics of selling cars over the Internet? Sure, but I don't think that's the issue. People still want to see what they're buying. They want to go for a test drive. We have 5,000 dealers offering sales and service to customers throughout the U.S. Our job is to support them. You don't jeopardize the largest part of the equation for the sake of another, smaller part.

Another manager from Ford questioned the viability of the business model of new cyber-intermediaries such as Auto-By-Tel:

> One-off arrangements to sell vehicles, such as those done by Auto-By-Tel, are not sustainable in the long term. The life cycle cost of owning a car is typically three times the purchase cost. During this life cycle, the actual purchase of the new car is the least profitable element. We are going after a lifetime relationship where we build an extended set of relationships with customers.

However, auto manufacturers are doing little to utilize the richness of the information interface via the Internet with customers. They typically view the Web as an adjunct layer to the traditional distribution system. There is little integration of customer preferences and requirements into product design processes and production planning schedules.

Feedback from the GM BuyPower Pilot

Since September 1997, when GM BuyPower went online, the site has had 10.5 million visitors, and 240,000 of them have stayed an average of 13 minutes. However, the company has acknowledged that GM BuyPower was not as easy to use as it should have been,[36] and did not generate as many sales as originally hoped.[37] Only about 200 GM vehicles were sold directly under GM BuyPower in the program's first 45 days. These problems have caused GM to delay the nation-

---

[35]http://hpcc940.external.hp.com/Ebusiness/october/index_auto.html.

[36]For example, it requires every visit to the site to follow a precise route, something awkward for an Internet-savvy surfer.

[37]http://www.jrnl.com/news/98/Feb/jrn156270298.html.

wide roll-out of BuyPower. Lyle Pennington, Buick Western Regional Manager noted:[38]

> We have not had as many online shoppers as we anticipated. It has not been up to expectations, and if we are to roll it out nationally, it needs to be a significant piece of our business.

GM hopes BuyPower eventually will account for as much as 30 percent of GM's sales. And a rocky start will not deter BuyPower's long-term mission as noted by Lyle Pennington:[39]

> We might have to change the emphasis and focus, but we'll be on the Internet. The Internet is here to stay. We wouldn't be investing the amount we're investing if we wanted it to be just 5 percent of our business.

The trial program is not a total failure either. BuyPower averages about 2,300 interactive sessions with consumers daily, averaging about 11 minutes each. For comparison, Chrysler Corp.'s trial Get a Quote Web program gets about 20,000 hits nationally per week. However, for GM and other auto-makers, hits are not nearly as desired as web sessions in which more information is exchanged.

In spite of the success of its site with respect to sites put up by rival auto manufacturers, GM's BuyPower has largely failed to lure away customers from new Internet intermediaries such as Auto-By-Tel. In a bid to increase the popularity of its site and make it more efficient as a source of revenue, GM re-engineered it as a part of its Internet marketing plan. In early 1998, they tried to capture more mileage out of the information potential of their page through a new functionality called the "Shopping Kit" which allowed visitors to customize the "ideal" vehicle. This prompted the potential buyer to invest little time and gave GM data on popular user choices, colors, options etc. GM also introduced a feature permitting the consumer to have a one to one dialogue on the Net with a dealer.

Creating the Future

> *I don't think automakers will use the Internet to try to sell cars directly. Most people want to see the car, feel the car, test-drive the car. The dealerships are the ones that inventory the cars. And dealers carry the cost of transporting those cars.*[40]
>
> Peter Kitzmiller, Director of Regulatory Affairs,
> National Automobile Dealers Association

---

[38]html http://www.jml.com/news/98/Jan/jm61090198.html.

[39]http://www.jml.com/news/98/Jan/jm61090198.html.

[40]Software Magazine, Dec. 1997, Electronic Commerce, http://www.sentrytech.com/97issues/Dec97/sml27f6.htm.

EXHIBIT 5   Fall in U.S. New Car Dealerships

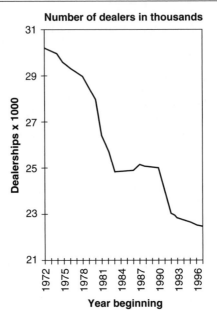

Source: © *The Economist,* London, February 14, 1998.

> *If you can see that going on the Web will increase your sales by 50 percent, then you're going to tailor your process to get that extra profit out of the system. If it's purely a gimmick and it's only going to raise profits by, say, 10 percent, then it doesn't make sense at all to change your supply-chain model.[41]*

> Claire Gooding, a U.K.-based analyst with Ovum

Automotive retailing is clearly in a state of turmoil. About 850 American dealerships have disappeared since 1992, and the number of survivors will probably halve to around 11,000 over the next five years (see Exhibit 5). Several questions are relevant in this context:

- What will be catalyst for radical change—both among dealers and automobile manufacturers?
- How will the different players in automotive retailing (manufacturers, dealers, consolidators, Internet intermediaries and consumers) converge towards the elusive "pot of gold" squeezing out the inefficiencies in the retailing and distribution of automobiles?

---

[41]Software Magazine, Dec. 1997, Electronic Commerce, http://www.sentrytech.com/97issues/Dec97/sml27f6.htm.

- What kind of a role will the Web play in building a "relationship over a lifetime" with customers?
- How will the role of dealers evolve as online commerce becomes increasingly commonplace?
- How should automobile manufacturers react to dynamic Internet start-ups such as Auto-By-Tel?

Automobile dealers and manufacturers are observing the trends in the Internet game but have not yet made any concrete moves to radically transform their business. Compounding this "wait and see" attitude is the fact that GM and other manufacturers probably lack the organizational dynamism for change. Notes the *Economist:*[42]

> . . . the one area where GM's managers have often not been brutal enough is in their own ranks. For years, the car maker was known by its white-collar workers as "Generous Motors." The "layer of clay" made up by GM's middle management has actively resisted many changes.

---

[42]"The Decline and Fall of General Motors," *The Economist,* October 10th, 1998.

Looks.com (A): Building Asia's First Health, Beauty and Fashion E-Tailer

By Professor John Hullard and Donna Everatt

Ian Smith, founder and managing director of looks.com, a soon-to-be-launched Asian e-commerce site for brand name cosmetics, fragrances, skin-care and fashion products, had just finished a video conference with his buyer, Robbie Jessel. Their discussion had, as usual, focused on how to attract brand name manufacturers of health and beauty products to list their goods for sale on looks.com.

Smith was very pleased with the development of his concept to date. Looks.com had been tremendously well received among the investment and Internet community. As a matter of fact, Smith had secured so much seed capital that in order to retain his target equity level in the company, he had been forced to return the last few subscriptions of US$100,000 each. Partnerships had been established with some of the most highly recognized global Internet brands, including AOL, Netscape, Hongkong.com, China.com, and Taiwan.com. An internationally renowned and award-winning web design firm had designed a splashy, professional, and well laid-out site, and Smith had attracted a highly talented and experienced team of professionals to support it. He had a solid first-mover advantage, and was poised to launch looks.com within weeks to capitalize on the 1999 Christmas shopping rush. The biggest challenge that the start-up company now faced was attracting vendors to list their products on the site.

Jessel had already successfully attracted the attention of several key brand names. However, in order for looks.com to really take off, it was imperative that many other major brands agree to list their products on the site as well. Smith and Jessel were confident that looks.com offered strong competitive advantages over traditional retailers. Their job now was to persuade manufacturers and consumers alike of this conviction.

The Internet Industry in Asia Heading into the Next Millennium

The e-commerce boom experienced in the U.S. was expected to hit Asia with full force in 2000. "While 1998 was the year that online shopping first rose to prominence in the U.S., the 1999 holiday season is shaping up to be the launching point for an expansion of global consumer e-commerce" according to a senior analysis for the Gartner Group, a high profile Internet consulting firm.

It was estimated that in 1999 there were between 20 million to 30 million Internet users throughout the Asia-Pacific region (almost half of whom were located in Japan) (see Exhibit 1). Though growth of the Internet had surged from a year earlier—up from 8.6 million users in 1997—this number accounted for only about 15 percent of the world's total Internet-user population.[1] Internet usage in the region, however, was expected to rise significantly in the foreseeable future, most markedly as consumers became less skeptical of e-commerce (something that was expected as sites offered better customer service). There remained the outstanding issues of security (a key concern globally with regard to e-commerce) and a relatively less developed e-commerce infrastructure to support credit card payment as well.[2] Thus, in 1999,

---

[1]Despite the fact that almost half of the world's population lived in the region.

[2]Specifically, many Asian-based websites still did not have payment gateways—electronic paths that directed credit-card charges to the card's bank, from an electronic site, which made sites more secure. Without an electronic payment gateway, customer service representatives typed credit card numbers into a terminal, which then relayed the data to a bank.

EXHIBIT 1   Industry Statistics

Growth in Number of Internet Users

1997 — 8.6 million
1998 — 14 million
1999 — 20 million
2000e — 26 million
2001e — 35 million
2002e — 48 million

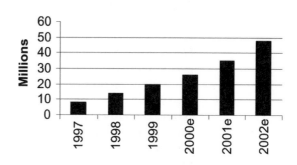

Internet Spending in Asia

1998 — US$ 700 million
2003 — US$ 32 billion

Source: IDC, GS estimates

E-COMMERCE REVENUES IN ASIA

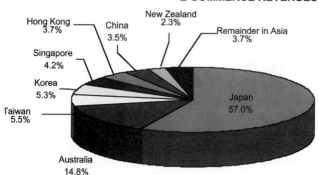

Women Online

1996 — 15% women online
1998 — 47% women online

Cosmetic Sales in Asia HK$30 billion 1998

Japan — 54%
Rest of Asia — 24%
China — 12%
South Korea — 10%

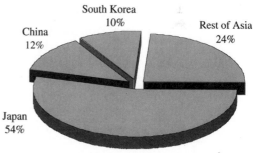

Source: Market Tracking International, Euromonitor.

e-commerce in Asia accounted for just 7 percent of the worldwide total of over $US12 billion (whereas the U.S. accounted for 70 percent of on-line purchases and Europe 23 percent). Asia, however, was forecast to be the second largest Internet growth opportunity in the world (after western Europe) and by 2002, the region was widely expected to have 50 million users, whose purchase activity would account for almost 10 percent of the value of global e-commerce activity.

Several environmental factors encouraged this trend. Besides the sheer size of several key markets located in Asia,[3] regional governments were expected to gradually lower tariffs and loosen restrictions, opening markets to foreign competition, paving the way for knowledge transfer of information technology (IT). Public sector initiatives to strengthen the technological infrastructure of many countries' economies within the region were also under way.[4] The increased adoption of e-commerce would make products and services that had previously been sold only in Western markets readily available to Asian consumers, and the pent-up demand among consumers and businesses alike for imported goods and services (especially those from the Western world) was expected to lead to strong sales in the foreseeable future.

Many Asian consumers and retailers alike welcomed this trend. Companies engaged in e-commerce were afforded several competitive advantages over their "bricks and mortar" competitors, including minimal leasing, leasehold improvement and overhead costs, centralized and highly efficient order processing and inventory controls, and lower cost, highly targeted marketing campaigns.[5] These competitive advantages, combined with a solid first mover advantage and the attractive margins available in the fashion industry, convinced Smith that looks.com was a tremendous opportunity.

Looks.com

Smith planned to offer the most popular brands of cosmetics, fragrances, skin-care and fashion-related products at "comparable prices to retail with value-added perks" (including samples and testers, attractive packaging, gifts-with-purchase, and gift-wrapping) on his secure site. Looks.com would offer "fast delivery to any destination around the world," although Smith expected that at least 50 percent of looks.com's initial sales would come from the Hong Kong market. Advertising and promotional campaigns, as well as "hotlinks"[6] on the web pages of looks.com's strategic partners (see Exhibit 2), would increase awareness of the site in this and other key Southeast Asian markets. Smith was very excited to have secured these strategic partnerships,

---

[3]Including China, Japan, Hong Kong, Taiwan, and South Korea.

[4]Including Singapore's "wired island," Malaysia's "Multimedia Super Corridor," and Hong Kong's "Cyberport."

[5]Web-based technologies allowed sites to capture a tremendous amount of knowledge on customer buying habits and preferences, as well as valuable demographic information that could be obtained through registration with the site.

[6]A "hotlink" is an icon or the name of a site listed on the screen of another site that allows users to directly access the former with the click of a mouse.

EXHIBIT 2   Strategic Partners

China.com Incorporated

Highly regarded, NASDAQ-listed, Internet portal with high traffic volume. Provides looks.com with exclusive cosmetic, makeup and fragrance territory within four portals—China.com, Hongkong.com, Taiwan.com and Netscape Guides to China. (An initial investor in looks.com.)

The Web-Connection

Leading Asian Internet solutions provider with extensive experience in e-commerce enterprise development and systems integration. Provides development and systems integration, engineering and graphic design for looks.com.

24/7 Media Asia

Leading Internet advertising agency in Asia, 24/7 Media oversaw all aspects of a global online advertising campaign for banners on the looks.com site.

AOL Asia

Highly regarded, NYSE-listed parent company, Internet portal with high traffic volume. Provides looks.com with exclusive cosmetic, makeup and fragrance territory within the popular portal.

---

since these sites provided him with an opportunity to reach a significant portion of his primary target market.

Because of its high e-commerce activity, one of the first market expansion plans was for Japan, for early 2000 with the development of a "mirror" site (in Japanese), with a company-owned server housed at a Japanese Internet service provider (ISP). Though he planned on organizing the Japanese site as a wholly or majority-owned subsidiary of Looks.com Holdings Limited, Smith did not rule out the possibility of the participation of a Japanese joint venture partner. In looks.com initial target markets (including Singapore and Taiwan), Smith did not foresee duties and import tariffs as major constraints to sales; however, Japan was a high tariff market. Therefore, Smith planned on establishing a distribution centre within Japan, which would also significantly reduce distribution costs and delivery times within Japan.

According to Smith, while China remained another attractive market for the sale of consumer products, it remained a challenging market for online sales. The lack of credit card processing facilities, post-sale distribution logistics, low Internet penetration and adoption rates, and high tariffs posed significant hurdles to effective penetration in the short term.

Though looks.com would initially focus on the markets in Hong Kong, Singapore, and Taiwan, as e-commerce transcended geographic boundaries, Smith considered the five million women with middle- to high-incomes, aged 17 through 35 in the Asia Pacific region, to be looks.com's target market. Smith felt that this segment of women was more likely to have Internet access and to be early adopters of online shopping. Smith grouped looks.com target market into four tertiary market segments—"Trendies," "New Women," "Mothers," and "Sophisticates."

EXHIBIT 3   Sample Page from www.Looks.com

Source: Company website, November 1999.

Trendies, aged between 17 and 25, were inclined to adopt new trends and were able to do so because they had a relatively high amount of disposable income. New product availability, extensive choice, and value were meaningful benefits to Trendies. New Women were a little older (between 25 and 30), had careers, relationships, and family commitments, hectic lives and a wide range of interests. They valued the benefits of convenience, availability of their brand, quality, and expected value for their money. Mothers and Sophisticates were considered secondary target markets. These segments were highly brand loyal, and sought quality and convenience.

The looks.com site would offer two fully integrated and complementary components: the "Looks Boutique" and "LooksZone" (see Exhibit 3). The Looks Boutique—the retail component of looks.com—would present brand name cosmetics and fragrances, and health and beauty products to consumers using extensive product descriptions, photos, and, where appropriate, digital demonstrations.

LooksZone, the entertainment component of the site, was designed to promote both "stickiness"[7] and repeat visits to solidify looks.com as a web-based community by providing information on various issues

---

[7]A site's ability to hold a user's interest.

EXHIBIT 3   *(continued)*

Source: Company web site, November 1999.

concerning Asian women, including, but not limited to, health and beauty. Various articles focusing on self-help and self-improvement, image consulting, fashion and trend reports would be written by looks.com in-house writers, and other articles would be written by guest dermatologists, gynecologists, and other medical professionals, augmented with content aggregated from other sites. Smith's objective was to become a portal for Asian women.[8] Smith's vision for looks.com was as an e-commerce site that sold a myriad of health and beauty-

---

[8]A portal is a web site that is intended to be the first place people see when using the Web. Typically, a portal site has a catalogue of web sites, a search engine, or both. A portal site may also offer e-mail and other services to entice people to use that site as their main "point of entry" (hence "portal") to the Web.

related products including baby and maternity products and services, and fashion accessories. Looks.com's ability to grow as a portal attracting the lucrative and fast-growing Asian female market was a key consideration in Smith's original choice of cosmetics as a product to sell via the Internet.

Why Cosmetics?

Smith had "no particular affinity for cosmetics" and no prior experience in the industry (or with the Internet for that matter). However, he had been working in Asia for over a decade, since he was 24 (see Exhibit 4). Knowing that he would somehow be involved in an Internet venture to capitalize on the incredible momentum of the industry in Asia, Smith wanted to "strike while the iron was hot" to capture a first mover advantage in such a rapidly growing industry, and he began research into what type of site he would launch. After examining "30 or 40 different site concepts," including pure portal plays, auction sites, and e-commerce opportunities for products and services (such as real estate, Asian art, sporting goods and "factory direct stuff out of China"), he found that cosmetics offered the most promising e-commerce opportunity. Smith explained the many reasons looks.com made the most sense to him:

> In cosmetics, 80 percent of the sales are repeat purchases—customers are highly brand loyal. Moreover, cosmetic brands are highly recognizable—the

---

EXHIBIT 4   The Looks.com Team

Ian Smith, Managing Director

Most recently, Smith had been an associate director of a Hong Kong-based direct equity investment firm for a number of years, after a two-year term as the managing director (Asia) of a car park operation. Smith's decade of experience in Asia had exposed him to establishing, financing and managing Asian-based organizations.

Mr. Robbie Jessel, Vice-President Brand Development

Leading cosmetics buyer, who brings over 10 years of sales and marketing experience to the company, including duty-free, department store and boutique sales.

Ms. Margaret Yeung, Beauty Editor

Successful color and makeup expert with international duty-free and global brand development and sales training experience.

Mr. David Ketchum, Marketing & Communications

Highly respected marketing and communications professional with a background in a leading international public relations firm and direct operating experience with leading international brands.

Ms. Cadena Wong, Marketing Manager

Background in retail merchandising and brand development in Europe and Asia. MBA from SDA Bocconi in Milan, Italy.

Ms. Eva Yuen, Logistics Manager

Experienced inventory and supply-side management control expert with cosmetic and fast-moving consumer goods experience.

---

industry spends about the highest percentage of revenue on promotion, so most of the products that would be listed on the site would already have a high profile in most Asian markets. Fraud was not as much of an issue as with other e-commerce sites—you can't download cosmetics, and statistics have proven that male sites are much more susceptible to fraud.

Moreover, health and beauty products are very small generally, so they're easily shipped and received (a consideration especially in Asia where most people have very small mail boxes in apartment buildings), and had a high value to weight ratio. Inventory management is made easier with such small products, and styles change each season so you don't have to carry products 10 years old (like Amazon does with books). Importantly, manufacturers are doing their damnedest to keep prices high; it was the profit margins that ultimately convinced me to sell cosmetics online.

Another attraction to selling cosmetics online was the fact that direct competition was scarce. Although several manufacturers of cosmetics and health and beauty products had created their own websites, and a myriad of sites had been created that sold name brand cosmetics, none catered specifically to Asian women as a rule, and few sites shipped outside of North America. Smith considered traditional cosmetic retail outlets including department, drug, and variety stores as well as beauty salons, supermarkets and discount cosmetic outlets to be indirect competition for looks.com, as he believed the site held a distinct competitive advantage over more traditional distribution channels. Thus, Smith considered the concept behind looks.com an "overlooked Internet opportunity in Asia." One of the most important considerations in the development of the business plan was whether looks.com would be a parallel importer, or would deal directly with manufacturers and authorized distributors to source products for sale on the site.

Parallel Importing or Dealing Direct

Parallel importing, sourcing products wholesale from authorized distributors through the "grey" market, was a popular practice in Asia in most industries, including cosmetics. It allowed retailers to offer products at up to 70 percent off retail, and, thus, consumers loved it. However, many manufacturers (who had little recourse to stop the unauthorized distribution of their products) were incensed at their inability to achieve an appropriate return on investment, control their distribution channels, or protect their brand image. On the other hand—driven by a desire for increased sales and to allocate costs over higher production levels to achieve economies of scale—some brand managers looked the other way when it came to grey market sales. Generally speaking, however, their official stance was one of hearty contempt for the practice.

The key disadvantages of parallel importing were two-fold. First, profit margins would likely be less than if authorized distribution channels were used, given that at least one more link (and, hence, another level of cost) was added to the value chain. Moreover, though products bought on the grey market could be sold at any price, often (especially if their packaging was damaged, or they had expired, or were last season's lines for example) grey market products were sold at a discount to full manufacturers' suggested retail prices (MSRP). Thus, even though Smith's costs would be lower, often his markups would be less than if he dealt with authorized dealers (and selling at full MSRP). Smith stated that if he chose to source his products through grey markets, "the game would be to drive up the volume, and get your profit that way." This was a key part of the business model of a very successful bricks and mortar cosmetics retailer—Sa Sa.[9]

Sa Sa's 25 locations throughout Hong Kong and the New Territories had the distinctive character of a discount retailer. Sa Sa's stores were located in very high pedestrian traffic locations, in a confined "no frills" environment, where cosmetics counters and bins brimming with health and beauty products retailed those items at 25 percent to 70 percent off the MSRP. This business model had served the company well—1998 profits were HK$250 million on sales of HK$1.25 billion. With a 20 percent after-tax profit, Smith referred to Sa Sa as "the best-known and most successful parallel importing retailer in Asia." Although consumers loved the practice followed by Sa Sa, distributors and manufacturers alike detested it. Thus, parallel marketers were often ostracized by manufacturers, angry at the loss of control over the price and the positioning of their products. Nonetheless, the practice was very popular in Asia, and was, according to Smith, not really illegal:

> The distributors really fight it, but many of the products bought on the grey market are highly sought-after brands, including Christian Dior, Shiseido, and Lancome, among others. Consumers don't really care about where the product comes from if it means they can buy their favorite brand at 30 percent up to 70 percent below MSRP for what appears to be an authentically branded product in its original wrapping, prior to (or close to) its date of expiry in most cases.

The second key disadvantage in using parallel importing was the fact that in the minds of potential investors, suppliers and consumers, this would put looks.com in Sa Sa's league. One consequence of this would be that when Sa Sa inevitably went online, looks.com would be going head to head with a well-established and deep-pocketed industry

---

[9]Though Sa Sa did purchase some brands directly from the manufacturer, they purchased the prestige brands—Lancome, Estée Lauder, and Polo Ralph Lauren, for example—on the grey market.

leader. Moreover, attracting leading industry professionals to work for looks.com would become considerably more challenging. For example, Jessel stated that he would never have tainted his reputation in the industry by joining looks.com if they had been a grey marketer. Jessel was a key player on the looks.com team, bringing over a decade of industry experience in Asia. Jessel had managed the distribution of products from high profile manufacturers such as Orlane, Club Monaco, Benetton, Ahava (a popular brand from Israel), Nina Ricci, Paco Robane, and Giorgio Fragrances, and Smith was not willing to forego Jessel's services. Jessel would apply his knowledge of markets, pricing and the structure of deals to the looks.com venture, and would establish key contacts with various international suppliers through his extensive personal network. Smith recognized that Jessel's experience and expertise were required to overcome what was clearly becoming the number one issue in the manufacturers' minds when deciding whether they would list their products with looks.com—whether the Internet would cannibalize existing sales agreements with previously authorized distributors.

Internet Sales versus Existing Distribution Channels

The issue of the extent to which the existing sales of "bricks and mortar" retailers would be displaced by the Internet was a hot topic in the retail industry. To avoid a conflict of interest with retailers, manufacturers often priced their products sold online at parity with the price at which their products were being sold in other channels. Moreover, many manufacturers that engaged in e-commerce were careful to avoid offering any special incentives that would entice consumers away from traditional retail channels.

A high profile example of how one manufacturer managed its initial foray into Internet distribution is Nike, the world's largest producer of athletic footwear and apparel. Nike established an exclusive alliance with Fogdog.com[10] to sell Nike products online, granting Fogdog.com volume discounts normally given only to Nike's top sales partners. In doing so, Nike reversed its policy of banning sales to Internet-only retailers. For six months, Fogdog.com was the only Internet retailer with access to Nike's full line of products. In return, Fogdog granted Nike the right to acquire 12.3 percent of the company at $1 per share,[11] a seat on its board, and undisclosed fees. Prior to this, Nike had moved cautiously into e-commerce, partly to avoid upsetting their existing

---

[10]Fogdog was a popular e-commerce site that sold a myriad of brand name sporting goods at close to the prices set for these products in more traditional retail locations.

[11]In late 1999, Fogdog's shares were selling in the low teens on the NASDAQ stock exchange.

distribution partners and retailers. However, the general consensus among industry analysts was that the Nike arrangement with Fogdog.com had little or no impact on traditional retailers.[12]

By late 1999, an increasing reliance on the Internet as a distribution channel seemed to be an inevitable trend in many industries, including the computer sector. Firms such as Compaq and CompUSA were slow to utilize this new channel. In contrast, Dell Computers, the number one U.S. supplier of personal computer systems, saw its shipments grow more than 100 percent in the second quarter of 1999. Half of those sales were generated online, through www.dell.com. This growth outpaced the industry, and led to record operating results in the fiscal second quarter. Internet sales to Dell customers reached $30 million per day, representing nearly 40 percent of the company's revenue. Dell's online sales were double the combined revenue of the other top 20 Internet shopping sites, as measured by Media Metrix.[13] Dell's business model of direct sales—with a focus on the Internet—was expected to become increasingly successful for many companies across a wide range of industries.

However, despite the quantifiable benefits of e-commerce, and specifically of manufacturers listing their products on looks.com (including increased sales and heightened promotion of the brand), Smith and Jessel were finding that many manufacturers had deep concerns regarding online distribution of their products. First, they feared the cannibalization of their existing sales through traditional distribution networks was dampening their enthusiasm for dealing with looks.com. Importantly, given that prices were significantly higher in, say, Japan and Korea than in Indonesia, for example, Japanese and Korean distributors feared that Internet distribution would adversely affect their sales (i.e., revenue).[14] Jessel appreciated these concerns firsthand, and having been a distributor for almost a decade, he was able to develop strategies to more successfully manage looks.com's relationships with them.

The Distributor's Perspective

Jessel appreciated why distributors would be protective of their territory if they perceived that they could lose revenue. First, distributors claimed that the terms of their (exclusive) distribution contracts protected them against sales in their regions by any other parties. This

---

[12]This was due in part to the fact that athletic footwear, which accounted for about two-thirds of Nike's revenues, was difficult to sell over the Internet. Consumers generally needed to try the shoes on in person prior to purchase.

[13]According to Dell's annual report.

[14]Manufacturers also had a fear of increased arbitrage with e-commerce, commensurate with their further loss of control of their distribution channels. However, Smith explained that looks.com was a business-to-consumer (B2C) site, and that any large bulk purchases could be red-flagged easily on the system.

protected their ongoing investments in the selling and promoting of the product lines they carried. Although expenses varied according to the region and the contract terms, the following costs were often incurred by distributors:

- Co-op brand-building advertising and promotions[15]
- Salaries and/or commissions of sales clerks (a portion of these expenses were generally paid by the manufacturer)
- Fixtures and supplies for the display counter
- Leasing of display counters in department stores (generally, a fixed amount per square foot, a percentage of sales or a combination thereof)

According to Jessel, a distributor's expenses were generally higher in Asia, because space in the department store was leased by the manufacturer, whereas, in the U.S., as a rule, it was not. It did not help matters that commercial real estate in Asia was perhaps the most expensive in the world.

Nonetheless, distributors had little or no legal recourse to fight Internet sales in their region. Given that the Internet was a relatively new phenomenon in Asia, there was no provision for e-commerce written into distributors' contracts according to Smith (see Exhibit 5):

> A standard distribution contract was not *ex*clusive, but *in*clusive. It delineated what sales were authorized, as opposed to what sales were not. The contract's focus was price rather than distribution. Alternative channels such as the Internet were not seen as viable until as recently as six months ago, whereas the retail pricing issue had been hotly contested by manufacturers and distributors for years on account of the influence that parallel marketing had on the retail environment in Asia.

Smith pointed out that the issue of alienating distributors could not be entirely avoided, even if looks.com dealt with the Hong Kong-based authorized distributors or directly with the manufacturer. According to Smith, even if looks.com did go "legit"—buying product from manufacturers and/or the authorized Hong Kong distributor—given the geographic scope of Internet sales, looks.com would still be considered a parallel importer by the regional distributors outside of Hong Kong. Smith stated that "you become a parallel importer without even trying—by entering markets through the back door."

The Organization of Distributor Agreements

According to Jessel, a single manufacturer often owned more than one brand, heightening the importance of attracting that particular manufacturer. For example, L'Oreal owned a number of the most popular

---

[15]A portion of the advertising costs are borne by the retailer and the brand manufacturer alike (often 50-50).

EXHIBIT 5   Excerpts from Standard Looks.com Contractual Letter

---

Beyond the standard trademark, non-disclosure and indemnification segments, the following exhibit outlines a condensed version of other terms of the contract between looks.com and manufacturers.

This letter summarizes the terms of sales between looks.com Limited, a Hong Kong registered limited liability company and _____ (the "Vendor"). The terms of this agreement shall be one year from the signing.

Product Sales

. . . Vendor grants looks.com the Internet distribution rights for products (as listed in Appendix X) . . . and agrees to allow looks.com to sell these products to customers internationally from its warehouse facilities in Hong Kong . . . and by entering into this agreement, and granting such rights to looks.com, the vendor will not be in breach of any other agreement or obligations to any third party.

Price and Payment Terms

Vendor agrees to sell to looks.com at the MSRP, less X^* percent, net 30 days on receipt of goods in Hong Kong.

Freight

. . . F.O.B. vendor's plant . . . international air courier shipping charges paid by looks.com.

Frequency of Shipping

Vendor agrees to ship products to looks.com's warehouse on a bi-monthly basis. . . . Vendor agrees to process and ship orders from Vendor's facility within five business days.

Returns

Vendor agrees to reimburse looks.com for the wholesale price of any product returned due to manufacturing defects and overstock, subject to prior authorization from the vendor.

Product Samples

Vendor agrees to provide looks.com with samples of products free of charge.

Market Research and Customer Sales Data

Looks.com agrees to make sales and performance reports to the vendor on a country-by-country basis.

Termination and Renewal

This agreement may be terminated for any reason by either party after receiving 60 days' written notice.

---

*This figure would generally be between 50 percent and 75 percent, in line with the industry average.

brands (including Bobbi Brown, MAC, and others) and, like many other multinational cosmetic manufacturers, had their own in-house distributors. For smaller players (e.g., Club Monaco, Cargo, Benetton), it made more sense to contract-out distribution, either through an Asia-Pacific distributor based in Hong Kong with sub-distributors in each region throughout Southeast Asia, or directly with regional distributors throughout Asia.

Distributors (predominantly based in Hong Kong) either had rights to all of Asia (depending on the manufacturer's presence in the region) or sub-distribution agreements with regional distributors under the Hong Kong distributors. Thus, dealing with regional distributors could get "a little complicated." To provide an example of a typical Asian distribution network with sub-agreements through the Hong Kong distributor, Smith pointed to Urban Decay, a "really hot brand in the U.S." with colors like "vomit" and "roach" that had one distributor in the U.S. and another in Hong Kong. The Hong Kong distributor had sub-division distribution agreements throughout Asia in each country. Smith acknowledged that he particularly appreciated the position of the sub-distributors because he knew that they were "getting squeezed" on their margins, after purchasing their products from the Hong Kong distributor.

Nonetheless, both Smith and Jessel felt that Asian distributors had to "see beyond their immediate, emotional reaction that it's their territory and that we're encroaching on it," feeling that the practice of grey marketing was the greater threat in Asia. According to Smith:

> In the short term, we don't expect our business to adversely impact any one distributor to any great extent. Not like Sa Sa did. Distributors should worry about the Sa Sas of the world rather than looks.com. We will be selling at very close to MSRP.

> When Sa Sa came to the market, it really caused problems. Local distributors were consistently frustrated and angry, both at seeing their lines at the local Sa Sa stores—knowing that they did not sell the products to them[16]—and having Sa Sa undercut their prices. But consumers loved it, and when Sa Sa became so successful, manufacturers became ever more vigilant in protecting the way their products were retailed, heightening their desire to deal only with reputable, well-known retailers.

Smith was confident that looks.com could offer manufacturers an alternative distribution channel that increased not only their revenue, but also the profile of their brands throughout Asia. According to Smith, as consumers browsed on looks.com and saw any given manufacturer's brand, it would keep the brand "top of mind," and they may even be more likely to purchase that brand the next time they saw it (i.e., in bricks and mortar retail location). Smith felt this exposure to be valuable in such a highly competitive, brand-focused industry. Moreover, manufacturers could trust that looks.com was a professional and well-designed site that would position the brand according to the manufacturer's desired brand personality.

Looks.com's layout facilitated an increased brand profile for each brand listed on the site with a "site-within-the site" (SWS)—the online version of cosmetic counters within a department store. With a link from the site's main page, customers could go directly to the SWS of any particular brand (see Exhibit 3) where special promotions and deals could be promoted.

---

[16]The origin of Sa Sa's products for sale could not be traced, since the uniform product codes (UPC) assigned to each product were routinely rendered illegible.

Thus, Smith felt that once the vendors' concerns regarding managing their distributor network in Asia were addressed, they would come to see that the advantages of listing their products for sale on looks.com outweighed the perceived disadvantages of doing so. Moreover, Smith and Jessel proposed strategies to manufacturers to mitigate any potential adverse reaction to sales through looks.com in their territory.

Working with the Distributors

Given the high margins in the cosmetic industry, Jessel proposed that manufacturers could afford to distribute a small percentage of their wholesale proceeds to the distributors. Jessel described his plan:

> What we're saying is that until we establish our credibility in the marketplace, and until we reach minimum order lots for bulk purchase discounts, we will often have to pay the top end wholesale price. This leaves the manufacturer with a slightly higher margin. Normally, most of the extra margins are reinvested in brand-building exercises. In this case, I propose that another effective use of that extra margin would be to distribute it to various regional distributors.

> It gets a little complicated, but what we are going to try to do is to buy directly from a manufacturer in, say, the U.S., and give credit for sales that are made in each of the regions in Southeast Asia. If we dealt directly with the Hong Kong distributor, they would want us to pay the same markup that they were charging their sub-distributors—up to 30 percent. This would make it unfeasible for us to sell the line.

Smith explained that looks.com had software capable of tracking sales of each line in each region, thus allowing manufacturers to provide credits to their sub-distributors in direct proportion to sales of their lines in each particular region. Smith and Jessel felt that this move would be a win-win-win situation for the vendor, distributor and looks.com. The vendors could increase their sales, the distributors would receive consideration for sales of their lines in their region(s) for which they expended very little effort, and looks.com would increase product listings, brand name recognition, and revenues.

Both Jessel and Smith felt that another effective way to assuage the manufacturers' concerns that sales through looks.com in their territories were infringing on exclusive distribution rights was to position looks.com in the minds of manufacturers and distributors alike as a Hong Kong-based duty-free retailer. Given that sales through duty-free outlets were excluded in distributor contracts, their hope was that this positioning would be seen as a natural evolution for a company operating out of Hong Kong, a region historically renowned as the "freest economy in the world" in terms of tariffs and duties according to several surveys.

Smith described an example of the interactions between the distributor, manufacturer and Jessel in the case of Orlane, a high-end brand that targeted women over 30. Recognizing that it was not a brand that fitted looks.com's primary target market, Jessel felt that it would nonetheless lend credibility to the site, given that it was a sophisticated, globally recognized brand:

> During our discussions, we went after "fair" margins and we positioned ourselves as a duty-free retailer. This positioning would essentially circumvent the local distributor (in Hong Kong), but we're not going behind their back—we've let them know that we are talking directly to the head office in France.

In the final analysis, if Orlane did join looks.com, Jessel explained "there is very little the Hong Kong distributor can do about it." He continued:

> Nonetheless, we want to take a reasonable stance. We approached distributors and said: "Look, let's work together on this. If you help build the brand by providing samples, participating in our sponsored trade shows, doing make-overs, or providing inventory when we're in a pinch, then we will push your case with the manufacturer to distribute that extra margin (the difference between the price the distributor pays and the price looks.com would pay) to you."

According to Jessel, the initial response of the Orlane distributor was "promising." Both parties recognized that ongoing antagonism would not be very productive for either side. Moreover, Jessel expected that Orlane's sales on looks.com would not materially impact their distributors in any region, given that the brand's primary target market was not a precise fit with that of looks.com.

Smith's Next Steps

Smith pointed to the U.S. experience, stating that Internet sales had not adversely impacted sales of bricks and mortar operations to the extent that many retailers and industry analysts had feared. Smith was hoping that Jessel could effectively persuade manufacturers and distributors alike that this would be the case in Asia, and that the advantages of listing their products for sale on looks.com outweighed the potential adverse impact on their existing distribution agreements. According to Smith:

> Even in the case of a popular brand that is right in line with our target market, our best case scenario is, say, 1 percent of the sales in Asia. That's insignificant to any one distributor, yet that would be a monstrous number for us. The market is that big.

I'm very optimistic. We've got the financing, management talent, high profile strategic partners, and a solid first-mover advantage. Now it's just a matter of attracting the brands onto the site.

The Richard Ivey School of Business gratefully acknowledges the generous support of The Richard and Jean Ivey Fund in the development of this case as part of the RICHARD AND JEAN IVEY FUND ASIAN CASE SERIES.

Blinds to Go: Evaluating the BlindsToGo.com Retail E-Commerce Venture

By Professor Michael Pearce and Ken Mark

Introduction

Senior management at Montreal-based Blinds To Go (BTG) had received sales, spending and survey results from their retail e-commerce venture, BlindsToGo.com. In early July 2000, Nkere Udofia, vice-chairman of BTG, wanted to evaluate the results of this online venture.

Surpassing US$100 million in store revenues, Blinds To Go, a retailer and fabricator of window dressings, had achieved a blistering pace of retail growth in the past few years, sparked by an infusion of capital from Harvard Private Capital, the investment arm of Harvard University. Continuing this trend towards an eventual initial public offering (IPO) in the next few years, they were aiming to add 40 to 50 retail stores per year, funded entirely out of current cash flow, to their current complement of 120 stores across North America.

When BlindsToGo.com, the online project of BTG, was first proposed in mid-1999, its board of directors was lukewarm to the idea. However, after six months of operation and seeing other retailers start to go online, and the tremendous valuation being given to dot.coms, the board was now encouraging BTG to devote more resources to this venture.

IVEY   Ken Mark prepared this case under the supervision of Professor Michael Pearce solely to provide material for class discussion. The authors do not intend to illustrate either effective or ineffective handling of a managerial situation. The authors may have disguised certain names and other identifying information to protect confidentiality.

Ivey Management Services prohibits any form of reproduction, storage or transmittal without its written permission. This material is not covered under authorization from CanCopy or any reproduction rights organization. To order copies or request permission to reproduce materials, contact Ivey Publishing, Ivey Management Services, c/o Richard Ivey School of Business, The University of Western Ontario, London, Ontario, Canada, N6A 3K7; phone (519) 661-3208; fax (519) 661-3882; e-mail cases@ivey.uwo.ca.

Montreal's Shiller Family, Originators of the Blinds To Go Concept

Consummate salesmen, David Shiller and his sons took this high-touch retail concept that Shiller had started in 1954 and turned it in to a multimillion-dollar business. "In our original 'Au Bon Marche' store," explained Stephen Shiller, president of BTG, "we fed our customers, kept them busy while they waited for about an hour for their blinds to be ready. The factory was literally next to the store and we offered one hour delivery—we certainly kept the customer happy!" The aggressive commission-based approach to sales had resulted in a high-energy environment where above-average salespeople sold Cdn$10,000 worth of blinds per week with a 6 percent commission.

BTG was capitalizing on a niche in the US$2 billion market for window coverings dominated by large manufacturers and similarly large retailers. A retail fabricator, BTG manufactured and sold only their own brand of blinds, and was able to offer 48-hour delivery of their customer's customized orders. BTG took six separate steps and between one to three hours to manufacture a set of blinds, versus the industry average for a customized order turnaround (assuming they had the parts in stock) of four to six weeks.

BTG's retail fabricator competitors included 3 Day Blinds with US$100 million in sales, House of Blinds with US$20 million in sales, and the rest of the smaller retail fabricators accounting for another US$220 million in sales.[1]

Blinds To Go Retail Stores

With over 20,000 varieties of blinds in stock, BTG's sales associates could offer almost any choice of blinds to their walk-in customers. Each associate was trained to bond with the customers, shepherd them through the choices, offer advice, answer any questions—ultimately, the goal was to address all customer objections and finish the encounter with an average sale of Cdn$226.

Retail stores' sales average over $1.0 million per store with an advertising budget comprising between three to 8 percent of revenues. Blinds To Go achieved average weekly store traffic of 300 to 900 people. The company leased real estate and built each store for an average of US$500,000. Refurbished stores (located in already established buildings) usually cost US$300,000 to build. Maintenance, including rent, utilities and staff expenses, generally cost BTG in the range of US$300,000 to US$400,000 per year. The biggest issue BTG faced in its expansion campaign was attracting, hiring and retaining qualified staff. Some new stores had delayed openings because of this staff shortage.

---

[1]1997 figures. Sullivan Marketing Group. In 1997, Blinds To Go achieved US$32 million in store sales.

EXHIBIT 1 Setting Up the Sale (BTG Company Files)

Bonding

Greet the customer and welcome them to Blinds To Go. Determine their needs by asking open-ended questions.

Product Selection

Work with the customer to find the perfect product for their needs. Address any objections as they come up. Ensure that the worksheet is properly and completely filled out.

Present Price with Confidence

Reaffirm factory-direct pricing and lifetime guarantee.

Deduct Coupon

Verify and approve coupon if customer has one.

Introduce Customer to Manager

Walk through the order with the manager and have the manager greet customer.

Source: Blinds To Go company files.

BTG staff had an average close rate of 30 to 40 percent, with low performance stores at 20 to 30 percent and high performance stores at 50 to 60 percent (see Exhibit 1.)

BlindsToGo.com—The Internet Initiative

In January 2000, BlindsToGo.com was launched. BTG approached a small website builder in Chicago to develop and host the site (development of functionality), and another small company in Boston to design the layout of the site (see Exhibit 2). The process was managed by BTG and the site cost US$500,000 to build and US$40,000 per month to host and maintain. The BTG e-commerce site allowed people to browse the varieties of blinds, put in their specifications and purchase blinds online (www.blindstogo.com[2]).

The site was created with the customer interface and ease of ordering as the main objectives. With this in mind, sections of the site were built in an attempt to replicate the in-store experience (see Exhibit 3). BTG's site was designed to be the leading blinds site that leapfrogged its fragmented online competition with focus and functionality. Jeff Rayner, vice-president of marketing at BTG, placed his online blinds website competition in two camps—order taking sites that received customer orders and passed them on to manufacturers, and catalogue sites that posted their houseware catalogues online.[3] Neither group

---

[2]Site accessed August 20, 2000.

[3]These sites included http://www.blindsgalore.com, www.americanblindsandwallpaper.com, and www.smithandnoble.com. Rayner believed that there were about three other sites with similar functionality.

EXHIBIT 2   Blinds To Go Homepage

Source: www.blindstogo.com, January 2001.

had sites with any substantial functionality, save for an online order form. Rayner felt that, currently, the field was wide open for a nationally branded blinds solution.

When it was created, BTG set out that the measures of success for the site would rank in the following order: total sales, number of catalogue requests, closing rate and shopping cart rate.[4] Because this was their first online venture, BTG did not set specific targets for each metric at this early stage. BTG management felt that sales associates who answered the incoming phone calls originating from the site should always refer customers to stores in their region, gaining synergy between site and stores in established markets.

Some BTG store managers (all stores were corporately owned and store managers were compensated based on revenues) were concerned about the impact of BlindsToGo.com cannibalizing their store sales. But senior management was able to ease the concerns of the stores by explaining that BlindsToGo.com was a new venture that would support the brand and was meant as a complement and support to store operations.

---

[4]The Shopping Cart Rate referred to the percentage of sales that occurred online without human assistance.

EXHIBIT 3 Ask the Blinds Expert

Whether in a Blinds To Go™ Superstore or on the website, our sales associates are the most knowledgeable sales associates in the industry. Each has completed intensive training in one of our Blinds To Go™ Universities. For help with choosing the right blind for you, contact one of our sales associates via email or at 877-842-0411 or try our new interactive wizard by answering the questions below.

I want a blind that is:

○ Room Darkening   ○ Adjustable   ○ Light Filtering

Which room are you decorating?

○ Living Room   ○ Dining Room   ○ Bedroom   ○ Den
○ Kitchen   ○ Bathroom   ○ Other

I am primarily concerned with:

○ Good Value   ○ Both - but mostly Value   ○ Both - but mostly Style   ○ Style

▶ find my blind! ◀

Existing Worksheet | Ask the Blinds Expert | Customer Reviews | Why Blinds To Go | Order the Idea Book

Source: www.blindstogo.com/blindstogo/products/expert, January 2001.

Six months after launch and selling over US$60,000 per month, BTG had received some site results. They had in their hands a slice of daily data from June (Exhibit 4), weekly website data from June (Exhibit 5), year-to-date results (Exhibit 6), Live Person Chat results (Exhibit 7), and the results of their online survey conducted in April 2000 (Exhibit 8).

BTG believed that the people who visited the site were the same people who visited their stores. With regard to fulfilment, it took equal time to fulfill an online order versus an offline order, with the exception that the online order would need to be shipped to the customer.

EXHIBIT 3   *(continued)* As the Blinds Expert

Why Shop at Blinds To Go™?

Our History: Blinds and shades are in our roots. Since 1954 our mission has been to provide you, our customer with the best quality, value and customer service.

The largest selection: We search across the world and research the latest fashion trends to bring you the best and largest selection of blinds and shades. Visit us often, as we build our online product lines with the latest styles!

The lowest prices: We manufacture everything you see on our site, so you get the lowest price! No middleman, no retail markups!

We are The Experts: We understand blinds. Every Blinds To Go salesperson/service rep goes through Blinds To Go University, and is trained to be blinds and shade experts and to "treat the customer like family".

The Fastest Delivery: We use national carriers like UPS to get your order from our factory to your door, and everything is custom made to your needs!

A Lifetime Guarantee! : All our products are backed with a 100% lifetime guarantee. So, you can rest assured that you are buying the best window treatments that will last for years!

Source: www.blindstogo.com, January 2001.

EXHIBIT 4   June 11 to 17 Website Results

	Totals	*Sun.*	*Mon.*	*Tue.*	*Wed.*	*Thu.*	*Fri.*	*Sat.*
				June 11th to 17th 2000—Week 3				
Total Net Sales (US$)	12,860.0	2,125.0	3,025.0	2,542.5	722.5	75.0	4,037.5	332.5
Number of Sales	42.5	5.0	7.5	7.5	7.5	2.5	7.5	5.0
Average Sale (US$)	308.0							
In Region Sale	30	3	8	5	8	3	3	3
Out of Region Sale	12.5	3	–	3	–	–	5	3
% out of Region	29%							
Advertising (US$)	1,648							
Online	1,648							
Offline	–							
Advertising as % of sales	13%							
Unique Visitors	6,028	648	1,103	1,003	913	910	850	603
Click Thru Rate	740	70	88	100	120	125	133	105
Sales as % of Unique Visits	0.70%							
Phone calls	135	5	30	13	25	30	10	23
Live Chats	80	13	15	10	8	18	18	–
E-mails	155	13	28	30	28	33	20	5
Phone Catalogues	58	–	10	18	13	10	5	3
Total Call Centre	428	30	83	70	73	90	53	30
Web Catalogue Requests	350	40	65	50	63	60	38	35
Phone Catalogues	–							

Source: Blinds To Go company files.

EXHIBIT 5 June Month-to-Date Website Results

	Totals	June—Month-to-Date			
		Week 1	Week 2	Week 3	Week 4
Total Net Sales (US$)	48,388	15,723	19,805	12,860	
Number of Sales	102	32	27	43	
Average Sale (US$)	258				
In Region Sale	127.5	52.5	45.0	30.0	
Out of Region Sale	60.0	27.5	20.0	12.5	
% out of Region	32%				
Advertising (US$)	5,050				
Online	5,050	1,955	1,448	1,648	
Offline	–				
Advertising as % of sales	10%				
Unique Visitors	17,726	5,890	5,808	6,028	
Click Thru Rate	2,105	818	548	740	
Sales as % of Unique Visits	1.07%				
Phone calls	315	68	113	135	
Live Chats	158	38	40	80	
E-mails	333	70	108	155	
Phone Catalogues	253	145	50	58	
Total Call Centre	1,058	320	310	428	
Web Catalogue Requests	1,078	400	328	350	
Phone Catalogues	195	145	50		

Source: Blinds To Go company files.

EXHIBIT 6   2000 Year-to-Date Website Results

	Totals		*2000 Year to Date*				
		Jan.	*Feb.*	*Mar.*	*Apr.*	*May*	*Jun.*
Total Net Sales (US$)	226,640.2	852.5	12,662.2	41,502.5	61,797.5	61,437.5	48,388.0
Number of Sales	917.0	10.0	40.0	212.5	295.0	257.5	102.0
Average Sale (US$)	228.0						
In Region Sale	675.0	10.0	32.5	130.0	202.5	172.5	127.5
Out of Region Sale	327.5	–	7.5	82.5	92.5	85.0	60.0
% out of Region	33%	0%	19%	39%	31%	33%	32%
Advertising (US$)	555,528	375	36,770	324,503	113,290	75,540	5,050
Online	75,643	375	25,270	18,888	19,293	6,768	5,050
Offline	479,883	–	11,500	305,613	93,998	68,773	–
Advertising as % of sales	245%						
Unique Visitors	149,249	3,125	16,998	35,043	32,325	44,043	17,726
Click Thru Rate	46,133	–	–	11,253	12,330	20,445	2,105
Sale as % of Unique Visits	0.87%						
Total Call Centre	4,650	–	–	1,688	1,308	598	1,058
Web Catalogue Requests	4,763	–	–	1,508	920	1,258	1,078
Phone Catalogues	213	–	–	–	103	235	195

Source: Blinds To Go company files.

EXHIBIT 7   Live Person Chats

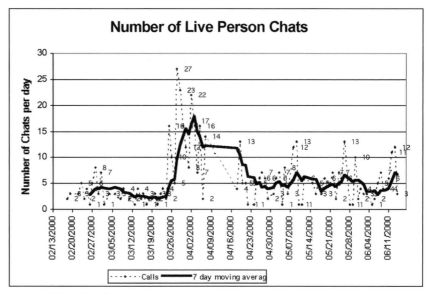

Source: Blinds To Go company records.

Conclusion

Udofia thought,

> We have now dipped our toes into the water. Is the board right—should we push forward aggressively? Is this going to be a break-even business? Or is this just a distraction to the organization? We are people constrained—do we continue to divert valuable management time to this opportunity?

EXHIBIT 8 Online Survey—April 10, 2000

Q1 — How did you hear about blindstogo.com | Q2 - Rating of overall experience

	Sample Size		Store	Friend	Banner	Newspapers/Mailer	TV	Catalogue	Others	Very Good	Good	Average	Bad
IN REGION (STORES)	35												
20%	7	TORONTO	5	2		4				4	3		
14%	5	DC/BALT	2			3					3	2	
6%	2	BOSTON	1			1				1	1		
9%	3	RICHMOND	1		1	1	1				1	1	1
31%	11	NY METRO	5	2		4				6	4		
6%	2	PHILLY	1				1				2	2	
14%	5	DETROIT			1	3	1			2	2		1
	15	*subtotal*	**15**	**4**	**2**	**16**	**3**	-	-	**13**	**16**	**3**	**1**
OUT OF REGION (NO STORES)	19												
5%	1	CHARLOTTE							Magazine			1	
42%	8	AUSTIN			2	3	3			3	5		
26%	5	ORLANDO				5					5		
21%	4	LAS VEGAS			1	1	3			2	2		
5%	1	OTHERS			1						1		
		subtotal	-	-	**4**	**9**	**6**	-	**1**	**6**	**13**	-	-
UN-IDENTIFIED	13	*subtotal*	**1**	**3**	-	**3**	**2**	-	**2**	**3**	**3**	**5**	**1**
	67	***Category Total***	**16**	**7**	**6**	**28**	**11**	-	**3**	**22**	**32**	**8**	**2**

EXHIBIT 8 *(continued)*

Q3—Why did you choose not to buy from us? N=67; ANS = 83

	Price	Unclear Shipping Selection	Site Policy	Security Troubles	Just Looking Concerns	for Info	Others	Total
All Regions 16%	13	8	1	3	1	25	32	83
	10%	1%	4%	1%	30%	39%		100%

Q4—Open-ended comments

	Site Visuals			
IN	15	4	–	3
OUT	7	3	1	–
Un-identified	7	–	–	1
Category Total	**29**	**7**	**1**	**3**
				48%

	Site Visuals	Not Enough Subtotal	Selection	Need Price	Skeptical About Cdn$	Positive Quality	No Online Disposition	Security Help	Site Problems	Navigation	Total
IN	2	24	6	5	3	–	1	2	1	3	45
OUT	1	12	6	5	–	–	1	–	2	1	27
Un-identified	–	7	2	2	2	1	–	2	1	3	18
Category Total	**3**	**43**	**14**	**12**	**5**	**1**	**2**	**2**	**4**	**7**	**90**
	16%	**13%**	**6%**	**1%**	**2%**	**2%**	**4%**	**8%**	**100%**		

Source: Blinds To Go company files.

Chapter 6

Business-to-Business E-Commerce and E-Commerce Strategy

While the popular press has focused heavily on business-to-consumer (B2C) e-commerce in recent years, the *real* story has actually been business-to-business (B2B) electronic commerce. The widespread acceptance of the Internet as a business platform has given organizations new mechanisms for reducing their costs, improving productivity, and streamlining their internal as well as inter-organizational business processes. The terms "intranet" and "extranet" entered the business lexicon, referring to the application of Internet technologies and standards to business processes within and without the organization, respectively. Surveys of global electronic commerce activity invariably indicate that the B2C space is many times larger—in terms of transaction volume, dollar volume of transactions, or any other measure—than is the B2C space. Because B2B e-commerce often impacts workflow or supply chain processes that are fundamental to a firm's competitive capability, implementing B2B e-commerce solutions is a nontrivial undertaking and demands close attention and support from senior management.

The cases in this section address B2B e-commerce as well as the question of e-commerce strategy development. Finding and implementing appropriate e-commerce strategies have been difficult challenges for senior executives. Conventional strategic thinking is often at odds with the realities of electronic commerce. The rules are simply different—and yet, perhaps not *so* different as some people supposed. The recent meltdown in market value of electronic commerce companies—especially "born on the Web" firms—suggests that, while some e-commerce rules may be different, basic business realities are still with us in the world of e-commerce, too. The manager's challenge is figuring out just *which* rules are really different here, and which parts of conventional wisdom still apply.

The five cases in this section illustrate a number of issues involved with the adoption and rollout of B2B business solutions, and with the formation and implementation of e-commerce strategy.

The first case focuses on the giant Ford Motor Company, and describes Ford's examination of its supply chain to evaluate whether the company should "virtually integrate," on the Dell Computers model. The case provides valuable insights into the challenges of virtually integrating supply chains in established industries.

The second case involves Metropolitan Life Insurance. In 1998, that company's first vice-president of Interactive Commerce faced a plethora of opportunities, challenges, and decisions in charting MetLife's strategy for e-commerce. He wanted to move quickly into transacting Web-based commerce, but he had to consider executive support, infrastructure requirements, possibly disenfranchising the sales force, fast-moving competitors, and the frenzied rate of technology change. The case covers almost all e-commerce start-up issues, but from the perspective of a large, established "bricks and mortar" business.

The third case in this section concerns eLance.com. eLance.com was created to allow buyers to find sellers for time-sensitive project work without limiting bids to local-area sellers. The company was just finishing the beta test of its website, which had facilitated over 30,000 transactions in the past year. However, before the concept could go fully operational, eLance needed to find a way to prevent, or at least minimize, disintermediation. For eLance, disintermediation occurred when buyers and sellers, after being introduced on the eLance site, would decide to conduct future project-related transactions offline (and hence avoid paying fees to eLance). eLance had already implemented several customer-focused online and offline features to deter disintermediation. The co-founder and vice-president of business development had to determine which incentives to keep, which to add, and which to drop.

The fourth and fifth cases are a companion pair of case studies of the Reuters organization. The first of these cases, set in late 1999, describes the financial market's anxiety about the Internet eroding Reuters' business. It describes the firm's history and competitive landscape. The second case, set in early 2000, describes Reuters' Internet strategy, which includes a decision to expand from B2B to B2C. The first case raises the question of how an old economy firm might transition to the new economy. The second case challenges the reader to assess the appropriateness of Reuters' strategy for Internet business.

Ford Motor Company: Supply Chain Strategy

By Professor Robert D. Austin

Teri Takai, Director of Supply Chain Systems, had set aside this time on her calendar to contemplate recommendations to senior executives. The question they'd asked was widely agreed to be extremely important to Ford's future: how should the company use emerging information technologies (e.g., Internet technologies) and ideas from new high-tech industries to change the way it interacted with suppliers? Members of her team had different views on the subject.

Some argued that the new technology made it inevitable that entirely new business models would prevail, and that Ford needed to radically redesign its supply chain and other activities or risk being left behind. This group favored "virtual integration," modeling the Ford supply chain on that of companies like Dell,[1] which had aggressively used technology to reduce working capital and exposure to inventory obsolescence. Proponents of this approach argued that although the auto business was very complex, both for historical reasons and because of the inherent complexity of the automotive product, there was no reason such business models could not provide a conceptual blueprint for what Ford should attempt.

Another group was more cautious. This group believed that the differences between the auto business and relatively newer businesses like computer manufacturing were important and substantive. Some noted, for example, that relative to Dell the Ford supplier network had many more layers and many more companies, and that Ford's purchasing organization had historically played a more prominent and independent role than Dell's. These differences and others posed complications when

---

[1]Information on Dell included in this case was obtained by Ford from public sources, including the 1997 Dell Annual Report, the Dell website (www.dell.com), and from "The Power of Virtual Integration: An Interview with Dell Computer's Michael Dell," by Joan Magretta, *Harvard Business Review,* March–April 1998 (reprint 98208).

examined closely, and it was difficult to determine the appropriate and feasible scope for redesign of the process.

As she read through the documents provided by her team, she thought about CEO Jac Nasser's recent company-wide emphasis on shareholder value and customer responsiveness. It was widely acknowledged that Dell had delivered on those dimensions, but would the same methods deliver results for Ford?

Company and Industry Background

Based in Dearborn, Michigan, the Ford Motor Company was the second largest industrial corporation in the world, with revenues of more than $144 billion and about 370,000 employees. Operations spanned 200 countries. Although Ford obtained significant revenues and profits from its financial services subsidiaries, the company's core business had remained the design and manufacture of automobiles for sale on the consumer market. Since Henry Ford had incorporated in 1903, the company had produced in excess of 260 million vehicles.

The auto industry had grown much more competitive over the last two decades. Since the 1970s, the Big Three U.S. automakers—General Motors (GM), Ford, and Chrysler—had seen their home markets encroached upon by the expansion of foreign-based auto manufacturers, such as Toyota and Honda. The industry was also facing increasing over-capacity (estimated at 20 million vehicles) as developing and industrialized nations, recognizing the wealth and job-producing effects of automobile manufacturing, encouraged development and expansion of their own export-oriented auto industries.

Although manufacturers varied in their degree of market presence in different geographical regions, the battle for advantage in the industry was fast becoming global. Faced with the need to continue to improve quality and reduce cycle times while dramatically lowering the costs of developing and building cars, Ford and the other large automakers were looking for ways to take advantage of their size and global presence. One element of the effort to achieve advantage in size and scale was a movement toward industry consolidation. In the summer of 1998, Chrysler merged with Daimler-Benz to form a more global automaker. In early 1999, Ford announced that it would acquire Sweden's Volvo, and there were rumors of other deals in the works.

Previously, in 1995, Ford had embarked on an ambitious restructuring plan called Ford 2000, which included merging its North American, European, and International automotive operations into a single global organization. Ford 2000 called for dramatic cost reductions to be obtained by reengineering and globalizing corporate organizations and processes. Product development activities were consolidated into five Vehicle Centers (VCs), each responsible for development of vehicles in a particular consumer market segment (one VC was in Europe). By making processes and products globally common, Ford intended to eliminate organizational and process redundancies and realize huge economies of scale in manufacturing and purchasing. Major reengineering projects were initiated around major company processes, such as Order-to-Delivery (OTD) and Ford Production System (FPS), with goals such as reducing OTD time from more than 60 days to less than 15.

Ford's new global approach required that technology be employed to overcome the constraints usually imposed by geography on information flow. Teams on different continents needed to be able to work together as if they were in the same building. Furthermore, in virtually every reengineering project, information technology (IT) had emerged as a critical enabler. The link between reengineering success and the company's IT groups was made explicit in the Ford 2000 restructuring—IT was placed within the process reengineering organization. In the supply chain area, there was general agreement that IT could also be deployed to dramatically enhance material flows and reduce inventories—substituting information for inventory, as the expression went.

As Ford 2000 unfolded, the Internet revolution unfolded in parallel, creating new possibilities for reengineering processes within and between enterprises. Ford launched a public Internet site in mid-1995; by mid-1997 the number of visits to the site had reached more than 1 million per day. A company-wide *intra*net was launched in mid-1996, and by January of 1997 Ford had in place a Business-to-Business (B2B) capability through which the intranet could be extended in a secure manner beyond company boundaries into an *extra*net, potentially connecting Ford with its suppliers. Ford teamed with Chrysler and General Motors to work on the Automotive Network Exchange (ANX), which aimed to create consistency in technology standards and processes in the supplier network, so that suppliers, already pressed to lower costs, would not have to manage different means of interaction with each automaker.

On January 1, 1999, Jac Nasser took over the CEO job from Alex Trotman. Nasser had been Trotman's second-in-command throughout the Ford 2000 rollout, and had a longstanding reputation as a tough-minded cost-cutter and a capable leader. Even before taking the helm, he had begun to focus Ford senior management on shareholder value. In the period between 1995 and 1999, Ford had seen companies with fewer physical assets and much lower revenues and profits achieve market capitalization well in excess of Ford's. Corporate staff members began to study models such as Cisco and Dell to try to understand whether Ford could produce shareholder value in the ways that these newer companies had.

As the end of 1998 approached, Ford had amassed profits of $6.9 billion, employees enjoyed record profit sharing, and return on sales (3.9 percent in 1997) was trending solidly upward. The company was the world leader in trucks. It had taken over the U.S. industry lead in profit per vehicle ($1,770) from Chrysler, and it was the most improved automaker on the 1997 J. D. Power Initial Quality Study (in fourth place overall, behind Honda, Toyota, and Nissan).

Ford's Existing Supply Chain and Customer Responsiveness Initiatives

Ford had a number of initiatives underway that were aimed at positioning the company favorably for success in integrating with the extended enterprise that also included suppliers and customers. In addition, there were historical factors that would need to be taken into account in any virtual integration strategy.

Ford's Existing Supply Base

The existing supply base was, in many respects, a product of history. As the company had grown over the years so had the supply base, to the point where in the late 1980s there were several thousand suppliers of production material in a complex network of business relationships. Suppliers were picked primarily based on cost, and little regard was given to overall supply chain costs, including the complexity of dealing with such a large network of suppliers.

Beginning in the early 1990s, Ford had begun to actively try to decrease the number of suppliers the company dealt with directly. Rather than fostering strong price competition among suppliers for individual components, there was shift toward longer-term relationships with a subset of very capable suppliers who would provide entire vehicle sub-systems. These "tier one" suppliers would manage relationships with a larger base of suppliers of components of sub-systems—tier two and below suppliers. Ford made its expertise available to assist suppliers in improving their operations via a range of techniques, including Just-In-Time (JIT) inventory, Total Quality Management (TQM), and Statistical Process Control (SPC). In exchange for the closer relationships and long-term commitments, Ford expected yearly price reductions from suppliers. While first tier suppliers had fairly well-developed IT capabilities (many interacted with Ford via Electronic Data Interchange links), they were not able to invest in new technologies at the rate Ford itself could. Also, the IT maturity (understanding and modernity of technology) decreased rapidly in lower tiers of the supply chain. As more cautious members of Takai's staff had often observed, this supply base was different in its nature and complexity from Dell's supply base.

Another major difference between Dell and Ford was organizational. At Dell, purchasing activities reported into the product development organization. At Ford, purchasing was organizationally independent of product development and had been—historically and up to the present—a powerful force within Ford. Because of the sheer volume of materials and services that Ford purchased, a very slim reduction in purchasing cost could result in very significant savings. Consequently, purchasing was involved closely in nearly every product decision. Engineers were counseled to avoid discussing prices in interactions with suppliers, as price negotiation was the sole province of purchasing agents. How this might work in a more virtually integrated system was unclear.

Ford Production System

The Ford 2000 initiative produced five major, corporation-wide reengineering projects. One of these was Ford Production System (FPS). Modeled roughly on the Toyota Production System, FPS involved a multi-year project that drew on internal and external expertise worldwide. FPS was an integrated system aimed at making Ford manufacturing operations leaner, more responsive, and more efficient. It focused on key attributes of the production process, aspiring to level production and move to a more pull-based system, with synchronized production, continuous flow, and stability throughout the process. One important part of FPS was "Synchronous Material Flow" (SMF), which Ford defined as "a process or system that produces a continuous flow of material and products driven by a fixed, sequenced, and leveled vehicle schedule, utilizing flexibility and lean manufacturing concepts." One key to SMF was "In-Line Vehicle Sequencing" (ILVS), a system that used vehicle in-process storage devices (such as banks and ASRSs[2]) and computer software to assure that vehicles were assembled in order sequence. By assuring assembly in order sequence, Ford could tell suppliers exactly when and where certain components would be needed

---

[2]A "bank" is a storage area into which partially assembled vehicles can be directed, for the purpose of removing them in a different order than the order in which they entered (i.e., resequencing). An "ASRS" or "Automated Storage and Retrieval System" is essentially a multi-level bank (vehicles are literally stored on top of each other); whereas an ordinary bank provides some resequencing flexibility, an ASRS provides the ability to access any vehicle in the bank at any time. As might be imagined, to hold a large number of vehicles and allow them to be accessed randomly, an ASRS must be very large (roughly the size of a several-story building).

days in advance, and buffer stocks could be dramatically reduced. If such sequenced assembly could be kept level and if it was well-forecasted, the benefits would be felt throughout the supply chain. The vision was of trucks constantly in motion throughout their lives, in continuous circuits between suppliers and Ford, stopping only to refuel or change drivers, feeding a process that worked like a finely tuned and smoothly running precision instrument.

Order to Delivery

Another key process Ford reengineering initiative was Order to Delivery (OTD). The purpose of the OTD project was to reduce to 15 days the time from a customer's order to delivery of the finished product—a significant reduction versus the present performance of 45–65 days. Ford took a holistic approach to the reengineering. Pilots studies in 1997 and 1998 identified bottlenecks throughout Ford's supply chain, including its marketing, material planning, vehicle production, and transportation processes. Ford's approach to implementing an improved OTD process relied on several elements: 1) ongoing forecasting of customer demand from dealers—before OTD Ford had never officially involved dealers in forecasting demand; 2) a minimum of 15 days of vehicles in each assembly plant's order bank to increase manufacturing stability; gaps in the order bank are filled with "suggested" dealer orders based on historical buying patterns; 3) regional "mixing centers" that optimize schedules and deliveries of finished vehicles via rail transportation; and 4) a robust order amendment process to allow vehicles to be amended for minor color and trim variations without having to submit new orders. The OTD vision was to create a lean, flexible and predictable process that harmonized the efforts of all of Ford's components to enable it to provide consumers with the right products in the right place at the right time. Ford believed that success in achieving this vision would provide better quality, higher customer satisfaction, improved customer selection, better plant productivity, stability for its supply base and lower dealer and company costs.

Ford Retail Network

On July 1, 1998 Ford launched the first of its Ford Retail Network (FRN) ventures in Tulsa, Oklahoma under the newly formed Ford Investment Enterprises Company (FIECo). Ford Investment Enterprises was formed to take advantage of the changing face of retail vehicle distribution systems in North America. FIECo had two primary goals: 1) to be a test bed for best practices in retail distribution and drive those practices throughout the dealer network; and 2) to create an alternate distribution channel to compete with new, publicly owned retail chains such as AutoNation. Ownership in the FRN varied from market to market; in some Ford would be the majority owner and in others Ford would be the minority owner. In Rochester, New York, Ford was partnering with Republic—another large, publicly owned corporation. One of the principles of the FRN was to buy all the Ford dealers in a local market so that the dealers were in competition against the "real" competition (i.e., GM, Toyota, Honda), rather than with each other. The overriding goal was for the consumer to receive the highest level of treatment and to create an experience they would want to come back to again and again. Showrooms would have a consistent look on the outside, with customized interiors for the different Ford brands—Ford, Mercury, Lincoln and Jaguar. The number of showrooms would be consolidated to focus resources on creating a superior selling experience, while the number of service outlets would increase to be closer to customer population centers. Ford expected personnel and advertising cost savings, as well as inventory efficiencies due to economies of scale and greater use of the Internet. Ford also believed that the FRN would provide an opportunity to increase business not just in new and used vehicles, but also in parts and service, body shop operations, and Ford Credit.

Dell's Integrated Supply Chain

See "The Power of Virtual Integration: An Interview with Dell Computer's Michael Dell," *Harvard Business Review,* March–April 1998, pages 72–84.

The Decision

Takai perused the neatly prepared documents that had been provided by her staff. There was a broad-based comparison between Dell and Ford on many important dimensions (Exhibit 1). Virtual integration would require changes in fundamental operations; some of the changes, framed as a shift from "push" to "pull" processes, were identified in another document (Exhibit 2). Whatever she decided, she would have to do it soon. Meetings were already scheduled with the VP of Quality and Process Leadership, and from there the recommendations would move upward, eventually to Nasser.

EXHIBIT 1 Dell and Ford Compared

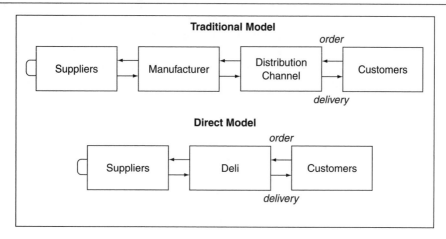

Comparative Metrics (latest fiscal year)

	Dell	Ford	
		Automotive	*Fin. Services*
Employees	16,100	363,892	
Assets ($mils)	4,300	85,100	194,000
Revenue ($mils)	12,300	122,900	30,700
Net Income ($mils)	944	4,700	2,200
Return on Sales	7.7%	3.8%	7.2%
Cash ($mils)	320	14,500	2,200
Manufacturing Facilities	3 (Texas, Ireland, Malaysia)	180 (in North and South America Europe, Asia, Australia)	
Market Capitalization ($mils)	58,469	66,886	
P/E	60	10*	
5 Year Avg. Revenue Growth	55% per year	6% per year	
5 Year Avg. Stock Price Growth	133% per year	33.4% per year	

*Excludes earnings from Associates spin-off.

Sources: Dell 1998 Financial Report, Ford 1997 Annual Report, Wall Street Journal Interactive.

EXHIBIT 1   *(continued)*

Enterprise Model Comparison

A high-level comparison of the Dell and Ford Motor enterprise models is shown below. Besides the lack of a dealer distribution channel, other key differences are Dell's ownership of assembly plants only—all component/sub-assembly manufacturing is done by its supply base—and the more integrated nature of Dell's Sales, R&D, and Manufacturing Operations. All of the operating principles that underlie Dell's success have counterparts in Ford's breakthrough objectives and key business plan initiatives.

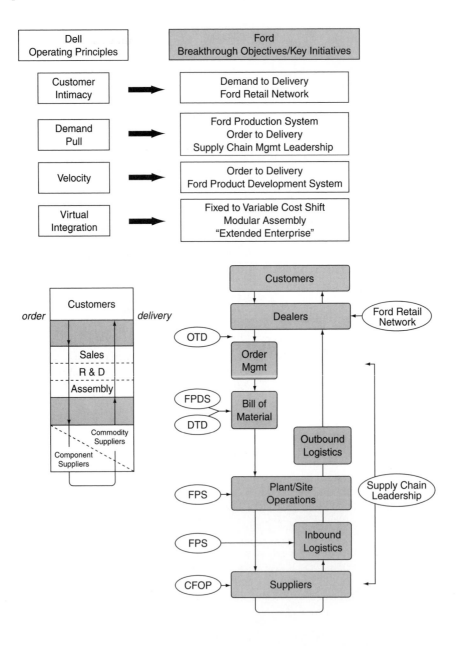

EXHIBIT 1 *(continued)*

Dell Processes	Ford
Suppliers own inventory until it is used in production	
Suppliers maintain nearby ship points, delivery time 15 minutes to 1 hour	✓
External logistics supplier used to manage inbound supply chain	✓
Customers frequently steered to PCs with high availability to balance supply and demand	✓
Demand forecasting is critical—changes are shared immediately within Dell and with supply base	
Demand pull throughout value chain—"information for inventory" substitution	
Focused on strategic partnerships: suppliers down from 200 to 47	✓
Complexity is low: 50 components, 8–10 key, 100 permutations	

EXHIBIT 2 Moving from Push to Pull

		Process	
Process	*Process*	*Push*	*Pull*
Design	Design strategy	Please everyone	Mainstream customer wants
Marketing	Vehicle combinations	More is better	Minimal
	Pricing strategy	Budget-driven	Market-driven
	Vehicle purchase incentives	Higher	Lower
Manufacturing and Supply	Capacity planning	Multiple material/ capacity constraints, driven by program budget	Market-driven (no constraints, FPV/ CPV+10% for vehicle, +15% for components
	Schedule and build stability	Maximize production— make whatever you can build	Schedule from customer-driven order bank, build to schedule
Dealer Network	Dealer ordering	Orders based on allocations and capacity constraints	Orders based on customer demand
	Order to delivery times	Longer (60+ days)	Shorter (15 days or less)
	Inventory	High with low turnover	Low with rapid turnover
	Dealership model	Independent dealerships, negotiations with company	Company controlled dealerships (Ford Retail Network)

Metropolitan Life Insurance: E-Commerce

By Professor Scott L. Schneberger and Murray McCaig

A study by Ernst & Young LLP revealed that despite considerable spending on Internet ventures, most financial companies don't have a clear idea of what they're doing or why they're doing it. Only 1 percent of the companies listed "selling more products and services" over the Internet as a top e-commerce goal. Thirty-three per cent listed retaining existing customers and 23 percent cited reducing operational costs as driving forces behind their Web strategies.

Meanwhile, 40 percent hadn't coordinated their Web offerings with their other distribution channels, and 70 percent had not come up with a pricing strategy for their e-commerce efforts. Still, financial companies are budgeting twice as much money for e-commerce this year as last, and by 2001, they predict they'll spend about 14 percent of their technology budgets on Internet commerce.[1]

Deep in thought, Richard Painchaud gazed out the window of the train on his return trip in June 1998 from Metropolitan Life Insurance Company (MetLife) headquarters in Manhattan. Richard was contemplating the difficult questions posed to him by Jim Valentino, the Senior VP of Corporate Marketing.

In 1995, as MetLife was assembling the Interactive Commerce department, Jim had asked Richard what he knew about the Internet. "Not much; I'm a marketer. Why?" That honest reply got Richard appointed as first VP of Interactive Commerce (IC), a position that was originally considered to be low stress. Richard's initial mandate was simply to create an informational website that would feature MetLife's extensive LIFE ADVICE® program for customers.

At that time, developing an information-based Web venue had required only limited coordination with other business units and departments. Moving the web venue to the next level where it could generate revenue as a fully transactional (see Glossary of Terms) and interactive

---

[1]*Wall Street Journal,* September 9, 1998.

site would require complex integration and interaction with many departments. Between coordinating departmental integration and trying to keep up with the unprecedented rate of change in the Internet, Richard's position became one of the most demanding roles of his career. As he looked out on the countryside, Richard wondered what strategy he should take both internally and externally to answer Jim Valentino's most difficult question, "When is this thing going to make money?"

Richard knew he needed to have a comprehensive solution in the works by year-end that clearly demonstrated to upper management that the MetLife Web venue was moving towards profitability. To meet this deadline, he figured he had two months to lay out his strategy.

MetLife

MetLife was a mutual company that had been a leader in the life insurance industry since its inception in 1868. The MetLife family of companies currently had offices throughout the United States and operations in North and South America, Europe and Asia. Its prized team of associates worldwide served millions of people. In the United States, MetLife served 86 of Fortune's top 100 companies. MetLife was the second largest North American life insurer (behind Prudential) with over $1.6 trillion of life insurance in force as of December 31, 1997, and ranked 15th on the Fortune 500 list in terms of assets (Exhibit 1).

EXHIBIT 1   Fortune's 1997 Corporate Rankings (Top 45 Ranked by Assets)

	(in millions)			
Company	*Revenues*	*Profits*	*Assets*	*Employees*
1. Fannie Mae	$ 27,777	$ 3,056	$ 391,673	3,500
2. Travelers Group	$ 37,609	$ 3,104	$ 386,555	67,250
3. Chase Manhattan Corp.	$ 30,381	$ 3,708	$ 365,521	69,033
4. Citicorp	$ 34,697	$ 3,591	$ 310,897	93,700
5. General Electric	$ 90,840	$ 8,203	$ 304,012	276,000
6. Morgan Stanley Dean Witter	$ 27,132	$ 2,586	$ 302,287	47,277
7. Merrill Lynch	$ 31,731	$ 1,906	$ 292,819	56,600
8. Ford Motor	$153,627	$ 6,920	$ 279,097	363,892
9. NationsBank Corp.	$ 21,734	$ 3,077	$ 264,562	80,360
10. J.P. Morgan & Co.	$ 17,701	$ 1,465	$ 262,159	16,943
11. BankAmerica Corp.	$ 23,585	$ 3,210	$ 260,159	77,000
12. Prudential Ins. Co. of America	$ 37,073	$ 610	$ 259,482	79,000
13. General Motors	$178,174	$ 6,698	$ 228,888	608,000
14. TIAA-CREF	$ 29,348	$ 1,227	$ 214,296	4,824
15. Metropolitan Life Insurance	**$ 24,374**	**$ 1,203**	**$ 201,907**	**44,979**

EXHIBIT 1 *(continued)*

	(in millions)			
Company	*Revenues*	*Profits*	*Assets*	*Employees*
16. Federal Home Loan Mortgage	$ 14,399	$ 1,395	$ 194,597	3,200
17. American International Group	$ 30,520	$ 3,332	$ 163,971	40,000
18. First Union Corp.	$ 14,329	$ 1,896	$ 157,274	43,933
19. Lehman Brothers Holdings	$ 16,883	$ 647	$ 151,705	8,340
20. Bankers Trust New York Corp.	$ 12,176	$ 866	$ 140,102	18,286
21. Hartford Financial Services	$ 13,305	$ 1,332	$ 131,743	25,000
22. Bear Stearns	$ 6,077	$ 613	$ 121,434	8,309
23. American Express	$ 17,760	$ 1,991	$ 120,003	74,000
24. Banc One Corp.	$ 13,219	$ 1,306	$ 115,901	56,600
25. First Chicago NBD Corp.	$ 10,098	$ 1,525	$ 114,096	33,962
26. Cigna	$ 20,038	$ 1,086	$ 108,199	47,700
27. State Farm Insurance Cos.	$ 43,957	$ 3,833	$ 103,626	72,655
28. Wells Fargo & Co.	$ 9,608	$ 1,155	$ 97,456	33,100
29. Washington Mutual	$ 7,524	$ 482	$ 96,981	19,880
30. Exxon	$122,379	$ 8,460	$ 96,064	80,000
31. Aetna	$ 18,540	$ 901	$ 96,001	40,300
32. Norwest Corp.	$ 9,660	$ 1,351	$ 88,540	55,729
33. Nationwide Ins. Enterprise	$ 12,644	$ 806	$ 87,830	29,051
34. Fleet Financial Group	$ 8,095	$ 1,303	$ 85,535	32,317
35. New York Life Insurance	$ 18,899	$ 651	$ 84,067	7,003
36. Intl. Business Machines	$ 78,508	$ 6,093	$ 81,499	269,465
37. Allstate	$ 24,949	$ 3,105	$ 80,918	51,400
38. American General	$ 8,927	$ 542	$ 80,620	16,200
39. Lincoln National	$ 6,437	$ 934	$ 77,175	8,120
40. PNC Bank Corp.	$ 6,859	$ 1,052	$ 75,120	24,814
41. KeyCorp	$ 6,568	$ 919	$ 73,699	24,595
42. U.S. Bancorp	$ 6,909	$ 839	$ 71,295	25,858
43. Northwestern Mutual Life Ins.	$ 13,430	$ 689	$ 71,081	3,818
44. Loews	$ 19,648	$ 794	$ 69,577	29,747
45. BankBoston Corp.	$ 6,727	$ 879	$ 69,268	21,500

MetLife was established by Simeon Draper, a New York merchant, following the Civil War. From its inception, aggressive sales were a MetLife hallmark. The company even imported polished British salesmen in the early 1900s when no suitable Americans could be found.

Throughout the 1900s MetLife experienced consistent growth in a highly regulated, and thus stable, environment. The most significant changes were becoming a mutual company, owned by policyholders, in 1915 and expanding to Canada in 1924.

Beginning in 1970, MetLife began to make some major organizational changes beginning with decentralizing its operations by setting up a number of regional service centers across the country. By the end of the decade, MetLife had head offices in seven cities across the United States. At the same time, regional computing centers were established in four different cities.

By the end of the decade, the flaws of MetLife's decentralization program became apparent. Spreading out the company's bureaucracy had caused frustration among employees, and the sales staff was defecting at a rate of about 40 percent per year—very high turnover for MetLife. In 1979, a major effort was begun to reduce bureaucracy, and the number of managers between the chief marketing officer and the sales representatives was reduced from six to three over the next five years. Executive vice president Pierre Maurer, in charge of the reorganization, told employees in 1983, "Always wage war against paper—it's the greatest waster of management time and energy." This began the trend towards centralization of operations at the Manhattan, New York-based corporate headquarters.

Deregulation of financial services throughout the 1980s gave impetus to a number of new subsidiaries and products. During this period, MetLife acquired numerous financial service operations; many of these, like Century 21 real estate, were unrelated to their core insurance business. By the late 1980s, the trend was towards globalization of financial markets. In keeping with this trend, MetLife initiated operations in Tokyo, Spain, and Taiwan.

MetLife undeniably had one of the most effective sales forces in the industry. MetLife placed immense value on this sales force, because it was central to the company's competitive position. Many of the senior executives in the organization had been involved in sales at one point in their careers, which further reinforced their commitment to the sales agents' interests. However, there were a few executives who believed MetLife should be exploring new channels of distribution that would allow them greater control.

MetLife Interactive Commerce Development

From the website's inception, MetLife decided marketing should drive its electronic commerce efforts (Exhibit 2). About this time, in 1995, there were a few individuals in the marketing department monitoring MetLife's experiments with new technologies like interactive television and kiosks. One of the most promising of these new technologies was the Internet. MetLife decided that a formal Internet experiment was required; IC was officially formed in 1995 as a division of the corporate marketing department with Richard at the helm. The Internet experiment was initiated without a stated goal in mind, but it was implied that IC should evaluate this new medium as a distribution channel.

Realizing that he did not have the capabilities to develop a user-friendly website in-house and wanting to act quickly, he decided to seek

---

EXHIBIT 2   MetLife Organizational Chart

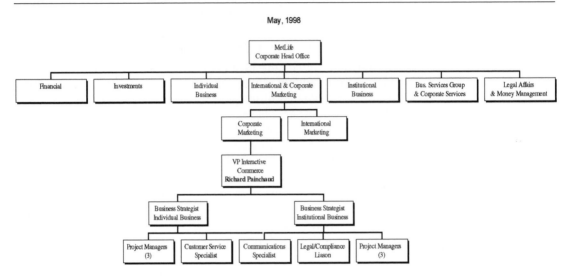

May, 1998

help outside MetLife. Richard interviewed several traditional and new media agencies. Eventually, his search led him to Chan Suh and Kyle Shannon. Chan and Kyle were two entrepreneurs who had recently founded the online communications agency called AGENCY.COM. After a series of introductory meetings, MetLife became AGENCY.COM's first major client as they helped create MetLife's first web site, known as MetLife Online®. The site was launched on December 17, 1995, just one day before MetLife's primary competition, Prudential Insurance, launched theirs. The MetLife web venue focused on the Life Advice program that provided consumers with valuable information on everything from family matters (like *Caring for Your Aging Parents*), to money matters (like *Creating a Budget*). The site was a success from the beginning and won numerous awards and accolades for its design from both the media and company executives.

Much of IC's efforts in 1996 were focused on building credibility internally through extensive promotion of the web venue. The purpose of this internal promotion was to solicit projects from other divisions, increasing the demand for IC's services and allowing Richard to justify a larger budget request. Merchandise like posters, videos, and t-shirts was created while an informational booth was set up in the lobby of MetLife's downtown Manhattan office tower.

By 1997, website usage was growing exponentially; there were more site visitors in the first month of 1997 than during the entire year of 1996 (Exhibit 3). Under pressure to take advantage of site acceptance and to demonstrate returns through cost savings, Richard began to con-

EXHIBIT 3 MetLife Web Venue Usage Statistics

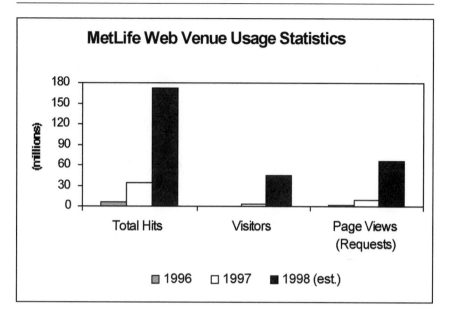

sider moving MetLife IC beyond simply providing information to delivering customer service. By allowing customers to service themselves through the website, substantial cost savings could be realized. For example, it was more cost-effective and quicker to have consumers download forms from the site than to mail them. Part of this initiative was the creation of the business-to-business section of the site, which was one of the main efforts of 1997. The business-to-business section was highly practical, allowing corporate clients to download forms (like claim forms) and submit changes through the Web to speed processing. These features had direct and measurable returns, and enabled MetLife IC to track the savings being created by the site.

The rate of growth had other effects. Richard had to rapidly add people to the IC staff to support its growing popularity and meet the increased demands for Web projects from almost every department. MetLife IC was coordinating everything from major business-to-business projects requiring systems integration, to banner ad creation for supporting marketing promotions in other channels. By early 1998, MetLife IC was working on more projects than the group could handle given their staff and budget. In addition, each project had become significantly more complex, time-consuming, and expensive. There was little time left for an overall Internet strategy or for the planning required by large projects; development was becoming more like patchwork.

Insurance Competition on the Internet

Competition in the insurance industry had been increasing rapidly due to deregulation, globalization, and shrinking demand in developed markets caused by an aging generation and introduction of non-insurance products. This increased competition started a trend towards consolidation and specialization worldwide. For many of the larger insurers, the Internet was an unwelcome addition to these competitive forces. More troubling, perhaps, was that the nature of competition on the Internet was very different and unfamiliar. However, with the online insurance industry expected to reach $4 billion by 2002 (Forrester Research), new entrants were flocking to the Internet and developing innovative solutions to serve the customers' needs for comparison and convenience.

The Internet was bringing together traditional, other financial, virtual, and indirect competitors in the insurance industry (Exhibit 4). Traditional competitors were being forced to compete in new ways

---

EXHIBIT 4   Web Venues Examples

MetLife®
Copyright 1997, 1998 Metropolitan Life Insurance Company
One Madison Avenue, New York, NY 10010
* MetLife Securities, Inc., One Madison Avenue, NY, NY 10010
All Rights Reserved

| Home | Contact Met | Search Met | Site Guide | * **Metgician**℠★ | **Meet** with **Met** |

Source: www.MetLife.com, October 1998.

EXHIBIT 4 *(continued)*

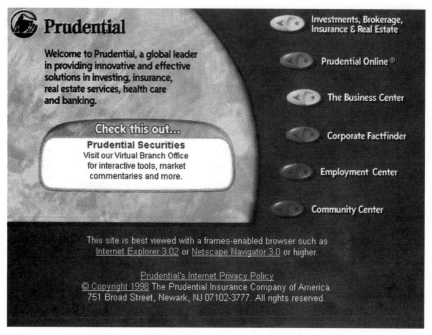

Source: www.prudential.com, October 1998.

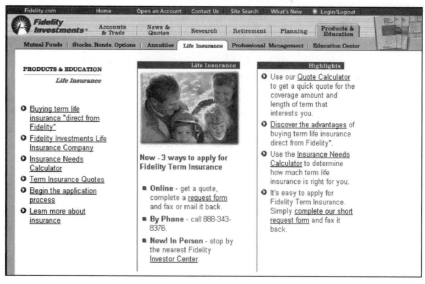

Source: www.fidelity.com, October 1998.

EXHIBIT 4 *(continued)*

Source: www.BudgetLife.com, October 1998.

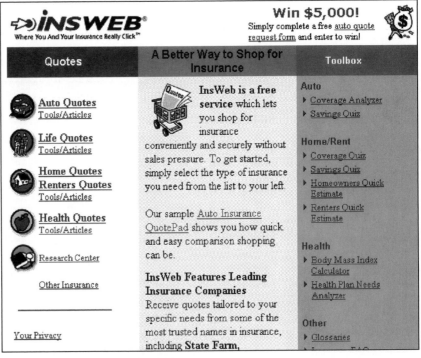

Source: www.insweb.com, October 1998.

EXHIBIT 4 *(continued)*

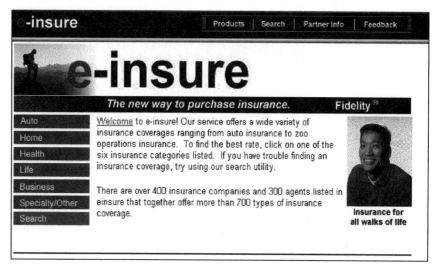

Source: www.e-insure.com, October 1998.

and in greater scope. Large financial institutions, like banks and mutual fund companies, were leveraging the Internet to market insurance to existing and new customers. New entrants to the insurance marketplace like virtual insurers, e-brokers, and aggregators were quick to exploit new technologies on the Internet. Finally, there was increasing indirect competition from infomediaries who, though not selling insurance, were positioned to take a percentage of the sales margin.

Traditional Competitors Online

Competition between the major insurers on the Internet in 1998 was weak, as each of the big players seemed to wait for the other to make a move before following. According to Booz·Allen, "just 1 percent of current insurance websites and fewer than 30 per cent of those planned for the year 2000 will allow users to purchase insurance policies."[2] Most of all, insurance companies were reluctant to embrace the Web as a legitimate sales channel for fear of aggravating their sales associates, who were at the time the main source of sales. If the agents felt they were being disintermediated by the Internet and thus losing sales

---

[2]Booz·Allen & Hamilton Study Says Insurance Industry Building Internet Presence—but Not Realizing Full Cyberpotential New York, NY, February 24, 1997 (http://www.bah.com/press/insurance.html).

commissions, there could be a mass exodus. Most insurers were using the Web to provide information, to support sales agents by providing qualified leads, and to perform limited customer service. Only one of the major insurers, John Hancock, was offering quotes online, and none of the major insurers was selling insurance directly online. The general attitude that top insurance executives possessed towards the Internet could be summed up by William F. Yelverton, CEO of the individual-insurance group at the Prudential Insurance, the country's largest life insurer, who said that computers may be fine for gathering and exchanging information but rejected the Internet as a vehicle for sales and, therefore, did not see it coming between Prudential and its 12,500 agents. "We see the agents as the preeminent way to distribute life insurance, now and in the future," he said.[3]

Banks

Banks (especially conglomerates such as Citigroup) were expanding their efforts in the insurance industry quickly due to deregulation. The leading banks were far ahead of insurers online, and strong online competition between them was pushing innovation. They offered full account access, transactions, brokerage services and many new innovative Web-only services—like life insurance quoting. The Internet was making it easier for banks to become one-stop financial centers because they could quickly expand their offering in the virtual market space.

Banks had a number of competitive advantages in the online financial services industry. The banks had been able to quickly embrace the Internet because their information systems were well prepared by systems work required to introduce the Automatic Teller Machine standard. Banks were ahead of insurers in the use of advanced data mining tools to finely target their marketing efforts. These data mining skills were being transferred to the Web environment, allowing banks to personalize their sites for customers. In addition, online customers typically visited their bank Web venues on a regular basis for common transactions, which allowed the banks to learn more about customer habits and to market specific products (like insurance) to them with each visit.

Mutual Fund Companies

Mutual fund companies were another new source of competition. They were merging insurance with other investment products to create all types of annuities that added new value to traditional insurance offerings. Mutual fund companies were beginning to successfully differenti-

---

[3]"When the Agent of Change Is a Click of the Mouse," *The New York Times,* September 6, 1996 (http://nytimes.com).

ate these insurance products by associating them with successful and recognized funds. Their Web venues had become popular sites that customers repeatedly visited to learn about their investment performance. Mutual fund companies were also significantly ahead of insurers online since most allowed Web account transactions.

Virtual Insurers

New, totally virtual entrants to the insurance industry, like Budget Life, posed a major threat to the established players in the insurance industry. These new entrants had thin operating structures and were not constrained by commitments to other channels or by large investments in fixed assets. They could be compared to online brokerages, which at the time, were successfully capturing a substantial share of the retail stock and mutual fund trading business from established brokers by drastically cutting margins. If these online insurance brokers gained a critical mass, they could have the same effect on the insurance industry.

New technologies were even threatening insurer price positions. For example, "intelligent agents" could further increase price competition by allowing customers to send out searches for the best-priced insurance products that would meet their stated criteria.

Keeping E-Brokers

What appeared to be the most formidable new competitors in the online financial services industry, however, were online brokers including companies like E*trade, Schwab, and Datek. A then recent study by Jupiter Communications predicted that online brokerages would control more than 50 per cent of personal finance activity online by 2002, taking significant market share away from banks. Online brokers were doing a superb job of rapidly implementing new technology, creating needs-based solutions, and marketing their products and brand online. Expansion into insurance and other financial products was a natural direction for these competitors. Recently, E*trade signed on one of InsWeb's insurance shopping services, making a major step towards the insurance market. Christos M. Cotsakos, President and CEO of E*trade, once provided all new accounts with a free copy of the book, *Boot Your Broker,* with a new message: "boot your agent."

Aggregators and Infomediaries

Aggregators and infomediaries, like InsWeb, Quicken, e-insure, Quote Smith and others were working to become insurance gateways or portals. These Web venues presented a strong value proposition to customers by providing convenience, selection, and comparison at a single location. It was thought they had the potential to act like independent "mega-agents," marketing a huge selection of products from many different providers and taking profit margin on each contract sold. By gaining a significant bargaining position with insurance underwriters, they could also capture a larger share of the margin. Major insurers would have to participate in these sites, as they were becoming the first and only stop for many customers online. InsWeb had been forming partnerships with everyone and at the time had signed deals with both Yahoo and E*trade.[4] "Until the Internet, there has not been an easy way to shop for insurance," said Enan Hussein, chairman and CEO of InsWeb. "Our goal is to do end-to-end insurance sales (competing directly with the major insurers), but now we're focused on what consumers really want, and that's comparison shopping."

Independent Brokers

A few small "Net savvy" independent brokers were creating well-designed Web venues to support their operations and marketing and to attract new customers in the marketspace. Transferring current customers to the Web was easier for these agents, because the customers knew they could always visit the agency or agent in person. Their strengths had always been in cultivating loyal customer relationships, which, if transferred to their Web venues, would provide them the same advantage online. The threats posed by independent brokers were much the same as aggregators but on a smaller scale. On the upside, these small independent brokers could become valuable online associates, using a strategic model similar to the web bookseller, Amazon.com.

Richard was well aware of the drastic effects that fierce competition on the Web could have on other distribution channels. In the worst-case scenario, the Web would lead to extreme price competition in all segments, customers would be encouraged to purchase on the Web, agents would begin to feel the crunch, the insurers would begin unsustainable cross-subsidization of their other channels, and slow their adoption. Richard knew he would have to be prepared for all scenarios, even the unlikely "guys down the street in their garage," who might be inventing a new method for risk management.

Emerging Internet Technology

Internet technology was evolving at such a frenzied pace that corporate Web venues were often outdated by the time they were launched. Discerning those technologies that would create value for the consumer was a daunting task that required the full-time attention of someone who clearly understood the broader picture.

Dynamically generated content, personalization, data mining of site usage statistics, collaborative filtering, and automated response e-mail

---

[4]C/Net News.com, "Yahoo Launches Insurance Center," April 6, 1998 (http://www.news.com).

software were just a few of the new features that were required to be a player in the online game. Being able to determine relevant technologies and quickly implement them was in itself a competitive advantage. It was certain that more advanced systems, tools, and ideas would be required to continuously renew competitive advantages going forward.

Ubiquitous Internet video conferencing was an example of evolving technology that could change the nature of competition by enabling "face-to-face" Internet contact between sales representatives and customers. This could return a somewhat personal touch to insurance sales, but would require large investment in personnel and training. Large insurers might again be capable of differentiating themselves through this close interaction.

New technologies were even threatening insurer price positions. For example, "intelligent agents" could further increase price competition by allowing customers to send out searches for the best-priced insurance products that would meet their stated criteria.

Keeping up with new developments was becoming a crucial activity, but unfortunately one that was often the first to be squeezed off the priority list as it did not provide immediate returns. As part of his overall strategy, Richard felt IC needed a plan for monitoring these technological developments.

Internal Challenges

Whichever Internet strategy Richard pursued would have to be one that could also be successfully implemented internally. Richard felt there were many internal barriers that significantly reduced his options. First, and foremost, was the challenge of convincing senior management that the Internet should be viewed as an opportunity, not a threat. Secondly, IC had to deal with MetLife's legacy systems and the task of integrating them with the Web. Then there was the urgent Y2K problem, the growing complexity of the Internet projects, and internal challenges from IT and other divisions to IC's total control over MetLife's Internet presence.

The first and highest level challenge was convincing upper management that the Internet was a viable sales channel and that it would not necessarily have to disintermediate the sales agents. MetLife highly valued its sales agents and was nervous of how its actions in other channels would be perceived by its agents. Top management had not yet supported the concept of selling insurance directly on the Internet; instead, they had opted for the indirect lead generation approach. This approach was to invite those individuals interested in MetLife's insurance products to submit their contact information so that an agent could contact them. Harry P. Kamen, CEO of MetLife, had repeatedly told sales agents he did not believe the Internet was a viable channel for selling insurance and would thus not be pursued by MetLife. According to Mr. Kamen, "Selling insurance requires face time."

Secondly, MetLife's information systems software was both complex and proprietary and many departments had incompatible software applications leading to poor information integration within the company. Most of these systems processed data in batches rather than in real time, which meant they were not ready for real time integration into the Web. Furthermore, the company's Internet server was not even connected to MetLife's systems. For example, each sales lead generated by the web venue had to be manually keyed into MetLife's information systems and sent electronically to a sales manager for printing and finally passed to a sales agent. Due to many incompatible systems and duplicated customer accounts, MetLife could not then offer consolidated account reporting for individuals. This feature, however, would be a minimum expectation of customers on the Web.

A third complication was the urgent Y2K problem, which was consuming the majority of IT resources. There was a lot of systems and web integration work required, but with Y2K on the horizon, IT would not be of any assistance in this process. Richard might have to outsource any systems integration work—which would be costly with the current demand in the marketplace, could rob his staff of valuable experience, and could diminish his control over the final product. It might also make him dependent on the outsourcer.

A fourth challenge surrounded the rapid increase in project complexity that required more extensive communication and coordination efforts with other departments and AGENCY.COM. This issue was only likely to get worse since the next stage of development would require significantly more complex integration with many areas within the organization. Moving the web venue to a transactional stage would require participation and cooperation from all departments like marketing, product development, and customer service.

Finally, other departments were beginning to question IC's total control over the web venue and all Internet projects, especially as many projects were far behind schedule. Some departments were asking to work directly with outsourcing agencies of their choice. Richard would have to be wary of challenges to gain control of part or the whole of the web venue, or attempts to outsource projects that should be managed by IC. Losing the support of the many departments IC served would mean the end of IC. Without the concentrated and coordinated effort that IC provided, MetLife's goal of profitability from the web venue, Richard thought, would be seriously hindered.

The Dilemma

Richard believed all along that the Internet had the potential to "make money," but daily management had become so chaotic that there was little chance to think about a strategy for accomplishing this goal. Jim Valentino's questioning about Internet profitability, however, was an indication that top management was beginning to look for concrete results from the IC department. Moreover, popular literature increasingly trumpeted the potential for Internet business profits.

Richard was certain the Internet would become a key component of MetLife's future corporate strategy, and that the pressure for that component to create revenue would build. It was clear to him that the Internet was a lower-cost delivery channel and would put pressure on margins in all channels. "The Internet could cut costs across the insurance value chain by more than 60 per cent,[5] with the most dramatic savings in distribution and customer service," according to Booz·Allen. These cost savings, combined with convenient and customized service, could encourage consumers to buy policies on the Web. Companies that offered online policies would undercut traditionally priced products and threaten insurers' profitability. Richard believed MetLife would be precluded from competing in an entire market segment if it did not wholly embrace the Internet as a legitimate sales channel. Richard understood the worst-case scenario, but he also felt there were many best-case scenarios where he could lead the organization.

The Main Options

Richard felt there were many strategies he could pursue to generate revenues from the MetLife web venue and establish it as a viable sales channel. They seemed to coalesce into three types: selling insurance directly to customers through the Web venue, the indirect strategy of keeping salespeople in the loop, and the strategy of selling through new intermediaries.

The first strategy, selling directly through MetLife's Web venue, had a number of benefits. MetLife could increase its margins and thus have more flexibility for competing on price. It could build relationships and interact directly with its customers, eventually transferring customer loyalty from the agents to the company. However, this move would likely be viewed negatively by the sales agents and could cause many MetLife agents to leave MetLife and independent agents to end distribution of MetLife products. Attracting customers to purchase products at the MetLife site could be difficult unless it matched the price and other comparison services that many aggregators currently offered.

The second strategy, which could avoid resistance by the sales agents, would be to involve them in the sales process either by allowing them to close deals arranged over the Internet (for smaller margins), or by creating Web pages for them to utilize in selling directly to customers.

---

[5]"Booz·Allen & Hamilton Study Says Insurance Industry Building Internet Presence—but Not Realizing Full Cyberpotential," New York, February 24, 1997 (http://www.bah.com/press/insurance.html).

The former transmediation strategy would transfer customers to agents once the limits of the Web were reached for a particular product. Thus, customers would be directed to agents only for complex or customized insurance needs that could not be provided via the Web venue, while simple sales could be performed through self-service at the Web venue. This would maximize utilization of both channels. The latter strategy would help to maintain sales agent relations in the short term, and build strong customer relations. And if done properly, MetLife could later strip out the sales agents from the process by moving to the first strategy.

The third strategy—selling through online intermediaries like associates or aggregators—also had some potential benefits. "If MetLife could build a powerful sales network online through associate programs, it could create a sustainable competitive advantage just as it has with its current sales network. It is really the same thing, but in the virtual world," said an Internet strategist at AGENCY.COM. MetLife could enable any website, whether an insurance broker or online community site, to set up a sales office for marketing its products. This could even allow some of MetLife's more technical agents to move their clients on to the Web. Any customers who chose to purchase through these online offices would be transferred to the main MetLife site to finalize their purchase. Many online organizations including Amazon.com, U-Frame it! and many shopping sites, were using this strategy with huge success.

Aggregators offered many benefits, like selection and convenience, to the customer and could thus attract the majority of insurance buyers. Not all aggregators were the same; some were solely infomediaries offering comparison services, while others sold the products and took a commission. Regardless, all aggregators had the potential to pit insurers against each other in direct price competition, and in the process, increase their bargaining power and capture a growing share of the sales margin. Richard had considered purchasing one of these aggregators, but he felt that competitors would quickly end their participation, as MetLife would obviously have the motivation to promote its products first and foremost. Without participation from the majority of leading insurers, the site would not be able to attract customers looking for selection.

Other Opportunities

Richard also pondered a number of other Internet opportunities for MetLife. One interesting alternative was to set up a virtual sales office on the Web to target the European market where the company had no sales agents. This would get around the sales agent problem, and could lead to a significant increase in European sales. One problem would be that prices would be open to inspection from individuals in all other areas of the world, and sales could be made to individuals outside of Europe—quite easily cutting into other markets. In addition, the Internet was less developed in Europe, perhaps limiting the possibilities for experimenting with new Web technologies.

Another interesting option was to partner, or even purchase, a successful online broker like E*trade. This could provide MetLife with a customer base, technological expertise, and a more complete Web offering. However, this would not likely solve the major problem of integrating MetLife's current systems with the Web—and could still be perceived by the sales agents as a move into their territory.

Richard knew he had plenty of options. His challenge was to choose the best ones—those which would provide MetLife with a profitable return on the required investments, enthuse and maintain a forward-looking IC group, and generate sustainable competitive advantages for MetLife. "I am confident that with all the options we have, we can get the MetLife Web venue making money."

GLOSSARY OF TERMS

aggregator Aggregator is the term for online operations that provide information and sometimes the sale of the majority of products/services in a given industry. Aggregators are an online equivalent of "category killers" like HomeDepot or PetsMart.

associate Associate is the common term used to describe an online partner who promotes the products of a larger vendor at its site in return for a commission on sales or a "bounty." Associate programs can allow companies to organize large proprietary sales networks. These associate programs are being built in cooperation with many types of Web venues including community sites (e.g., Association of Retired Persons), personal home pages, non-profit sites, and other business sites of all sizes.

collaborative filtering Collaborative filtering occurs when both a consumer and the database of that consumer's former interaction with the Web venue collaborate to personalize the data or Web venue for that consumer. This could involve knowledge learned from a consumer's interaction with the site and the specific requests of the consumer at that time.

disintermediation Disintermediation is the process of by-passing an agent or middleman, and occurs when a middleman is no longer adding sufficient value relative to the open market. Insurance agents could be disintermediated by the Internet where consumers can easily find the services that previously were delivered by the agent.

dynamically generated content Dynamically generated content is created in real-time in a process where a database is queried for relevant information and this information is then posted into a standard Web page framework or template.

infomediary   An infomediary provides information on products or services, but does not sell them. An example would be *Consumer Reports* which provides consumer product information, but does not endorse, advertise, or sell commercial products. One theory is that in the virtual world the information regarding a product is as valuable as the product itself.

marketspace   Marketspace is a term for describing the virtual marketplace on the Internet.

personalization   Personalization is the customizing of content and/or context to each individual's preferences. There are obviously many levels of personalization, but the tendency on the Web is towards further customized interactivity.

portal   An Internet portal acts as a gateway to other sites. Portals vary from general gateways such as search engines, to gateways dedicated to a specific industry, product, or consumer interest. They do not contain information at the site; they only provide links to relevant sites.

server   In general, a server is a computer that provides services to computer programs in the same or other computers. Specific to the Web, a Web server is a computer that provides, or serves up, requested HTML pages or files. The Web browser in a computer is a client that requests HTML files from Web servers.

transactional   Transactional refers to the commerce ability of a Web venue. A Web venue that is transactional allows the purchase of information, products, or services entirely over the Internet.

Y2K   Y2K refers to the problem that many software applications will encounter due to the year being expressed in a two-digit format (e.g., 98 vs. 1998). In the year 2000, some software programs may incorrectly interpret the "00" or freeze some information systems.

eLance.com: *Preventing Disintermediation*

Professor Scott Schneberger and Ken Mark

Introduction

"What's the best way to prevent buyers and sellers from executing transactions outside of eLance's site?" wondered Beerud Sheth, cofounder and vice-president of business development for Sunnyvale, California's eLance.com. It was July 21, 2000, and eLance was completing a beta test of its site, having facilitated over 30,000 transactions between project buyers and sellers since its August 30, 1999, site launch.

eLance was in the midst of closing its second round of venture financing which would allow it to execute its plan to become the premier online global services marketplace. In order to achieve this goal, it needed to prevent disintermediation—instances when eLance buyers and sellers, after being introduced on the eLance site, would decide to conduct future project-related transactions offline. Offline transactions would prevent eLance from mediating these transactions and gaining revenue from them.

To combat disintermediation, eLance had already put in place several onsite and offline features. As this was eLance's number one concern, Sheth wanted to know what more it could do.

Overview of the Traditional Staffing Industry

In 1946, William Russell Kelly, anticipating a post-Second World War business and industrial boom, moved to Detroit and founded the Russell Kelly Office Service. The firm, a service bureau that sent its employees to fill in for vacationing or sick employees, set the standard for the newly created staffing industry, and coined the term "Kelly Girls" to identify its staff, most of whom were female secretaries.[1]

The staffing industry was divided into two categories—temporary staffing agencies who hired workers and outsourced them to companies in return for a fee, and talent matchmakers who received a fee for matching freelance independent professionals with companies who required their specialized services.

There were basically two classifications of temporary workers whom the staffing industry counted on: agency-dependent contract employees and independent professionals. In the agency-dependent model, the agency located the assignment, recruited the contractor, negotiated with and billed the client. The agency also withheld applicable taxes from the contractor's regularly scheduled payroll check, with the

[1]Jennifer L. Laabs, "Father of the Staffing Industry—William Russell Kelly—Dies;" *Workforce,* Costa Mesa, March 1998, Volume 77, Issue 3.

difference between the client bill rate and the contractor pay rate (minus taxes) being the agency's revenue. Contractors were responsible for all of the above non-work related items. (See Exhibit 1: Traditional Staffing Industry.)

EXHIBIT 1   Traditional Staffing Industry

Overview

- 6 percent annual growth overall; 24 percent growth in professional/technical markets.
- 7,000 firms in industry with 17,000 locations.
- Top 10 firms control 29 percent of US$72 billion industry (Manpower Inc., Adecco Staffing Services, Interim Services, Norrell Corp, Kelly Services).
- 100 firms with revenues exceeding US$100 million.
- 90 percent of firms offer training programs.

Examples

Company	Type	Focus	Financial Performance	Other
Roth Staffing Company	Traditional temporary staffing service	75% of demand was for clerical or secretarial workers 25% of demand was for higher-skilled workers Company focused on driving volume of placements	Achieved US$74 million in 1998 20% revenue growth from 1994 to 1998 Expected to approach US$240 million in sales by 2003	Roth placed 5,000 temporary workers in 1999 65 offices in seven states
Robert Half International	Traditional temporary staffing service	Focused on high-priced financial and accounting talent	Achieved US$1.3 billion in 1997 43% CAGR from 1995 to 2000	Market capitalization US$5 billion
Aquent (formerly MacTemps)	Talent matchmaker	Focused on creative and technical talent	US$100 million in 1998, expected to top US$190 million in 2000	Offices in nine countries 110% money-back guarantee Offers additional services such as training and factoring

Sources:
- *U.S. Bureau of Labor Statistics.*
- *Linda Davidson; "Maximize the Return on Temp Staff Investments,"* Workforce, Costa Mesa, November 1999, Volume 78, Issue 11.
- *Edward O. Welles,* Number 1 company: The People Business Inc., Boston, October 19, 1999, Volume 21, Issue 15.
- *www.aquent.com, December 2000.*

The independent professional phenomenon became a fundamental socio-economic shift in the American workforce. In 1999, there were an estimated 25 million independent workers in the United States, including 14 million self-employed, eight million independent contractors, and three million temps.[2] Within this group, an estimated eight million were highly skilled independent professionals. In addition, there were approximately four million untapped professionals—people actively thinking about freelancing—for example, moonlighters and work-at-home moms.

E-Lancing Emerges

Freelancers weighed the freedom to be able to work on different, temporary projects against the absence of a fixed revenue stream. Professionals who chose this lifestyle most often relied on personal contacts or staffing agencies as a source for project work. These sources usually limited the freelancer to short-term contract work in his or her immediate geography and network. The emergence of the Internet in the early 1990s promised to remove this barrier of space and time.

Much was written about the opportunity to exchange employment information over this new medium. An excerpt from the article "The Dawn of the E-Lance Economy" by Thomas Malone and Robert Laubacher read:

> The fundamental unit of such an economy is not the corporation but the individual. Tasks aren't assigned and controlled through a stable chain of management but rather are carried out autonomously by independent contractors. These electronically connected freelancers—e-lancers—join together into fluid and temporary networks to produce and sell goods and services. When the job is done—after a day, a month, a year—the network dissolves, and its members become independent agents again, circulating through the economy, seeking the next assignment.

Formation of eLance.com

Wall Street traders Beerud Sheth and Srini Anumolu founded eLance.com with a private placement in late 1998. On August 30, 1999, eLance.com launched the beta version of its global services marketplace from New York City. Its website proclaimed: "eLance is the premier global services marketplace. From business, computer and creative needs to family, financial and much more, eLance provides the resources for people to connect, communicate and complete their project." It continued: "Buyers can post a project description and receive bids from service providers or buy directly from thousands of

---

[2]U.S. Bureau of Labor Statistics.

fixed-price service listings. eLance support features include the Work Space for project development and remote delivery, service provider certifications, feedback ratings, and an international billing and payment system. Service providers find a global market at eLance, and can build their reputation through our feedback system."

The Online E-Lancing Competition[3]

These new e-Lancing e-marketplaces were a way for independent professionals to increase their exposure to potential clients while limiting the amount of resources normally required for self-promotion and advertising and transaction costs. In some cases these sites also served as an effective and efficient way to access necessary services for business survival, including bill payment, insurance purchasing and tax report filing, in a convenient one-stop shopping location. A short list of some of eLance.com's online competition follows.

Ants (Formerly Job Swarm)

The personnel at JobSwarm.com had constructed a fully functioning site and its goals were to build traffic and membership. The opportunities posted on the site covered marketing, IT and writing. The site's main source of revenue seemed to be the 5 percent finder's fee on all billable work completed by registered freelancers. Another possible source of revenue was the private label services it aimed to provide to partners like Startupbiz.com. The primary business model difference between Ants.com and eLance.com was that Ants recruited freelancers to offer the services that clients needed. The site had chosen to offer a program that promised to pay the individual referring another freelancer to the site royalties on the long-term work of that person.

Guru

Guru.com had focused on building a community that promoted freelancing as a lifestyle. By designing a visually appealing site, it sought to brand itself as the leading destination for freelancers. It also offered freelancer advice and support through numerous alliances with other content providers. It charged buyers to post projects that were staffing sites and a high percentage of its staffing was on location. Being a destination site for freelancers, it was expected to offer them additional services such as 401(k) plans, health benefits, and product advice. Guru.com was expected to focus on matching independent professionals (known as "gurus") with hirers.

---

[3]The foundation of this section was outsourced on eLance.com on August 15, 2000.

FreeAgent

FreeAgent.com offered many of the same services as its competition via a basic interface. It had been developed by Opus360, a company that placed IT contractors and provided benefits, including 401(k) plans and insurance for its contractors. Posting an opportunity on the site provided a client with project exposure to thousands of providers. As with the other services in this category, each provider was encouraged to provide an e-portfolio to help the client choose a potential partner. One of the key noticeable differences in its approach versus that of eLance.com's was the effort to promote repeat business to the site by charging clients for posting freelance opportunities on a sliding scale. This sliding scale offered the client, who might otherwise have been inclined to look elsewhere for talent, a clear option to reduce freelance recruiting costs for an ongoing business operation.

eLance.com Overall Site Features

Since its launch date (late August 1999), eLance.com had the set of online tools shown in Table 1 available to users. In addition, eLance.com planned to add billing and payment systems that allowed buyers and sellers in different countries to pay each other (with different currencies, if they so wished). Most improvements were done with the intention of eLance.com keeping buyers and sellers on its site throughout the transaction. To that end, it even offered both parties an online virtual workspace for them to transfer their documents and files.

TABLE 1   eLance.com Site Features, July 1999

Description	Platform upon which buyers and sellers post, review and bid on projects. Includes auction-style bids for projects, messaging, bid acceptance and notification.	File-sharing capability (50 MB space limit), messaging capability, and online scheduling. Can conduct online meetings.	Credit Card Billing and rating system allowing buyers and sellers to rate each other.
Primary Objective	Matching of buyers and sellers of project transactions.	To facilitate transfer of work between buyers and seller (especially international ones).	Develop the primary stream of revenue and put in place a self-managing rating system.

The development of additional functionality could aid the buyer, the seller, its partners or internal operations. Within these four groupings, the co-founders wondered what additional functionality would look like. Initial thoughts created the following list of possibilities:

- Launch regional sites. This would require eLance.com to facilitate personnel matching in various geographies and customize content to each particular geography.
- Provide robust independent professional profiles. This would allow buyers to research the sellers, reviewing their work experience and previous projects.
- Provide search engine. Using keywords, sellers and buyers could search for each other's project postings.
- Provide response management tool. Because of the number of project bids and postings that eLance.com was expected to attract, the response management tool would help buyers and sellers filter through the bids and posts.
- Provide quality control tool. The actual functionality of this product was not yet confirmed but the objective was to build a tool to aid buyers in assessing the quality of a seller. At the time, a rating system had been rolled out by eLance.com.
- Content. One way to attract buyers and sellers was to create specific content relevant to each audience. This would involve in-house writing or syndication of content from other providers, posting articles on topics such as training, selection, workplace improvement or humor.
- Support different languages. eLance.com was considering launching foreign language sites including German and Spanish sites. This was still a new idea and eLance.com intended to explore it within a year.

Registered Users of eLance.com

eLance believed that any registered user could be both a buyer and a seller of services. Thus, there was no distinct demographic profile of eLance buyers. However, eLance noticed that buyers generally shared several common characteristics. The first two were time sensitivity and budget constraints—they wanted the electronic project completed and delivered on-time and on-budget. "These early adopters are often fast-growing tech-savvy start-ups, although many large corporations were using eLance as well," commented Sean Jacobsohn, business development manager. "In addition, buyers are users with limited time and financial resources, and limited employees. Seventy per cent of all buying requests originated in the United States, with an average amount of US$1,000 per transaction."

Projects ranged in price from US$5 to US$500,000. Sellers could design PowerPoint presentations, write a press release, help a small- or medium-sized business develop a website or do piecemeal software engineering. These independent professionals were part of the aforementioned 25 million independent workers in the United States. They ranged in profession from financial consultants, clerical staff and business writers, to graphic designers. Because of their independent status, they were constantly searching for new projects. With its growing number of buyers and its site functionality, eLance believed that its marketplace would draw many of these professionals in search of project work.

Leveraging the Power of the Internet

In creating eLance, Sheth and Anumolu sought to harness the power of the Internet. Here was a medium that allowed global, immediate access to buyers and sellers. Not only were buyers able to find sellers for time-sensitive project work, they were able to choose between competing bids from anywhere in the world. Because each listed project was intended to be completed remotely, there was no need to limit bids to sellers within the vicinity of the buyer's physical office. In addition, the availability of eLance site tools allowed immediate, electronic delivery of projects via a shared Workspace.

There remained, however, several barriers to eLance's success. First, the notion of dividing a person's workload into several projects remained fairly new—eLance would have to ensure that its potential users were familiar and comfortable with posting and bidding for projects.

But more importantly, even if they were at ease with the concept of projects, eLance would have to present enough of a value proposition to buyers and sellers to dissuade disintermediation. There were several key features already incorporated into the eLance model.

Preventing Disintermediation

Sheth explained:

> Well, let me put it this way. You can never really prevent this disintermediation. You can just kind of mitigate the risk. Even an active large market place like eBay still grapples with a grey market as they call it. I think what we will do is make sure we give our users enough reasons that they don't need to go away, allowing them to stick around. We need for our users to arrive at that point where the easiest way to get the job done is through the site rather than off the site. In spite of the added cost, the user gains in terms of convenience, amount of time spent, effort exhausted, money spent—the cheapest way to transact is through our site.

So that's kind of the challenge that we as a company face and the way we address it is by providing a lot of value-added features. For example, our workspace component facilitates development and delivery, our billing and payment features make it easy to pay for the product once it's done, and both buyers and sellers leave feedback for each other. Leaving the feedback allows sellers to build a rating that will get them access to more work.

Sheth listed the onsite and offline features that eLance currently possessed to deter disintermediation.

Onsite

Marketplace

The goal was to create a platform to support project transactions. Because it was open to anyone in the world with an Internet connection, eLance hoped that the marketplace dynamics (real-time, remote bidding, always the prospect of a "better deal") would continue to persuade buyers to post their projects onsite in the hope of getting the best bid.

Workspace

eLance provided the parties of each transaction in progress with 50 megabytes of workspace where projects could be shared and discussed.

Feedback Rating

Buyers and sellers were encouraged to rate each other on a scale of one to five (higher score denoting higher satisfaction with work completed). Because each subsequent project added to one's feedback rating, it was hoped that sellers would continue to bid for onsite projects to maintain their feedback rating and command higher prices.

Online Chat

This function allowed buyers and sellers to speak with each other—eLance.com's site dialed the phone number for both parties at the appointed time. Thus, no telephone numbers had to be exchanged.

Billing and Payment

eLance's site supported credit card payment by buyers—in essence, buyers could pay the seller's bill (generated and sent electronically via eLance) onsite. In addition, an icon appeared beside buyers preregistered with credit cards, providing a higher level of assurance of payment.

Sample Templates

A collection of templates outlining typical bid requirements for various projects was available to both buyers and sellers to help them structure and manage their project transactions.

Online Arbitration

eLance provided online arbitration for disputed transactions via a third-party service, SquareTrade.com.

Offline

Market Makers

eLance market makers facilitated transactions between buyers and sellers, intervening to prompt parties to clarify bids and replies.[4]

Account Managers

One idea was to focus on buyers involved in the majority of transactions. Using the 80:20 rule—80 percent of your volume comes from 20 per cent of your customers—eLance intended to provide these "power buyers" with an account manager to assist them in projects posting.

Electronic Newsletter

eLance provided an electronic newsletter to its members filled with spotlights on recent projects, upcoming functionality and tips for buyers and sellers. It also sent an e-mail notifying sellers of projects postings which met their criteria.

Conclusion

In the following few weeks, eLance would be progressing to a live site from its beta version. It intended to start charging sellers 10 percent of the cost of each project, but keep the service free for buyers. Because eLance felt that it was still in a testing phase for the next few months, it did not want to set any short-term goals for its live site.

Jacobsohn emphasized,

> We're very customer-focused. That's why it took us a year to start charging and see what value-added services we want on site—we will keep monitoring the customer experience so we have a high retention rate. Once we test it long enough, we will be able to set internal goals for these numbers.

Since an increasing number of projects would be transacted on the eLance site, senior management wanted to address the issue of disintermediation before it became an issue. Sheth concluded, "Once they develop a relationship with a buyer or seller, they will be tempted to take the relationship offline. What incentives (or disincentives) can we use to keep these people on our site?"

---

[4]In the stock trading world, the market maker was the person who provided liquidity to the marketplace—a bank or trading firm might have a market maker to keep transactions flowing.

Reuters' Internet Strategy (A)

By Associate Professor Subramanian Rangan
and Brian Coleman

On 21st October 1999, as Internet fever was sweeping through the financial markets, Reuters Group PLC Chief Executive Peter Job held a conference call with investment analysts from New York. As Job discussed the group's third-quarter results, analysts peppered him with questions about how the London-based news and financial information company was preparing for the Internet age.

Observers perceived that Reuters faced a serious challenge with the arrival of the Internet. Some of the financial information that Reuters provided—charging customers between $200 and $1,500 a month—was coming available for free on the Internet.[1] For example, stock prices and an array of breaking news stories could be obtained free of charge at web sites like Yahoo!Finance, TheStreet.com, and cnnfn.com. Likewise, some of the other services the company offered, such as stock trading through its Instinet electronic-trading service, were also coming under pressure from new web-based competitors. Analysts wanted to know how Reuters was responding to the challenge. Job reportedly confessed that it was "hard to be clear about strategy because there are so many changes in our markets at the moment."[2]

The response left analysts nonplussed and worried that Reuters did not have an Internet strategy. More so because just four weeks earlier, on September 23rd, the company had held a briefing that had triggered related concerns and led analysts to revise downward their profit forecasts for Reuters.[3] Rather than reversing those sentiments, this Octo-

---

IVEY   This case was written by Brian Coleman, INSEAD MBA 2000, and Subramanian Rangan, Associate Professor at INSEAD. It is intended to be used as a basis for class discussion rather than to illustrate either effective or ineffective handling of an administrative situation.

Copyright © 2000, INSEAD, Fontainebleau, France

Copies may not be made without permission.

Distributed by The European Case Clearing House, England and U.S.A.

North America, phone: +1 781 239 5884, fax: +1 781 239 5885, e-mail: ECCHBabson@aol.com.

Rest of the World, phone: +44 (0)1234 750903, fax: +44 (0)1234 751125, e-mail: ECCH@cranfield.ac.uk.

All rights reserved. Printed in UK and USA. Website: http://www.tech.cranfield.ac.uk.

---

[1]Information on price of Reuters' services from Peter Job, "Reuters Group PLC: Preliminary Results Presentation to Analysts," 8 February 2000, published on www.reuters.com. For an account of the rise of web-based information providers see Gregory Zuckerman and Rebecca Buckman, "Financial-Data Firms Face Challenges From Web Rivals," *The Wall Street Journal Interactive Edition,* 21 September 1999.

[2]"Reuters Shares Lose 13% after Warning," *Financial Times,* 22 October 1999, p. 1.

[3]"Reuters Shares Plunge after Briefing: Exchange Probes Whether Analysts' Meeting Breached Rules," *Financial Times,* 24 September 1999, p. 1.

ber conference further fueled concern about the company's future in the wake of the Internet.[4] By the end of the day, Reuters' shares were sharply down. In fact, in a span of a few weeks, the company's shares had lost more than a third of their value. Clearly, the 150 year old Reuters was under pressure to fashion a response to the Internet and do so rapidly.

History and Growth of Reuters: 1850–1980[5]

Using carrier pigeons to send stock prices between Aachen, Germany and Brussels, Belgium, Paul Julius Reuter founded his company in the German city around 1850. The pigeons were faster than the train, and Reuter's business was off to a flying start. Soon thereafter telegraph lines filled the gap and rendered the pigeons obsolete, but Reuter rose to the challenge by making use of the new technology. He moved the company to London and began using the newly laid cross-channel telegraph to transmit closing stock prices between London and Paris. Soon he was also supplying a wealth of other market-relevant information, ranging from corn prices to political news to shipping reports. With success came funds to invest in the company's own telegraph network. And so the pattern was set. With the arrival of each new technology, such as teleprinters and radio, Reuters would be among the pioneers in putting it to use.

During the 1880s, to better cater to the growing number of newspapers that subscribed to his service, Reuters introduced longer, more detailed news stories. During the last years of the 19th century and the first two decades of the 20th century, this "general news service" grew to be the largest of Reuters' businesses. Newspapers took to the service for several reasons. First, it offered a single source of prompt and accurate information. Reuter was obsessed with timeliness and accuracy, and newspapers had come to rely on his news service for both.[6] Reuters' reputation for speed and accuracy was bolstered when, in 1865, it became the first news service in Europe to report the assassination of U.S. President Lincoln. Moreover, Reuters pledged that any market-moving news would be delivered at the same time to all of its customers, a policy that helped broaden the company's customer

---

[4]"Lex Column: Reuters," *Financial Times,* 22 October 1999, p. 24.

[5]Material for this section taken mostly from Donald Read, *The Power of News: The History of Reuters,* Second Edition (New York: Oxford University Press, 1999).

[6]In an 1883 memo that is still quoted by the company today, Mr. Reuter instructed his correspondents to cover affairs in the following manner: "It is requested that the bare facts be first telegraphed with the utmost promptitude, and as soon as possible afterwards a descriptive account, proportionate to the gravity of the incident. Care should, of course, be taken to follow the matter up." Source: www.reuters.com, 24 June 2000.

base. A second factor behind the success of Reuters news was its use of the latest technology, which in the mid-19th century consisted of overland telegraphs and undersea cables. Reuter ensured that his network had sufficient capacity to handle the wealth of information it transmitted and he built in backup systems to guard against line failure. Last but not least was the extensiveness of Reuters' network of correspondents. In those early days, Reuters pursued a policy known as "follow the cable." As the global cable network expanded, so did the coverage Reuters provided, with reporters as far afield as India (as of 1866), the Far East (as of 1872), and Latin America (as of 1874). No other organization could provide such coverage and few newspapers could afford to build themselves such a global network of correspondents. More than a century later, Reuters remained the largest news organization in the world, reporting news from nearly 100 countries in 23 different languages.

Yet profits were perennially difficult in the general news business and for most of its first century in existence the company was looking for ways to boost earnings. The company experimented with banking and private telegrams among other activities. Those efforts, however, weren't as successful as the company's oldest service: providing data from the financial markets.

It wasn't, however, until the 1960s and the arrival of computers that the "commercial services" business truly took off. In 1964, Reuters entered into a joint venture with Ultronic Systems Corp., a U.S.-based firm that provided computer-based stock quotes. In exchange for exclusive use of Ultronic's market information outside of the U.S., Reuters brought to the joint venture access to the company's extensive international network of communication cables. The machines—dubbed the Stockmaster—were rudimentary by standards of the late 1990s. They had a display of just three digits. This was eventually upgraded to 72 digits with the partnership's second-generation product, the Videomaster. The Stockmaster was a big hit because it allowed customers to retrieve information on demand rather than having to receive stock prices only when Reuters chose to send them. Stock brokerage houses bought multiple terminals for their trading rooms, paying subscription fees for each machine. By the end of the 1960s, revenue from the commercial services business was greater than that of the general news division. In both cases, still, the businesses relied upon a combination of content and technology.[7]

Subsequently, Reuters developed a specialized computer terminal product designed for the foreign exchange markets. Launched in 1973, the Monitor service, as it was called, featured yet another leap forward

---

[7] Read, pp. 354–359.

EXHIBIT 1   Reuters Group Profits and Revenues, 1979–1999
(in millions of pounds)

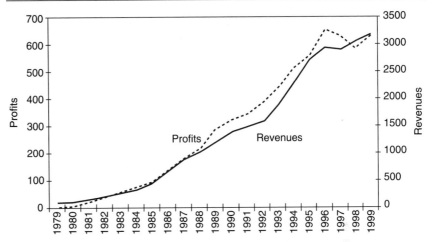

Sources: Based on figures from Donald Read, 1999, *The Power of News: The History of Reuters,*
second edition, New York: Oxford University Press, pp. 485–486; and company annual reports.

in technology with screens able to display 170 words at a time. Later, the
Monitor service was expanded to include prices for bonds, equities, com-
modities, and U.S. government securities. Reuters had discovered its
magic formula for profits. By 1983, the operating profit on the Monitor
service since its launch totaled £100 million and the company's revenue
was 14 times what it had been in 1973.[8] As in the general news business,
Reuters' reputation for extensive and reliable coverage (in this case, of
market price data) propelled the company forward. (See Exhibit 1.)

Even as Monitor took off, Reuters was looking for new ways to grow
its business. The breakthrough came with the addition of "trading services" to the news and financial content business. This was done in 1981
with the launch of Reuter Money Dealing Service that allowed institutional customers (mainly banks) to trade (buy, sell, and lend) foreign
exchange.[9]

Thus, as the 1980s arrived, Reuters was becoming a one-stop shop for
financial transactions. It provided customers with general and financial news, market data, and currency trading services. Importantly to
make it all work, Reuters had assembled under its ownership one of the
world's largest dedicated telecommunications networks with all the
necessary hardware and software.

---

[8]Read, p. 365.
[9]Read, pp. 366–370.

Deregulation, Boom Markets, and Competition: 1980s–early 1990s

The decade of the 1980s brought new threats and opportunities. Deregulation swept through the financial markets, generating a boom and a host of sophisticated new financial products. Users became more demanding of their information service products. They were performing increasingly complex analysis—much of it made possible by the growing power of computers. Against this backdrop, the Reuters terminal appeared simple. It wasn't capable of providing historical data, making calculations, identifying arbitrage opportunities, or performing many of the sophisticated analysis that traders desired.

Spying an opportunity, a former Salomon Brothers banker named Michael Bloomberg entered the market. Frustrated with the limitations and the difficulty of using the Reuters terminal and other information products, Bloomberg launched his own financial information terminal product in 1981. His idea was to create a terminal that was user-friendly and capable of performing sophisticated data analysis. With the early backing of Merrill Lynch, the "Bloomberg" (as traders called it) took off and quickly became a favorite tool on the trading floors and the sales rooms of investment banks.[10] Bloomberg's success was, among other things, attributed to the fact that his product allowed traders to quickly calculate the impact of any change to a portfolio by running a variety of "what if" scenarios. Eventually, Bloomberg broadened his offering to include everything from stock prices to live television feeds to movie reviews. This was the first serious challenge to Reuters' supremacy in the world of financial information services.

Bloomberg wasn't the only rival. Others too were trying to take a chunk out of Reuters' commanding lead in the information services market. Dow Jones & Co. Inc. (publisher of *The Wall Street Journal*) owned a majority stake in Telerate, which specialized in prices on U.S. government securities. (In the 1990s, Dow Jones sold Telerate to private investors, who renamed it Bridge Information Systems.) And in many countries, numerous firms were competing on a national basis for a piece of the financial information business.

In the face of these developments, Reuters was also changing. One significant change occurred in its ownership structure. Over the years, Reuters had undergone several ownership changes. The Reuter family had controlled the company until the 1915 suicide of Paul Reuter's son, after which professional management took control of the enterprise. In 1941, Reuters was acquired by a trust representing UK newspapers,

---

[10]For a detailed account of the rise of Bloomberg LP, see Michael Bloomberg and Matthew Winkler, *Bloomberg by Bloomberg* (New York: John Wiley & Sons, 1997).

many of which were worried about preserving the independence of Reuters' news coverage. But by the mid-1980s, this structure looked outdated, and the newspapers that owned Reuters saw in the boom market an opportunity to collect on their investment. In 1984, Reuters went public with a share offering.

The trust structure prevented a straight forward public offering, so a complex structure was used. In the end, the newspaper associations retained most of the voting rights and 25 percent of the equity while the general public was offered 75 percent of the equity with limited voting rights. Upon listing, Reuters had a market capitalization of £770 million.[11] Now, under the light of shareholder scrutiny, Reuters' financial performance would be watched more closely.

The company also responded to the changing environment by making a number of acquisitions. In a three-year span during the mid-1980s, Reuters spent heavily to acquire a range of companies in information, communication, and related businesses. The aim was to add quickly to the company's product and service portfolio those things that competitors like Bloomberg offered but that were not yet part of the Reuters arsenal.[12] But the most important acquisition, unrelated to competitors' moves, was the 1987 purchase of the agency brokerage Instinet. Instinet offered financial institutions the ability to anonymously trade large blocks of stock over a secure network even when other markets were closed. It offered institutional investors an inexpensive, convenient, and around-the-clock alternative to the traditional brokerage houses. It bought Reuters a powerful presence in yet another part of the wholesale financial service business. As mutual funds and other institutional investors grew in number and influence, Instinet became a valuable component of the Reuters group.[13] (See Exhibit 2 for Reuters' financials.)

The Arrival of the Internet: 1995–1999

Even as Reuters was responding to those challenges, another trend that would alter the financial services landscape was gaining momentum. Throughout most of Reuters' history, investing was an activity undertaken by financial institutions or wealthy individuals.

---

[11]Read, pp. 432–434.

[12]Read, pp. 474–479.

[13]In 1969, the year Instinet was founded, individual households held 69.1 percent of the market value of U.S. equities outstanding. Institutions held the remaining 30.9 percent. By 1998, households held 48.2 percent, institutions 57.2 percent. Source: Instinet website, www.instinet.com, 24 June 2000.

EXHIBIT 2 Reuters Group Financials, 1989–1999 (in millions of pounds, unless stated otherwise)

	1989	1990	1991	1992	1993	1994	1995	1996	1997	1998	1999
Income Statement											
Revenue	1,187	1,369	1,467	1,568	1,874	2,309	2,703	2,914	2,882	3,032	3,125
Net interest (payable)/receivable	19	30	49	66	60	51	60	61	80	2	(4)
Profit before tax	283	320	340	383	440	510	558	652	626	580	632
Taxation	102	112	110	123	140	162	185	210	236	196	207
Profit after tax	181	207	230	236	299	347	373	442	390	384	425
Balance Sheet											
Fixed assets	484	531	488	499	571	687	999	1,026	1,046	1,098	1,205
Net current assets	(33)	81	289	419	151	176	387	525	790	(577)	(232)
Long-term creditors	(22)	(27)	(30)	(26)	(32)	(87)	(135)	(41)	(37)	(16)	(284)
Provisions	(20)	(30)	(25)	(23)	(32)	(36)	(39)	(51)	(120)	(116)	(88)
Net Assets	409	555	722	869	658	740	1,212	1,459	1,679	389	601
Free Cash Flow	54	227	339	276	224	321	455	494	449	490	402
Key Ratios											
Basic EPS (pence)	10.9	12.4	13.7	14.0	18.0	21.7	23.2	27.3	24.0	26.7	30.2
Cash flow per ordinary square (pence)	23.6	27.4	31.7	33.6	40.3	45.6	52.7	60.7	61.0	68.3	71.6
Book value per ordinary share (pence)	24.5	32.9	42.7	51.2	40.6	44.7	73.7	88.3	99.9	23.3	36.1
Pretax profit margin (percent)	23.8	23.4	23.2	24.4	23.5	22.1	20.6	22.4	21.7	19.1	20.2
Return on fixed assets (percent)	40.9	41.3	45.4	53.2	57.2	57.6	55.2	60.0	49.0	48.2	57.5
Return on equity (percent)	53.6	43.2	36.2	29.9	39.5	50.8	34.8	33.7	25.6	78.5	102.0
Outstanding shares (millions)	1,724	1,735	1,743	1,753	1,662	1,668	1,677	1,689	1,694	1,422	1,423
Employees	10,071	10,731	10,450	10,393	11,306	13,548	14,348	15,478	16,119	16,938	16,546
User Access Count	194,800	200,900	201,800	200,800	227,400	296,700	327,100	362,000	429,000	482,000	521,000

Source: Reuters Group PLC, 1999 Annual Report, pp. 86–87.

Only professionals working at banks, insurance companies, trading houses, or in other financial service firms needed or even understood the kind of information Reuters provided. But by the 1990s that started to change. Small investors, especially in the United States, began pouring into the market.

The boom in private investment was fueled by several factors. The bull market of the mid-1980s obviously helped. So too did the fact that the baby boom generation in the United States was entering its middle-age years and starting to have savings to invest. The preferred investment vehicle was the mutual fund. In 1980 there were 458 mutual funds in the United States; by 1990 there were 2,343.[14] By the mid-1990s, the number of funds was greater than the number of stocks quoted on U.S. exchanges. Eventually this trend spread to Europe, where privatization was leading to a further expansion of the equity markets. (See Exhibits 3 and 4.)

EXHIBIT 3   Mutual Funds in the United States, 1980–98

Year	Number of Funds	Number of Accounts (000s)	Net Assets (billions of US$s)
1980	458	7,326	58
1981	486	7,176	55
1982	539	8,190	77
1983	653	12,065	114
1984	820	14,424	137
1985	1,070	19,828	252
1986	1,350	29,700	424
1987	1,771	36,746	453
1988	2,103	36,107	471
1989	2,236	36,821	553
1990	2,343	38,995	567
1991	2,587	44,778	851
1992	2,965	56,285	1,096
1993	3,617	69,633	1,505
1994	4,366	89,013	1,544
1995	4,732	101,115	2,059
1996	5,266	117,977	2,625
1997	5,671	134,897	3,409
1998	6,288	155,007	4,174

Source: "1999 Fact Book," Investment Company Institute, p. 70.

---

[14] *1999 Fact Book,* (Washington, D.C.: Investment Company Institute, 1999) p. 70.

EXHIBIT 4   Worldwide Assets of Open-end Investment Companies (mutual funds)
(all figures in millions of U.S. dollars)

	1993	1994	1995	1996	1997	1998
Total Non-USA	2,086,382	2,315,443	2,574,445	2,815,661	2,788,978	2,761,738
Total USA	2,070,069	2,155,435	2,811,537	3,526,270	4,468,201	4,889,880
Long-term	1,504,750	1,544,430	2,058,519	2,624,463	3,409,315	3,622,978
Short-term	565,319	611,005	753,018	901,807	1,058,886	1,266,902
Total World	4,156,451	4,470,878	5,385,982	6,341,931	7,257,179	7,651,618

Source: "1999 Fact Book," Investment Company Institute, p. 102.

Then, on top of these developments, came the Internet and the dot-com craze.

The abrupt emergence of the Internet in the mid-to-late 1990s threatened to have a profound impact on Reuters, its customers, and its competitive landscape. One effect was to accelerate a trend that began in the 1980s: the growth of private investors. Indeed, as Internet stocks and the number of paper millionaires rose, millions of new investors entered the market. Only this time they wanted to invest in individual stocks rather than in mutual funds. According to one study, the number of Americans that owned equities had risen from some 42 million in 1983 to 79 million in 1999.[15]

Importantly, the Internet offered those individual investors a new way to "play" the market. Internet-based brokerages offered stock-trading to private investors at less than $15 per trade—far below the $100 to $400 per trade charged by traditional, full-service brokerage houses like Merrill Lynch. Seemingly, overnight, the market was invaded by a whole new and assorted group of retail investors. A report by the Securities Exchange Commission noted that at the end of 1999 assets in online accounts totaled $415 billion. The report projected that the figure would grow to $3 trillion. The document also reported that by the second quarter of 1999 online activity had grown to nearly 16 percent of all equity trades.[16] Many of those trades were being made by a new class of investors known as "day-traders." In a search for quick profits, day-traders bought and, within minutes or even-

---

[15]*Equity Ownership in America* (Washington, D.C.: Investment Company Institute and Securities Industry Association, 1999) p. 5.

[16]Securities Exchange Commission, *On-Line Brokerage: Keeping Apace of Cyberspace* (Washington, D.C.: SEC, 2000), p. 1.

seconds, sold the same shares. Suddenly, the financial services industry—the target market for Reuters' services—was going through a new revolution.

The market for information was also being transformed. Whereas Reuters had previously profited from its role as an intermediary delivering real-time quotes from the New York Stock Exchange and other markets, the Internet opened up a new distribution channel for that information. Other news organizations that weren't previously in direct competition with Reuters were using the Internet to enter the electronic information business. *The Wall Street Journal* launched a web site that it claimed reached a new group of readers that were not subscribing to the print edition. While the *Journal* charged for its news, many other credible news organizations, such as *The Financial Times, The New York Times,* and *Handelsblatt* (Germany's top business daily), were putting their information on the Internet for free. And entirely new competitors, like TheStreet.com, were also using the Internet to break into the information business.

Lastly, equipped with a computer and an Internet connection, individuals and institutions were becoming linked. While Reuters had invested heavily in its dedicated network, which had some 60,000 connections to financial institutions around the globe, many of those institutions were increasingly relying on Internet vendors with lower cost bases for their information needs. One survey of 900 financial institutions published in mid-1999 found that Internet-based data providers already accounted for 14 percent of the financial information market.[17] Thus, the Internet was impacting all three elements of Reuters' business core—infrastructure, information, and institutional trading.

On the other hand, as an established information and media company, Reuters also appeared well positioned to take advantage of this technological revolution. Indeed, keeping with its pioneering tradition, in 1994 Reuters established what it called the Greenhouse Fund. The fund's mission was to invest in companies that would either pipe Reuters news and data to new customers or that were developing technologies deemed potentially useful to Reuters. As luck would have it, the fund began by investing $1 million in Yahoo!, which subsequently went on to become one of the most popular Internet portals. Other investments in companies like Phone.com (online telephony) and VeriSign (online security software for brokerage firms) suggested that Reuters had a keen eye for Internet start-ups.

---

[17]*The Waters Survey,* Waters Information Service, July 1999.

By February 2000, the Greenhouse Fund held investments with a quoted value in the hundreds of millions of dollars. In addition, the fund also held a number of investments in ventures that had yet to go public.[18]

An equally if not more noteworthy financial success was Reuters' spinoff of a previously acquired now in-house software unit, TIBCO. That unit's expertise in developing software for dealing rooms had other applications, including such activities as creating Internet portals and the handling of on-line transactions. In July 1999 Reuters took TIBCO public and sold 37.7 percent of the unit's shares on the NAS-DAQ. Less than a year later, in June 2000, TIBCO boasted a total market value of $15 billion.

But skeptical observers viewed these moves as "asset plays," and they were starting to ask how, in the wake of the Internet, Reuters would reshape its core businesses. At the time, however, Reuters itself was focused on its Reuters 3000 and 3000Xtra products (launched in 1997 and 1999 respectively). These products, targeted at financial institutions, were sophisticated counters to Bloomberg. While they exhibited the group's commitment to countering competitive challenges, to the investment community they did not convey sufficient urgency around the Internet issue. (See Exhibit 5 for Reuters' financials by major division.)

To be sure, observers could see that Reuters was already providing information—mostly news stories—to websites, more than 900 in all. But otherwise it appeared to be business as usual at the company. Thus, even though the group's 1996 annual report spoke about "embracing the net," the section summarizing the company's competitive environment and strategy in the 1998 annual report did not mention the Internet. Then, when Peter Job, during that fateful conference in October 1999, failed to convince analysts that the company had an Internet strategy, the investment community took fear and Reuters' stock cratered.

As *The Economist* later put it: "The Internet and Reuters have much in common. Both are electronic networks, operating in real time, whose job is to transmit information. In fact, they have so much in common that it is easy to imagine how the Internet could replace Reuters."[19]

---

[18]*Reuters Group PLC Annual Report and Accounts 1999,* p. 15; Bill McIntosh, "Corporate Profile: Reuters," *The Independent,* 16 February 2000, p. 3; and Job.

[19]"Reuters: Setting Up Shop," *The Economist,* 12 February 2000, p. 71.

EXHIBIT 5   Reuters Group Financials by Major Division, 1997–99
(financial figures in millions of pounds)

	1997	1998	1999
Reuters Information (1)			
Revenue	1,477	1,531	1,619
Costs	(1,320)	(1,373)	(1,366)
Contribution	157	158	253
Contribution Margin (%)	11	10	16
Employees	8,863	9,306	9,239
Trading Systems (2)			
Revenue	800	827	780
Costs	(524)	(541)	(550)
Contribution	276	286	230
Contribution Margin (%)	35	35	30
Employees	3,870	3,887	4,105
Instinet (3)			
Revenue	383	446	525
Costs	(234)	(291)	(396)
Contribution	149	155	129
Contribution Margin (%)	39	35	25
Employees	1,086	1,181	1,379
Reuterspace (4)			
Revenue	167	154	157
Costs	(196)	(181)	(172)
Contribution	(29)	(27)	(15)
Contribution Margin (%)	(17)	(18)	(10)
Employees	1,484	1,541	1,344

(1) Includes revenue from the sale of information products to financial institutions and their clients.
(2) Includes all revenue from foreign exchange and equity trading (other than Instinet) as well as revenue from technology and software support for financial institutions.
(3) Instinet is the world's largest agency brokerage, allowing institutions to anonymously buy and sell blocks of equities.
(4) Previously Reuters Ventures: Includes revenue from sale of content (text, photos, and video footage) to news media and Internet sites, and the Greenhouse Fund.

Source: Reuters Group PLC, 1999 Annual Report, pp. 10–14.

Reuters' Internet Strategy (B)

By Associate Professor Subramanian Rangan and Brian Coleman

You might almost believe the Internet was created for Reuters.

Peter Job, CEO Reuters Group PLC, 8 February 2000.[1]

On 8 February 2000, just three months after the infamous October 1999 presentation to investment analysts, CEO Peter Job made another presentation to the financial community. "This presentation is all about the Internet and what it means for Reuters," Job began. He then proceeded to lay out a bold and ambitious Internet strategy that promised to catapult the 150 year old enterprise into the thick of the hot new, dot-com economy.

From "Trading Room to Living Room"[2]

At the heart of the strategy lay a decision to offer to the growing mass of individual investors many of the same online real-time data, analysis, news, and trading services Reuters offered professionals via dedicated terminals. Thus, in the language of the Internet, Reuters would expand from B2B into B2C, that is, from business-to-business to business-to-consumer markets. In Job's words, this was a "breakthrough mission," the first of its kind in the company's long history.

---

[1]Excerpt from presentation entitled "Reuters Group PLC Preliminary Results Presentation to Analysts," Reuters.com/investors/presentation/chiefexec.asp, March 2, 2000.

[2]Thom Calandra, *CBS MarketWatch.com,* March 15, 2000. "Reuters Already Winning Its Net Bet."

EXHIBIT 1   Electronic Trading Value Chain

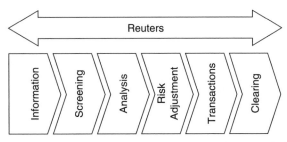

Source: Reuters Group PLC, March 2, 2000, www.reuters.com/results/2000/slides/pj/05.asp.

Excerpt from Reuters Group PLC CEO Peter Job's February 8, 2000 presentation

"The value chain is very clear. It starts with things hitting the dealing room—in Reuters alone about 6,000 changes per second now. Somehow or other people are only interested in, say, Spanish stocks and only want 400 changes per second; instantaneously you have to deliver those, without any delay, to the right position. That requires fairly complex software. Then you have to be able to feed directly into spreadsheets to facilitate analysis. Analysis generates the prospect for buying or selling successfully. You adjust your risk positions and at the touch of a button you transact, you clear and you settle."

Source: Reuters Group PLC, March 2, 2000, www.reuters.com/investors/presentation/chief. exec.asp.

To compete in the already crowded retail market, Reuters would establish an Internet financial portal and offer a "one-stop shop." Referring to the "electronic trading value chain" (see Exhibit 1), Job explained: "Reuters is present throughout this value chain. In effect, it is a complete e-commerce strategy already. It is about linking the process of 'knowing' to 'doing' in a few seconds or, at most, a few minutes." Job elaborated later, "All of [our] assets can be deployed to do the new thing. We hope to send our products right into the living room."[3]

Toward this vision, Reuters would invest £500 million: £300 million in reorganizing the company and £200 million over four years in Internet technologies.

If the costs were high, so were the projected rewards. Reuters estimated that the "audience" represented by the professional investment community numbered 1.1 million. Growth in that segment was forecast

---

[3]Calandra, March 15, 2000.

at 5 percent a year. By contrast, the retail investor market was projected to be in an entirely different league. Reuters estimated that there were as many as 65 million customers that might be interested in online investing. "We believe that market will be worth $1 billion within three years," Job told analysts. Beyond those 65 million individuals, he reckoned that there were as many as 125 million individuals who would use the Internet at work for various activities and could therefore be exposed to the Reuters brand.

Joint Ventures

"One law of the Internet is that you cannot succeed all on your own: you need partners." With that claim, Job discussed four joint ventures: one related to content, another related to a new service, and two to technology. To boost content, Reuters had formed a 50-50 joint venture with Multex.com, a U.S.-based firm that provided private investors electronic versions of equity research from investment banks. The Multex-Reuters jv would distribute this content to investors in Europe. On the service side, Reuters entered into a 60 percent-owned jv with U.S.-based W. R. Hambrecht to extend to Europe the latter's "Dutch auction system" for IPOs.

On technology, Job discussed two joint ventures. A 40 percent Reuters-owned jv with Aether (another U.S. based firm) would provide *mobile* information and transaction services in Europe. The other, in which Reuters would hold 51 percent, was with Equant, "the world's largest [communications] network, providing voice, data and Internet services . . ."[4] This New York-based joint venture would provide *secure* Internet Protocol services to the financial community (including banks, trading houses, and insurance companies). The idea, Job explained, was to offer financial institutions the ease of use and familiarity of the Internet with the security of a private network. The secure "extranet" that Reuters-Equant would own and manage would work "closely" with TIBCO to help customers enter the digital, Internet-based, new economy.

New Organization Design

As Job unveiled the company's Internet strategy, he also announced the restructuring of Reuters into three broad business areas. Reuterspace, a newly named area, would be charged with conquering the Internet. This area would house the financial portal, the Greenhouse Fund, which was now renamed Reuters Venture Capital, and TIBCO hold-

---

[4]Equant.com, press release of 3 February 2000. "Reuters and Equant Create New Global IP Network Company for Financial Markets," June 30, 2000.

ings. The Reuters Media unit, responsible for the sale of news stories to the media and web sites, would also report into Reuterspace.

Reuters Financial would house the core businesses of Reuters Information and Reuters Trading Solutions (so renamed from the previous Reuters Trading Systems). The third business area would be Instinet, the electronic institutional brokerage that Reuters had acquired in 1987 and that was expected to play a key part in the company's plan to capture a share of the retail brokerage market.

On a concluding note, Job remarked: "People very often ask the question of Reuters . . . whether it is a content company or a technology company . . . the question is irrelevant: content and technology are completely indivisible at Reuters, as they have to be in an e-commerce company." As for the old and new economy dichotomy, he commented thus: "We are seeing a forking of the ways . . ." Reuters would manage for value in the old business, while, at the same, "unconstrained by P&L," the group would "fearlessly invest in the land grab on the Internet . . ."

Altogether, it was a sweeping set of changes for Reuters but one that the stock market applauded. In a report headlined "Nice Job Peter," Morgan Stanley Dean Witter wrote that "the 22% rise in the share price [on February 8] in our view reflects the market's appreciation of Reuters' strengths in an Internet environment as well as Peter Job's clear and convincing articulation of the strategy."[5] By mid-February the stock hit an all-time high of 1445 pence up from a low several months earlier of 516 pence.

---

[5]V. Padiachy, et al., Morgan Stanley, Dean Witter, 9 February 2000. *Reuters Group.*

Chapter 7

Virtual Work

Economists have long argued about why there isn't free market competition for labor services *within* a firm. After all, the argument goes, free market conditions provide the most efficient allocation of resources. Why shouldn't a secretary, for example, accept bids for secretarial work and choose the ones that would give him or her the greatest reward for projects with the highest worth? The consensus has been that the costs of advertising and transacting for competitive labor within a firm would be greater than the efficiencies gained. If there are times when the secretary is paid for being idle, it averages out to be less costly than trying to link labor and work, and negotiating the optimal free market rate. But what might happen if the cost of finding labor and work approached zero, and the cost of negotiating fees was also close to zero? And what if the pool of available labor and work was essentially unlimited? In theory, global connectivity can provide those conditions.

This chapter addresses virtual work in an e-commerce environment where labor projects can be carried out autonomously by independent contractors—Internet freelancers sometimes called "e-lancers." Buyers of labor post projects that e-lancers bid for, and sellers of labor post their skills that buyers with projects bid for. When a job is done, the network dissolves and the buyers and sellers become independent agents again.

The first case, "eLance.com: Projects versus Personnel," addresses the key issue of whether an intermediary web service site should focus on being project oriented or personnel oriented. With two different groups—buyers and sellers of labor, both of which are needed for a viable site—should the intermediary focus on projects or personnel or both? What revenue model should they pursue—fees from buyers, fees from sellers, fees from both, intermediary services, or advertising? One way or another, these intermediaries must reach a critical mass of users to become viable. While eLance decides to focus on the buyer (project-centric), the firm at the center of the second case, Guru.com, decides to focus on the seller (guru-centric). The company aims to be the world's largest online database of independent, professional, virtual workers. Therefore, Guru.com chose a revenue model based on buyers with projects paying a fee to post their projects on the company's web site (somewhat akin to career sites). These two cases provide a good matched pair to explore many of the online virtual work issues.

The third case, Scantran (A), provides another perspective on virtual work from the view of a virtual company based on hiring online freelancers for doing language translation work. Scantran receives proposals electronically for translation work (into and out of Scandinavian languages), they find and hire translators online, electronically deliver the work, and electronically receive the translated product. The Scantran model can occur across the traditional boundaries of space and time, providing huge opportunities for growth—or huge opportunities for overextension and competition. This case addresses lifestyle, management, and growth strategies for virtual work businesses.

eLance.com: Projects versus Personnel

Professor Scott Schneberger and Ken Mark

Introduction

eLance.com had just opened its online services marketplace to the public. It was August 30, 1999, and there were six projects over the first three days. Suddenly, there appeared three requests for temporary positions.

Beerud Sheth, co-founder and chief executive officer (CEO) of eLance.com remarked,

> We have to take these three requests for temporary positions down. We don't want anyone mistaking us for a recruitment site like Monster.com; we're a project-based site where projects are bought and sold. We have to carefully form our product in the early stages.

Srini Anumolu, the other co-founder and president retorted,

No, you're wrong. I believe that we should leave it completely open at this stage; let the market govern itself. After all, we are a trading platform and we want to encourage liquidity. Let the market forces decide.

Both founders knew that the choices they made now would directly affect future website development, as features to support a projects-only site would be somewhat different from a combined projects and personnel site. The founders had to decide if they were going to take down the three requests for temporary positions or let the market proceed unchecked.

Overview of the Traditional Staffing Industry

In 1946, William Russell Kelly, anticipating a post-Second World War business and industrial boom, moved to Detroit and founded the Russell Kelly Office Service. The firm, a service bureau that sent its employees to fill in for vacationing or sick employees, set the standard for the newly created staffing industry, and coined the term "Kelly Girls" to identify their staff, most of whom were female secretaries.[1]

The staffing industry was divided into two categories: temporary staffing agencies who hired workers and outsourced them to companies in return for a fee, and talent matchmakers who received a fee for matching freelance independent professionals with companies who required their specialized services.

There were basically two classifications of temporary workers on whom the staffing industry counted: agency-dependent contract employees and independent professionals (IPs). In the agency-dependent model, the agency located the assignment, recruited the contractor, negotiated with and billed the client. The agency also withheld applicable taxes from the contractor's regularly scheduled payroll check, with the difference between the client bill rate and the contractor pay rate (minus taxes) being the agency's revenue. Contractors were responsible for all of the above non-work related items. (See Exhibit 1: Traditional Staffing Industry.)

The independent professional phenomenon became a fundamental socioeconomic shift in the American workforce. In 1999, there were an estimated 25 million independent workers in the United States, including 14 million self-employed, eight million independent contractors, and three million temps.[2] Within this group, an estimated eight

---

[1]Jennifer L. Laabs, "Father of the Staffing Industry—William Russell Kelly—Dies," *Workforce,* Costa Mesa, March 1998; Volume 77, Issue 3.

[2]U.S. Bureau of Labor Statistics.

EXHIBIT 1   Traditional Staffing Industry

Overview

- 6 percent annual growth overall; 24 percent growth in professional/technical markets.
- 7,000 firms in industry with 17,000 locations.
- Top 10 firms control 29 percent of US$72 billion industry (Manpower Inc., Adecco Staffing Services, Interim Services, Norrell Corp, Kelly Services).
- 100 firms with revenues exceeding US$100 million.
- 90 percent of firms offer training programs.

Examples

Company	Type	Focus	Financial Performance	Other
Roth Staffing Company	Traditional temporary staffing service	75% of demand was for clerical or secretarial workers 25% of demand was for higher-skilled workers Company focused on driving volume of placements	Achieved US$74 million in 1998 20% revenue growing from 1994 to 1998 Expected to approach US$240 million in sales by 2003	Roth placed 5,000 temporary workers in 1999 65 offices in seven states
Robert Half International	Traditional temporary staffing service	Focused on high-priced financial and accounting talent	Achieved US$1.3 billion in 1997 43% CAGR from 1995 to 2000	Market capitalization US$5 billion
Aquent (formerly MacTemps)	Talent matchmaker	Focused on creative and technical talent	US$100 million in 1998, expected to top US$190 million in 2000.	Offices in nine countries 110% money-back guarantee Offers additional services such as training and factoring

Sources:
- U.S. Bureau of Labor Statistics.
- Linda Davidson, "Maximize the Return on Temp Staff Investments," *Workforce,* Costa Mesa, November 1999, Volume 78, Issue 11.
- Edward O. Welles, *Number 1 Company: The People Business Inc.*; Boston, October 19, 1999; Volume 21, Issue 15.
- www.aquent.com (December 2000).

million were highly skilled independent professionals. In addition, there were approximately four million untapped professionals—people actively thinking about freelancing—e.g., moonlighters and work-at-home moms.

E-Lancing Emerges

Freelancers weighed the freedom to be able to work on different temporary projects against the absence of a fixed revenue stream. Professionals who chose this lifestyle relied on personal contacts or staffing agencies as a source for project work. These sources usually limited freelancers to three-to-six-month contract work in their immediate geography and network. The emergence of the Internet in the early 1990s promised to remove this barrier of space and time.

Much was written about the opportunity to exchange employment information over this new medium. An excerpt from the article, "The Dawn of the E-Lance Economy" by Thomas Malone and Robert Laubacher read:

> The fundamental unit of such an economy is not the corporation but the individual. Tasks aren't assigned and controlled through a stable chain of management but rather are carried out autonomously by independent contractors. These electronically connected freelancers—e-lancers—join together into fluid and temporary networks to produce and sell goods and services. When the job is done—after a day, a month, a year—the network dissolves, and its members become independent agents again, circulating through the economy, seeking the next assignment.

Formation of eLance.com

Meanwhile, Wall Street traders Sheth and Anumolu founded eLance.com with a private placement in late 1998. On August 30, 1999, eLance.com launched the beta version of its global services marketplace from New York City. Its website proclaimed:

> eLance is the premier global services marketplace. From business, computer and creative needs to family, financial and much more, eLance provides the resources for people to connect, communicate, and complete their project.

It continued,

> Buyers can post a project description and receive bids from service providers, or buy directly from thousands of fixed-price service listings. eLance support features include the workspace for project development and remote delivery, service provider certifications, feedback ratings, and an international billing and payment system. Service providers find a global market at eLance, and can build their reputation through our feedback system.

The Online E-Lancing Competition[3]

These new e-marketplaces served as a way for IPs to increase their exposure to potential clients while limiting the amount of resources normally required for self-promotion and advertising. In some cases these sites also served as an effective and efficient way to access necessary services for business survival, including bill payment, insurance purchasing and tax report filing, in a convenient one-stop shopping location. Here was a short list of some of eLance.com's online competition.

JobSwarm

The personnel at JobSwarm.com had constructed a fully functioning site, and its goals were to build traffic and membership. The opportunities posted on the site covered marketing, information technology (IT) and writing. The site's main source of revenue seemed to be the 5 percent finder's fee on all billable work completed by registered freelancers. Another possible source of revenue was the private label services the company aimed to provide to partners like Startupbiz.com. The primary difference in how JobSwarm.com worked its business model was that it recruited freelancers to offer the services that clients need. The site had chosen to offer a program that promised to pay the individual referring another freelancer to the site royalties on the long-term work of that person.

Guru

Guru.com had focused on building a community that promoted freelancing as a lifestyle. By designing a visually appealing site, it sought to brand itself as the leading destination for freelancers. It also offered freelancer advice and support through numerous alliances with other content providers. They charged buyers to post project staffing sites and a high percentage of their staffing was on location. As a destination site, for freelancers, they were expected to offer additional services such as 401(k) plans, health benefits and product advice. Guru.com was expected to focus on matching independent professionals (known as "gurus") with hirers.

FreeAgent

FreeAgent.com offered many of the same services as its competition through a basic interface. It had been developed by Opus360, a company that placed IT contractors and provided benefits, including 401(k) plans and insurance for their contractors. Posting an opportunity on

---

[3]The foundation of this section was outsourced on eLance.com on August 15, 2000.

the site provided a client with project exposure to thousands of providers. As with the other services in this category, each provider was encouraged to provide an e-portfolio to help the client choose a potential partner. One of the key noticeable differences in their approach compared to that of eLance.com's was the effort to promote repeat business to the site by charging clients on a sliding scale for posting freelance opportunities. This sliding scale offered the client, who might have otherwise been inclined to look elsewhere for talent, a clear option to reduce freelance recruiting costs for an ongoing business operation.

eLance.com Overall Site Features

As of its launch date (late August 1999), eLance.com had a set of online tools (shown in Table 1) available to users. In addition, eLance.com planned to add billing and payment systems that allowed buyers and sellers in different countries to pay each other (with different currencies if they so wished). Most improvements were done with the intention of eLance.com keeping buyers and sellers on its site throughout the transaction. To that end, it even offered both parties an online, virtual workspace by which to transfer their documents and files.

The development of additional functionality could aid the buyer, the seller, its partners, or internal operations. Within these four groupings, the co-founders wondered what additional functionality would look like. Initial thoughts created the following list of possibilities:

- Launch regional sites—This would require eLance.com to facilitate personnel matching in various geographies and customize content to each particular geography.

TABLE 1 eLance.com Site Features, July 1999

	Marketplace	*Workspace*	*Billing and Post Feedback*
Description	Platform upon which buyers and sellers post, review and bid on projects. Includes auction-style bids for projects, messaging, bid acceptance and notification	File sharing capability (50 MB space limit), messaging capability, and online scheduling. Can conduct online meetings.	Credit Card Billing and rating system allowing buyers and sellers to rate each other.
Primary Objective	Matching of buyers and sellers of project transactions.	To facilitate transfer of work between buyers and seller (especially international ones).	Develop the primary stream of revenue and put in place a self-managing rating system.

- Enable e-lancers to provide robust profiles—This would allow buyers to research the sellers, reviewing their work experience and previous projects.
- Search engine—Using key words, sellers and buyers could search for each other's project postings.
- Response management tool—Because of the number of project bids and postings that eLance.com was expected to attract, the response management tool would help buyers and sellers filter through the bids and posts.
- Quality control tool—The actual functionality of this product was not yet confirmed, but the objective was to build a tool to aid buyers to assess the quality of a seller. Currently, a rating system had been rolled out by eLance.com.
- Content—One way to attract buyers and sellers was to create specific content relevant to each audience. This would involve in-house writing or syndication of content from other providers, posting articles on topics such as training, selection, workplace improvement or humor.
- Support different languages—eLance.com was considering launching foreign language sites including German- and Spanish-language sites. This was still a new idea, and eLance.com intended to explore it within a year.

Key Challenges for eLance.com

In running a project site, Sheth identified several key challenges:

Building Liquidity

In order for the site to function as a transaction platform, a critical mass of buyers and sellers, termed "liquidity," would have to be transacting on the site.

Alex Hacking in business development inquired,

> How are we going to attract these people? Building liquidity will be a real challenge—we're going to build transaction volume. The concern is that when we convey our message to them, they will try to associate it with what they have experienced before with other job placement agencies. The challenge will be educating our customers to treat us as a project matching site and not a personnel site.

Hilary Krant, eLance.com's market maker, was charged with facilitating transactions and communications between buyers and sellers. In the stock trading world, a market maker was a person providing liquidity to the marketplace. Each bank or each trading firm might have a market maker in a specific stock. If there was no counter party for a trade, then a market maker would often step in and take the other side of the trade so that the trade gets completed, keeping supply and demand flowing.

We needed someone who was going to really pay attention to the marketplace and all the transactions and make sure that the projects that got posted received an up bid quickly—so facilitating information and then going outside of eLance.com to get people to come in to place bids, etc.

Payment and Quality Disputes

Although eLance.com would not mediate payment disputes, it offered buyers the opportunity to list a valid credit card on its site as a guarantee of payment. Sellers would be able to identify these people by a tiny credit card symbol beside their buyer identities, indicating that the buyer was pre-qualified. This was intended to assure sellers that they would be paid for rendering services. Thus, if the buyer was pleased with the delivered project, payment could be made via credit card right on eLance.com's site.

Sheth outlined another issue eLance.com would face:

> I think that we have an attractive model, but then quality will become an issue. Can you make sure you can get good quality stuff in the right time frame and the right time line and have it delivered? So now you are relying on hundreds of unseen developers, writers and designers halfway around the world and when you've actually made a commitment to deliver a product in a certain time frame, do you do this, or do you not?

An arbitration process did not yet exist to mediate disputes if the buyer was not pleased with the delivered project. eLance.com intended to create this system in the first six months. One option was to provide buyers with online arbitration through a third party arbitrator like Square Trade.

Instilling Loyalty

When a transaction between eLance.com buyers and sellers occurred offline, eLance.com would be unable to capture a portion of the transaction cost. At eLance.com, there were specific initiatives aimed at reducing offline transactions:

- Having an online workspace for buyers and sellers.
- Enabling buyers and sellers to post a feedback rating on each other.
- Ensuring that billing and payment occurred; service providers usually had difficulty receiving payment.
- Not allowing buyers or sellers to exchange contact information until the transaction occurred.

Current eLance.com website rules stipulated that no identifying information (e-mail or street addresses) would be exchanged and this was monitored by eLance.com's "market makers." This was because eLance.com wanted to be a platform for the end-to-end delivery of services. If it were able to keep each side on the site, it would be in the position to capture more transaction fees. Sheth explained:

Well, let me put it this way. You can never really prevent this disintermediation. You can just kind of mitigate the risk. Even an active large market place like eBay still grapples from a grey market, as they call it. I think what we will do is make sure we give our users enough reasons that they don't need to go away, allowing them to stick around. We need our users to arrive at that point where the easiest way to get the job done is through the site rather than off the site. In spite of the added cost, the user gains in terms of convenience, amount of time spent, effort exhausted, money spent. The cheapest way to transact is through our site.

So that's kind of the challenge that we as a company face, and the way we address it is by providing a lot of value-added features. For example, our workspace component facilitates development and delivery, our billing and payment features that make it easy to pay for the product once it's done, and both buyers and sellers leave feedback for each other. Leaving the feedback allowed sellers to build a rating that would get them access to more work.

The Main Question: Projects or Personnel?

With its decision to focus its efforts on buyers of services, eLance.com was forced to define even more clearly its business model. The key issue was this: should eLance.com allowing buyers of services to engage the e-lancer as a temporary onsite employee (hence, allowing for personnel postings like "marketer needed for a period of three months in New York City")? Or limit the buyer's contact with e-lancers by allowing only project postings (for example, "direct mail marketing plan required")? Contractors willing to work onsite usually came from within 15 miles of the job site. It would be difficult to attract candidates from afar due to the temporary nature of the placement. Having the buyer post a personnel request for a contract total of US$10,000 might give eLance.com a transaction fee of 10 per cent, or US$1,000. On the other hand, insisting that the buyer break up the listing into four or five different projects would certainly increase the number of postings, but would lower each individual project's transaction fee.

Another difference between the two approaches lay in the amount of information that the e-lancers would provide to the buyer of their service. By allowing the buyer to contact the e-lancer directly, eLance.com risked that the transaction would be taken offline, thereby losing any future transaction fees. But by limiting the buyer to project postings only, the company risked alienating itself from a significant portion of the buyer market.

eLance.com's project posting model was new to the market and as yet untried. Sheth conceded that trust might be an issue. If a buyer did not have enough trust to hire a person to finish the assignment, would that buyer hire several e-lancers to handle several projects? Sheth believed that this obstacle could be overcome through an education process. But what would happen if people were not ready to switch to project-based work? What if eLance.com could not educate them to switch from staffing. Last, what if people needed to have an onsite presence? Would eLance.com be able to capture that transaction fee?

Thus, the management team at eLance.com had to decide if they were to allow the additional three job postings to continue on their site.

Conclusion

Sheth and Anumolu wanted to resolve the projects-versus-personnel dilemma before the close of business. The site had been up for three days, and there were many other priorities that required attention. To make their decision, Sheth and Anumolu had to think beyond the present to the strategic and IT implications of each choice. What would their site objectives be and what products would they need to launch? Already, they were hearing of imminent competitive e-lancing site launches. There remained no dominant site in the rapidly growing e-lancing space, and the two founders felt that they had a chance to become the market leader.

Guru.com: Power for the Independent Professional

By Professor Mary Crossan and Ken Mark

There's a new movement in the land—as fast growing as it is invisible. From coast to coast, in communities large and small, citizens are declaring their independence and drafting a new bill of rights. Meet some of the 25 million residents of Free Agent, U.S.A.

Dan Pink, Author, *Free Agent Nation*

Introduction

With only a small team of people and a big vision, Guru.com believed it was on the brink of a huge opportunity. They intended to transform the global labor market by creating the world's largest online marketplace for independent professionals (IPs)—freelancers, consultants, "knowledge workers" and "hired guns." Affectionately known internally as "gurus," independent professionals were one of the fastest growing segments of the North American workforce.

In August 1999, one month into the launch of its preview site (version 0.5), Guru.com was preparing for its first major release, scheduled for November 1999. Their goal was to build a home on the Web for independent professionals, providing the essentials for running a guru business. Jon and James Slavet, co-founders of Guru.com believed that catering to the needs of gurus was the key to achieving market leadership and revolutionizing the traditional contingent staffing business. Turning to a recent hire, Jennifer Tyler, Jon and James wanted her opinion on Guru.com's product strategy.

Jennifer Tyler

Jennifer Tyler was brought into Guru.com as one of its first team members in July 1999. Having graduated from the Ivey Business School in 1995, Tyler joined Monitor Company where she focused on developing emerging technology strategies for clients. Tyler recognized the IP trend and brought an intimate knowledge of the market to this early-stage team—she developed a similar concept and strategy for a company who was in a market closely aligned with Guru.com's. Tyler believed that focusing on the IP market was a tremendous opportunity and believed that Guru.com's approach, focusing on attracting the gurus, was going to allow them to capture market leadership. Tyler commented on her initial thoughts about the business:

> I saw Guru.com as a tremendous opportunity to catalyze the emerging freelance market. I had explored many approaches to the business, and felt strongly that focusing on the guru would allow us to achieve market leadership. For most traditional companies finding the talent was the toughest part. Pulling together a fragmented population like independent consultants would be incredibly valuable. Guru.com had a vision for connecting with people, speaking their language, empowering the independent professional. It was energizing at a personal level, and I believed the approach would differentiate the business.

Overview of the Traditional Staffing Industry

In 1946, William Russell Kelly, anticipating a post-Second World War business and industrial boom, moved to Detroit and founded the Russell Kelly Office Service. The firm, a service bureau that sent its employees to fill in for vacationing or sick employees, set the standard for the newly created staffing industry, and coined the term "Kelly Girls" to identify their staff, most of whom were female secretaries.[1]

Kelly set the mould for the temporary staffing business, which remained relatively unchanged through most of the 1970s and 1980s. Temporary staffing was typically used for clerical and administrative work. However, the downsizing trend in the late 1980s, coupled with the technology boom in the 1990s, dramatically changed the way that companies worked with contingent staff. Instead, companies relied on outside expertise to guide their companies through uncharted territory, and to bring in knowledge that didn't exist within the corporate walls and to help projects move at a speed that was not possible using internal resources alone.

The staffing industry was broken down into three categories—temporary staffing agencies who hired workers and outsourced them to companies in return for a fee (usually a markup on the consultants hourly rate), talent matchmakers who received a bounty for matching freelance independent professionals with companies who required their specialized services, and independent consultants that relied primarily on their personal networks to find work for themselves.

There were basically two classifications of temporary workers whom the staffing industry counted on: agency-dependent contract employees and independent professionals. In the agency-dependent model, the agency located the assignment, recruited the contractor, negotiated with and billed the client. The agency also withheld applicable taxes from the contractor's regularly scheduled payroll check, with the difference between the client bill rate and the contractor pay rate (minus taxes) being the agency's revenue. Alternatively, IPs were personally responsible for managing the entire process from sourcing work to billing clients and managing taxes (see Exhibit 1).

The Rise of the Guru Nation

According to Guru.com, the independent professional phenomenon was a fundamental socio-economic shift in the American workforce. By 1999, there were an estimated 25 million independent workers in the United States.[2] Within this group, an estimated eight million were considered highly skilled independent professionals, or IPs. In addition to the existing group of IPs, it was thought that there were

---

[1]Jennifer L. Laabs, "Father of the Staffing Industry—William Russell Kelly—Dies," *Workforce:* Costa Mesa, March 1998, Volume 77, Issue 3.

[2]U.S. Bureau of Labor Statistics.

EXHIBIT 1   Traditional Staffing Industry

Overview

- 6 percent annual growth overall; 24 percent growth in professional and technical markets.
- 7,000 firms in industry with 17,000 locations.
- Top 10 firms control 29 percent of US$72 billion industry (Manpower Inc., Adecco Staffing Services, Interim Services, Norrell Corp, Kelly Services).
- 100 firms with revenues exceeding US$100 million.
- 90 percent of firms offer training programs.

Examples

Company	Type	Focus	Financial Performance	Other
Roth Staffing Company	Traditional temporary staffing service	75% of demand was for clerical or secretarial workers 25% of demand was for higher-skilled workers Company focused on driving volume of placements	Achieved US$74 million in 1998 20% revenue growing from 1994 to 1998 Expected to approach US$240 million in sales by 2003	Roth placed 5,000 temporary workers in 1999 65 offices in seven states
Robert Half International	Traditional temporary staffing service	Focused on high-priced financial and accounting talent	Achieved US$1.3 billion in 1997 43% CAGR from 1995 to 2000	Market capitalization US$5 billion
Aquent (formerly MacTemps)	Talent matchmaker	Focused on creative and technical talent	US$100 million in 1998, expected to top US$190 million in 2000	Offices in nine countries 110% money-back guarantee Offers additional services such as training and factoring

Sources:
- U.S. Bureau of Labor Statistics.
- Linda Davidson, "Maximize the Return on Temp Staff Investments," *Workforce,* Costa Mesa, November 1999, Volume 78, Issue 11.
- Edward O. Welles, "Number 1 Company: The People Business," *Inc.* Boston, October 19, 1999; Volume 21, Issue 15.
- www.aquent.com.

still a large number of professionals-to-be, people on the cusp of going "guru." This potential market included "moonlighters" and work-at-home parents.

There were a number of factors fueling the rise of "gurudom." Affected by corporate downsizing in the 1990s, entrepreneurship tendencies were on the rise, while career-long allegiance to big corporations was fading into American corporate history. Hyper-competitive companies were increasingly looking to selectively hire "expertise" for short stints as a way to outsource their workload, thus improving profitability and "speed to market." In addition, information technology was making tremendous strides as a powerful enabler and equalizer for IPs. And an increased awareness and concern for balancing career with personal interests was leading people to choose careers with more flexibility.

The result was that proven IPs were a new breed of American worker—non-traditional, highly skilled, and able to garner astronomical fees for much sought after advice. While millions of people were benefiting from this trend, and enjoying the freedom of shaping their own careers, the transition to this new way of work came with some challenges. Guru.com's initial research indicated that gurus faced a number of hurdles in their pursuit of an independent lifestyle. These included: accessing professional community, generating a steady flow of consulting projects, and managing business logistics. Guru.com aimed to focus on solving these problems for gurus, through a combined online and offline strategy.

The Creation of Guru.com

The founding members saw dramatic changes in the market and an opportunity to revolutionize the way that independent professionals connected with the clients that needed to hire them. James and Jon Slavet, together with Al Yau, co-founded Guru.com in April 1999.[3]

Jon Slavet, Co-CEO

In the three-ring circus that is Guru.com, Jon Slavet waves the baton. As co-CEO, he manages Guru.com's marketing, sales, and business development teams. From 1997 until 1999, Jon worked at E! Online in Los Angeles as vice-president responsible for advertising sales, business development, and international content syndication. As a senior executive for strategic development at Wired Ventures, Jon built a great department and sold lots and lots of ads. He has also worked as director of corporate sales for National Public Radio in New York. Jon graduated with honors from Dartmouth College.

---

[3]From Guru.com's website: www.guru.com/content/about/about_team.jhtml, January 2001.

James Slavet, Co-CEO

James Slavet develops the strategies that power Guru.com's growth. Today, he oversees Guru.com's financing, human resources, operations, product and engineering teams. Previously, he was a member of the launch team at Drugstore.com. Before that, he served as manager of business development at Wired Ventures. James has also worked in marketing and operations for Vivid Studios, a San Francisco web development firm, and as a strategy consultant with Monitor Company. He graduated from Brown University and has an MBA from Harvard Business School.

Al Yau, Vice-President of Product Management

Al Yau knows how to run a tight ship. As a manager of business development at Peoplesoft, he helped the company migrate its software from a client/server architecture to the Internet. At Sun Microsystems, he identified acquisition targets and learned to appreciate casual dress. He also worked as an associate at McCown DeLeeuw & Co., a private equity investment firm, and in the mergers and acquisitions group at Goldman Sachs. As a former U.S. Army Airborne Ranger, Al can go for very long periods without food. He graduated from Stanford University with a degree in industrial engineering and has an MBA from Harvard Business School.

All three believed that the Internet was the perfect platform on which to build an online contractor-professional marketplace. Jon commented on this opportunity,

> We'd tried to get expert help on projects in our past lives and found it was a really difficult process. You relied on your personal network and hoped you found a good person. Also, a lot of our friends had left corporate America and gone off on their own, so we knew about the frustrations of the guru. With the Web, we figured we had a perfect opportunity to streamline this process.

While the experience and network of the founding team members was strong on the business side, they recognized the challenge of building a technology company without engineering or product experience under their belts. Jon continued,

> We are determined to pull together the right set of resources to make the business successful. Our top priority in the summer of 1999 is our investor network—bringing in experienced Internet angels to back the company and to give us advice. We also need technology experts. It is going to be incredibly difficult to find a talented engineering lead given the tightness in the market. So we made the decision to outsource development of the website.
>
> Marketing is our strength. We know we can build a brand that is compelling to the gurus. The challenge for us is to build a product that can back up our promises. We are pulling together a team of people that have a strong connection with the IP trend—nontraditional trend-setters with a touch of irreverence.

The early team has set the voice and culture for the company, and it is a company that the gurus can identify with. We can't create a corporate-style company when our customers are trying to free themselves from that environment.

James concluded,

Our strength is that the brand has connected with gurus in terms of engendering trust—even from the first day. Our model is focused on helping gurus achieve independence and it is important that our product reflected that commitment.

In August 1999, backed by US$3 million of angel funding, the team wanted to draft out a list of priorities, particularly related to the product. The vision was compelling, but turning the vision into a successful product was no small task. The next round of investors would also want clarity around what Guru.com was going to build and how they planned to generate revenue. The stakes were higher now, with Guru.com in discussions for US$10 million to US$15 million in their first venture round with firms such as Greylock and Kleiner Perkins. Guru.com's first step was to analyse the market.

Guru Characteristics and Needs

I work in my robe
While all my friends toil away
In starched monkey suits.

Guru haiku submitted by Michelle Goodman, writer, Seattle, WA

In addition to being a large, rapidly growing market, IPs were a highly attractive target group for many reasons. According to the U.S. Bureau of Labor Statistics, IPs were ahead of the rest of North American households on every measure of income, technology optimism and education. They were generally a higher-skilled demographic and they appeared to have significant unmet needs (see Exhibits 2(a) and 2(b)). Tyler commented on the initial customer findings,

I was overwhelmed with the positive response we received—with only the promise of what was to come. Customers would write to us telling their stories about how we had given them the motivation and support to venture out on their own and how the site we were creating was going to be a cornerstone for them in building their independent careers. It raised the bar, putting a lot of pressure on the product team to deliver what our customers envisioned and needed.

Early research on the market, combined with feedback from the preview site helped to develop the team's understanding of the guru (see Exhibit 3). Three primary needs were identified: finding work, accessing community and managing day-to-day business logistics. Guru.com next looked at hirers and their needs.

EXHIBIT 2(A)   Guru Characteristics and Needs

- **They are affluent and high spending**—IPs are twice as likely as corporate employees to earn more than $75,000 per year. According to a Guru.com survey, a large per centage of this population spends between 10 percent and 15 percent of their annual income on business related products and services.
- **They are "connected"**—Independent professionals are highly connected, with nearly 90 percent of the market owning a computer for business purposes (Freelance Centre Survey) and a large percentage of the online population using high-speed Internet connections.
- **They are experts working in high-demand job categories**—In addition to being concentrated in large metropolitan areas,[*1] over 85 percent of Guru.com's user base has expertise in the Web, IT, creative, sales, marketing and public relations, and management consulting categories—areas of high corporate demand. Furthermore, these professionals are experienced in their fields, with many having worked independently for more than five years.
- **They adopt this workstyle by choice**—Contrary to popular belief, independent professionals actively choose the solo workstyle, consciously rejecting the confines of corporate life. According to industry surveys, less than 10 percent of independent consultants cited downsizing as the reason for going solo.[**] Gurus cited flexibility and freedom as their primary reasons for wanting to go solo (Guru.com survey and focus groups), and 76 percent said that their quality of life improved dramatically after becoming an independent (U.S. Bureau of Labor Statistics).

[*]50 percent of Guru.com's user base was located in one of 10 major metropolitan areas. These included Austin, Boston, Chicago, Dallas, DC, Houston, LA, NY, Seattle, and SF.
[**]Penn Schoen & Berland's survey.

EXHIBIT 2(B)

Needs

While they enjoyed the freedom of shaping their own careers, gurus faced three major challenges:

Generating a Steady Flow of Consulting Projects

Gurus cited their biggest challenge as being the ability to maintain a steady flow of quality jobs. Moreover, they do not currently have effective mechanisms for marketing themselves and sourcing jobs. For most, the process of finding clients is at best a "word-of-mouth" proposition—80 percent cited their personal network or referrals as their primary source of jobs (Guru.com survey)—an often inefficient channel. Additionally, they reported that current online sites do not deliver the type and quality of projects that match their needs and qualifications—often being contacted by companies looking for full-time candidates. Typical gurus have a limited marketing budget and would rather focus on doing the work they love. The combination of tight project deadlines and operating a small business leaves scarce time for networking and lead generation.

EXHIBIT 2(B) *(continued)*

Accessing Professional Community

I just read about you today via The Industry Standard, *and I must say, I'm impressed. I'm spreading the news about your site, as I think it has real promise in building the community we home-based workers need.*

Wendy J., User Feedback, August 1999

Isolated (70 percent work from home, according to industry surveys) and without effective means to collaborate with their peers, independent professionals had a high need for finding and teaming with a professional community. They rated this solitude one of the top dislikes of their profession. In focus groups conducted by Guru.com, gurus suggested that they wanted to find ways to collaborate with each other to learn, to share experiences, and to form virtual project teams; however, they did not have an effective way to do this.

Managing Business Logistics

Freelancers need tools. Providing links as a first step is good, but I think the real sticky business, where the margins are, is in providing mission critical services to these independent virtual companies. Financial tools and banking partnerships . . . [or] partnering with Office Depot for supplies and discounts. From my research, there is a definite need for such services.

Marc L., User Feedback, July 1999

The day-to-day hassles of running a solo business prevented gurus from focusing on working with clients and honing their expertise. These administrative tasks were also listed as a top dislike of their profession. Almost all participants in Guru.com's focus groups reported having problems collecting fees from clients. Additionally, the process of completing quarterly tax reports and dealing with legal contracts and business forms was considered tedious.

Gurus independently manage the details of running a business, and they often lacked the time, expertise, and operating leverage to do so efficiently. Gurus lack purchasing power, and often make purchase decisions in an information vacuum. Major products and services purchased by gurus included: computer hardware and software, telecommunications, office equipment and supplies, business gifts, travel and entertainment, insurance, legal advice, tax and financial planning services, magazines and books, industry research, conferences and networking events, continuing education and career certification. With respect to many of these categories gurus expressed a strong desire to be able to purchase at a discount.

EXHIBIT 3 Selected Customer Feedback

- How did you know so well what we need? I have been on for 10 minutes and all I can do is mumble Yes!!! Yes!!! Yes!!! —Gene Russell
- What a terrific idea! I'm excited about the potential for your new site. Keep up the great work—I'll be around for the long term. —Deborah Mayfield
- Great work! Finally, a web site worth surfing. Hope you will continue to provide insightful and helpful hints. I wish you all the best and please continue with the great website. Although still in its infancy stage, I can see a huge potential for it. —Steven C, Strategy Consulting Guru, Boston
- I love your website! I have been procrastinating over starting a financial consulting biz targeting women and you have given me the inspiration to go for it! I have made you my homepage. —Nia Barrameda, Soon-to-Be Virtual CFO, LA
- This is too cool! I'm tap dancing in my living room. Go guys! —Louise Marchildon
- Funny. I always thought of myself as a whore, a mere utensil at the hands of the highest bidder, a body, an overglorified typist. And whenever I met someone under social circumstances I inevitably ended up labeled as a guru. But I never thought of myself as one—until this morning when I found your site. I love your site. It's new think for the new world I live in. —Erick Calder
- Your site is chock full of useful info and I love the tasty tidbit sidebars. Fast. Easy. Useful. Entertaining—that's Guru.com. Keep up the good work and continue practicing those pushups—the better to carry our guru banner onward into the battle for freedom and fun! —Juliet McCleery
- All I can say is, "Finally." —Suzanne Petrizzi Wilson

Hirer Characteristics and Needs

I know where the creative people hang out, and where the techies hang out, and I go there to network and recruit candidates. I don't care where these people go; if they are using Toiletbowl.com, I'll go to Toiletbowl.com.

Corporate user, Guru.com Focus Group, August 1999

Guru.com's target corporate customers were companies with a high demand for project-based workers. These companies ranged from small to mid-size businesses with fewer than 500 employees, to large corporations such as Microsoft. The defining characteristic of these companies was their need for specialized workers on a project basis. It was thought that as companies increasingly moved to an outsourced model and felt heightened pressure to find resources in high demand areas such as web development without paying astronomical placement fees, there would be an increasing demand for the services offered by Guru.com.

The outsourced labor market was growing at 6 percent annually, and professional and technical outsourcing was growing at 24 percent, four times faster than the broader market. These businesses relied heavily on professional/technical outsourcing to access essential skills while limiting overhead expenses. Furthermore, outsourcing allowed these companies to focus full-time human and financial resources on their core competencies. The use of outsourced expertise could also provide substantial personnel cost savings versus hiring full-time employees. These savings could be achieved through lowered training and benefits costs, plus the ability to smooth out labor expenses during volatile operating periods. In this bull market,[4] traditional staffing firms were continuing to increase rates, garnering a 30 percent to 50 percent markup on the contractors' fee (see Exhibit 4).

At present, staffing agencies had a stronghold on the hiring companies, with long-term contracts and onsite resources to keep each other's competitors at bay. Jon and James thought their best chance was to attract the talent—who were typically hard to find and highly fragmented in terms of geography.

The Competitive Landscape

In August 1999, Guru.com believed that there was no brand that embodied the guru movement, or effectively delivered on the core needs of independent professionals and the corporate hirers who depended on them. Thus, although there were many different online competitors, Guru.com believed that no one firm dominated this nascent online market. Tyler stated,

> There were a number of companies that were trying to create a marketplace for independent work—but they were all limited by the constraints of their core business strategy, which usually didn't put the independent professional first. Guru.com was the first company in the space to approach the problem from a blank slate—our whole business was about the independent professional, which gave us a huge advantage.

Their competitive analysis revealed the following two charts (Table 1 and Table 2). Both map out Guru.com's competition, strengths and weaknesses, and market positioning:

From Guru.com's perspective, there was no effective service that provided: (1) a place for gurus of all types to band together to share knowledge and experiences, and (2) tools, services and tips for gurus that are needed to run their businesses more efficiently and profitably. From the corporate users perspective, Guru.com also held the promise of a much-needed solu-

---

[4]In 1999, the American economy was enjoying a period of expansion unrivaled since the 1950s.

EXHIBIT 4   Hirer Characteristics and Needs

Hirer Needs

Although these companies covered a broad range of industries and varied widely in terms of size and revenue, their core needs with respect to finding, hiring and working with independent professionals were fairly similar. Guru.com also believed that most companies would be price insensitive.

Sourcing Quality Candidates

> *How am I finding developers? I'm wandering the halls at MIT.*

> David Kelly, Founder, Net Startup

Consistently, the feedback received from corporate managers through focus groups and interviews was the tremendous challenge associated with finding qualified candidates. Word-of-mouth, temporary staffing agencies, and online sites were all mentioned as channels used to find candidates. However, all were deemed inadequate. Word-of-mouth was the most frequently cited method of sourcing candidates, but was also considered to be highly inefficient and limited. Many communicated frustration with the process of using temporary staffing firms, due to high fees and an inability on the part of these firms to deliver qualified candidates. Furthermore, managers communicated dissatisfaction with most online sites because of their inability to deliver a manageable set of qualified candidates.

Time Sensitive versus Price Sensitive

Research found that hiring managers were relatively insensitive to price when it came to finding quality candidates. Managers were typically under significant time pressure to find contract resources, and would sacrifice cash to find qualified people in a timely manner. Moreover, they were frequently forced to use unsatisfactory channels, such as temporary staffing agencies, when faced with a tight situation. As quoted by one focus group member, "There is a love-hate relationship with agencies. I'll turn to them in a tight situation, but I'd prefer not to use them due to the cost, hassle and their general inability to deliver the high level candidates that I need."

Support on the Legal Requirements of Hiring Independent Contractors

Heightened by concerns generated from the recent Microsoft ruling, hiring managers increasingly recognized their need for guidance with respect to the requirements of hiring and managing independent contractors. Most hiring managers were unclear about the differences between freelancers and independent contractors and did not have adequate resources, outside of consulting an expensive legal firm, for getting clear information about the technical distinctions and their responsibilities as employers. Furthermore, hiring managers reported that it was sometimes difficult for them to confirm that an independent professional was a qualified independent contractor.

TABLE 1

Category	Value Proposition	Sample Competitors
Online career sites	• Job matching • Heavy orientation towards full time positions • Limited: no community, tools, content or commerce	• Monster.com (Talent Market) • HotJobs.com • Dice.com • Headhunter.net
Professional service automation (PSA) companies	• Focus on enterprise software customers • Tools focus—migrating enterprise applications to the Web • Limited: no community, content	• Opus 360 • Niku • Evolve • Portera
Staffing agencies	• Job matching • Agency model (high fees on signed deals, recruiters) • Heavy offline infrastructure • Online access to agency-sourced jobs • Basic tools for independents such as billing, 401Ks • Onsite services and dedicated account reps	• Aquent (Mac Temps) • Manpower • Adecco and Olsten
Independent professional job sites	• Job matching • Typically focused on a specific vertical, such as IT • Limited/no community, content, or commerce	• eWork • IC Planet • Brainpower

TABLE 2 Independent Contractor Market Map

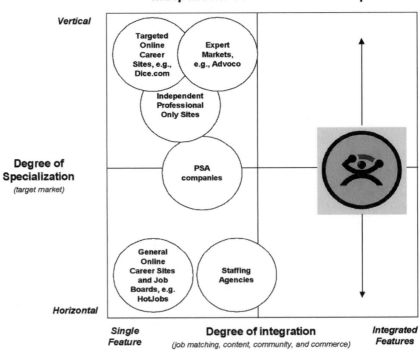

Independent Contractor Market Map

tion—a place to locate talent. Guru.com's analysis had revealed that hirers employed a variety of methods for finding and hiring gurus and drastic measures were often used to find and recruit these people (see Exhibit 5).

EXHIBIT 5   Competitive Landscape

Guru.com considered its primary competitors in the space to be:

- *Professional services automation (PSA) software companies* (i.e., Evolve Software (EVLV), Opus360 (OPUS), and Niku (NIKU)): These companies were developing enterprise software for automating professional services firms such as MarchFirst (MRCH). Each of them had developed an online strategy to source additional resources for their clients and to boost their potential valuations (at the time, enterprise software companies needed to have an Internet strategy in order to garner attention in the public markets). It was thought that PSA software companies would be at a disadvantage due to a lack of focus, as their core business was servicing the corporate customer side with enterprise software applications.
- *Major online career sites (i.e., Monster.com):* Online career sites such as Monster.com and HotJobs were mass classifieds businesses focused primarily on full-time job placement and international expansion. They were not building the content, community, tools or commerce features to provide a home for gurus, and their brands didn't target solo professionals. Vertically focused job sites such as Dice.com were also included in this segment. Some of these companies were making efforts to target the independent professional market (e.g., Monster's Talent Market—eBay style bidding on independent professionals); however, their products and brand positioning were failing to address the core concerns of high-end independent professionals.
- *Temporary staffing firms (i.e., Manpower):* Guru.com viewed their business as disintermediating the staffing industry, which was based upon marking up placement services 30 to 50 per cent. Temporary staffing firms were focused on consolidating the temporary staffing industry for W-2 employees, rather than building web-based solutions for independent professionals. However, many were hiring expensive management consultancies to study the impact of the Web on their core businesses. Some companies in this market, such as Aquent (formerly MacTemps), were attempting to launch online businesses. However, the legacy of an agency model remained, which served as a disadvantage for these players. Due to their reliance on the agency model (and its associated margins), corporate and guru reluctance to use staffing agencies, and their limited Internet capabilities, these companies were not viewed as a strong competitive threat.
- *IP focused job sites:* A series of start-ups were emerging to serve job seeking independent professionals, such as eWork and eLance. Again, these companies appeared to lack the ability to integrate interesting and relevant content with community, commerce and gigs. These were typically new entrants; therefore, it was important to keep a close watch on movements in this area. However, at the time, these competitors were not viewed as a major competitive threat.

Guru.com Launches Its Preview Site in July 1999

Against the advice of investors who advised Guru.com to wait until it had a more robust product, the Guru.com team launched a preview site in July 1999 to begin spreading the word about Guru.com's service and acquiring customers.[5] According to James,

> It has no functionality—there is some content aimed at IPs and a place for people to preregister for our service, but we decided not to do project matching at this stage.

Tyler added,

> Our initial site, which was entirely content driven, was getting a huge response from the guru community. We figured that we'd keep bringing in the gurus and then start acquiring hirers.

The Guru.com Strategic Approach

Now that they had a "placeholder" site that was beginning to sign up hundreds of IPs per week, Guru.com's next step was to build a functional website.

The brand was to be guru-centric. With the goal to create the largest database of independent professionals, customer acquisition would focus on gurus initially, with hirer acquisition following not far behind. The goal was to establish a 10:1 (guru:hirer) ratio in key markets such as San Francisco, Boston and New York by the end of the year. Guru.com's revenue model would be based on project posting, with hiring companies paying a fee to post projects on Guru.com. Additional revenue would come from online advertising and offline events. Upon reviewing the business model, Tyler commented,

> We are building something new and different, but we can look to other markets for proxies. For example, Monster has built a successful business on project postings for full-time positions. This gives us, and our investors, confidence that we could use a similar model to build a marketplace for contract work.
>
> As for focusing on gurus or hirers, it is a classic "chicken and egg" scenario. Without the gurus, the hirers wouldn't take us seriously. Without the projects, the gurus wouldn't be interested.

James added,

> The staffing industry has changed and the difference between Guru.com's product and traditional staffing industries is that our product will be automated and boundary-free—there will be no physical locations. To start, there won't be much screening, vetting, handholding—it'll be low touch. But we won't have the markups that temp agencies charge.

---

[5]In this first version, gurus could sign up with Guru.com by filling out a registration form.

The Guru.com Version 1.0 Product

Working with a small technical development company, Guru.com started to build its first major product (Version 1.0).

The product goals were to provide:

- A place for gurus of all types to band together to share knowledge and experiences
- Access to "hot," exclusive gigs for all types of gurus
- Tools, services and tips for gurus to run their businesses more efficiently
- Content to provide advice and perspective on issues that are relevant to gurus and to generate lively discussion within the community, and
- A place for corporate hirers to find top quality gurus

Implementing the Plan

To achieve these goals, Guru.com planned to launch a series of online products that covered four major areas: project matching, community, tools and services, and commerce. The first release would establish a basic project matching system, and to build on the existing content infrastructure to enhance its community features. They planned to roll out tools and commerce products within six to nine months from the initial release.

Release	Timing	Focus
1.0	Nov. 1999	Project matching and community
1.5	Dec. 1999	Added project matching functionality
2.0	Mar. 2000	Tools and services offering, commerce phase 1
3.0	Jun. 2000	Full commerce offering

Version 1.0—Project Matching and Community

Project Matching Features

The cyclical "feast and famine" nature of the guru's workload would be the first issue addressed. To help generate a steady flow of consulting projects, Guru.com planned to provide IPs with a variety of methods to increase their access to quality projects. These key features would include:[6]

- Guru Profiles: Guru Profiles would serve as a vibrant showcase through which gurus could highlight their skills and expertise—a résumé on steroids.
- Gig Postings: The gig posting system would allow hirers to easily create project postings via a simple-to-use, modular interface. Postings would be accessible to all gurus via the Guru.com project

---

[6]From Guru.com's 1999 business plan.

database. A basic messaging system would allow gurus to easily apply for projects by sending a link to their Guru Profile and a brief message.

- Guru Search: Searching and browsing capabilities would be provided to allow hirers to quickly locate gurus that matched their project requirements. Hirers would be able to conduct searches based on key criteria such as skills, availability and location. Additionally, hirers would be able to specify attributes and request notification of new gurus that met their criteria on an ongoing basis.
- Gig Search: Gurus looking for new clients or projects would be able to proactively seek out new work by searching the Guru.com project database. Through an easy-to-use, searchable database, gurus would be able to identify interesting opportunities posted by hirers or other gurus. Gurus would have the option to specify target project characteristics and receive notifications of postings that met these criteria.
- Response Management: Guru.com planned to build an online response management system to give hirers the ability to manage responses from candidates.

Community Features

Community at Guru.com would extend far beyond the typical confines of chat rooms and message boards. Thus, content, community, tools and services, commerce, and jobs would be tightly integrated. Guru.com intended its community to drive the creation and flow of content, giving Guru.com access to a perpetual source of granular, timely, relevant, low-cost material:

- Relevant and timely content: Content would be provided to give guidance and generate discussion within the Guru.com community. Features included Guru Guides, which provided how-to instructions on topics of interest to gurus; Guru Portraits, which showcased interesting gurus; cartoons to provide comic relief; and special features to provide more in-depth coverage of key topics.
- Interactive community forums: Moderated community forums, led by Guru.com community leaders, would provide gurus with the opportunity to voice opinions and share knowledge relevant to the entire guru community. Guru.com also planned to rely upon topical experts to answer specific questions from users and to post responses. For example, Dan Pink hosted a forum, answering questions from gurus across a range of topics from how to moonlight to how to protect your intellectual property. Experts were recruited to host community channels in five major areas: workstyle, tax and finance, legal, tech and gear, and lifestyle.

Future Website Features Proposed

These were the features that Guru.com proposed for their future website versions (1.5 and higher). Although they would have liked to include these features in version 1.0, Guru.com recognized that their time and financial resources were not unlimited (from Guru.com's Business Plan).

- Quality control: Guru.com planned to pursue a variety of methods to ensure that both gurus and hirers received quality leads. Guru.com would create a feedback loop through which customers could rate their experience with a contractor and vice versa. In addition, gurus and hirers would have access to credit and background check information through a Guru.com partner.
- Collections services: Collecting from non-paying clients was another major problem for gurus. Guru.com planned to offer services via partners to help gurus collect on unpaid invoices.
- Time and expense management: Guru.com was considering offering web-based time and expense tools to ease the burden for gurus of tracking hours and invoicing clients. They had not determined whether they would buy or build this product.
- Rate advice: Once they had achieved a critical mass of data in the system, Guru.com would consider offering a rate advisor to provide gurus with aggregate information about market rates for relevant projects and skill levels.
- Project management tools: Guru.com was considering offering gurus and hirers access to shared workspace for file sharing and collaboration.
- Commerce: Through partnerships with leading e-commerce vendors, and the ability to leverage an aggregated buying model, Guru.com planned to provide access to discounted products and services through a store targeted to independent professionals. Product areas under consideration included:
  - Insurance and financial and retirement planning services
  - Tax and legal services
  - Computer hardware and software
  - Communications products and services
  - Continuing education, training and certification programs
  - Industry research, conferences and events
  - Office equipment and supplies
  - Business gifts and greetings

Recommendation Time

As Tyler started to think about Guru.com's product strategy, her extensive consulting experience prompted her to link product with business strategy. Was focusing on the guru the best place to start? Were they making the right choices about prioritizing the product features?

Tyler commented,

We have to make some tough choices. We don't have a lot of time because competitors have started to launch their products, the customers are getting restless, and we've only got a small team to build this product. We've also got aggressive goals, but we can't build it all at once. If we choose to build a bit for the gurus and a bit for the hirers, we'll end up with a lot of nothing. I think we're starting in the right place, but we've got a long way to go.

Scantran

By Professor Sid L. Huff and Mike Wade

"This is a purely virtual company," said James Warren, vice-president of Scantran. "We are completely dependent on the Internet; it is our business lifeline. We never see or speak with our clients; we never meet with or talk to our translators. All the work is done out of our apartment, most of it by my wife Heidi, and all of it is passed back and forth electronically over the Internet, or sometimes by fax. Our web page *is* our marketing and advertising. Our growth rate is phenomenal, to the point where we are having to turn away more business than we can accept. While we started out doing the translation work itself, Heidi does very little actual translation any more; she just manages others, remotely. And the business is doing *very* well financially, thank you, far better than we ever imagined when we started. Our biggest problem right now is, how should we manage growth? We'd like to stay the size we are, but can we? If we decide to get bigger, we'll need to move to a new business model, and we're not exactly sure what that should be."

Background

James Warren was born in England, and moved to Canada when he was 14. After earning an undergraduate business degree at the University of Western Ontario in 1991, he moved to Japan and took a job teaching English there. On the side, he started a small business, translating documents for Japanese companies. Since his circle of friends and acquaintances in Japan included people from a number of different countries, he was easily able to locate people who could translate text from English to other languages. He would hire one of his Japanese friends to translate a Japanese document into English. He would then edit the English version, then pass it to other friends to translate it to German, Italian, or whatever the Japanese client wanted. Since the age of the Internet had not yet dawned, he did most of the work using his fax machine. The biggest frustration, he found, was constantly having to type and re-type text, in English as well as other languages, since fax was essentially a paper-based (not electronic) medium.

He left Japan in early 1994 and spent six months in Costa Rica, mainly studying Spanish and learning about the country. A short time later he accepted a job with a consulting firm in Norway, where he spent much of his time helping Norwegian businesses better understand North American and Japanese business practices. At a Christmas party in 1994, he met Heidi Bjerkan.

Heidi Bjerkan was born in Copenhagen, Denmark. Her mother was Danish, her father Norwegian. She spent her early years in Denmark, three years in Greece, then moved to Norway when she was 14. She had to master Norwegian in order to complete high school there. She completed a year of university in Norway, and three more years at U.B.C. in Vancouver. After completing her degree she returned to Norway to work. On the side she did some freelance translation work, in which her fluency in three languages—English, Norwegian and Danish—was an obvious advantage.

Towards the end of 1995, James accepted a job with a Canadian company that manufactured mining equipment. Because the firm did substantial business with companies in Latin America, it had decided to establish a presence in Costa Rica. James was the "point man" whose job it was to move there, find a suitable location, and generally pave the way for the firm's establishment of its Costa Rican-based operations. Consequently, James moved to Escazú, near San José, the capital of Costa Rica, and began the scouting work for his employer. Heidi joined him in January 1996, for what was originally to be just a few weeks. However, they soon decided to get married, which they did on April 1 of that year, in Costa Rica.

James was very busy with his work, and Heidi soon became bored working on her garden and her tan. She also discovered that, as a blonde woman, blending into the local social fabric was next to impossible. Both James and Heidi were quite familiar with the Internet, and hit on the idea of Heidi picking up freelance translation work via the Net. Heidi added her name to a few of the translator name and address lists that existed on the World Wide Web (WWW) and waited for the work to come in. Eventually, she was contacted by e-mail from a

Japanese company wishing to have some material translated from English into Norwegian. The company e-mailed the material to Heidi, who translated it and e-mailed it back. A few weeks later, to Heidi's delight, a check arrived in the mail for the work done.

Leveraging the Internet

James, who had dabbled with web page design and HTML programming in his spare time, decided to create a web page advertising Heidi's translation services. They realized that since Heidi could already translate between Norwegian, Danish and English, they only needed someone who could translate between English and Swedish to cover all the Scandinavian languages.[1] A quick look on the Web indicated that there were no other companies focused exclusively on the Scandinavian tongues, so they felt they had found a nice niche market. They decided to call their venture Scandinavia Translations, or Scantran for short. James hoped that they might make an extra US$500 a month; however, Heidi was more optimistic, and thought the figure would be closer to US$1,000.

James and Heidi obtained access to the Internet through a service provided by the Costa Rican telecommunications monopoly. However, the quality of the service left something to be desired. They were limited to a single telephone line into their home (getting a second telephone line in Costa Rica was essentially impossible for ordinary people, even when bribes were offered). Even the one telephone line they had was unreliable, and often stopped working during the frequent Costa Rican rainstorms.

While they used a local Internet Service Provider (ISP) for Internet connection services, they contracted with a site in California to host their web page. James explained:

> The main reason we used the California server was cost. Because once you're on the Internet it doesn't really matter where you store your web page files, your web host can be totally separate from your access point. Our California host charges us one dollar a month to store our web files. Typically, web hosts charge $25 or more, and in fact Sympatico, the Canadian ISP we currently use, charges over $200 a month!

The company's home page is shown in Exhibit 1.

After setting up their home page on the server in California, James set to work making sure that the Scantran home page came up in the top 10 results of the most popular search engines when key criteria such as "Norwegian," "translation," and "language" were used.[2] Driven

---

[1] While many people would naturally assume Finnish to be a Scandinavian language, in fact it is not. Finnish has its roots in Mongolian, as do the languages of Estonia and Hungary.

[2] There are ways of "seeding" search engines, such as including the appropriate key words frequently in the web page's front-end text, or using "meta tags" in the document, or submitting information to directory search engines such as Yahoo. Some of these change over time as search engines change their indexing strategies.

EXHIBIT 1   Scrantan's Home Page—Norwegian Version

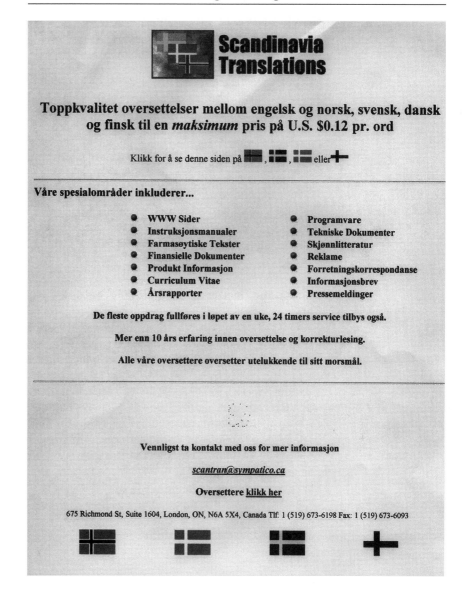

solely by advertising provided by their home page, and by Heidi's listing of her name in translation lists on the Web, by the end of 1996 she had more work than she could handle. Through the Internet she managed to find other translators who could take some of the load, but found that she was becoming more and more constrained by the level of Internet service available in Costa Rica.

For example, it was not uncommon to have to dial repeatedly, for over an hour, to get connected. Sometimes, inexplicably, the connection wouldn't work at all. Other times, especially when it rained, there would be no phone service whatsoever. The fact that they were limited to a single telephone line made juggling the telephone, fax machine and modem a challenge. When the connection did work, it was often painfully slow. Large files from clients might take an hour and a half to download, and then the same again to upload, if the material had to be sent to another translator. Heidi recalled:

> I remember one time, playing backgammon all day, waiting for a set of large files from one key client to download. Often a file would make it 80 to 90 percent of the way through, then "die," and we would have to start it all over again.

Despite these restrictions, during the first months of 1997, Scantran was making in excess of US$5,000 a month in revenue, and almost all of that was profit.

James' project was scheduled to finish in the summer of 1997. Although they were tempted to remain in Costa Rica to enjoy the tropical climate and low living costs, they eventually decided to move back to Canada. James enrolled in the MBA program of the University of Western Ontario. They decided that Heidi would work full-time for Scantran while James concentrated on his studies. James would provide part-time marketing help and provide support functions on an as-needed basis.

Upon arrival in Canada they rented a roomy apartment with a large area they could use as an office, and filled it with the necessary computer and communications equipment. They arranged for multiple phone lines to be installed, and obtained a high speed connection to the Internet. Once everything was set up, Scantran resumed operations.

Scandinavia Translations' Business Dynamic

A typical translation project cycle began when a large corporation needed a document, say a user manual, translated into all major world languages. They normally contracted with a large translation agency such as Harvard Translations of Boston, Team International in Germany, or Omega International in Monterey, California, to do the entire job for them. The large agency executed some portion of the translation work in-house (most large agencies covered the major European and Asian languages in-house), and looked for subcontractors to do the rest.

Scandinavia Translations' business usually came from such large agencies, with the request to translate the document into all the Scandinavian languages.

The proposal to Scantran would have included the size of the project in number of words, the source and target languages, per-word rate, completion deadline, and perhaps some other special requests specific to that project. Scantran then either agreed to take on the contract, or declined. If Scantran accepted the project, the large agency sent the document to Scantran by e-mail attachment. Scantran then located individual translators for the project, typically one translator for each of the four Scandinavian languages. Once a translator was found, Scantran sent the project to him or her, usually in the form of a text document attached to an e-mail message. The translator completed the translation, then sent the translated file back to Scantran by e-mail attachment. Scantran (Heidi) then checked the work to make sure the format was as requested by the client, skimmed the translated text for obvious errors, and forwarded the complete translation back to the client. Payment was received from the contracting agency, and made to the individual translators, by mailed check. Exhibit 2 summarizes the process.

Prices and Revenues

Scantran had a simple pricing system. It charged its clients US$0.10 per English word for translation, and paid its translators US$0.05 per English word for the same work. Both these rates were well below the industry average. Typical industry practice was to charge on a sliding scale depending on the total number of words in the project, subject matter complexity and deadline. Rates for the Scandinavian languages were generally somewhat higher than for other European languages. Typical rates for medium-sized jobs (5,000 to 10,000 words) were US$0.15 to US$0.25 per word. Typical rates paid to the individual translators were US$0.07 to US$0.15. Precise competitor rates were somewhat hard to determine, since very few companies followed Scantran's practice of posting its rates on its web pages.

Scantran's only variable costs were the fees paid to the translators. Fixed costs included office rent, Internet connection costs, and general overhead. The combination of low fixed costs, healthy margins and a high volume of business meant that the business had a solid positive cash flow. The business had no bank debt.

An income statement for the time period June 1, 1997, through February 28, 1998, is shown in Exhibit 3. Monthly gross revenues for the same time period are shown in Exhibit 4.

EXHIBIT 2   Diagram of the Process Flow for a Typical Translation Job

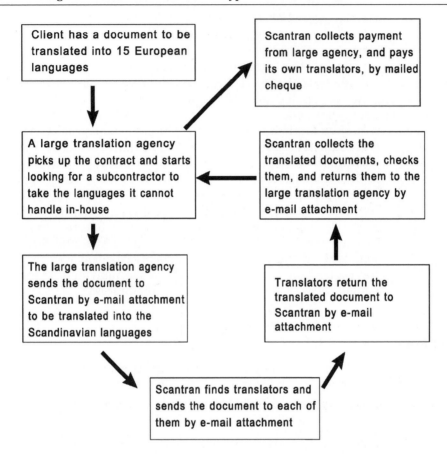

EXHIBIT 3   Recent Scantran Income Statement

Scandinavia Translations
Income Statement for the Nine-Month Period from
June 1, 1997 to March 1, 1998

Total Revenue:		$163,070
Payments to Translators	$58,245	
Gross Profit		$104,825
Expenses		
Start up expenses	$5,121	
General overhead	$8,514	
Total expenses		$13,635
Net Profit		$91,190

Notes: All figures in U.S. dollars. "Payments to translators" does not include payment to the co-owner, Heidi, for translation work, calculated at $23,290.

EXHIBIT 4   Chart Showing Scantran's Recent Revenue Growth

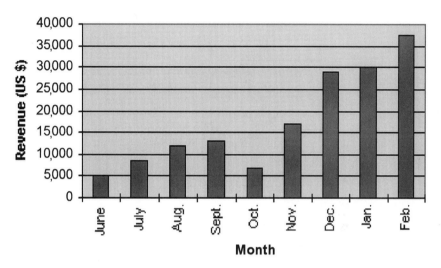

Scantran Revenue Growth, June 1997–Feb. 1998

Notes: During the same time period, Scantran completed 417 translation jobs for 39 clients using 25 translators. They managed the translation of approximately 1.6 million words, or approximately 4,000 pages of text.

Scantran's Strengths and Weaknesses

What did it take to be successful as a translation agency? James commented:

> Translation is an unusual business in that the quality of the work done is very hard for most customers to determine. Typically, translation services are seen by clients as a "cost of doing business." Translation is often somewhat of an afterthought that usually comes at the end of a large project such as a new software product development, and companies do not generally give it a lot of attention. Plus, there are almost always tight deadlines involved. The factors that matter most to our clients include customer service, speed and price.

Most clients underestimated the time required to translate a document. Translation companies were constantly working under tight deadlines, and those agencies that worked well under this kind of pressure were popular with clients. Customer service, too, was a very important part of the translation business. Those agencies that provided prompt and courteous service invariably attracted repeat business.

Prices for translation varied widely throughout the industry. Most clients did not shop around, but if they did, they would have found that translation rates varied considerably from agency to agency. Prices tended to depend on project size, complexity, language, client profile, and deadline. The market for translation services was very elastic. If a client seemed desperate, the prices went up dramatically; if a project was being "shopped around," the prices dropped.

Scantran tried to address the market using a number of tactics. It focused heavily on service. Among other things, Scantran had never missed a deadline, a common occurrence in the translation business. The company was always civil and courteous in its communications with clients, and had a policy of replying to e-mail messages within one hour. Scantran's geographical location in southwestern Ontario facilitated the company's ability to respond quickly to requests. As Heidi noted,

> Our clients are all over the world, and they all expect a response from us in 30 minutes. They forget about time zones and things like that. So we have to be able to conduct business 24 hours a day. Living here we are just 3 to 4 time zones away from the west coast, and 5 to 6 time zones for most of Europe and Scandinavia. If we lived in Vancouver, we probably couldn't run this business at all. Bermuda would be perfect!

Also, Scantran was the only translation agency on the Internet exclusively dealing with the Scandinavian languages. Other agencies generally offered one language, or all languages. For big translation agencies, it was a huge bonus that Scantran could take care of all their subcontracted Scandinavian work.

Thanks to low operating costs, Scantran was able to profitably charge less than its competition for comparable translation work. Also, their pricing policy was transparent. There was no need for clients to request a quote.

Scantran was not perfect. Some of the weaknesses the Warrens were well aware of included:

Quality: The quality of Scantran's translation work was very good for most types of work. Translation of highly technical material—e.g., medical or pharmaceutical documents containing a preponderance of technical terminology—was the most challenging, and Scantran sometimes turned down requests for such work for that reason. James commented, wryly, "If you're translating a document describing a new type of heart treatment, it's got to be right!"

Range of Services: Scantran was a "translation factory" with limited capability to take on added value work such as desk top publishing, audio work and the like.

Size: Due to its small size and lack of access to constantly available full-time staff, Scantran could not easily take on great numbers of large projects concurrently without reaching operational bottlenecks. The biggest bottleneck was usually the availability of translators. The company was currently attempting to increase its number of on-call qualified translators.

Competition

On the Internet, the search directory Yahoo listed hundreds of translation agencies, varying in size from a single translator to large publicly traded multinationals. However, as far as James and Heidi were aware, there were no other companies exclusively covering the Scandinavian languages.

Scantran's main *direct* competition was independent translators. These translators, a fragmented group, usually covered one or two languages and, like Scantran, advertised on the WWW. Also like Scantran, they were usually contacted by larger translation agencies for specific translation projects.

Scantran's main *indirect* competition was the translation companies based in Scandinavia. However, these agencies tended not to advertise or represent themselves on the WWW. On a research trip to Scandinavia, the Warrens visited a few translation agencies, and concluded that they were rather "fat and happy." They got the impression that these companies were doing a brisk and profitable business translating from Scandinavian languages into English, mainly on behalf of Scandinavian multinationals. Rates for such translation averaged about US$0.70 per word, and ranged from US$0.50 to US$0.90 per word, with all kinds of complicated extras such as deadline premiums, minimum order costs, complexity surcharges and the like.

Both James and Heidi felt that there was excellent potential to steal business away from these companies, but they were unsure how to do so without an office in the region. They felt that companies in Scandinavia were less "Internet-friendly" than were companies in North America, less accepting of the Internet as a business tool. Consequently, they were wary of trying to sell these firms on the concept of the Internet in addition to translation services.

Where to from Here?

James and Heidi felt they had been quite fortunate to have succeeded as well as they had to date. They both thought that their current business "model" was working very well for them, but they weren't sure about where to try to take things in the months and years ahead.

Stay the Same

The Warrens were fairly confident that Scantran could simply continue forever at its current size and scale of operations. As long as the company continued to pay its translators piece rates, then fixed costs could be maintained at their present levels. The question in James's mind was whether anything might happen that would disrupt the business were they to try to keep it just as it was at present.

Also, the Warrens wondered whether they were "leaving money on the table." In other words, could they be doing more business, and making more money, using the same or a similar business model? Or had they reached the maximum of the opportunities available through the present business model?

At the current level of operation, there seemed to be little problem obtaining clients. Marketing was done over the Web to target clients, i.e., large translation agencies. In October 1997, James decided to try using the Internet to market Scantran in a more proactive way. He simply went through the Yahoo listings of translation agencies and sent an introductory e-mail to all the companies that seemed at first glance to be large. On a trial basis, he targeted only those companies between A and F. The response was immediate, and overwhelming. Business poured in so quickly that he suspended all further marketing efforts.

Clearly, there was still plenty of untapped opportunity (at a minimum, companies G through Z) out there. Expanded marketing through the Internet, coupled with continuous searches for new translators, could be one way to grow the business while maintaining the same operating model. However, Heidi had been working "flat out" in recent weeks, and had little, if any, excess capacity.

Expansion Options and Issues

Full-time Staff versus Contractors

If Scantran really wanted to expand its size, one option was to hire on-site, full-time translators. This represented a major change from their current policy of maintaining a simple home office and only hiring piece-work contractors.

The overriding advantage of using piece-work contractors to do the translating was that fixed costs were kept to a minimum. It also meant that the company didn't need to obtain and pay for expensive office premises. Nor did it require the company to deal with the contractual obligations of an employer-employee relationship, including the payment of payroll taxes. It allowed James and Heidi to operate the business literally from the den in their apartment. Another advantage was flexibility. Contractors could be added and removed quickly and cheaply, depending on the level of business. Furthermore, Heidi could handle the company's day-to-day operations from practically anywhere in the world. This allowed her the opportunity to spend some time in her native Norway each year, while taking the company's work with her. This was more than just a chance to visit her family; as well, it allowed her to keep her language skills sharp.

But there were disadvantages to this mode of business as well. Contracting with translators was somewhat inefficient. Since many had other jobs, part-time translators were often unable to take on assignments, especially on short notice, which was the usual *modus operandi* of the business. The process of sending and coordinating large e-mail attachments, or arrangements to courier or fax documents, could become quite cumbersome. In addition, since translators were not full-time employees, they sometimes did not feel a very strong sense of loyalty to the company. This was especially true of Scantran, since the translators were invariably located in a different country. In fact, James and Heidi had used 15 translators over the past six months, some practically full-time, and had never met any of them face-to-face. In most cases they had never even spoken to them on the telephone.

Another disadvantage was inconsistent quality. Although Scantran received few complaints from clients, there was a concern that since the translators they used were not full-time translators, nor were most of them officially qualified as translators, quality problems might crop up. In fact, Scantran had occasionally turned down lucrative, highly technical translation work due to concerns over quality.

Role of the Internet

One consideration for Scantran was to reduce its reliance on the Internet for the generation of business. Scantran had the option of locating and working with Canadian and U.S. firms directly, rather than through the Internet. One reason for considering this was the issue of payment. Even though bad debts to this point had been negligible, there was a considerable amount of trust and good faith required when running a business through the Internet. Since it was easy to hide behind e-mail and a web page, it was often difficult to determine the size and legitimacy of business partners. Getting paid was always a concern, especially with new clients. Scantran had found that a "communal trust" existed on the Internet—as if among pioneers—but how long was this likely to continue? Collection of bad debts and/or legal action across borders or through the Internet was an unappealing proposition.

Another reason for abandoning the Internet involved working with individual translators who were not knowledgeable about the Net. The Warrens knew from experience that there was nothing more frustrating than trying to walk a contractor through the process of zipping a file, then attaching it to an e-mail message, when the person knew little more about using a PC than how to operate the word processor. Multiple versions of Internet software such as e-mail programs, or capabilities provided by different Internet Service Providers (ISPs), further complicated things. For example, James pointed out that users of America Online, one of the largest ISPs in the world, were not able to handle messages with multiple file attachments, while other e-mail systems could handle such things easily.

Contractor or Subcontractor

Another choice facing Scantran was whether to continue its role as mainly a subcontractor for other translation agencies, or try to become a prime contractor by actively seeking contracts directly from end user clients. An important advantage of being a subcontractor was that it was easy for Scantran to remain a niche player dealing exclusively with Scandinavian language translation. If it were to deal directly with end clients it would likely have to expand, in three specific areas.

The first concerned the range of languages it handled. It would either have to offer other language options itself, or make strategic alliances with firms to take the non-Scandinavian language work. The Internet might facilitate such an alliance: the members of the alliance could create a "web ring" by cross-linking each other's web pages, referring work to each other over the Net, and so forth. A concern with this was that quality would become harder to monitor. Shortly after its inception in Costa Rica, Scantran started to offer Spanish, French and Portuguese translation services. Heidi and James found, however, that there was no easy way to check the quality of the work which was done by the translators. Scantran dropped all non-Scandinavian work when it moved to Canada (and added Finnish, which, though not considered part of Scandinavia, was frequently requested by clients).

The second area concerned the range of services it would have to offer. Usually a customer not only wanted a project translated, but also wanted the finished product to be delivered in a very specific format. Because of this, most translation agencies had desktop publishing staff and facilities on site to fulfill the often complex document formatting and layout requirements of the client. Scantran currently had very limited skills and equipment for handling anything but the most simple desktop publishing work.

The third area in which Scantran would have to change involved its sales and marketing presence. If it were to deal with end clients, especially large ones, it would likely have to shed its "back office translation factory" image. It would likely need to establish a proper office, hire a receptionist and perhaps full-time sales staff, take clients to lunch, and so forth.

The main advantage of dealing directly with end clients and being a contractor rather than a subcontractor was financial. Scantran would be in a position to charge client fees (e.g., US$0.20 a word) to such customers, as opposed to subcontractor fees (US$0.10 per word).

Agents in Scandinavia

While Scantran's clients were scattered around the globe, 90 per cent of its business consisted of translating documents from English *into* Scandinavian languages. James and Heidi believed that their failure to get much business *from* Scandinavia mainly stemmed from the fact that the company had no physical presence there. Scandinavian companies were much more hesitant to use the Internet as a vehicle for business, and relied on an "on-the-ground" presence when they went searching for translation firms.

Recently, one of Scantran's best Swedish translators, Erik Zettervall, raised the possibility of coming to Canada and working for the company full time. Erik had been one of the first people to contact the Warrens about translation work after Scantran had put its web page on the Internet. In fact, he had pointed out errors, and helped them correct the text on the Swedish version of their web page (which the Warrens had developed without the benefit of personal fluency in Swedish).

However, James and Heidi were concerned that, once they committed to taking on a permanent employee, they were starting down a "slippery slope" of changing their current business model, perhaps into something that would work less well for them. Consequently, they discouraged Erik, much preferring to keep him as a contract translator, in Sweden.

The risk they saw in doing this was that they might lose him as a contractor by turning down his request to become a full-time employee of theirs. He clearly was looking for a larger role, a bigger "piece of the action," than simple piece-work translation jobs. James and Heidi were worried that if they refused him a larger role in the company, he might turn away from them entirely, and take some of their business with him as well.

One possible way of keeping Erik working for them (and generating a portion of their profit) was to create an agency agreement, where Erik would represent Scantran in Sweden (use Scantran's letterhead, business cards and such); he would be paid commissions on business brought in to Scantran, but would not receive a salary from the company. Erik could continue to do English-to-Swedish translation, but more importantly, he could become an on-the-ground presence that might help generate Swedish-to-English translation work as well. However, it was unclear to the Warrens how they should structure such an arrangement. How should they arrange the cost and profit-sharing with Erik? And how should they monitor his efforts to make sure he wasn't "cheating" them by using the Scantran name but locating and doing translation work by himself, without telling James or Heidi Warren about it?

Sitting in their comfortable apartment watching their young son Christopher play, with the computers that constituted their company's existence humming away in the adjoining room, James and Heidi Warren thought about how far their "purely virtual" business had come in such a short time. Since James had decided to enter a Ph.D program in the fall, they knew they would continue to be dependent on Scantran for much of their income for the next few years. The decisions they faced were critical to their future.

Chapter 8

Virtual Communities

The "virtual community" is one of the more successful and enduring outcomes of global connectivity. In the beginning, virtual communities consisted mostly of newsgroups and e-mail-based discussion groups around an area of common interest. The focus of these groups was on discussion and collaboration. Later, advances in web-based technologies allowed virtual communities to become clearing houses for content as well as forums for discussion. The challenge for the operators of these communities was to introduce commerce into the community business model. In theory, virtual communities have great value; in practice, however, profitability has been elusive. This chapter contains two cases on firms which have attempted to use virtual communities to pursue commercial ends.

Stockgroup Interactive Media (SIM) is a financial services information broker. SIM's primary business is serving as a collection point for information useful to investors seeking to invest in small-cap firms—primarily mining companies. SIM, in effect, matches potential investors with firms looking for capital. SIM's revenue comes from the firms looking for capital, since on their own they are much less likely to attract much investor traffic. SIM is also in the business of developing web pages for these small-cap resource firms, since generally the companies do not have in-house expertise to create and maintain their own web presence. The company has been relatively successful establishing a virtual community in the mining sector. SIM's main challenges involve managing growth, deciding on appropriate future directions, and determining how best to lever the "virtual community" they have created.

The second case describes Celebrity Sightings, a web-based company which offers a virtual community to fans of teenage celebrities in the United States. The case describes the creation of the company and its evolution during the first two years of operation. The company provides a forum in which fans can read material about their favorite celebrities, purchase celebrity merchandise, and chat with one another. The company is also a "front" for many celebrity websites. Special features and promotions, such as interactive chat sessions with celebrities, help to attract premium (paying) members. A number of issues are brought up in the case. These include effective website design, marketing of web-based services, revenue models for content-based sites, online community building, and the necessity for continuous innovation.

Stockgroup Interactive Media

By Professor Sid L. Huff and Rob Attwell

"Our goal is to be a fifty million dollar company in five years," said Marcus New, president of Stockgroup Interactive Media (SRG), an Internet-based investor relations services firm whose physical offices were in Vancouver. Marcus had a great deal to celebrate. Three years ago he had started SRG to develop web sites for junior public companies. The firm had been profitable since its earliest stages, a significant accomplishment considering the money-losing reputation many Internet-based businesses had earned for themselves.

SRG had developed an enviable reputation as a leader in providing investor relations services to junior public companies via the Internet. Recently, however, Marcus and his partner, Craig Faulkner, had found it increasingly difficult to sustain the company's growth, and were becoming frustrated with the operating problems that SRG was starting to experience as it attempted to expand. As Marcus gazed out his office window at the spectacular Vancouver harbor, he wondered how he would achieve the fifty million dollar goal he had set for himself and for SRG.

The Investor Relations Industry

The investor relations industry served a number of important functions for public companies and investors alike. Investor relations firms worked for public companies, usually as sub-contractors, to make investors aware of the company's stock, to encourage them to invest in the stock and, once the stock has been purchased, to continue to hold the stock. The mission of the investor relations firm was to ensure that the stock was not under-valued by the market and that the price of the stock remained relatively stable. They were also responsible for raising additional interest in the stock when the firm had a good news announcement to make, or when the firm was seeking additional funding.

Investor relations firms were usually paid a monthly retainer by the public companies they represented, plus expenses incurred to promote the stock. However, they made most of their money by cashing in on stock options issued to them, which they were able to exercise after a specified period of time.

The Internet had much in common with financial markets. Both were largely borderless, operated 24 hours a day, and were essentially electronic media. Not surprisingly, the investment community was one of the earliest adopters of the Internet. In spite of this, most investor relations firms had been slow to recognize the potential of the Internet as a source of value to client firms and to their own operations. Rather than viewing the Internet as a way of delivering information to existing and potential investors quickly and at a relatively low cost, it was often seen as having a negative impact on financial markets, as a source of rumors and hype.

Junior Public Companies

There were at least 3,500 junior public companies in Canada, and over 12,000 in the United States, at the end of 1998. Junior public companies, or "small caps," are classified as a public company with a market capitalization of less than US$500 million. These companies passed through a predictable life cycle, starting with the funding of a new initiative, subsequent rounds of funding, and periods of dormancy and failure. A small minority of such firms became going concerns, grew larger, and graduated to senior markets.

Junior public companies ("juniors") faced a number of challenges not faced by established firms. These companies were usually run by entrepreneurs whose personal wealth was largely tied to the success of the venture. Their primary challenge was that of survival, since they were almost always under-financed. Juniors had a perpetual need to raise money, since their cash flows were usually insufficient to cover their operating costs. As a result, these firms went through regular cycles of promotion and fundraising to sustain operations until their cash flows grew sufficiently to operate the company, or until the company failed altogether.

Given the shoestring nature of their operations, most juniors directed little of their resources towards administration and support. Most operated out of small offices, typically with a staff of three to ten people. Management, product development, marketing and sales activities soaked up most of the available resources. The majority of support services and functions were supplied by outside service providers, with very few of these kinds of functions performed in-house.

Juniors also had difficulty finding additional funding on acceptable terms, since few were closely followed by investment analysts and the business press. It was very difficult for investors to wade through the sea of scattered information about junior public companies and be confident about investing in the firm. As a result, all but the most informed investors tended to avoid investing in these types of firms.

Investors in small-cap stocks (i.e., the publicly traded stock of junior public companies) typically possessed a sophisticated understanding of investing and financial markets. They were usually well informed and up-to-date about developments in the sectors in which they invested. Since comprehensive information about the junior markets and the firms involved in them was not available, investors in the sector obtained information from multiple sources. They also spent a lot of time talking with other investors in the sector, often by attending investment conferences where they could speak to analysts as well as company representatives and management.

Many Canadian juniors found it extremely difficult to gain access and exposure to U.S. investors, the largest pool of risk capital in the world. The opportunity to become known by U.S. investors was limited to a small number of investment shows in major U.S. cities. By the same token, U.S. investors found it difficult to locate good, reliable information about Canadian juniors.

Recently, the Internet had emerged as a channel through which U.S. investors could obtain useful information about Canadian junior companies. Fifteen-minute delayed quotes and charts were available through various investment web sites. Investors were able to "chat" via sites such as The Silicon Investor.[1] And of course any junior which wished to could create a web site to promote the company and its products or services. That was where Marcus New first spotted an opportunity.

Marcus New and Craig Faulkner

Marcus New graduated with a bachelor in commerce from Trinity Western University, a small private university in Langley, British Columbia. Marcus's career as an entrepreneur started at age 17, when he worked as a branch manager for Triple 'A' Student Painters, a small painting company which hired university students over the summer. Marcus was one of the youngest branch managers ever hired by Student Painters.

---

[1]The Silicon Investor is located at www.techstocks.com. Subscribed users can participate in discussion forums for US$20.00/year. Only subscribed users can post to the site; however, read-only use of the site is available to anyone (such users must first register at the site).

In his first summer with the company Marcus's branch produced revenues of over $100,000, and Marcus was named the Western Canadian Rookie Manager of the Year. Marcus returned to Student Painters each summer through his university career, as a branch manager in his second year, and then as a district manager. In his final year with the company Marcus was general manager for the entire Western Canadian division, generating four-month revenues of $1.5 million.

Since the age of 16, Marcus had been an active investor in the stocks of small companies. Through his interest in investing, he had developed a good understanding of financial markets, and particularly the special challenges faced by the juniors. After completing his commerce degree at Trinity, he had the opportunity to join Student Painters full time, but instead looked for opportunities in the financial markets community surrounding the Vancouver Stock Exchange (VSE). He joined a small public relations firm whose main business was the promotion of VSE-listed junior public companies.

Craig Faulkner met Marcus at Trinity Western University. Like Marcus, Craig was an entrepreneur and had been a successful branch manager with Triple 'A' Student Painters. Craig graduated from Trinity and joined Construction Select Software as a consultant specializing in database applications.

The Creation of SRG

Marcus and Craig started Stock Research Group (SRG, later re-named Stockgroup Interactive Media) in 1994, out of Marcus's apartment. The purpose of the original business was to create web sites for junior public companies. Marcus hired Scott Larson, a former classmate from Trinity Western University, as the company's first salesman. Initially Scott was paid on a commission-only basis. The company's first client was Exor Data. Within six months SRG had 15 accounts, and 25 accounts after 12 months, at which point Marcus moved the company's operations into a modest 800 square foot office in Vancouver's financial district.

From the outset Craig was a minority partner in the business. Initially, he worked for SRG on a part-time basis early each morning and in the evenings after his day's work at his "regular" job. Craig performed all of the technical work in this fashion until February 1996, when he quit his other job and joined SRG full time.

Marcus soon discovered that his clients gained little value from the web sites SRG developed for them, since nobody visited the clients' sites. His first client received fewer than 100 visits to its web site during the first month the site went live. Not surprisingly, the client was unimpressed. It was evident to Marcus that if SRG was to be successful, he had to find a way to channel "eyeballs" to his clients' sites. That, he felt, would be a far more valuable service for his clients than simply designing and maintaining their websites.

Marcus came up with the idea of a special website, which he envisioned as an online "world" of financial information for small-cap investors. He chose a name for his concept: Stockgroup. The financial world that Marcus envisioned was based on the concept of a retail shopping mall. The idea was to create traffic, in the same way that a shopping mall establishes traffic that is part and parcel of its offering to its retailers. Marcus' vision was to provide a one-stop site on the Internet, through which investors interested in junior public companies could find all the information about the markets and companies they needed on a daily basis. The entire purpose of this online community was to bring value to his clients by directing traffic from Stockgroup to the client sites, so as to enhance the value of the website design and maintenance side of the business.

Stockgroup,[2] the small-cap financial "world" envisioned by Marcus, was developed quickly and went live on the Internet in August 1995. Considerable effort was put into developing the initial traffic base. Once Stockgroup went live, everyone involved with SRG spent hours each day trying to build traffic to the site by registering the site with various search engines, establishing cross-links with related financial sites, promoting the site in chat rooms and on subject related bulletin boards, and placing banner advertisements on related websites.

Stockgroup was also promoted in the mainstream media. Press releases were issued to the local business press and also to the national and international media, which led to a number of feature articles in local business publications (see Exhibit 1). Marcus also recognized that success on the Web could be achieved by advertising in print media, which SRG did by taking out small advertisements in the national Canadian newspaper *The Globe and Mail,* as well as in Canada's leading daily financial publication, *The Financial Post.*

Early Successes

Traffic to the site grew steadily. In June 1996, SRG got its first big break when Point Communications, the owner of the popular search engine Lycos, rated Stockgroup the top Internet financial site for that month. A surge of traffic resulted immediately. Following the award the growth of traffic flattened out but did not decline as these new users continued to visit the site. The next big break came in August 1996, when Stockgroup was picked as the Microsoft Network "Site of the Day," and was featured on the MSN member start page. The result was another significant surge in traffic, with a similar retention of the new traffic volume.

---

[2]www.stockgroup.com.

EXHIBIT 1   Article from *Business in Calgary* Magazine about Stock Research Group

Stock Research Group offers Internet window for public companies

By Business in Calgary Staff

We started Stock Research Group (SRG) in April 1995 to help investors find and research information on small cap companies. We had found that research on Vancouver, Alberta and Toronto small caps was virtually non-existent and that the Internet provid-'ed a medium where the investor could find information at one site."

With that vision and two home computers, company president Marcus New and partner Craig Faulkner began an entrepreneurial project that has led them to open offices recently in Calgary and San Francisco, with plans to open a third branch in Toronto next spring.

While the head office remains in Vancouver, the de facto core of its business is the bastion of Cyberspace and a spot on the World Wide Web accessed at http://www.stock group.com.

There, retail investors avidly and anxiously seeking the next Bre-X flier can access a wealth of information: company profiles, investment newsletters, Hot Topics, client products, charting and current quote services, market reports and a wide variety of linked financial sites from across the web and consequently the globe. A point which distinguishes it from other Internet services is that SRG is focusing on smaller cap companies. This said, they do have one client with a market cap of more than $1 billion.

"Rather than focus exclusively on the market cap, we are primarily attracting investors with a certain risk capital who are interested in stocks that are trading below $10," says Karen Hounjet, SRG's Calgary Account Manager.

New characterizes his firm's core services as focused, efficient, cost effective, third party connectivity and marketing strength. "The vision of Stock Research Group is to become a dominant supplier of small cap information in the Internet and to help the investment community learn more about these public companies."

The site has now evolved into a meeting ground where investors receive quotes on a 15 minute delay, the latest stock charts and news releases and Q&A sessions with company executives. The Real Audio button on the site accesses a variety of interviews with company presidents.

What they provide is a professional quality interview for computer users to hear. The only prerequisite is a free download of the Real Audio software which users can easily accomplish from the SRG site.

Much of what distinguishes SRG from the myriad of competitive services is the lengths to which the company actively markets to third-party resources. Stockgroup.com is featured on more than 70 other financial sites including Quote Com, UK Financial, Wall Street On-Line and Equity Magazine.

Source: Business in Calgary, October 1996. Reproduced with permission.

Determined to maintain their ranking at Lycos, Marcus and Craig continued to upgrade and develop the Stockgroup site, and consequently managed to hold the top financial site ranking for 17 months straight, until it was bumped to number four, with The Motley Fool site[3] taking over the number one position. In spite of losing Lycos's number one ranking of all financial sites, Stockgroup continued to gain recognition, winning 19 different Internet awards. Exhibit 2 illustrates a web site rating placing SRG's site at the top. Exhibit 3 shows a portion of the home page of SRG's website as of late 1998.

SRG's Products and Services

SRG began business strictly as a website design and maintenance service for junior public companies. As the client base expanded and a close working relationship developed between SRG and its clients, it became evident to Marcus and Craig that SRG was in a strong position to compete with traditional investor relations service providers. As a result, SRG expanded its line, and developed a portfolio of web-related and non-web products and services. These included:

Website Design and Development
From the beginning, web development and design has been SRG's core business and the source of its profitability. In late 1998, website development continued to provide over 70 percent of the company's revenues. This service was responsible for bringing in many new clients who at the time had no web presence (although the proportion of junior public companies without a website was declining continually). SRG's focus on investor relations for junior public companies allowed it to offer a number of specialized products and services tailored specifically for this segment.

Website Maintenance Service, Updates, Quotes and Charts
It was essential that information on any investor relations site be kept up-to-date and accurate, in part to comply with securities regulations, and also to maintain good relations with investors. Junior public companies usually lacked the personnel and expertise to update their own websites in a timely manner. As a result, SRG offered a site maintenance package, which ensured that the client website was updated regularly. Material changes in the state of the company, new press releases, and other such information of interest to investors were added to each maintenance client's website in a timely manner.

---

[3] www.fool.com.

EXHIBIT 2   Website Rating Showing SRG as the Number One Site

Click on graphic to visit site.

POINT review   Top Ten Sites of the Week

Top 10 Investment Sites

Forget everything you learned watching Michael Douglas in *Wall Street*: the modern high roller no longer has to suit up for a downtown New York brokerage firm. Those flannel PJs and fuzzy slippers will do just fine while you browse the Web for late-breaking company news and stock market quotes. And — if you've got the guts — it doesn't take an expensive suit to be your own broker and invest online using the Web's many discount trading houses.

If research, tracking and trading are the cornerstones of personal investing, the Web can help with all three. Sites that keep tabs on particular niches can be a boon if your interests happen to coincide. The highly ranked Stock Research Group - our number-one site — is such an example, focusing on high-growth businesses, while Silicon Investor (a Top 10 honorable mention) is renowned as home base for the latest happenings in technology companies. Similarly, another runner-up The SmallCap Investor monitors the riskier, but potentially lucrative game of trading in smaller companies, along with the even smaller "microcap" stocks.

Once you've chosen your investments, you'll want to watch them closely. You can fire up your own stock ticker and watch the quotes roll across your computer screen, or you can stop by popular "free" quote services such as our no.-8 site, CheckFree's Investment Services Quote Server, for the latest updates. Our no.-10 site, Quote.com, last week announced a free, *real-time* stock-quote service. Now, at-home investors only have to pay standard stock-exchange levies to get the same up-to-the-second data as the big boys. Lycos's own StockFind serves up quotes on equities and popular mutual funds, along with the all-important news dished out by corporate public relations departments.

Unless you're faint of heart, the real fun is in buying and selling. Palo Alto-based E*Trade pioneered online trading on CompuServe before Wall Street denizens had even heard of the Internet. The outfit still has a reputation as one of the lowest-commission brokerage firms around for investors who don't need a lot of hand-holding. More-tony advisors, like the team at Smith Barney, are now getting Net-wise and are eager to offer their sage advice ... for a price.

New Search • TopNews • Sites by Subject • Top 5% Sites

City Guide • StockFind • PeopleFind • Companies Online

Rating out of 50

1. Stock Research Group
Info on high-growth stocks
Rating: 44.5

2. Chicago Board of Trade
Futures exchange site
Rating: 44

3. Investors Edge
Free investment information
Rating: 43.5

4. Wells Fargo
California bank homepage
Rating: 43

5. Douglas Gerlach's Invest-o-Rama
Tons of investment links
Rating: 42.5

6. StockMaster
Historical charts for publicly traded stocks
Rating: 42

7. NumaWeb
Resources for investors from U.K. firm
Rating: 41.7

8. CheckFree Investment Services Quote Server
Handy service from Security APL
Rating: 41.5

9. Smith Barney Access
Market insights from investment firm
Rating: 41.3

10. Quote.com
Voluminous financial, investment info
Rating: 40

Source: Point Review, http://point.lycos.com, March 1997.

EXHIBIT 3 Portion of SRG Home Page (as of October 1998)

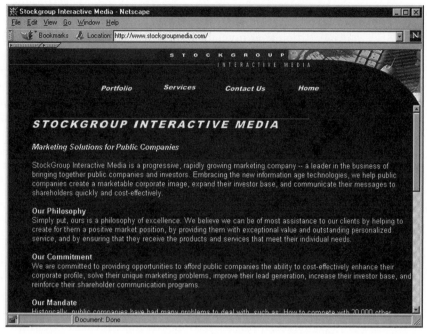

Source: SRG.

The maintenance service was a key to SRG's profitability. An initial web site design typically generated a fee of $1,200 to $1,500 on a one-time basis. In contrast, the maintenance package generated $300/month and required considerably less effort, since most of the functions were automated. Each SRG client site used a standard quote and chart format, which was customized to match the client's website design. Most clients required three updates per month, usually in the form of press releases, which could be uploaded with a template in a matter of minutes. Still, this service was extremely valuable to clients, since they could count on having their websites updated in a very timely manner. Many small web developers took days just to return client phone calls, and longer to update the sites, while SRG was able to update its clients' sites seamlessly, within hours.

Sector Specific Financial Worlds

Based on the data provided by its member profiles, SRG possessed useful information on the specific sectors preferred by its users. From these data it developed specialized sector-specific sites catering to narrow investor segments, with an emphasis on small-cap stocks. Through these sites, SRG provided information, drawn from the wider market, which it thought likely to have an impact on its clients' companies.

The first such "super site" to go live was DiamondStocks.com, followed by PetroleumStocks.com and, most recently, MiningAuthority.com. The idea behind these super-sites was to create "category killers" of investment information for each of these sectors, providing all of the information that investors in the sector need to stay informed and up-to-date.

SRG invested considerable resources gathering accurate data and information about each company in the entire sector. Each of these sector-specific sites contained information about each of the companies in the sector, but featured SRG clients. SRG also sold links to non-client sites. By the end of 1998 the majority of SRG clients in the diamond sector and the oil sector had been listed in the new financial worlds; however, only a few non-clients had signed up for the linking service. Marcus was considering hiring a dedicated sales force to sell these links. He was also considering outsourcing sales of this product to a telemarketing firm on a straight commission basis.

Banner Advertising

Stockgroup's large volume of narrowly focused traffic made it a very attractive site for banner advertising. The profile of its users made it ideal for advertising by both offline and online brokerage businesses, junior public companies seeking to gain additional exposure for their stocks, and online and offline financial publications. However, interest in SRG was not limited to the financial world. IBM and Lotus Development Corp. were also regular advertisers at the SRG site.

Advertising revenue had almost no cost associated with it other than the 20 percent sales commission. The client purchased a given number of impressions for $35 per 1,000 impressions, which was a common rate on the Internet for banner advertising. Once the ad was sold the client would e-mail the banner to SRG's webmaster, who would upload it for rotation on the site. Banner advertising was, however, limited to a few key pages on the site and was restricted from client sites. As a result ad revenue was limited by Stockgroup's traffic.

E-mail Blasts

Although the Stockgroup financial world was a free site, which did not require registration, users were given the opportunity to register for the SRG Club. These members received a monthly newsletter and periodic information about events and companies in industry sectors that they had specified. This provided SRG the opportunity to sell another product, e-mail blasts, to corporate clients. A client company was usually interested in sending out an e-mail blast when it had a major "good news" announcement it felt would help build momentum for the stock. For $1,500, SRG would e-mail a press release to those of its 21,000 SRG Club members interested in the corporate client's industry sector.

One of the challenges of this product was managing its impact on the SRG Club members. SRG had to balance its desire to gain additional revenue with the tolerance level of the club members for unsolicited information. Too many e-mail blasts per week, Marcus thought, was likely to lead to a lack of effectiveness of the e-mail blasts, an increase in club member attrition and an erosion of club member trust.

Quote-and-Chart Applications

In order to improve efficiency internally, SRG developed a number of software applets, small downloadable browser applications that could provide certain website functions such as quotes and charts. It turned out that being able to provide this capability in this fashion gave SRG an important competitive advantage.

Numerous established companies, as part of their corporate web presence, included features on their websites of interest to potential investors. In particular, investors often wanted to be able to get near-real-time quotes of the price of the company's stock, and to be able to view various graphs of the stock's performance. To provide this, the company's site would normally include a link to a separate quote-and-chart site, outside the corporate site. However, once an investor reached the quote-and-chart site, he or she would often spend time checking the price of other stocks, or would choose to access various other financial information provided at the quote-and-chart site, and might not return to the company's site. As a result, the quote engine site pulled traffic away from the corporate site, effectively stealing its traffic.

SRG's quote-and-chart applets allowed SRG to provide the same service, but actually imbedded the quote-and-chart feature on the client's own site, by reposting the client's quote-and-chart page every 15 minutes. SRG could package its quote-and-chart applet software for its client firms as an add-on to their sites. SRG provided the data feed required by its software through a satellite link at the Vancouver office. Early in 1998 SRG decided to package and to sell the quote-and-chart applets as a separate product for an annual fee of $1,200.

Electronic Newspaper

Marcus had developed (but not yet implemented) another idea for a vehicle which would draw more users to the SRG site: publishing an online investment newspaper. Since Stockgroup's visitors had the same profile as investors who subscribed to small cap analyst newsletters which were mailed to the investor via Canada Post, Marcus felt they were a community of people primed to buy such a service online from SRG. Marcus thought an appropriate price for the newspaper would be $9.95 per month. The newspaper would be delivered via a password protected web site. The web format was chosen instead of an e-mail format to allow for additional banner advertising revenue. As well as an electronic newspaper, Marcus intended to establish a virtual news-stand of newsletters and analyst reports to sell to visitors to the site. Launching the services would require nine full-time staff to write and publish the content and operate the business. The new division of SRG would also need operating capital for office space, computers and start-up operations.

Investor Market Place

The first non-web product SRG developed was called the *Investor Market Place (IMP)*, a high-quality four-page color brochure delivered as an insert in *The Financial Post* (see Exhibit 4). Space in the brochure was sold to web clients, and utilized text and graphics supplied by the client company. Each edition contained a profile of 24 small-cap companies, and included a detachable postage-paid reply card which prospective investors could fill out and mail to receive more information about the companies listed. The brochure was supported by a web site which contained the same features, along with a direct link to each company.

The IMP service competed directly with Stockdeck, a traditional investor relations service provider. Stockdeck, however, had not yet identified the Web as a key to its future success. Over a three month sales cycle SRG's web service sales force cross-sold IMP spots to its existing web clients and targeted non-clients and vice versa.

Investment Shows

One of the most effective ways for junior public companies to reach new investors was by attending investment shows. The shows were designed to give the juniors an opportunity to present their company to investors, and to give investors an opportunity to speak directly to employees of the company, including management.

Companies featured at such shows were charged a fee for space and services in a convention hall. Attendees were charged a registration fee, which was often waived in the interest of ensuring that the event was well attended by potential investors and investment analysts and since the featured companies were the primary source of revenue for the show promoter.

By the middle of 1997, Marcus realized that SRG was in a unique position to compete effectively in this business. It already had a corporate client base of over 300 public companies which were all seeking more exposure to investors at one time or another; many of these clients were regular purchasers of trade show booth space. As well, SRG attracted a large volume of Internet traffic, some proportion of which would surely be interested in attending investment trade shows. Stockgroup site had been generating over five million page views per month, and was visited by over 170,000 unique visitors per month. Furthermore, SRG could use the investment shows to further promote the Stockgroup community, as well as SRG's other services, creating a "virtuous circle" of on- and off-web services.

EXHIBIT 4   Example *Investor Market Place* Document

Source: SRG company documents.

Marcus decided initially to partner with investment show promoters, thus providing SRG an opportunity to test the strategy with less risk. The success of the first two shows led to the acquisition of an investment show business. This was done in order to leapfrog many of the development stages of this new line of business. The first two shows following the acquisition were successful in terms of attracting companies to feature at the shows; however, both shows were poorly attended by investors.

Full Investor Relations Services

The ultimate extent of backward integration for SRG was to become a full-scale provider of investor relations services. Marcus was considering taking SRG into the mainstream investor relations business in a limited way, since two key clients indicated interest in having SRG handle their investor relations. This was a potentially lucrative business, since companies typically paid a monthly retainer plus expenses and offered a significant number of stock options. However, Marcus was not yet convinced that this was the right move, given the state of the junior markets in Canada, the businesses' lack of scalability and the amount of SRG management time full investor relations might require.

Revenue Model

Unlike the majority of Internet-based startups, SRG enjoyed solid initial revenues, generated primarily through its website design and maintenance businesses. As a result it did not experience as much pressure to generate revenue from visitors to the Stockgroup website as it otherwise would have. Marcus continually reminded himself that the purpose of the Stockgroup site was to generate traffic and channel potential investors to SRG's clients' corporate sites, thereby providing added value to client companies in order to sustain the design and maintenance revenues. Still, it was not lost on Marcus and Craig that the large number of visitors to the Stockgroup site was a potential source of revenue in its own right as well. The question of whether and how to generate revenues from the Stockgroup traffic, which had become an investor community with a life of its own, was a nagging issue for SRG.

In the interest of allowing traffic to continue to develop, Marcus and Craig decided that Stockgroup would always be free to the user, based on the firm belief that charging users a fee to access the Stockgroup site was a sure way to kill the virtual community in its infancy (for further information on virtual communities, see the Appendix). As a result almost no revenue was generated from the investors who visited the Stockgroup website.

As of August 1998 more than 70 per cent of SRG's revenues were generated by fees charged to corporate clients for the design and maintenance of their websites. Site design fees ranged from $1,200 to $7,500, and maintenance typically cost each client $300 per month. SRG's remaining revenue came from selling banner advertising on four key

EXHIBIT 5 SRG Financial Performance through 1997, and Projection for 1998

Year	Sales	Profit	Net Margin
1995	$78,000	($1,500)	(2%)
1996	$458,000	$110,000	24%
1997	$1,340,000	$152,000	11.3%
1998 (est.)	$4,200,000	$800,000	19%

Source: SRG.

pages on the Stockgroup site, by selling e-mail advertising (e-mail blasts) which was sent to SRG's 21,000 registered users, and by selling the low margin IMP to web clients. Revenue from trade shows was only starting to build and the quote-and-chart software applets had not yet been launched.

Less than 1 percent of SRG's revenue was generated through online transactions with visitors to the site. The online transactions that did take place centered on the online sale of two analyst newsletters through the Stockgroup community, which were not produced by SRG. Although Craig and Marcus had not been able to find a way to generate revenue directly from the Stockgroup traffic, they were convinced that it had considerable, and possibly the most significant, upside potential in the long run.

SRG's financial performance projected through 1998 is illustrated in Exhibit 5.

Competition

SRG's unique product and service mix meant that it had no direct competition. However, it did face competition in each of the segments of its business from different competitors.

Web Design Firms

Local website design firms frequently competed with SRG for the initial development of clients' corporate websites. The number of these small, local web design companies was growing rapidly. They ranged in size from one individual working part time or evenings at home, to a handful of people working out of a low-rent office. Marcus felt that these design firms were not well equipped to match SRG's range of products and services.

While many such firms competed to do initial web site design work, none was focused on ongoing maintenance, the most profitable service. The difficulty was in convincing clients that ongoing maintenance was important, not just for regulatory compliance, but more importantly to bring their existing or potential investors back to the site regularly.

A number of larger design houses, such as Agency.Com in New York and Cyberplex Interactive Media in Toronto, catered to the needs of Fortune 500 or TSE 300 companies. These firms had sophisticated services designed to meet their clients' entire corporate web service needs, including investor relations. While these larger firms had the capability to provide a complete range of services, their offerings actually went well beyond the needs (and budgets) of junior public companies; and their services were not tailored to the specific needs of this market.

Traditional Investor Relations Firms

Traditional investor relations firms were not seen as a major threat to SRG, even though they served the same clients and performed some of the same functions. SRG could also be seen as a service provider to these firms, and these firms as gatekeepers to the clients. This industry was quite highly fragmented, and most of the companies were only beginning to see the need to be online, largely as a result of "investor pull" rather than an industry recognition of the Internet as a competitive weapon. Given their relatively unsophisticated understanding of the Internet, the industry remained largely unaware of the potential of virtual communities (such as Stockgroup) as a source of value for clients. Moreover, the industry had not yet perceived the potential threat posed by competitors backward integrating from the Internet—competitors such as SRG.

Online Financial Sites

Investors have been very rapid adopters of the Internet. A number of financial virtual community sites have been developed, and online investors have begun to amalgamate at these investment sites. Popular investment web sites included the Silicon Investor,[4] TheStreet.Com,[5] the Wall Street Journal Online[6] and The Motley Fool.[7]

Portals

Internet portals such as Yahoo, Altavista, Lycos, Excite and the portal services of Microsoft and Netscape aggregated information and generated content on a wide array of topics, including investing. Portals were

---

[4]www.techstocks.com

[5]www.thestreet.com

[6]www.wsj.com

[7]www.fool.com

increasingly becoming destination sites for many purposes. So far, how-ever, Marcus felt that these portal sites were less a source of competi-tion than they were a source of traffic through their links to Stockgroup and SRG clients.

The Challenge of Growth

SRG's success with its web business had led to an array of opportuni-ties, each of which included its own set of challenges. The greatest over-all challenge facing Marcus and Craig was that of deciding which op-portunities to pursue first, and how to assess opportunities appropriately. However, rapid growth of the business had created a number of challenges and each of the opportunities required cash.

SRG Operations

In less than four years SRG had grown from a two-man company oper-ating out of an apartment, to a $1.3 million operation with a full-time staff of 21 and offices in the financial districts of Toronto, Calgary and Vancouver. All of the computer and communications technology for op-erating the web sites and the administration of the business was lo-cated in Vancouver, while the Calgary and Toronto offices handled only sales and marketing functions. The Vancouver office had moved three times in two years to accommodate new staff, and recently had taken over the adjoining space in its current office building, doubling its workspace to 5,000 square feet. Soon after securing the new space Mar-cus wondered if it would be big enough.

Management of the daily operations increasingly consumed Marcus's time, while Craig spent most of his time managing the array of com-puters which ran the site, the data feeds and the networks upon which the site depended. A full-time webmaster administered the content of the SRG website and managed the design, development and mainte-nance of client sites with five full-time site designers.

Recently Marcus had become frustrated by SRG's inability to attract and retain qualified staff, particularly sales staff. Turnover of sales and marketing staff required Marcus to devote a considerable amount of his time to recruitment. He was considering hiring a national sales man-ager whom he could put in charge of managing the sales and market-ing functions. He was also considering hiring a human resources man-ager. However, finding and attracting highly qualified staff was time-consuming, difficult and expensive for a relatively small company like SRG. A very positive sign was that Marcus seemed willing to hand over functions and control to professional managers.

SRG's difficulty in retaining qualified sales staff was driven in part by the competition for salespeople due to the robust state of the Cana-dian economy, but also by SRG's cash constraints. Since SRG's growth was financed entirely by operating cash flows, it could not offer aggressive salaries. The sales staff had the potential to earn substantial commissions; however, only a small proportion of their salaries was guaranteed. The commission structure put considerable pressure on sales staff to produce in the short term, and made it difficult to attract the most capable sales staff, who were able to command higher salaries and more guarantees elsewhere.

Furthermore, with the growth of the account base for the core business had come the problem of account attrition and the need to secure additional accounts just to "stand still." The problem of account attrition had been exacerbated by the relatively poor performance of juniors in Canada during 1998, following the collapse of the infamous Bre-X mining company.[8] The Vancouver Stock Exchange Index, mainly comprising junior public company stocks, had fallen over 60 percent during that period. Many junior firms had failed to raise the capital necessary to continue operations, and others had had to scale back their stock promotion (investor relations) activities until market conditions improved. This had resulted in a higher than normal rate of account attrition for SRG.

Need for Financing

SRG was starting to come under cash flow pressure in the third quarter of 1998. Marcus attributed this to a number of factors. The high level of account attrition experienced recently had forced the company to spend additional time and money on customer acquisition and retention. Overhead costs had been expanding rapidly. The Calgary office had been added in October 1996 and the Toronto office in January 1997. Sales volume from these offices had not yet grown sufficiently to cover their costs. Toronto in particular was only producing 50 per cent of its budgeted revenues. Furthermore, the Vancouver office had been expanded and required leasehold improvements. The additional site traffic also meant that SRG's hardware and software had to be upgraded constantly.

The expanding volume of product development initiatives undertaken by SRG was a concern, as it was consuming rapidly increasing amounts of resources. These product and service developments included: the further development of quote-and-chart applets, the development of three additional "category killer" sector-specific financial

---

[8] The website http://www.brexclass.com/ provides information and background on Bre-X, and on the ongoing class action lawsuit.

worlds, and the move into the trade show business. All of the new projects had been undertaken without having secured additional financing.

Raising Additional Financing

According to Marcus, SRG had a number of advantages in raising capital. Most importantly, the firm had been quite profitable for over two years, a rarity among Internet companies. The success of the Stockgroup virtual community, and its high volume of traffic, made it quite attractive, especially in light of the premiums being paid for Internet stocks. Investors also seemed to be rewarding Internet category leaders, such as Stockgroup, with disproportionately high valuations.

In spite of those advantages, SRG had had trouble convincing Canadian sources of funding about the merits of the company. While there had been some interest from Canadian venture capitalists, in general, when it came to the Internet, "(Canadian sources of funding) just don't understand," according to Marcus. "Your best bet is to go to the U.S.," he continued.

For over a year, Marcus had been seeking additional financing to provide SRG the resources it needed to progress to the next stage of development. Both Marcus and Craig spent a lot of their time speaking to everyone they knew in the financial community about financing the business. While the firm had received considerable interest, no major financing agreements had yet been reached. Marcus had been able to secure a line of credit with a major bank for $150,000, secured against accounts receivable and personally guaranteed by Marcus. Recently, Marcus engaged PriceWaterhouseCoopers to assist in securing financing, and to help SRG establish a credible valuation of the firm for the negotiation process.

The need for additional financing was a long-standing issue for SRG; however, SRG's profitability and positive cash flows had, until now, allowed Marcus to wait until he could get additional funding on acceptable terms. For Marcus, acceptable terms meant a valuation which reflected his understanding of the value of the company, and being able to meet SRG's funding needs to implement his vision.

As Marcus returned to his desk, he reviewed his travel agenda for the next two weeks, which would take him to Calgary, Toronto, New York and Seattle. The problems of the business didn't simply seem to be accumulating, but rather to be compounding. Although it had never seemed that there was enough time in the day to put in place all of the plans Craig and Marcus had for the business, it now seemed that there was no longer time in the day even to sustain operations at the current level. Marcus wondered what it would take to get SRG to its $50 million goal.

Appendix

VIRTUAL COMMUNITIES AND THE PRINCIPLE OF INCREASING RETURNS

Virtual Communities

A distinguishing feature of SRG has been its ability to develop and maintain a virtual community of and for small-cap investors. Hagel and Armstrong, in their book *Net Gain,*[9] argue that virtual communities should have five distinct characteristics, all of which are necessary for success.

Distinctive Focus

The community must have a distinctive focus, making it easy for users to understand what they can expect to find on the site and the kind of resources it contains.

Capacity to Integrate Content and Communication

Virtual communities are sources of content and information for customers. Furthermore, they provide an environment for communication between users and members of the site.

Appreciation of Member Generated Content

In addition to providing for communication, virtual communities should provide an environment in which users/members can generate and post content. The community site should facilitate interaction and communication between members.

Access to Competing Publishers and Vendors

Virtual communities comprise an aggregation of information about an entire area of interest for the users/members. In order to provide for the needs of users, Hagel and Armstrong argue that it is essential to offer access to competing publishers and vendors in order to enhance the value of the community for users.

Commercial Orientation

Similar to many other Internet facilities and services, virtual communities originated as volunteer ventures, provided for free or at cost to members. Increasingly, however, they have been organized as commercial enterprises; the community organizer seeks a financial gain from the community.

---

[9]*Net Gain: Expanding Markets through Virtual Communities,* John Hagel III and Arthur G. Armstrong, Harvard Business School Press, Boston, MA, 1997.

The Principle of Increasing Returns

One of the key elements of the concept of a virtual community is the principle of increasing returns. According to this concept, the larger and more concentrated the virtual community becomes, the more valuable it becomes as a potential source of profits. To this end, a virtual community can develop increasing returns in four ways, according to Hagel and Armstrong. These are:

Transaction Offerings

One way to increase the value of a virtual community is to provide transaction offerings. Users will value the community increasingly if they can act on the information provided in the community immediately.

Content Attractiveness

Hagel and Armstrong emphasize the need for attractive content to increase the value of the virtual community. This can be achieved by offering a comprehensive collection of information about the distinctive focus of the community, content which is updated regularly, to give reason for members to return regularly.

SRG fully understood the need to provide content which was up-to-date, relevant to users and constantly changing to enhance the value of the community to users. To this end the site provided constantly changing news, quotes and charts. Regular news and features were updated every day throughout the day. The information supplied was carefully chosen to meet the distinctive focus of the community; it was very focused and relevant to the members. Links to even more focused and specific information for different users was available at Stockgroup in the form of SRG-developed sector-specific sites, and links to other sector-specific resources.

Member Generated Content

The third means of increasing returns is to capture user profile information on an individual and aggregate level. On the individual level, this information can be used to customize and tailor the site for individual users to enhance their experience. On an aggregate level the information can be used to determine how to enhance the community for all users. The aggregated information can also be used to attract advertisers and to target advertising to portions of the user group.

Member Loyalty

The fourth way to increase the returns of a virtual community is by continually building user loyalty. This can be achieved by customizing interaction with the user, by encouraging member interaction and by giving power to the user in the purchasing process.

Celebrity Sightings

Professor Arnoud De Meier, Professor SoumitraDutta, and Lieven Demeester

Introduction

Celebrity Sightings provides entertainment on the World Wide Web. In July 1997, after eight months of operation, the site had over 16,000 members with ages ranging from 8 to 25 years. Members visited the site to read the latest stories, see the latest pictures and get the inside scoop from their favorite teenage celebrities. They also visited to chat with each other, shop in the Star-Store, play interactive games or quizzes and participate in announced chats with the teenage celebrities themselves. With the membership growing steadily, Robert Landes, the CEO of Celebrity Sightings, believed that the first sponsoring deals that would allow him to cover his costs were in sight.

In an important move, Robert Landes had recently set up a merger between Celebrity Sightings and its main supplier and technology partner, Guidance Solutions. In many ways Celebrity Sightings had become the flagship of the new company. Further building the success of Celebrity Sightings would surely require the best of Robert's extensive marketing and sales skills. More than before, however, Robert now also found himself thinking about how to shape the new company's organization.

The Vision of Robert Landes

The idea for Celebrity Sightings had come fairly naturally to Robert Landes. In his function of Chief Marketing Officer at LA Gear, a sport shoes and clothing retailer, he had worked frequently with young celebrities in his effort to create brands for a teenager market. Later on,

IVEY This case was prepared by Lieven Demeester under the supervision of Professor Arnoud De Meier and Professor Soumitra Dutta. It is intended to provide a basis for class discussion, not to illustrate positive or negative administrative practices. The authors would like to thank Karen Barber, Rob Bynder, Barry Burchell and Robert Landes for their time and their support. Some information has been disguised to protect the interests of Celebrity Sightings. Celebrity Sightings ™ is a trademark of Celebrity Sightings Inc.

Copyright © 1998 INSEAD, Fountainebleau, France.

Distributed by The European Case Clearing House, Cranfield University, Wharley End, Bedford MK43 OJR, England.

To order copies, phone: +44 (0)1234 750903, fax: +44(0)1234 751125, e-mail: ECCH@cranfield.ac.uk.

All rights reserved. Printed in England.

his leadership had been at the source of a new group of designers that focused on interactive multi-media marketing applications. Obviously his attention had been drawn to the Internet and the World Wide Web as an excellent medium for these applications.

While surfing the net for ideas, Robert noticed the multitude of "unofficial" celebrity web pages. He wondered if he would be able to create some attractive content on the Web by bundling a set of "official" web pages in cooperation with the celebrities. In his idea, these web pages would contain exclusive and authentic pictures, stories and interviews for fans to read and look at. In March 1996 he started thinking seriously about a market and a competitive strategy for this business idea.

Robert realized that the best market would be the one centered around teenage celebrities. Teenagers, it turns out, have quite an interest in teenage celebrities. In the United States alone, a total of 6 million youngsters read one of several teen magazines whose content is heavily focused on teenage celebrities. Each of these magazines (such as *Super Teen, Tiger Beat, Six Teen,* etc.) is published monthly, bi-monthly or quarterly and costs $3 per copy. Observing also that the TV shows in which these celebrities star have growing audiences all over the world, Robert was confident that there was a promising market.

The website Robert had in mind would be a mix between a magazine and a fan club but with clear advantages over both. The website would have some areas of general interest and also special areas for each celebrity. Exclusive contracts with the celebrities would guarantee a lot of authentic material that would generate a sense of closeness that no magazine could copy. In the meantime, because the site would contain information about many different celebrities, it would retain a flavor of independence that is not always present in a fan club.

It was the Web technology, however, that would give the site its major advantages. The communication technology behind the Web would allow fans to interact through e-mail or through electronic chat, not only with each other but also with the celebrities themselves. Web technology would also enhance the entertainment that would be offered. Alongside text and pictures, the site could also use sound and video to report on the lives of the celebrities. In addition to these multimedia elements, the medium would also allow for all kinds of interactive games, contests or live quizzes. All this with a technology that would make it no harder to reach Australian teenagers than it would be to reach the kids in Beverly Hills. Robert figured he would be able to attract 100,000 surfing teenagers at least.

Robert's vision reached further than the website, however. He believed that he could use the "Celebrity Sightings" website to create a "Celebrity Sightings" brand. He envisioned Celebrity Sightings print editions, radio and television shows. "Build the proprietary content on the Web and then fan it out to the traditional media," was the picture in his mind.

Launch

The Celebrity Sightings website was launched November 13, 1997. The website was designed and implemented in a joint effort between *Bright Interactive,* Robert's own design group for interactive media, and *Guidance Solutions,* a provider of website design and programming services. Bright Interactive was a spin-off of the Bright Design group and contained all the artistic and creative talent needed to create the "look" and structure of the website. Guidance Solutions contained the IT experience, programming skills and project management capabilities that were necessary to make the website into a technical reality.

Present at the launch party were Jonathan Taylor Thomas (ABC's "Home Improvement"), Tatyani Ali (NBC's "Fresh Prince of Bel Air"), Jodie Sweetin and Candace Cameron (ABC's "Full House"), Danielle Fishel (NBC's "Boy Meets World"), Tia and Tamera Mowry (WB's "Sister, Sister"), Larisa Oleynik (Nickelodeon's "The Secret World of Alex Mack") and Andrew Keegan ("Independence Day"). The nine celebrities had all signed two-year contracts with Celebrity Sightings. Also present at the launch were reporters from ABC, CNN, MSNBC and Family PC. The presentation of the website was a success and reporters all covered the story on their separate networks. In its first six weeks of operation, Celebrity Sightings realized 880,000 user hits and by July 1997 the web site was attracting 880,000 user hits per week (see Exhibits 1 and 2).

EXHIBIT 1

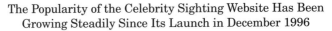

The Popularity of the Celebrity Sighting Website Has Been Growing Steadily Since Its Launch in December 1996

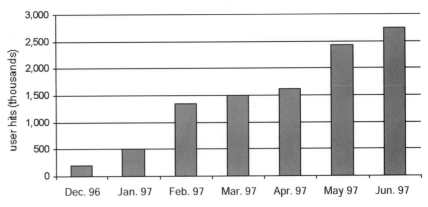

EXHIBIT 2

Many Celebrity Sightings members visit the site more than once a week. When they visit they spend an average of 14 minutes on the site.

Site Statistics for July 1997

Basic members	14,000
Premium members	2,200
User hits per week	880,000[1]
User-sessions per week	22 000
Average length of user session	14 minutes
Members who chat	400–500

[1]Among the 10 percent most hit sites on the WWW.

The Website

Celebrity Sightings had succeeded in creating an entertaining website for its members. Both look and content were appealing and the promise of interactive fun had been realized. Exhibit 3 gives an overview of the Celebrity Sightings website as it was in August 1997.

On the entrance page, members can enter the site by using their login ID and password. Others can register online to become a member. Members choose between basic membership which is free, and premium membership for which they pay $12 a year. Credit cards are accepted online. Their $12 a year provides premium members with access to the electronic chat facilities, higher resolution pictures as well as a set of special privileges.

The site is organized as follows. Each one of the celebrities has his or her own dedicated area, each with a similar structure but with a personalized look. Exhibit 4, for instance, shows Tia and Tamara Mowry's homepage. A **celebrity's home page** contains pictures, character and lifestyle descriptions, interviews, answers to frequently asked questions, career information, sighting reports and a fan mail section. Premium members can write e-mails to the celebrities. The electronic fan mail is screened and then posted on the site. The celebrities read their fan mail on a regular basis and write an answer to typical or especially interesting letters. Their answers get posted too, for all members to read.

Each of the stars can sell memorabilia in the **StarStore** section (Exhibit 5 shows Jodie Sweetin's store). Most stars offer autographed pictures and posters but some also have T-shirts, caps or even sports

EXHIBIT 3   Website Overview

Entrance

Join the club	Membership registration center. Those who join choose between the free, basic membership, and the $12 a year, premium membership.
Open Sez Me	Members enter with ID and password they choose for themselves while registering.

Home (with an official home page for each one
of the celebrities, see Exhibit 4)

Up-Close	In-depth look into the life of the celebrity. Topics include dreams, wishes, character, etc.
Snapshots	This section has the latest set of exclusive pictures. Only premium members can see the pictures full size.
Event update	Information about the latest activities of the celebrity and about his or her upcoming schedule.
A day in the life	Report of a one-day visit to see the celebrity in action in the studio.
FAQ	Answers to the most frequently asked questions about the celebrity.
Word up	Reports by fans of their own personal "celebrity sighting."
Article archives	Archives of articles that have previously appeared in Up-Close, Event Update or a Day in the Life.
Read fan mail	Screened fan mail as well as the celebrity's answers to a few of the letters.
Write Fan mail	Option to send a fan mail letter. Only for premium members.

Calendar

Table of events. Events include celebrity chats, celebrity appearances, radio-show broadcasts, contests, etc. (See Exhibit 7.)

Fan Central

Cool list	E-mailed member reviews for movies, TV shows, music, books, places and other stuff.
CS-radioshow	Broadcast and scheduling information for the CS-radioshow on AAHS-radio. Excerpts available on *RealPlayer* format.
The Buzz	Celebrity centric articles on dating, sports, movies, etc.
Chat transcripts	Transcripts of previously scheduled celebrity chats.
Contests	Rules of contests. Announcements of winners and winning submissions.
Comics	Two CS-created characters show up in a new cartoon every week.
Teen-seen	Reports of Celebrity Sightings Special Events, reported by Bazza (online personality created by Barry).

Chat (premium members only)

Rules of the road	A set of rules are communicated in order to foster a pleasant chat-culture. Because of the young audience specific safety guidelines are also communicated (see Exhibit 5).
Celebrity chat room	In their favorite celebrity's chat room, fans can chat with each other about different topics. Sometimes the celebrity will pay a surprise visit.
Auditorium	The auditorium is a chat room used for planned celebrity chats, games and contests. Members "reside" in the auditorium to participate.

EXHIBIT 3   *(continued)*

Games	
Fashion puzzles	Players put celebrities in six different outfits by combining the right tops, bottoms and shoes. (Enabled by Shockwave from Macro-media).
Jigsaws	Players complete jigsaws of their favorite celebrities. (Enabled by Shockwave from Macromedia).
Other games	Word games. Matching games (e.g., which nose belongs to which celebrity).

Star Store	
Celebrity stores	Each celebrity has a "store" with their own merchandise. Merchandise ranges from signed pictures, posters and T-shirts; with online ordering.

Information Station	
Membership information	Membership agreement. Option to change from basic to premium membership
Instructions for down-loading software	In order to fully enjoy the site members need to have (1) the Macromedia Shockwave Plug-in for games and (2) the I-chat plug-in for chatting.

EXHIBIT 4   Each one of the celebrities has an official website that is part of the Celebrity Sightings website.

Below is the "home page" of twin sisters Tia & Tamara Mowry, who star in "Sisters" on Warner Brothers Network.

EXHIBIT 5   Jodie Sweetin's Star Store

Just fill out the quantity you want to order and click on "check-out" to place
your order automatically.

bottles.Celebrity Sightings also presents a selection of its own brand
name merchandise such as T-shirts, caps, pictures, videos, etc. Fans can
pick out the items they like and order them online.

The section called **Fan Central** contains event reports, articles, letters and information not specifically related to one of the celebrities. It
caters to the teenage audience by covering topics such as movies, music, dating, etc. In this section Celebrity Sightings goes beyond being a
collection of fan clubs and creates an identity of its own.

Another section where a kind of common culture is created is in the
"rooms" for electronic **chat.** An electronic chat room is a virtual room that
you enter by clicking on the appropriate icon on your screen. Once you
enter, your presence is announced to the others in the room and you can
see who is there. You can make conversation by typing. As soon as you hit
the return key, your words appear on the screens of those in the room. An
example of a "chat session" can be seen in Exhibit 6. To make up for the

EXHIBIT 6 Transcript of a Moderated Chat Session in Which One of the CS Celebrities Answers Questions from Her Fans online

Larisa Oleynik; August 19, 1997
(In the transcript below **Karisa-cs** identifies Larisa Oleynik who stars in "The Secret World of Alex Mack" on Nickelodeon's Cable Network. **Momoney-cs** and **Monkybutt-cs** identify two Celebrity Sightings associates. This chat session was "seen" by online premium members who were in the "auditorium"—chat room. The members in the auditorium could not participate directly in the chat but they were allowed to type questions, which, if selected, were presented to the celebrity.)

Momoney-cs says, "Welcome back to CS Melissa!!!"

Momoney-cs says, "Ooops"

Larisa-cs says, "Melissa?"

Momoney-cs says, "She's a special CS member Larisa"

Larisa-cs bops Mo-money

Monkybutt-cs says, "So, Mo, lets get this show on the road!"

Momoney-cs presents questions #160 from Amyr
If you were stranded on a deserted island what 3 things would you bring?

Momoney-cs says "This one is becoming another CS standard question"

Larisa-cs says, "A phone . . . my stereo system and a cute boy!"

Momoney-cs presents question #163 from Crono
Hey how are yah? do you remember me? Crono? Anyhow WB to CS!!! How was your summer and what did you do?

Larisa-ca says, "I remember you . . . how are you? My summer? I worked all summer . . . now I have some time off"

Momoney-cs presents the speakers with question #212 from Yankees
What do you like to do in your spare time?

Larisa-cs says, "I like to go and hang out with my friends and go to concerts . . . right now we are OBSESSED with JumbaJuice . . . a juice bar in LA we go every night!"

Momoney-cs present the speakers with question #205 from So-fly
Where would you go or like to go if you want to spend time alone?

Monkybutt-cs love jamba juice too!

Momoney-cs says, "Yummy!!!!"

Larisa-cs says, "I love hanging out on the roof of my building . . . its really calm and relaxing"

Monkybutt-cs says, "On the roof??"

Momoney-cs presents question #225 from Dgol
Hey, Larisa, Hi) How come you don't come to CS more often? You otta just pop on sometimes, everyone here loves you!

EXHIBIT 6 *(continued)*

Larisa-cs says, "Ummm I am sorry . . . I just got my powerbook fixed . . . I will try as hard as I can"

Momoney-cs presents the speakers with question #226 from Harmony84
Larisa are you going to do any movies?

Larisa-cs says, "I would love to, but I have nothing planned right now."

Momoney-cs presents question #224 from Mr_t
Are you still single (please say yes)

Larisa-cs says, "Um . . . ."

Larisa-cs says, "Maybe"

Momoney-cs says, "Um . . . . ?"

Larisa-cs says, "Maybe not"

Momoney-cs presents question #228 from Jimstark
What would constitute the perfect date for you, Larisa?

Larisa-cs says, "Just something fun with no awkward pauses would pretty much rule right now."

Momoney-cs presents question #181 from Jimstark
Laris, do you think the world will be a better place 100 years from now? ;)

Monkybutt-cs says, "Larisa must be typing for herself . . ."

Momoney-cs says, "This is a serious question, requires some DEEP thought . . . ."

Larisa-cs says, "Actually, if it were up to me. I'd live 100 years in the past. As much as I love CS, technology sometimes moves toooo fast!"

Larisa-cs says, "Sorry my typing sux"

---

lack of nonverbal communication, you can also use special "emoticons" to do things like "frowning," "smiling" or even "flirting" with someone.

Each of the celebrities has his or her own chat room where members can chat with other fans. The announced chats during which fans can interact directly with the celebrities usually take place in a special room called the "auditorium." To make a chat session with a celebrity manageable, the chat is moderated. In this format, all members are made electronically mute but they can submit their questions for screening. The selected questions are presented to the celebrities and their answers come live on the screen for everybody (Exhibit 6 is an example of such a moderated chat session). Another special chat room is the trivia room. In this room weekly trivia contests are organized.

EXHIBIT 7   Calendar Section of the Celebrity Sightings Website

Teen-beat magazine and FAO Schwarz Toy Stores are partners in cross-promotional deals.

Members type answers to live questions and the best or fastest answers are rewarded with celebrity related prizes. All chat facilities are for premium members only.

The **Calendar** section gives a listing of past events (with links to the archives) and a list of announcements to future events. Most items announce electronic chat sessions with celebrities. Others refer to celebrity appearances that are sponsored by Celebrity Sightings. Exhibit 7 shows the events that took place in August 1997.

The **Games** section contains a set of celebrity-centric interactive games in which fans can test their celebrity knowledge in a playful way. Most of these games require a special software plug-in which members must download to their computers first.

Guidelines for downloading the plug-ins for the games and for the electronic chat can be found in the **Information Station** section. This section also contains general technical information and a link to the membership registration area.

Learning by Doing

By running, maintaining and further developing the website the Celebrity Sightings team members learned firsthand which capabilities they needed to build further. Technically, operationally and editorially important lessons were learned and decisions taken.

On the technical side, Celebrity Sightings learned to control the complexity of the website but also learned to create awareness about it. The two-type membership concept and its technical implementation provides a good illustration. In the original design, there were two web sites, one for premium members and one for basic members. This created a maintenance nightmare because every change had to be implemented twice, not only the content but also the underlying browsing logic and database links. After a costly redesign in January 1997 this complex double website system was replaced by the current one where there is only one website but where access is controlled for each page. The company also experimented several times with the extent of the privileges granted to premium members. Several sections were changed from "free for all" to "for premium members only" or vice versa. The difficulties in making these changes often surprised those with non-technical backgrounds. After a while everybody learned to think ahead and to work out a proposed change in detail before implementing it.

Operationally, it was quickly discovered that there was a need for specific skills and systems to operate the Star Store. Processes like order-tracking, inventory management and order-fulfillment required operational skills, systems and experience that were not available in the company at the outset. Originally Robert had planned to run the Star Store within Celebrity Sightings, offering the celebrities a 15 percent share in the profit from the store. After realizing the difficulty in building the necessary operational capabilities and considering the priorities, Robert negotiated a different formula with the celebrities. Under the new arrangement, orders are passed on to the celebrities who are responsible for fulfilling the orders and who pay a 15 percent commission to Celebrity Sightings.

On the editorial side, the Celebrity Sightings editors were learning more about the differences between an online magazine and a printed one. It was mostly good news. A big difference is the level of feedback you get from your readers, directly and indirectly. Writing an e-mail is very fast and many Celebrity Sightings' members enjoy giving direct feedback about their experiences with the site. The e-mail link with the "readers" not only generated useful suggestions but also provided encouragement and satisfaction for the Celebrity Sightings team members who were flooded with positive comments. Indirectly, "readers" provide a lot of information by clicking their mice. After introducing a horoscope feature in their Fan Central section, Celebrity Sightings found out that very few members were interested in it. Only a small number of user hits reached the horoscope. The feature was quickly discontinued. "You quickly find out what works and what doesn't," says the editor-in-chief. The contact with the readers is much closer than what printed magazines can achieve.

Another important difference with a printed magazine is the fact that there are very few internal delays between a story and its readers because there is no "waiting for the next edition." Celebrity Sightings is often able to bring stories to its readers within a week after the facts. For the magazines, which often have editorial cycles of three months, that would be impossible. The knife cuts both ways however. Without monthly "editions" and deadlines, the natural pressure to have a new set of stories every month disappears. In practice most of the articles on the site range from being "hot off the keyboard" to being several months old and updates are often not as fast as hoped. Because fresh content is crucial in attracting user hits from the growing group of loyal members, a need was felt to create some self-imposed editorial discipline, not only for the writers but also for the programmers who were often needed to bring new content to the site.

A very special and new set of skills Celebrity Sightings had to build was related to the electronic chat. It became clear that the electronic chat element provides real value to a sizeable group of members. Mastering the art of producing a large chat event and creating a safe, pleasant and exciting chat culture was seen as critical.

Members are definitely attracted to the interaction with the stars during the electronic chats. Their positive e-mail responses as well as the recurring presence at the chats were interpreted as strong approval signals. A chat event in April 1997, where several celebrities were online at the same time, attracted more than 300 members. Other entertainment in the chat areas is popular too. The weekly live "quiz" easily draws 30–50 members in the chat area and even on eventless nights anywhere from 10 to 30 members can be found chatting on the site. There are also signs of an online culture. One element in the culture is the complete denial of spelling, grammar and punctuation rules in the typed language. In response to a statement, it would not be unusual, for instance, to read something such as "WUT!?" on the screen. Members also look for small ways to express feelings online. The emoticons provided by the chat software are very popular and typed expressions such as "Ouch" or "Joan has a headache" are quite common in the conversations. "In some small way," says the editor in chief, "I believe the online chat activities satisfy some of our members' basic needs."

Providing successful chat entertainment was something that Celebrity Sightings learned by doing. That quite a few things can go wrong in a chat event was illustrated by the first announced chat with Jonathan Taylor Thomas (also known as "JTT"). The first problem was technical. When more than 50 members tried to access the chat room area, the software failed. There was hectic phone traffic between the facilities for the big PR event, the Guidance Solutions office, and the provider of the chat software. Only five minutes before the event was scheduled and after many added stress points for the Celebrity Sightings team, the right parameters in the Unix server were set to the required values. Once the chat had started, it was difficult to organize an orderly and interesting chat. "Our first chat with JTT was a mess," describes one of Celebrity Sightings' main chat moderators. After a few more experiences, Celebrity Sightings eventually became quite good at organizing chats. For chats with 30 members or more, the format of a moderated chat became the preferred solution (see description above and example in Exhibit 6). For smaller groups the presence of an experienced chat moderator was sufficient. Little tricks like typing "Ssssshhhhhhh" to ask for electronic silence now belong to the toolbox of each chat moderator at Celebrity Sightings. This accumulated experience means that, even after serious comparison, the Celebrity Sightings team can now count itself among the best chat organizers on the net.

To create a chat culture that is safe, pleasant and exciting, Celebrity Sightings publishes rules and safety tips, enforces the rules and uses online personalities to monitor, guide and stimulate conversations.

When a member enters the chat area he is encouraged to read the safety tips and the rules of the chat (see Exhibit 8). Members are also encouraged to report on infraction of the rules. So far only two people have had their membership retracted because of inappropriate chat-behavior and in general the online conversations are nice and good-natured.

To have a more direct impact on the chat culture, Celebrity Sightings team members have created online personalities who participate in chats regularly. They try to foster a non-sexist, non-racist, teenager friendly chat culture. In a neutral, low-profile manner the online personalities try to stimulate thinking, bring in new ideas and reinforce positive issues in the discussions. As one of the team members stated, "It is not very hard to raise the level of discussion because most online discussions are fairly mindless." The online personalities seem well liked and accepted and clearly add value to the chat experience of many members.

Celebrity Sightings had clearly succeeded in creating value for its members through the chat facilities. Two issues received continuing attention. Although sizeable as a group, only 20 percent of all premium members participated in chatting. The Celebrity Sightings editor-in-chief felt he needed to understand why the other 75 percent remained silent. Secondly, considering the age group of its members it was very

---

EXHIBIT 8   Celebrity Sightings tries to foster a pleasant and safe "chatting" environment for its members.

Rules of the Road

At Celebrity Sightings we want EVERYBODY to have a great time!

In the chat rooms you can flirt, gossip, joke, banter, flirt, argue, sing, smile, shout and giggle to your heart's content but please don't be offensive or rude to other members 'cuz that is just so un-cool.

If you do encounter people who are bugging you, using foul language or are threatening you in any way here is what you can do: First ask them politely but firmly to stop! If that doesn't work copy and paste the entire message including their screen name and e-mail it to chatguide@celebritysightings.com.

As a last resort members should simply ignore the comments and log off from that chat-room. Any members who are reported to Celebrity Sightings and who continue to break the rules of the road will be given the celebrity boot and their membership will be canceled.

At Celebrity Sightings we want EVERYBODY to be safe! Please take a couple of seconds to read the following tips and make sure you stay street smart!

- Just as you stay away from strangers on the street, be careful about strangers you meet in chat rooms.
- Don't believe anyone who tells you that they are one of the stars featured on Celebrity Sightings.
- Each of the celebrities have been given just one name which they will always use when they are chatting in the rooms. The celebrities are the ONLY people who have access to these screen names ending in "-cs." Other people who have "-cs" in their member names are Celebrity Sightings Staff members.
- Be aware that people are NOT always telling the truth. Sometimes guys will say they are girls and girls will say they are guys.
- If anyone uses nasty language or mentions things that make you feel uncomfortable, don't respond; just log off or ignore them.
- Never ever give your real last name, address, telephone number or fax number to anyone. If someone asks for this information (or for your password), don't respond. Log off and tell a trusted adult and/or Celebrity Sightings Staff at chatguide@celebritysightings.com.
- Remember, even if you call someone else's telephone number, with caller ID they can still get YOUR telephone number.
- Never agree to meet with someone you've talked with in chat rooms without asking permission from your parents first.

---

important to do everything possible to secure their safety. The publication of the safety tips was a good first step but continued alertness was necessary.

Partnership with the Stars

The contracts with the stars are clearly Celebrity Sightings' main asset. These contracts enable it to create the attractive content that is key to its revenues. The contract is basically an exclusivity agreement for content on the Internet. In exchange for a few commitments and for an agreement on exclusivity, the celebrities receive an interesting set of benefits.

Fifteen percent of membership revenues is divided among all participating celebrities based on the relative popularity of their personal web pages. Through the Star Store, celebrities are also provided with a new distribution channel for their merchandise at 15 percent commission. If they are interested in sharing further in the success of Celebrity Sightings they can become an investor (three celebrities have taken this option). In addition to these extra revenues celebrities benefit in other ways too. Celebrity Sightings offers a set of services, such as free publicity and contact with fans, that celebrities otherwise have to pay for or do themselves. Also, to have some control over what is shown about them and written on them in a prestigious new medium like the Internet is quite valuable to a young star. That they have to share space with other celebrities on the website is not perceived as a problem. Most celebrities understand that everybody wins in this situation. Robert Landes explains, "It is like a community. Everybody enjoys being part of it."

The young stars sign a two-year contract with annual renewal option after two years. Nine celebrities were signed on at the launch in November 1997, two more were added in the first six months of operation and several others have shown interest. The commitments the celebrities agree to are reasonable but not negligible. They include monthly information updates, one hour of electronic chat per month, two photoshoots per year for exclusive pictures, two interviews per year, two appearances per year and regular cooperation with respect to fan mail. The content that Celebrity Sightings creates this way becomes exclusive property and cannot be distributed without its consent. In addition, the celebrities agree to do this exclusively for Celebrity Sightings. They can still have one-time appearances on other websites but not without mentioning Celebrity Sightings.

So far there has been no need to enforce the contracts and most celebrities have cooperated enthusiastically. Celebrity Sightings manages these relationships very carefully. Apart from Robert himself, only one other experienced person at Celebrity Sightings deals with the celebrities directly.

Members

Although nowhere near the estimated potential, the total number of members had grown steadily to a respectable 16,200 in July 1997, 2,200 of which were premium members, and together with the other members they had purchased about $13,000 of merchandise online. Signals about member loyalty and member demographics provided good news but total member growth had been slower than expected.

About 6 million teenagers in the U.S. read one of several teen magazines whose content is heavily focused on teen celebrities. Depending on who is counting (Killen, Commercenet/Nielsen, Project 2000, Jupiter Communications), somewhere between 25 and 35 million Americans had access to the World Wide Web early in 1997. According to Louis Harris and Associates around 16 percent of all web users are under 25. Independent from them, Jupiter Communications estimates that around 5 million kids are online. This is in the U.S. alone. Morgan Stanley estimates that by the year 2000, 150 million people will be online worldwide.

Even in his most conservative estimations Robert Landes saw himself as the only player in a market with several hundred thousand potential "members" for his website. How many of the members would be willing to make online purchases? One indication comes from the same survey from Louis Harris and Associates, in which 24 percent of web users respond that they have already used the Internet to make purchases, a percentage that, it is estimated, will climb to 39 percent in 2001.

Members seem to have good potential for loyalty. More than readers from magazines, the members of the Celebrity Sightings website seem active, responsive and motivated to participate. When asked for contributions to the website in the form of movie reviews or stories of their personal celebrity sightings, responses have always been surprisingly numerous. It became clear however that current members have a rather narrow interest, focused on the celebrities. Most attempts to create interest outside the celebrity sphere were not so successful. Horoscopes on the website failed to attract readership and a photo-competition to win a Kodak camera received fewer than 30 submissions. A contest, however, in which you could win the jacket that Jonathan Taylor Thomas had worn in his last movie by writing a review of that movie, received hundreds of responses. "We must not forget that our members are generally strongly preoccupied with these celebrities," says the editor-in-chief, "sometimes even obsessed."

The demographics of the July 1997 member base came as a pleasant surprise, both in age and gender. Robert expected to get 8 to 14 year olds and instead the age of members ranged from 8 to 25 with most members between 12 and 18 years old. Robert was happy to get the important group of 18 year olds: "Once you get the 18 year olds, you also get the 12, 13 and 14 year olds." In gender, members were divided 50:50. This was a surprise since 95 percent of all teenagers that buy teen magazines are girls. Since in general more boys use the World Wide Web than girls (70 percent vs. 30 percent), a different proportion was to be expected, but no one hoped to get 50 percent boys. "I think I discovered a new market," says Robert Landes. It seems that, from the privacy of their own rooms, boys are more eager to check out their favorite celebrities than at the newsstand. Danielle Fishel, for example, has a majority of male fans.

Members need a lot of technical support. By July, around 20 messages a day were technical questions. The provision of step-by-step instructions in the Information Station on the website brought some relief but members still needed a lot of technical help. Someone even had to be refunded his membership fee after it turned out that he didn't have access to a computer.

Looking back, Robert was not unhappy with membership growth. "It is a little slower than I expected though. It took us eight months to achieve what I thought we would do in three."

Sponsors

In July 1997 there were no corporate sponsors yet. Robert was hoping to get around 14 sponsors at $20,000 a month by the end of the first year. In exchange for their contribution, sponsors would be offered a customized advertising and promotion mix with elements such as chat room or scheduled event sponsoring, banner ads with web interlinks, animated interactive ads, online contests and promotions or co-marketing programs. In addition sponsors would also get priority access to a range of market research programs that could be organized among Celebrity Sightings members.

Although no sponsoring deals had been signed, Robert remained optimistic. The Celebrity Sightings members were a targeted and attentive group of young consumers. Such an audience usually has no problem getting the attention of marketing managers of large consumer companies.

One reason for the slow progress was that advertisers had become more careful about advertising on the Web. After the initial rush many companies were rethinking their web advertising policies and rates. There was a general feeling among advertisers that web advertising rates were too high. In the first quarter of 1997 *Webtrack* reported web advertising rates of between $15 or more than $80 per thousand pageviews (a pageview happens when someone's browser program loads the page in question to be viewed by the user), with destination sites getting higher rates than search engines. In comparison, a 30 second spot on "NBC Evening News" costs around $5.50 per thousand households and a full page, four color ad in Cosmopolitan costs $35 per thousand paying readers. Obviously web advertisements have some clear advantages in their ability to convey news and information (this happens when a viewer clicks through the ad to receive more information), their ability to change content quickly and in their opportunity for audience response. Add to that the prestige of the medium and the possibility to really select your audience, and it is easy to imagine the advertising power of the Web. Setting the price per thousand pageviews remained controversial, however, and it seemed that advertisers were educating themselves more thoroughly and were waiting for lower rates to be established.

Strategies for Marketing Celebrity Sightings

In his original marketing strategy Robert Landes focused on using Celebrity Sightings' proprietary content and its agreements with the stars to "pay for" advertising in other media.

Celebrity Sightings has a cross-promotional deal with the publisher of seven teen magazines. In exchange for banner ads that allow the user to subscribe to a magazine online, Celebrity Sightings has full page ads in the editions of these magazines. With AAHS Kids Radio, a national radio station with 9 million listeners, Celebrity Sightings has another interesting marketing deal. In exchange for the appearance of a celebrity on a bi-weekly radio show for children, the show markets the Celebrity Sightings brand and provides recurrent information about the website on the air. Robert Landes is working on an even more extensive deal for television and cable with Samuel Goldwyn Mayer. The plan is to produce a Celebrity Sightings TV show. Already $125,000 has been put aside to produce a pilot show in August 1997. More than extra advertising, a successful TV show would also generate extra revenues. "If that pilot gets picked up, we're in the black right away."

Further promotion of the web site can come from celebrity appearances in malls, new stores, special events, etc. So far, Celebrity Sightings has set up two PR events of its own, one at the launch and another one in April. These included the presence of all the celebrities and were mainly directed at getting news coverage in other media. In another event, two celebrities appeared at the opening of a new toy store from FAO Schwarz in Las Vegas. This last promotional event was paid for by the toy store. When more sponsors for these kinds of events can be found, they can become an important element in the promotion of the website.

A second element of Robert's marketing strategy was the pricing of the premium membership. Initially premium membership, with chat privileges, was priced at $5 a month and $50 a year. Fearing after a while that $50 was too high, Robert reduced the price to $12 a year in order to attract more premium members. Lowering the price clearly had a positive effect on the growth of premium members but pricing remained a point of discussion. Another lesson about pricing changes was that they required a fair amount of administration and programming. Weighing the costs and benefits of further price changes clearly received more attention whenever changes were suggested.

Given the slightly disappointing member growth after a few months of operation, Robert decided to expand his original strategy. In April 1997 he started looking for other ways to increase member growth.

In a first step, Celebrity Sightings decided to buy advertising on Yahoo, one of the five most used search engines on the Web. When you buy advertising on a search engine, you usually "buy" a set of words. When a user makes a search for that word, your banner ad will be on top of the results page. Users may then click on the ad to go to your website. Celebrity Sightings started by buying the names of the celebrities it features. This turned out to be a success. The Celebrity Sightings banner ads obtained a 50–60 percent click-through rate (this is the percentage of users that, after seeing the ad, click on it to go to the web site). The average click-through rates for ads is less than 5 percent. At $15 per thousand pageviews, the Yahoo advertising seemed quite effective. After this successful first step Celebrity Sightings was now considering doing further advertising on the Web.

Another avenue that Robert started considering was to link the Celebrity Sightings web site to another highly successful entertainment web site. Such deals usually involve some form of revenue sharing and Robert started looking carefully at alternative options. Warner Brothers was a viable candidate and had already shown interest.

The Technology Partner

To make the Celebrity Sightings web site into a technical reality, Robert Landes hired Guidance Solutions, a small but growing provider of Internet services. Guidance Solutions was a promising start-up that originally specialized in database to web integration for business-to-business web applications, mainly for midsize distributors and manufacturers. The founders of Guidance were all top-trained engineers or computer scientists with several years of experience in software development and system applications. Their database expertise, in particular, made them stand out in the Internet services market. Guidance Solutions had been looking to expand their services to the business-to-consumer web application market and had expressed an interest in a partnership with Bright Interactive, a group of designers led by Robert and specializing in interactive multimedia applications. With skills that were almost perfectly complementary to the skills

Robert had access to in Bright Interactive, Guidance Solutions was asked to make a proposal for the technical realization of the Celebrity Sightings website.

It was clear from the start that the relationship with Guidance Solutions would not be a supplier relationship at arm's length. Guidance Solutions was to design, select, install, operate and maintain the information technology of Celebrity Sightings, an asset that would be key to its success. The project manager from Guidance Solutions would become almost an integral part of the Celebrity Sightings organization and communication would have to be frequent and intense. Since the stakes were high for both companies, the relationship was seen as a partnership from the outset.

As requested, Guidance Solutions designed and installed a hardware and software infrastructure that could be scaleable to a capacity of 1 million user hits a day. The Celebrity Sightings web site is hosted on a Sun Ultra Enterprise with multiple UltraSPARC processors, each with 512-Kbyte UltraCache connected to a T3 line with a direct connection to the Internet. The site was co-developed by Guidance Solutions programmers and Bright Interactive designers with C-based Common Gateway Interfaces, Unix scripts, Javascript, Oracle SQL, Netscape SSL encryption for secure transmissions, Macromedia Director and I-chat interactive chat software. It is an open architecture designed for future growth and scaleability. Originally a video and audio server were included in the plans, but their installation was postponed to limit the investment costs.

Choosing application software is difficult. Functionality, ease of development, availability of technical support are all important but so is browser compatibility. Celebrity Sightings uses Macromedia Director for the interactive games, I-chat for electronic chat and IC-verify for on-line credit card processing. Carefully selected by Guidance Solutions, these applications are compatible with most common browser software, such as those from Netscape or Microsoft (not all are compatible, however, with the WebTV or American Online browsers). By building relationships with these application software vendors but also by keeping an eye on new innovations or new standards, Guidance Solutions enables Celebrity Sightings to make the most of current technologies and to stay in sync with future developments.

Guidance Solutions also plays an important role in the operation of the website. It is responsible for the flawless technical operation of the web site and it also monitors and reports on how it is used by members. In addition, Guidance Solutions manages the member database and generates needed outputs from it, thereby taking on a set of administrative tasks and creating important management information.

Organization

Celebrity Sightings has a simple organizational structure, where practically all team members work directly with CEO Robert Landes. Robert is an enthusiastic leader and, although simple in structure, his organization has started to incorporate a set of unique skills and organizational capabilities.

As CEO of the company, Robert represents the vision for the company, provides leadership and manages most important external relationships, at least in their initial phases. He is the one who contacts the celebrities, makes the media deals, looks for sponsors and sets up the partnerships. The company's marketing strategy and plan are his and he takes the important steps in implementing the plan.

Barry Burchell is the editorial director. Barry has a strong media background. He has worked as a writer for magazines and as a researcher and producer for radio news. More recently he managed the LA office of a British film magazine. He joined Celebrity Sightings in November 1996 and has since then written over 90 percent of all the text that has appeared on the web site. He is the content guru. He does the interviews with the stars, reports on special events and organizes the semi-annual photo shoots to get exclusive pictures. His writing style is very much adapted to the teen audience but his texts clearly testify to a personal devotion to authenticity. He is also the one who manages the relationships with the celebrities and their parents, on a regular basis. Barry is probably also closest to the members. With his online personality "Bazza," Barry hosts most of the chat events and has become an "icon" in the Celebrity Sightings chat rooms. Together with two student interns who work with Barry and who have created their own online personalities, he manages the site's chat events and responds to all member e-mail that doesn't deal with administrative or technical questions.

Rob Bynder is the artistic director. Rob has a creative art background and knew Robert from Bright Interactive. Before joining Celebrity Sightings, Rob managed several projects in which he was responsible for creating the graphic identity of magazines or of corporate PR materials. This included setting up the pallets, style sheets and style guides that enable publishers to create a single unified "look" for their publications. As a freelance designer Rob has also done artwork for interactive applications such as kiosks or CD-ROMs. Rob is responsible for the look and feel of Celebrity Sightings. He did most of the artwork, not only for the web site but also for all PR and marketing materials. Through his work designing marketing materials for Celebrity Sightings Rob also started taking small responsibilities for marketing in general. Among other things, he is now responsible for identifying further advertising opportunities on the Web. Now that most of the design groundwork is finished Rob finds that he can spend more time in other areas, especially since he started to commission out some of the artwork to student interns or freelance designers.

Richard Parr is the production director. Also coming from the creative sector, Richard has the final responsibility for the production of the website. Where necessary he coordinates Rob, Barry and the programmers at Guidance Solutions.

Mo Whelan is the operations director. She is responsible for the day-to-day operations of the company in the areas of administration, public relations, membership services, and coordination of Celebrity Sightings events. She is the contact person for Celebrity Sightings and handles all promotions on the site. Having degrees in Fashion Design and Business Administration and having worked in an architectural design firm, Mo has the right combination of creative talent and business sense to keep the operations in gear at Celebrity Sightings.

Although theoretically not part of the organization, Karen Barber from Guidance Solutions took on major responsibilities in Celebrity Sightings. As project manager for the technical realization of the web site she has spent about 60 to 80 percent of her time working for Celebrity Sightings since September 1996. Before joining Guidance Solutions in early 1996 she held roles as technical team leader and technical developer in the systems application/business support unit of a large aerospace and defense company. In September 1996, after Robert had shown interest in working with Guidance Solutions, she specified the requirements, made a functional description and provided a cost estimate for the website that Robert's team had in mind. She selected the technical architecture, made all major software choices and managed the implementation project from start to finish. Even after the launch of the web site, several redesigns of the site and its continuous evolution meant that Karen remained active in Celebrity Sightings. During all this time she managed on average two programmers at Guidance Solutions. The partnership between Celebrity Sightings and Guidance Solutions worked very well and Robert encouraged Karen to be proactive about the continuous technical innovation of the web site.

The people at Celebrity Sightings are all selected for their talent and enthusiasm. Moreover, they all own stock in the company. "Everybody here has a vested interest in the company so I don't spend a lot of time checking in on people's work," says Robert, who sees himself more as an entrepreneur than a manager. "Being one of those one-idea-a-minute guys, I am the one who needs to be managed," he jokes.

Clearly Celebrity Sightings was building some unique skills and organizational capabilities. It was learning how to entertain a teenage audience over the Web. Nobody in the company would claim that they mastered the art yet but confidence was fairly high. A certain proficiency was clearly emerging, both in organizing chat-based entertainment and in creating the type of content that is attractive to teenagers. In another important skill domain Celebrity Sightings was learning how to build long-lasting partnerships with the celebrities. Having grown from nine celebrities at start, to two more after eight months, and several more celebrities considering participating, the Celebrity Sightings team felt it was making strong progress in this area too.

Another aspect of the Celebrity Sightings organization is that people from very different backgrounds need to work together to make the site a success. In the beginning it was clear, for instance, that the creative people were novices with regard to the technical aspects of a database-linked website, and that the technical people at Guidance did not fully understand the creative aspects of running an entertainment website. Not without some difficulties the different experts learned about each others' work, work style and added value. The mutual fine-tuning and cooperation that developed gradually between Robert Landes, Barry Burchell, Rob Bynder and Karen Barber had generated an organizational capability that takes a while to develop.

Moving Forward

In July 1997, the pressure to find a first big sponsor was slowly rising. The business model for Celebrity Sightings depended heavily on revenues from sponsors (see Exhibit 9 for an overview of sources of revenues and costs). Partly because the company was undercapitalized at first, but also partly to compensate for the current lack of sponsors, Robert organized two extra rounds of funding in the first eight months, raising the company's capital to $1 million.

In the meantime there seemed to be many opportunities to enlarge and improve member services. One idea was to enlarge the target audience by including sports and music celebrities. This would be especially exciting once the planned audio and video capabilities were installed. One of Robert's dreams was to let bands play live music on the web site.

Another set of ideas involved increasing the "community" features of the web site by allowing members to publish their own home page and by enabling them to send internal e-mails. The chat rooms demonstrated how much members enjoyed the interactive aspect of the service. By facilitating this effect further everybody could benefit.

Marketing, of course, remained one of the biggest points of focus. Robert kept targeting his energy towards making advertising deals with other media and recently also towards finding other ways to strengthen the Celebrity Sightings brand. More direct advertising on the Web or an important inclusion deal with a high-traffic entertainment site were some of the ways the exposure of the site could be increased.

EXHIBIT 9 Revenues and Costs for Celebrity Sightings

	Revenues	
Premium Memberships	$12 per premium membership	Considering to raise price to $19.95
Corporate advertisers	$10 per thousand pageviews (minimum rate based on current advertising rate on the WWW)	So far no advertisers were found
Merchandise	15% commission on all merchandise sold	In the first 6 months, the star stores grossed $14,000
	Celebrity revenue sharing	
Premium Memberships	15% of membership revenue	Divided among stars according to relative popularity
	Web site hosting and development costs	
Website hosting fee	$1,000 per month, includes hardware rental, telecom costs and software costs for operating systems, database systems and CGI's	Paid to Guidance Solutions, who owns the $35,000 hardware setup
Website development	$25,000 per month for programming and project management fees (average from September 1996 till June 1997)	Paid to Guidance solutions, who have one project manager and the equivalent of two full-time programmers working for CS
	Staff costs and commissioning	
Directors	Average of $45,000 per director per year	Currently five directors
Freelance writing or designing	Highly variable	So far less than $1,000 a month
Website operators	$20,000 per operator per year	Currently one full-time equivalent
Support staff	$20,000 per staff member per year	Currently one administrative assistant
	Software costs	
Software purchases	$20,000 in one time fees	Database software, web-application software, graphic design software, Administrative software
Software licenses	$10,000 each year	Most development and design software is licensed per computer. Licensing costs for operational software, such as the chat software depend on the number of supported concurrent streams (users)
Software upgrades	$2,000 per year	Around 20% of original purchasing price

---

EXHIBIT 9   *(continued)*

Office expenses

| Office space rental | $20 per square foot per year | $1,500 per month for current office |
| Travel, supplies etc. | $500 per employee per month | |

Advertising and promotion

| Advertising on WWW | $10 per 1000 page views | Currently $2,000 per month to Yahoo |
| P.R. events | $10,000-$15,000 per event | Three PR events in first half of 1997 |

There was also a feeling that none of this should wait too long. Although no real competitors were on the horizon, it was unlikely to stay this way. Most networks were seriously considering creating an Internet presence for their shows and might also be interested in claiming some Internet time and content from their stars. Also, many other community-based web sites targeting teenagers were emerging and becoming increasingly professional (Kidscom, Cyberteens, etc.). In order to become really credible for sponsors, Celebrity Sightings needed to grow further at a steady pace.

The Merger

In July 1997, Celebrity Sightings merged with Guidance Solutions. Robert Landes became the CEO of the newly merged company. For Celebrity Sightings the merger brought a couple of important advantages.

Financially the two companies were very complementary. Guidance Solutions was a profitable, low-debt company in the growing but competitive market of Internet services. Celebrity Sightings was a potentially highly profitable business in the entertainment business that needed a little time and resources to grow to viability.

In terms of capabilities, the synergies were very clear. Robert Landes and his creative team brought the sales and marketing experience and the graphic design skills that Guidance Solutions would need to grow its business. The system application and business support experience at Guidance Solutions would be of real value to Celebrity Sightings' growing operations. Having Guidance Solutions programmers and project managers in the same office as the Celebrity Sightings organization would also improve organizational efficiency quite drastically, given the need for frequent communication.

Finally, the merger provided important synergies in knowledge generation and exploitation. By merging with a web development firm, Celebrity Sightings could benefit from the knowledge Guidance Solutions was generating by working with other clients. Vice versa, in merging with an Internet entertainment business Guidance Solutions would gain a much deeper understanding for the needs of its clients, thereby improving its competitiveness.

Satisfied with the merger, Robert now needed to think hard about his new role. In the short run he would probably take important sales and marketing responsibilities for the two different companies. In the short run this would probably be the best use of his time, but he also realized that in the long run it would be difficult to keep running around with two different hats. Eventually he would have to redefine his role and reshape the organization of the newly formed company.

Chapter 9

Social and Legal Issues

Many of today's most pressing e-commerce issues are not the "hard" issues of financial performance, but the "softer" social, ethical, and legal issues. Among these issues are the protection of intellectual property rights, privacy, security, and online ethical practices. Today, consumer surveys consistently mention these issues as major deterrents to more widespread Internet commerce. This chapter focuses on five firms that are grappling with various legal, ethical, and moral questions.

DoubleClick is the largest and most visible advertising intermediary on the Internet. As part of its service to clients, it keeps detailed data on Internet consumers' surfing habits through the use of "cookies." Therefore, eyebrows were raised when, in 1999, the company purchased Abacus direct, a marketing research firm, with a database of detailed information on the purchasing habits of 90 percent of American households. The combination of the two databases would allow DoubleClick to conduct very precise "profiling" of individual consumers, in effect putting real names to hitherto nameless cookies. The case explores the trade-offs between new sources of revenue generation, advanced targeting techniques for advertising, resource use, and legal and ethical considerations over consumer privacy and the extent to which consent for use of online information is received.

"Canadian Imperial Bank of Commerce: Digital Employee Privacy" is written from the perspective of a large employer deciding whether or not to implement a surveillance system to monitor all employee electronic communications. The firm, a large multinational bank, must juggle the need to minimize inappropriate use of corporate resources (risking possible litigation) with the ethical desire to protect the privacy of employees. If the monitoring system is put in place, the organization must then formulate policies about how to deal with infractions. Various grey ethical and moral areas are examined.

The iCraveTV case explores the murky area of intellectual property rights between jurisdictions. The founders of iCraveTV took advantage of a provision in Canadian law that allowed them to retransmit U.S. network television broadcasts on the Web. There were several resourcing obstacles to overcome while entering the fiercely competitive broadcasting industry and building competitive advantage: obtaining rights to the programs, securing paying advertisers, retaining viewers, having sufficient cash, and management expertise. Several issues remained unresolved as they moved towards the launch of iCraveTV: negotiating rights from each of the content syndicators and attempting to pay Internet royalties for the programming. Perhaps the largest issue iCraveTV faced (legal, ethical, and technical) was preventing U.S. users from accessing the Canadian site since the company might face broad U.S. broadcast industry objections if U.S. audiences found access to the iCraveTV signal.

The next case is about Open Text Corporation, the company behind one of the Internet's first search engines, the Open Text Index. The case revolves around two basic issues: revenue generation for content providers and Internet culture. Revenue generation has been, and continues to be, a challenge for most content providers. Traditional models such as banner advertising, subscription fees, and usage fees have been dominant, but new models are being tried all the time. In order to increase revenues, Open Text came up with a revenue model that involved advertisers paying to have their sites appear at the top of search engine results when "bought" words were included in the search criteria. It was an innovative approach and a potentially lucrative departure from the dominant banner ad model. The second issue of the case concerns whether the prevalent culture on the Internet would allow search engine results, which are generally considered to be a free and accurate resource, to be influenced by advertisers. The case also describes the technical aspects of search engine technology, and thus can be used as a primer for a discussion on index, search, and retrieval techniques.

The Euro-Arab Management School case deals with some of the benefits and challenges of managing a virtual organization. The School is a virtual organization in that it does not operate bricks and mortar classrooms; instead, programs are offered in an innovative manner that combines web-based learning with local tutoring. The case contains a number of management and social issues. The management issues include how to manage a physically dispersed workforce, how to ensure academic quality and consistency, and how to market a system to attract qualified students. Some of the social issues concern the future of education and the need for close interaction among students and between student and teacher.

DoubleClick Inc.: Gathering Customer Intelligence[1]

By Professor Scott Schneberger and Ken Mark

Introduction

"This Monday, we revealed that the Federal Trade Commission (FTC) began a voluntary inquiry into our ad serving and data collection practices," explained Kevin Ryan, president of DoubleClick Inc. It was Thursday, February 17, 2000, in New York City and Ryan was preparing to answer media and investor questions.

"We are confident that our business policies are consistent with our privacy policy and beneficial to consumers and advertisers," he continued. "The FTC has begun a series of inquiries into some of the most well-known web companies, including DoubleClick, and we support their efforts to keep the Internet safe for consumers."

Several Internet privacy activists had filed a formal complaint with the FTC after being informed by media sources that DoubleClick had the ability to determine a person's identity through the use of "cookies" and other databases. Here was an excerpt of an article in an early January 2000 edition of *USA Today:*

Activists charge DoubleClick double-cross

Web users have lost privacy with the drop of a cookie, they say.

By Will Rodger, USATODAY.com

Say goodbye to anonymity on the Web.

---

[1]This case has been written on the basis of published sources only. Consequently, the interpretation and perspectives presented in this case are not necessarily those of DoubleClick Inc. or any of its employees.

DoubleClick Inc., the Internet's largest advertising company, has begun tracking web users by name and address as they move from one web site to the next, USATODAY.com has learned.

The practice, known as profiling, gives marketers the ability to know the household, and in many cases the precise identity, of the person visiting any one of the 11,500 sites that use DoubleClick's ad-tracking "cookies." What made such profiling possible was DoubleClick's purchase in June of Abacus Direct Corp., a direct-marketing services company that maintains a database of names, addresses and retail purchasing habits of 90 per cent of American households. With the help of its online partners, DoubleClick can now correlate the Abacus database of names with people's Internet activities.

DoubleClick Inc.

With global headquarters in New York City and over 30 offices around the world, DoubleClick was a leading provider of comprehensive Internet advertising solutions for marketers and web publishers. It combined technology, media and data expertise to centralize planning, execution, control, tracking and reporting for online media companies. Along with its proprietary DART targeting technology, DoubleClick managed Abacus Direct, a database of consumer buying behavior used for marketing purposes over the Internet and through direct mail.

The privacy controversy over DoubleClick began in the summer of 1999, when DoubleClick announced it was merging with Abacus Direct in a deal valued at more than US$1 billion. Privacy experts had feared that DoubleClick would begin merging the two databases at some point. But they said they were unaware that DoubleClick had begun its profiling practice in late 1999. Before its Abacus purchase, DoubleClick had made its money by targeting banner advertisements in less direct ways. DoubleClick ad-serving computers, for instance, checked the Internet addresses of people who visited participating sites. Thus, people in their homes may see ads different from those seen by workers at General Motors, or a machine-tool company in Ohio.

Every time viewers saw or clicked on those banners, DoubleClick added that fact to individual dossiers it built on them with the help of the cookies it stored on users' hard drives. Those dossiers, in turn, helped DoubleClick target ads more precisely still, increasing their relevance to consumers and reducing unnecessary repetition.

The "owner" of those cookies remained anonymous to DoubleClick until it bought Abacus.[2]

---

[2]These cookies were anonymous because although DoubleClick tracked the cookie (and subsequently, the user), it did not possess any means to identify the owner of the cookie. In effect, DoubleClick was cognizant of the user's surfing habits but not of the surfer's identity. With the additional database containing personally identifiable information, there existed a possibility that the information in the cookie could be matched with a surfer's profile, thus identifying the user.

Being tracked as they move around the Web "doesn't measure up to people's expectation on the Net," says Robert Smith, publisher of the newsletter *Privacy Journal*. "They don't think that their physical locations, their names will be combined with what they do on the Internet. If they (DoubleClick) want to do that they have to expose that plan to the public and have it discussed."[3]

A publicly listed company, DoubleClick traded under the symbol DCLK on the NASDAQ exchange.[4]

DoubleClick's DART

Developed by DoubleClick and awarded U.S. Patent 5,948,061, DART was a web-based, enterprise-class advertising management software package. It performed targeting, reporting and inventory management, allowing sites (or networks of sites) to manage all or some of their ad serving and reporting functions through DoubleClick's central servers. The benefit to advertising clients was the opportunity to build lifelong relationships with their customers (users) through personalization of advertising messages (see Figure 1). A client would begin by placing an advertising campaign with DoubleClick. With the use of DoubleClick's DART technology, advertising messages would be placed on sites most visited by the client's customers, and advertising results tracked. DoubleClick would then compile data gathered and present the results of the campaign to the client (see Figure 1).

Websites intending to sell banner advertisement could outsource the delivery of the site's online advertisement to DoubleClick. While serving the ads, DoubleClick would then utilize DART to collect, analyse and optimize online ads and their delivery.

Benefits of DART[5]

Streamlined campaign management, pinpoint targeting and real-time, actionable reports all add up to one important metric—increased return on investment (ROI.) DART For Advertisers gives you the process and tracking refinement that empowers you to continuously optimize your campaigns and tie your marketing programs to real dollars generated. Here are a few of the benefits of using DART for Advertisers:

- **A Web-based Service Offering**—DART for Advertisers is available from anywhere based on permissions you control. And because it's a service, you get instant upgrades without application deployment or maintenance costs.

---

[3]As reported in *USA Today,* Jan. 15, 2000.

[4]DoubleClick information and press releases were accessed from www.doubleclick.com.

[5]From www.doubleclick.com, February 29, 2000.

FIGURE 1   Central Campaign Management

CENTRAL CAMPAIGN MANAGEMENT

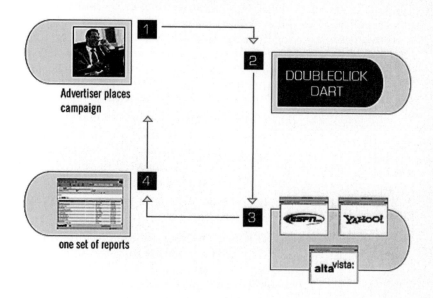

- **An Integrated Solution**—DART provides the industry's strongest ad management technology, built-in targeting and sophisticated reporting that, together, form the cornerstone of closed-loop marketing and enhanced ROI. Its constantly evolving feature set is based on the aggressive demands of leading-edge installed base.
- **Centralized Planning and Control**—No matter how extensive your media plan, DART for Advertisers provides a sophisticated media planning tool and enables you to buy and traffic ads across as many sites as you wish. So you can track requests for proposals (RFPs) and insertion orders, control creative changes and view standardized reports within and across campaigns like never before.
- **High-Level Targeting**—With built-in targeting capabilities, DART offers an unlimited array of targeting criteria to ensure you get the right message to the right person at the right time. DART's targeting capabilities are the best in the industry.
- **Consistent Reporting**—DART provides you a single set of real-time reports that span your entire campaign. Armed with detailed post-click, transaction and reach and frequency information, you can test different executions of selling messages, rich media and ad sizes—and then swap instantaneously to maximize campaign effectiveness.
- **Private Labeling**—With DART, agencies gain a competitive advantage by offering the leading online campaign management capabilities within their own suite of products and services.

Delivering DART

With an expansive team of engineers supporting DART's complex system, DoubleClick served up to 53 billion ads[6] to DART-enabled sites per month to companies in over 13 countries around the world. It accomplished this through the use of 23 global data centers, world-class hosting facilities like Frontier Global Center and Exodus Communications. It also possessed a network of nearly 800 media and ad servers (Microsoft NT Quad Processors) positioned around the world to assure reliability. The architecture it used was 100 per cent scalable, running Oracle databases hosted on Sun Solaris equipment. DART's front-end (user interface) was hypertext markup language (HTML) compliant and could be accessed from any browser and any platform.

DoubleClick had the ability to segregate ad serving from the site's back-end transaction processing, matching ads in under 15 milliseconds and serving ads at an average rate of one every 24 milliseconds.

DART in Operation

DART's user profile database recognized unique users by their cookies and delivered a precisely targeted ad every time the user accessed Web pages that were using DART. First, by accessing the web page, the user would trigger an ad "request" from DoubleClick. Next, if that user had previously visited DoubleClick sites, DoubleClick would recognize the user's cookie file and unique number, retrieving the IP address, country domain, company, browser and operating system. (If not, a cookie would be placed on the new user's computer at this time.) DART would match up a targeted ad to the user-profile, then deliver a targeted ad to the user (see Figure 2).

Using Cookies at DoubleClick

Cookies were small text files stored on a user's hard drive and were employed by thousands of sites. Cookies enabled sites to "remember" users across site pages and across multiple visits to a site. Using cookies did not damage user files nor could they read information from a user's hard drive.

This feature enhanced e-commerce and Internet advertising in numerous ways, including allowing personalization features such as stock portfolio tracking and targeted news stories, and enabling shopping sessions and quick navigation across multiple zones of e-commerce sites. Cookies could remember user names and passwords for future visits, control ad frequency or the number of times a user saw a given ad, and could allow advertisers to target ads to a user's interest.

---

[6]DoubleClick expected to serve over 53 billion ads per month by June 2000.

FIGURE 2 DoubleClick DART in Action

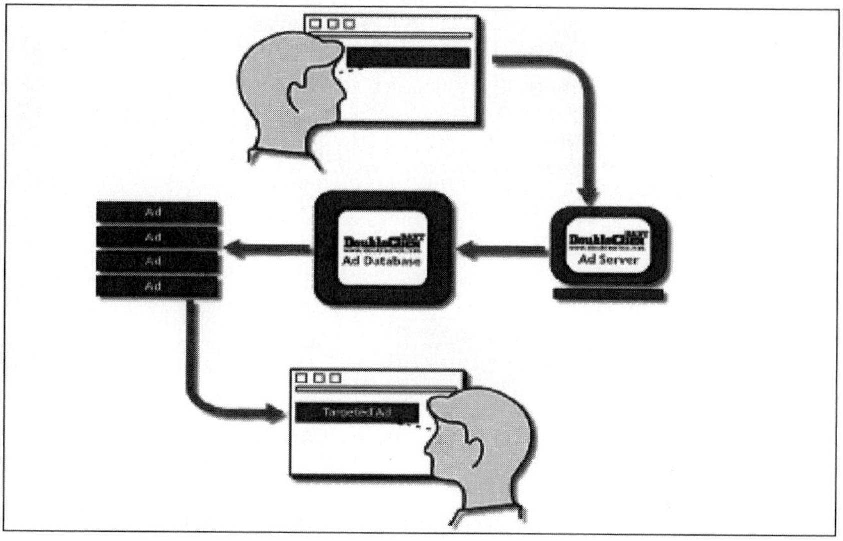

Ryan explained that DoubleClick did not employ cookies to exploit sensitive data.

> DoubleClick has never and will never use sensitive online data in our profiling. It is DoubleClick's policy to only merge personally identifiable information with personally identifiable information for profiling, after providing clear notice of a choice.

Selling Research on Collected Data

One of DoubleClick's business units collected traffic and usage data, and analysed the effectiveness of campaigns. From this research, the document produced for advertising clients was called Spotlight.

Spotlight allowed an advertiser to determine which media placement generated a specific type of post-click activity important to its media plan. Spotlight provided customizable metrics such as the number of registrations, number of sales, number of units purchased, types of services purchased, and actual sales revenue generated as a result of an advertiser's campaign.

Reports offered three levels of reporting including banner level, campaign level, and aggregate activity data at the advertiser level. Another feature offered conversion-to-activity rates by clicks, impressions and media costs. A third offered a counting methodology that credited activities to the last ad the user clicked on prior to performing the activity, for up to 90 days after the ad had stopped running (see Figure 3).

FIGURE 3

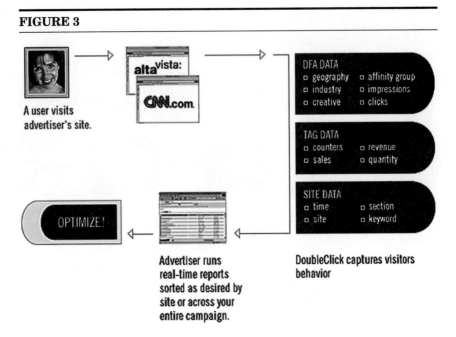

A user visits
advertiser's site.

DFA DATA
□ geography   □ affinity group
□ industry   □ impressions
□ creative   □ clicks

TAG DATA
□ counters   □ revenue
□ sales   □ quantity

SITE DATA
□ time   □ section
□ site   □ keyword

OPTIMIZE!

Advertiser runs
real-time reports
sorted as desired by
site or across your
entire campaign.

DoubleClick captures visitors
behavior

Abacus, the previously mentioned division of DoubleClick, would, on behalf of Internet retailers and advertisers, use additional statistical modeling techniques to identify those online consumers in the Abacus Online database who would most likely be interested in a particular product or service.

A Complaint Filed with the FTC

Jason Catlett of Junkbusters Inc. (an Internet privacy consultancy), David Banisar, deputy director of Privacy International, and the U.S. Electronic Privacy Information Center filed a complaint with the Federal Trade Commission charging that DoubleClick had deceived consumers by suggesting the company's technology let them remain anonymous. They expected to enlist a wide array of consumer groups to back their position.

More troubling to privacy advocates was DoubleClick's refusal to state which Internet sites were furnishing them the registration rolls that DoubleClick needed to link once-anonymous cookies to names, addresses, phone numbers and catalogue purchases. Catlett stated,

> The fact that DoubleClick is not disclosing the names of the companies who are feeding them consumers' names is a shameful hypocrisy. They are trying to protect the confidentiality of the violators of privacy.

Jonathan Shapiro, senior vice-president and Abacus unit chief bristled at Catlett's characterization, saying, "Any company that uses data from the Abacus database to target Internet ads must disclose it online." Moreover, he added, DoubleClick itself would hand over to privacy advocates the list of participating companies if it could. But as in many lines of business, partners frown when their relationships were disclosed without their permission. Shapiro concluded, "If they all bought a billboard and said they work with us, that would be great."

The New Privacy Policy

Ryan announced,

Earlier in February, DoubleClick announced what we believe is the most aggressive Internet privacy policy ever and committed ourselves to a national campaign to educate consumers about online privacy. We also announced that we will only do business with online U.S. publishers that have privacy policies. We have engaged PriceWaterhouseCoopers to perform periodic privacy audits so that consumers remain confident that we are living up to our commitment to protect users' privacy. In addition, we have announced the creation of the DoubleClick Privacy Ad Board, and we are adding a new executive level position of Chief Privacy Officer.

DoubleClick explained in its privacy policy (see Exhibit 1) that it did not collect any personally identifiable information about its users such as name, address, phone number or e-mail address. It did, however, collect non-personally identifiable information such as the server the user's computer was logged on to, his or her browser type, and whether the user responded to the ad delivered.

Non-personally identifiable information collected by DoubleClick was used for the purpose of targeting ads and measuring ad effectiveness on behalf of DoubleClick's advertisers and web publishers who specifically requested it. However, non-personally identifiable information collected by DoubleClick could be associated with a user's personally identifiable information if that user had agreed to receive personally tailored ads.

In addition, with the delivery of ads via DART technology to one particular web publisher's website, DoubleClick combined the non-personally identifiable data collected by DoubleClick from a user's computer with the log-in name and demographic data about users collected by the web publisher and furnished to DoubleClick for the purpose of ad targeting on the web publisher's website. DoubleClick had requested that this information be disclosed on the website's privacy statement.

There were also other cases when a user voluntarily provided personal information in response to an ad (a survey or purchase form, for example). "That person will receive notice that their personal information is

---

EXHIBIT 1 DoubleClick Privacy Policy

PRIVACY POLICY

DoubleClick Privacy Statement

Internet user privacy is of paramount importance to DoubleClick, our advertisers and our web publishers. The success of our business depends upon our ability to maintain the trust of our users. Below is information regarding DoubleClick's commitment to protect the privacy of users and to ensure the integrity of the Internet.

Information Collected in Ad Delivery

In the course of delivering an ad to you, DoubleClick does not collect any personally identifiable information about you, such as your name, address, phone number or e-mail address. DoubleClick does, however, collect non-personally identifiable information about you, such as the server your computer is logged onto, your browser type (for example, Netscape or Internet Explorer), and whether you responded to the ad delivered.

The non-personally identifiable information collected by DoubleClick is used for the purpose of targeting ads and measuring ad effectiveness on behalf of DoubleClick's advertisers and web publishers who specifically request it. For additional information on the information that is collected by DoubleClick in the process of delivering an ad to you, please click here.

However, as described in "Abacus Alliance" and "Information Collected by DoubleClick's websites" below, non-personally identifiable information collected by DoubleClick in the course of ad delivery *can be associated with a user's personally identifiable information* if that user has agreed to receive personally tailored ads.

In addition, in connection solely with the delivery of ads via DoubleClick's DART technology to one particular web publisher's website, DoubleClick combines the non-personally identifiable data collected by DoubleClick from a user's computer with the log-in name and demographic data about users collected by the web publisher and furnished to DoubleClick for the purpose of ad targeting on the web publisher's website. DoubleClick has requested that this information be disclosed on the website's privacy statement.

There are also other cases when a user voluntarily provides personal information in response to an ad (a survey or purchase form, for example). In these situations, DoubleClick (or a third party engaged by DoubleClick) collects the information on behalf of the advertiser and/or website. This information is used by the advertiser and/or website so that you can receive the goods, services or information that you requested. Where indicated, DoubleClick may use this information in aggregate form to get a better general understanding of the type of individuals viewing ads or visiting the websites. Unless specifically dis-

---

EXHIBIT 1 *(continued)*

---

closed, the personally identifiable information collected by DoubleClick in these cases is not used to deliver personally tailored ads to a user and is not linked by DoubleClick to any other information.

Abacus Alliance

On November 23, 1999, DoubleClick Inc. completed its merger with Abacus Direct Corporation. Abacus, now a division of DoubleClick, will continue to operate Abacus Direct, the direct mail element of the Abacus Alliance. In addition, Abacus has begun building Abacus Online, the Internet element of the Abacus Alliance.

The Abacus Online portion of the Abacus Alliance will enable U.S. consumers on the Internet to receive advertising messages tailored to their individual interests. As with all DoubleClick products and services, Abacus Online is fully committed to offering online consumers *notice* about the collection and use of personal information about them, and the *choice* not to participate. Abacus Online will maintain a database consisting of personally identifiable information about those Internet users who have received notice that their personal information will be used for online marketing purposes and associated with information about them available from other sources, and who have been offered the choice not to receive these tailored messages. The notice and opportunity to choose will appear on those websites that contribute user information to the Abacus Alliance, usually when the user is given the opportunity to provide personally identifiable information (e.g., on a user registration page, or on an order form).

Abacus, on behalf of Internet retailers and advertisers, will use statistical modeling techniques to identify those online consumers in the Abacus Online database who would most likely be interested in a particular product or service. All advertising messages delivered to online consumers identified by Abacus Online will be delivered by DoubleClick's patented DART technology.

Strict efforts will be made to ensure that all information in the Abacus Online database is collected in a manner that gives users clear notice and choice. *Personally identifiable information in the Abacus Online database will not be sold or disclosed to any merchant, advertiser or web publisher.*

Name and address information volunteered by a user on an Abacus Alliance web site is associated by Abacus through the use of a match code and the DoubleClick cookie with other information about that individual. Information in the Abacus Online database includes the user's name, address, retail, catalog and online purchase history, and demographic data. The database also includes the user's non-personally identifiable information collected by websites and other businesses with which DoubleClick does business. Unless specifically disclosed to the contrary in a website's privacy policy, most non-personally identifiable information collected by DoubleClick from websites on the DoubleClick Network is included in the Abacus Online database. However, the Abacus Online database will not associate any personally identifiable medical, financial, or sexual preference information with an individual. Neither will it associate information from children.

EXHIBIT 1 *(continued)*

Sweepstakes

DoubleClick's Flashbase, Inc. subsidiary provides automation tools that allow our clients to provide online contests and sweepstakes ("DoubleClick sweepstakes").

All DoubleClick sweepstakes entry forms must provide a way for you to opt-out of any communication from the sweepstakes manager that is not related to awarding prizes for the sweepstakes. Entry forms must further provide consumers with a choice whether to receive e-mail marketing materials from third parties. When you enter a DoubleClick sweepstakes, the information you provide is not to be shared with DoubleClick or any third party, unless you agree by checking the opt-in box on the sweepstakes entry form. If you enter a sweepstakes, you agree that the sweepstakes sponsor may use your name in relation to announcing and promoting the winners of the sweepstakes. See the official rules of the sweepstakes you are entering for additional information.

DoubleClick does collect aggregate, anonymous information about the sweepstakes. That information is primarily used to help sweepstakes managers choose prizes and make other decisions regarding the organization of the sweepstakes. DoubleClick does not associate information provided through the sweepstakes with your other web-browsing activities or click-stream data.

DoubleClick Research

DoubleClick Research is a subsidiary of DoubleClick, Inc. To review DoubleClick's privacy policy from the beginning, including information on opting out of the DoubleClick cookie, click here. DoubleClick Research provides surveys to users. All research survey responses are voluntary, and the information collected will only be used for research and reporting purposes, to help DoubleClick and our clients determine the effectiveness of our businesses, websites, or advertising campaigns.

If you participate in a survey, the information you provide will be used along with that of other study participants (for example, DoubleClick Research might report that 50 percent of a survey's respondents are women). DoubleClick may share anonymous individual and aggregate data with the company that requested the survey for research and analysis purposes.

The only individually identifiable information DoubleClick Research may use is the e-mail address you provide, in order to contact sweepstakes prize winners. DoubleClick Research may also contact you through your e-mail address for other purposes if you tell DoubleClick Research that it may do so; for example, if you indicate in the survey that you wish to join a DoubleClick Research online research panel. When you submit your survey, your e-mail address and your response to the "future contact" question described above are automatically stored in a database that is intentionally separated from your survey responses. Therefore, your e-mail address is not tied back to your survey responses. DoubleClick Research will not share the personally identifiable individual data you enter in response to survey questions with third parties.

EXHIBIT 1 *(continued)*

For all other purposes, only aggregate data that has been stripped of all personally identifiable information will be used.

DoubleClick Research uses DART ad server technology to transmit the survey. In the course of providing this survey to you, a DoubleClick cookie may be placed on your browser. DoubleClick utilizes cookie technology for many purposes, including targeting ads to you on other web sites. In connection with DoubleClick Research Surveys, the cookie is used to control the research process, primarily to stop people from being asked to take the same survey twice. In addition, the types of advertising you have viewed on web sites during the course of your normal web surfing, such as whether you have viewed a particular ad or how many times you have viewed a particular ad, may be connected to your anonymous survey responses. This information is strictly for research purposes and is totally anonymous.

If your cookies are turned off or you have opted out, DoubleClick Research will be unable to recognize whether or not you have been offered a survey, and may inadvertently offer you the same survey in the future. To read more about DoubleClick's cookies, including information on how to opt-out of a DoubleClick cookie, click here.

Please contact DoubleClick Research at surveyhelp@doubleclick.net if you have questions or comments about DoubleClick Research or your participation in the survey or if you wish to later choose not to receive future e-mail.

E-mail

DoubleClick uses DARTmail, a version of DART technology, to bring you e-mails that may include ads. E-mail is sent only to people who have consented to receive a particular e-mail publication or mailing from a company. If at any time you would like to end your subscription to an e-mail publication or mailing, follow either the directions posted at the end of the e-mail publication or mailing, or the directions at the e-mail newsletter company's website.

In order to bring you more relevant advertising, your e-mail address may be joined with the information you provided at our client's website and may be augmented with other data sources. However, DoubleClick does not link your e-mail address to your other web-browsing activities or clickstream data.

Information Collected by DoubleClick's Web Sites

The websites owned or controlled by DoubleClick, such as http://www.plazadirect.com/ and http://www.iaf.net/ may ask for and collect personally identifiable information. DoubleClick is committed to providing meaningful notice and choice to users before any personally identifiable information is submitted to us. Specifically, users will be informed about how DoubleClick may use such information, including whether it will be shared with marketing partners or combined with other information available to us. In most cases, the information provided by a user will be contributed to the Abacus Online database to enable personally tailored ad delivery online. Users will always be offered the choice not to provide personally identifiable information or to have it shared with others.

EXHIBIT 1   *(continued)*

Access

DoubleClick offers users who have voluntarily provided personally identifiable information to DoubleClick the opportunity to review the information provided and to correct any errors.

Cookies and Opt Out

DoubleClick, along with thousands of other websites, uses cookies to enhance your web viewing experience. DoubleClick's cookies do not damage your system or files in any way.

Here's how it works. When you are first served an ad by DoubleClick, DoubleClick assigns you a unique number and records that number in the cookie file of your computer. Then, when you visit a website on which DoubleClick serves ads, DoubleClick reads this number to help target ads to you. The cookie can help ensure that you do not see the same ad over and over again. Cookies can also help advertisers measure how you utilize an advertiser's site. This information helps our advertisers cater their ads to your needs.

If you have chosen on any of the websites with which Abacus does business to receive ads tailored to you personally as part of Abacus Online's services, the cookie will allow DoubleClick and Abacus Online to recognize you online in order to deliver you a relevant message.

However, if you have not chosen to receive personally targeted ads, then the DoubleClick cookie will *not* be associated with any personal information about you, and DoubleClick (including Abacus) will not be able to identify you personally online.

While we believe that cookies enhance your web experience by limiting the repetitiveness of advertising and increasing the level of relevant content on the Web, they are not essential for us to continue our leadership position in web advertising.

While some third parties offer programs to manually delete your cookies, DoubleClick goes one step further by offering you a "blank" or "opt-out cookie" to prevent any data from being associated with your browser or you individually. If you do not want the benefits of cookies, there is a simple procedure that allows you to deny or accept this feature. By denying DoubleClick's cookies, ads delivered to you by DoubleClick can only be targeted based on the non-personally identifiable information that is available from the Internet environment, including information about your browser type and Internet service provider. By denying the DoubleClick cookie, we are unable to recognize your browser from one visit to the next, and you may therefore notice that you receive the same ad multiple times.

If you have previously chosen to receive personally tailored ads by being included in the Abacus Online database, you can later elect to stop receiving personally tailored ads by denying DoubleClick cookies.

Your opt-out will be effective for the entire life of your browser or until you delete the cookie file on your hard drive. In each of these instances, you will ap-

---

EXHIBIT 1　*(continued)*

---

pear as a new user to DoubleClick. Unless you deny the DoubleClick cookie again, DoubleClick's ad server will deliver a new cookie to your browser.

If you would like more information on how to opt-out, please click here.

Disclosure

DoubleClick makes available all of our information practices at www.doubleclick.net, including in-depth descriptions of our targeting capabilities, our privacy policy, and full disclosure on the use of cookies. In addition, we provide all users with the option to contact us at info@doubleclick.net with any further questions or concerns.

Security

DoubleClick will maintain the confidentiality of the information that it collects during the process of delivering an ad. DoubleClick maintains internal practices that help to protect the security and confidentiality of this information by limiting employee access to and use of this information.

Industry Efforts to Protect Consumer Privacy

DoubleClick is committed to protecting consumer privacy online. We are active members of the Network Advertising Initiative, NetCoalition.com, Online Privacy Alliance, Internet Advertising Bureau, New York New Media Association, and the American Advertising Federation.

For more information about protecting your privacy online, we recommend that you visit http://www.networkadvertising.org/, http://www.netcoalition.com/, and http://www.privacyalliance.org/. If you have any additional questions, please contact us at info@doubleclick.net.

We also recommend that you review this Privacy Statement periodically, as DoubleClick may update it from time to time.

URL: corporate/privacy/default.asp
Copyright © 1996-2001 DoubleClick Inc.
DoubleClick's DART technology is protected by U.S. Pat. 5,948,061.
Source: www.doubleclick.com, February 2000.

---

being gathered," stated Shapiro. In those situations, DoubleClick (or a third party engaged by DoubleClick) collected the information on behalf of the advertiser and/or web site. This information was used by the advertiser, and/or website, to ensure that users received goods, services or information requested. Jennifer Blum, Media Relations, stated that only about a dozen of its affiliated sites had started to collect and use personal information. She acknowledged, however, that DoubleClick's goal was to gain agreement from all its partner sites to participate. Where indicated, DoubleClick could use the information in aggregate form to get a better general understanding of the type of individuals viewing ads or visiting the websites. Unless specifically disclosed, the personally identifiable information collected by DoubleClick in these cases was not used to deliver personally tailored ads to a user and was not linked by DoubleClick to any other information.

Opting out of Being Identified

DoubleClick did allow users the option of "opting-out" of being identified by DART. By logging on to DoubleClick's site, the user could enter information to allow DoubleClick to recognize the particular user and assign him or her an "opt-out" cookie.

On subsequent visits by the user to DART-enabled sites, the opt-out cookie would disallow DART from assigning other cookies or from identifying the user's computer uniquely. DoubleClick discouraged this approach by stating in its privacy statement:

> DoubleClick believes that all users should have a positive web experience. Because of this belief, we allow advertisers to control the frequency (the number of times) a web user sees an ad banner. We also deliver advertising based on a user's interests if that user has chosen to receive targeted advertising. We believe that frequency control, and relevant content makes advertising on the Web less intrusive by ensuring that users are not bombarded with repeat and irrelevant ad messages. Opting-out removes our ability both to control frequency of exposure to individual users and to increase the level of relevant content.

The opt-out would be effective for the entire life of the user's browser or until the user deleted the cookie file on his or her hard drive. In each of these instances, the user would then appear as a new user to DoubleClick—unless the user denied the DoubleClick cookie again, a new cookie would be delivered to the user's browser.

Disclosure and Security

DoubleClick made available all its information practices on its website, www.doubleclick.net, including in-depth descriptions of its targeting capabilities, privacy policy, and full disclosure on the use of cookies. DoubleClick was an active member of the Network Advertising Initiative, NetCoalition.com, Online Privacy Alliance, Internet Advertising Bureau, New York New Media Association, and the American Advertising Federation.

DoubleClick Confident in Face of Inquiry

Ryan concluded,

> We renew our challenge to other Internet players to adopt similarly strong privacy policies. We are taking these steps because we believe they are good for consumers, good for our customers and sound business practices.

In spite of the FTC's inquiries, DoubleClick was confident that its internal practices were sound.

DoubleClick shares, trading at a high of US$131 during the beginning of January 2000, had dropped to the US$90 range since the charge was announced. Would the move to establish the new privacy policy aid in placating the fears of advertising clients afraid of a consumer backlash? Would the new privacy policy hold up to scrutiny? Was DoubleClick doing enough to satisfy the privacy concerns of Internet surfers? Last, were investors satisfied?

Canadian Imperial Bank of Commerce: Digital Employee Privacy

By Mike Wade and Ken Mark

Introduction

"We could have a lively situation on our hands if some of these e-mail privacy scenarios come true," remarked Bob Jones, manager, Compliance at Canadian Imperial Bank of Commerce (CIBC). It was May 16, 2000, and Jones was aware that Toronto-based CIBC had implemented word recognition software in its U.S. broker to comb e-mail messages sent by employees for specified business words. What if these routine searches flagged an e-mail message that also contained personal information about an employee? In the wake of an e-mail "worm" that crippled corporate networks in the first week of May 2000, use of e-mail at work was a hot topic of discussion in management circles.

Canadian Imperial Bank of Commerce

As of May 2000, Canadian Imperial Bank of Commerce had 45,000 employees worldwide serving six million individual customers, 350,000 small businesses, and 7,000 corporate and investment banking customers. The bank had total assets of $250 billion, and a net income of $1.029 billion in 1999.

Formed out of a 1961 merger between The Canadian Bank of Commerce and Imperial Bank of Canada, CIBC was one of North America's leading financial institutions offering retail and wholesale products and services through its electronic banking network, branches and offices around the world.

Customer Privacy in the Banking Industry: The Tournier Case

Privacy practices in the banking industry could be traced back to the landmark 1924 "Tournier Case" (*Tournier* vs. the *National Provincial* and *Union Bank of England*). Common law and guidelines resulted from that decision, and thus the case had become necessary background for management employees in the banking industry.

The Tournier Case concerned a bank customer with a £10 overdraft, who, having no fixed address, gave his bank branch manager the name and address of his new employers. When he defaulted on repayments, the branch manager telephoned those employers to ask if they knew his customer's address. In the course of doing so he disclosed the overdraft and default, and expressed his opinion that his customer was betting heavily. As a result, Tournier lost his job, sued the bank, and won his case upon appeal.

What came out of the decision was a set of four exceptions on the banker's contractual duty of confidentiality where customer information could be disclosed without their consent:

(a) Where disclosure is under compulsion by law;
(b) Where there is a duty to the public to disclose;
(c) Where the interests of the bank require disclosure;
(d) Where the disclosure is made by the express or implied consent of the customer.

Since the Tournier decision, banks have become extremely sensitive about protecting customer information. Strict privacy policies have been put in place, and systems containing personal information have been protected from unauthorized use and manipulation. Recent advances in security and encryption technology allowed banking customers to access their accounts and conduct simple transactions though online and telephone banking systems.

Employee Privacy in the Banking Industry

Employee privacy was somewhat different than customer privacy. By design, in most banks, customers were provided with the best level of privacy protection available. However, there were legitimate reasons why banks might want to monitor what employees were doing on company time and with company equipment.

For banks like CIBC, providing employees with access to company e-mail had become a strategic necessity. However, with e-mail access came the possibility of unwittingly receiving or transmitting an e-mail worm or virus, much like the ones which swept across the world in early 2000. (For an explanation of worms and viruses, see Exhibit 1.) Computer Economics Inc., a research firm based in Carlsbad, California, reported that the ILOVEYOU virus alone had infected three million computers

---

EXHIBIT 1   Explanation of Worms and Virus

Viruses

A virus is a piece of programming code usually disguised as something else that causes some unexpected (and often undesirable) event, and which can automatically spread to other computer users. Viruses can be transmitted by diskette or CD, by sending them as attachments to an e-mail message or by downloading infected programming from the Internet. The source of the e-mail note, downloaded file, or diskette is often unaware of the virus. Some viruses wreak their effect as soon as their code is executed; other viruses lie dormant until circumstances cause their code to be executed by the computer. Some viruses are playful in intent and effect, while others can be harmful.

Generally, there are four main classes of viruses.

File Infectors

Some file infector viruses attach themselves to program files, usually selected COM or .EXE files. Some can infect any program for which execution is requested, including SYS, .OVL, .PRG, and .MNU files. When the program is loaded, the virus is loaded as well. Other file infector viruses arrive as wholly contained programs or scripts sent as an attachment to an e-mail note.

System or Boot-Record Infectors

These viruses infect executable code found in certain system areas on a disk. They attach to the DOS boot sector on diskettes or the Master Boot Record on hard disks. A typical scenario is to receive a diskette from an innocent source that contains a boot disk virus.

Macro Viruses

Macro viruses are the most common form of viruses. Each macro virus can only be spread through a specific program. Most common types are Microsoft Word and Excel viruses. These programs contain "auto open macros" and "global macro templates." Virus writers recognize that any macros stored in the global file will automatically execute whenever something is opened. Macro viruses exploit these two aspects to enable themselves to replicate.

Worms

A worm is a special type of virus that transfers itself from one computer to another via a network. Worms can replicate themselves very quickly (often through e-mail address books) and thus carry the potential to overload host systems. Normally, worms cannot attach themselves to other programs, and thus do not pose a threat to files or data.

around the world, causing US$2 billion in direct economic losses and a further US$6.7 billion in lost productivity. Insurer Lloyd's of London announced on May 8, 2000, that computer viruses would prove to be the biggest insurance risk in upcoming years, prompting business analysts to call for a widespread change in company e-mail policies.

In addition to protecting company systems from viruses, employers like CIBC had obligations to ensure that employees were not acting illegally, for example, in perpetrating frauds, or immorally. E-mail could be used by employees to make inappropriate or defamatory comments. It could also be used to transmit sensitive corporate information, without appropriate security.

CIBC's Electronic Communication Policy

E-mail and voice mail were both included in Section 4.6 of CIBC's *Principles of Business Conduct*. CIBC recognized that occasional personal use could not be avoided.

> E-mail and voice mail are essential ways to communicate with employees, customers, suppliers, and other parties. Although all e-mail and voice mail facilities supplied by CIBC are its property, CIBC recognizes that incidental or occasional personal use of both is unavoidable.

CIBC reserved the right to access and monitor both internal and external e-mail and voice mail, including stored messages, and to restrict the use of both, without prior notice. The company also reserved the right to produce all office communications in legal proceedings.

Assentor Software

To ensure that its brokerage employees were not acting inappropriately in their dealings with customers through e-mail communications, CIBC relied on software to screen and archive e-mail messages in a central database. The software had the ability not only to screen key words, but combinations of words and sentences (so called natural language technology). The software allowed CIBC to "flag" and hold potentially inappropriate e-mail communications, such as high-pressure sales tactics, insider information, as well as other potentially litigious issues, such as sexual harassment. These flagged e-mails were then held for human analysis and review before being sent.

The market for e-mail screening software was worth $17 million in 1999, and was growing at a rate of 45 percent per year. According to a report by the Tower Group (www.towergroup.com), natural language technology was a significant improvement in screening technology allowing for more flexible and accurate monitoring than keyword or phrase search alone.

An excerpt from a news release from SRA International Inc. (which markets Assentor e-mail screening software), dated Feb. 22, 1999, read:

> (Tower Group) predicts that natural language functionality will become the technology of choice for e-mail compliance tools. . . . Securities firms of all sizes are using Assentor to apply technology to the compliance review process and take advantage of the many benefits of e-mail technology for communicating with their clients. Assentor uses a sophisticated, linguistics-based natural language pattern matching engine and highly refined compliance patterns developed closely with securities industry associations, compliance experts, and major broker/dealers to ensure that the technology is effective for all types of compliance requirements.

Companies in the financial services industry which used Assentor included CIBC, A.G. Edwards, BancBoston, Southwest Securities, and the National Association of Securities Dealers. Many others used other, mostly less powerful, e-mail screening methods.

Call centers typically tape conversations for quality control, and most organizations announce to the customer at the beginning of the call that the conversation will be taped. Employees working at call centers knew when they arrived at work that their conversations would be taped due to the possibility of disputes—for example, replaying a taped call would confirm if the customer requested a "buy order" of 500 shares instead of a "sell order" for 5,000 shares of the same stock. It was much easier, on the other hand, to forget that e-mail use could be monitored.

CIBC had recently developed an "Electronic Mail Policy," which went into more detail than the previous entry in its *Principles of Business Conduct* document. This policy outlined appropriate and inappropriate use of this company resource. A short summary of the policy read:

> Electronic mail (e-mail) systems, provided by the CIBC Group of Companies (CIBC Group), are its property. Employees are to use these systems for company business primarily within the boundaries of this policy and its standards. Business information, and the ability to freely communicate it, are valuable assets that play a significant role in CIBC's success. The protection and appropriate use of these assets is everyone's responsibility.
>
> All messages sent or received by electronic mail are CIBC records and must be handled in a manner consistent with CIBC record management policies and practices. Caution and discretion should be used in the nature and content of all messages sent, stored or distributed.
>
> CIBC recognizes that incidental or occasional use of e-mail for personal communications is unavoidable. However, all users with access to CIBC e-mail systems should be aware that the CIBC reserves the right to access, to monitor and to archive all e-mail messages, transmitted, received or stored on its systems, without further prior notice.

"E-mail use is often similar to casual conversations rather than formal written communications," stated Jones, "because employees forget that it is recorded and can be monitored." Jones went on to stress that e-mail is a business resource covered by a separate e-mail policy. He concluded by asking, "How should employees be discouraged from inappropriate language, content and usage?"

Jones knew that these were not easy questions to answer. Recent articles in newspapers and trade journals on e-mail privacy, such as the following excerpt, had brought the issue to CIBC's attention once more.

"Prying Times: Those Bawdy E-Mails Were Good for a Laugh—Until the Ax Fell," *The Wall Street Journal,* Feb. 4, 2000.

> In the course of their inquiry, workers say, managers found a number of potentially offensive e-mails, some of which had been sent by or forwarded to other employees in the office. That led to a wider investigation, and ended Nov. 30th 1999 when the Times fired 22 people in Norfolk, plus one in New York. Roughly 20 more workers, who the company determined had received offensive messages but didn't forward them to others, got warning letters. Most of the fired employees were otherwise in good standing; one had just received a promotion, and another had recently been commended as "employee of the quarter."

Some corporations, like CIBC, used e-mail screening to catch e-mail misuse, but since these filters tended to slow down network traffic, the practice was not universal. A second option, according to Jordan Worth, an Internet analyst with International Data Corporation, an Internet research firm, was to put in place policies that banned certain "types" of attachments. A third approach was to archive e-mail, but only access it in the event of a complaint.

What Should CIBC Do?

Jones found that taking the decision to implement the Assentor software was a lot easier than deciding what to do in the event that the software found something improper.

"What if an employee sends a personal message using a business 'word' flagged by Assentor and his or her direct manager finds out about a private situation?" wondered Jones. "What are the legal ramifications if the employee is reassigned or fired and subsequently claims bias on the part of the manager? What about the question of company ethics? Should we be reading personal e-mail from employees?"

Jones was wondering how to best reinforce its e-mail policy at CIBC.

> The employee should know that e-mail is a business resource that *could* be monitored by the employer. But how would we enforce it?
> If we were to cease monitoring e-mail, it might seem to be a viable solution, but remember that we have a responsibility to our customers, shareholders,

and the regulatory agencies to ensure proper records are kept and to monitor business e-mail use. It is also a regulatory requirement in the securities industry. Should we consider taking that risk and not having an e-mail screen? Probably not. There are things that an employee legally can't say, and some things they shouldn't say. Assentor "sniffs" this out for us and our employees should understand this.

I believe it is all about how we present it to our employees. To best implement our Principles of Business Conduct, clear communication and upfront understanding from our employees will go far to prevent negative impressions. We want to be as upfront and clear as possible to them. How best, then, to do that?

Should we inform our employees once? Inform them once per year? Have them sign a code of conduct? Or inform the employee every time he or she logs on to a company computer?

The Richard Ivey School of Business gratefully acknowledges the generous support of the MBA '89 class in the development of these learning materials.

iCraveTV.com: A New-Media Upstart

By Professor Mary Crossan, Professor Margaret Ann Wilkinson, Ken Mark, and Tammy Smith

Be at the right place, at the right time. Take massive, immediate action.

Attributed to Bill Gates, Founder of Microsoft Corporation

Introduction

"We've got a plan to create a new extension market for the release of television programming. And in the process, we aim to become the dominant TV aggregator retransmitter on the Internet when we launch iCraveTV in two months," stated Ian McCallum. Located in Montreal,

IVEY Ken Mark and Tammy Smith prepared this case under the supervision of Professors Mary Crossan and Margaret Ann Wilkinson solely to provide material for class discussion. The authors do not intend to illustrate either effective or ineffective handling of a managerial situation. The authors may have disguised certain names and other identifying information to protect confidentiality.

Ivey Management Services prohibits any form of reproduction, storage or transmittal without its written permission. This material is not covered under authorization from CanCopy or any reproduction rights organization. To order copies or request permission to reproduce materials, contact Ivey Publishing, Ivey Management Services, c/o Richard Ivey School of Business, The University of Western Ontario, London, Ontario, Canada, N6A 3K7; phone (519) 661-3208; fax (519) 661-3882; e-mail cases@ivey.uwo.ca.

Canada, iCraveTV was founded by McCallum and William Craig. It was September 30, 1999, and McCallum was looking over his launch options.

iCraveTV was legally permitted to retransmit television signals already carried on Canadian cable channels. But, due to differences in regulation, iCraveTV might face U.S. broadcast industry objections if U.S. audiences found access to the iCraveTV signal.

History of iCraveTV

Buying a computer for the first time in May 1999, Craig was not at all tech savvy. But he asked a single question of his group of friends, who had 50 years of broadcast experience behind them: "Why can't you put television on your computer screen?" Reaction from others around Craig led him to think that they thought it an infeasible idea. With the advent of broadband and the realization that its penetration into households would allow the piping of quality streaming video, iCraveTV (Canadian Radio And Video Entertainment) sought to be the first-to-market solution. Taking guidance from watching the growth and penetration of Internet and cable television, McCallum knew that the penetration of fibre optics would rapidly spread, resulting in increased high-speed connections—it was estimated that by the start of 2001, broadband access would comprise 50 percent of the Internet Service Provider (ISP) market.[1]

An Overview of the North American Broadcast Industry[2]

As of January 2000, 98.2 percent of total U.S. households owned TV sets, and 75.6 percent owned two or more sets. Average daily U.S. TV household viewing was six hours and 57 minutes, roughly one-third of which was devoted to cable.[3] Neilsen Media Research measured the viewing habits of this audience and ranked audience sizes by "rating points" and "share points." (One rating point equaled 1 percent of the total television households in a station's designated market area, while one share point equalled 1 percent of the area's total TV households that were using a television at the time. Thus, rating points would be used by media buyers for the purpose of determining advertising rates at the television station level (potential target audience pool), while

---

[1] Ian McCallum, Speech Notes, Presentation to the Edmonton Business Council, circa May 2000.

[2] Year 2000 Outlook Upbeat for Cable, Radio, and TV, Broadcasting & Cable Industry Survey, January 27, 2000, *Broadcasting & Cable Magazine,* pp. 1–23.

[3] According to statistics supplied to the National Association of Broadcasters by Nielsen Media Research.

share points would be used by networks to determine the success of each individual television program.)

The U.S. television market was the largest in the world and was served by three main distribution channels: the national television networks, independent commercial television stations, and cable television services, including pay cable. A commercial broadcast television station might be affiliated with one of the four established national networks (ABC, CBS, NBC, Fox), with one of the two new networks (WB or UPN), or with no network at all. To maintain a network license according to Federal Communications Commission (FCC) rules, commercial TV stations must broadcast at least 28 hours a week and at least two hours every day. Canadian broadcasters regularly paid to rebroadcast syndicated American programs as established viewing trends showed that Canadians preferred American content—polls continued to indicate that up to 19 of the top 20 television programs in Canada originated from the United States. To encourage the continued production of Canadian-made programs, the government-funded Canadian Broadcasting Corporation (CBC) was given a mandate to purchase and air domestic content.

The radio and broadcast television industries were expected to increase their share of the total U.S. advertising market over the next five years. Broadcast television accounted for 20 percent of the total U.S. advertising spending, and radio accounted for approximately 8 percent. Combined, advertising spending in broadcast television and radio was expected to rise to US$67.5 billion in 2000, up 13 percent from the year before.

An Advertising-based Model

The entire North American broadcast industry worked on the assumption that advertisers would pay to promote their wares to consumers. Attracting these consumers required producing consumer-appealing content, acquiring the rights to that content, and finding a means to broadcast it to consumers. AC Neilsen acted as a paid referee, regularly polling consumers to determine the most popular programs. These poll results were termed "Neilsen ratings" and allowed the players in the broadcast industry to price their products appropriately.

A summary of the revenue flows in the broadcast industry would show that almost all stakeholders in the industry depended on advertisers. For example, a content syndicator could be in competition for advertising dollars against the network to which it sold its content programs. (See Table 1.)

By selling more advertising time, an independent station or new-network affiliate typically garnered a higher share of local advertising revenues than its audience ratings would suggest. But because it broadcast more syndicated programs than a major-network affiliate

TABLE 1   Revenue Flow in the Broadcast Market

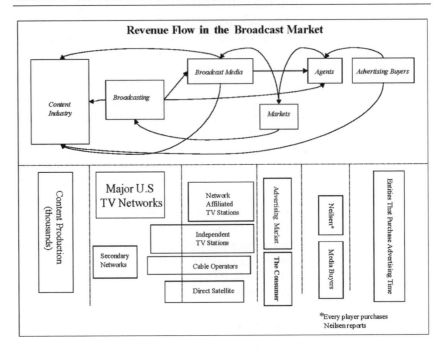

did, its total programming costs were generally higher than those of a major network affiliate in the same market.

Radio broadcasters, television broadcasters, and cable television operators were similar in that they sought to attract audiences to their programming. To stay in business, they had to satisfy subscribers, viewers or listeners by providing desirable programming. Where they differed was in their means of delivering programming and generating revenues. U.S. radio and TV stations typically got about 90 percent of their revenues from advertising. Cable system operators also sold advertising, but 65 percent to 70 percent of their revenues came from monthly subscriber fees paid by consumers. Content production companies that created basic cable programs received only 15 percent of their revenues from advertising; most of their earnings came from the carriage fees paid by cable system operators.

Relationships between Content Rights Owners and Broadcast Media

The broadcasting and cable industries comprised tens of thousands of individual companies, most of which were small business operations. Within each segment, however, the biggest players claimed a disproportionately large share of business, and the industry was becoming more top-heavy every year. The Big Three television networks—ABC, CBS, and NBC—generally accounted for more than 40 percent of the broadcast television industry's annual advertising revenue and as much as 47 percent or more during Olympic years. Although the Big Three would continue to see their future audience share whittled away by cable and other media outlets, they were still expected to dominate television viewership and advertising for the foreseeable future.

Because the major networks regularly bought and provided first-run programming during prime-time hours (generally 8 P.M. to 11 P.M. in the Eastern and Pacific time zones), network affiliates often achieved higher audience shares than their local rivals did. However, the major networks pre-empted most of their affiliates' prime-time schedule for broadcasting their programs and could sell most of that advertising time themselves. This meant that affiliates of the Big Three networks had substantially fewer prime-time advertisements ("inventory") to sell than did independent stations or affiliates of the newer networks. On the other hand, their large audiences meant higher rates for the slots that they did have, which helped compensate for their limited amount of prime-time advertising.

The newer networks also demanded a high percentage of their affiliates' advertisement inventory during network broadcasts. But because their programming consumed fewer prime-time hours, their affiliates had more slots to sell than did affiliates of the major networks. And despite their generally low advertising rates, new-network affiliates and independent stations enjoyed a large advertisement inventory, which gave them more prime-time slots than their major-network affiliates.

The Advertisers

Advertisers paid to place their television commercials on programs that would reach their target audience. AC Neilsen regularly polled consumers about their viewing habits and charted the popularity of various television shows. Thus, the future of a television series or program was tied to its Neilsen ratings.

Advertisers usually bought airtime through advertising agencies, for a commission of about 10 percent to 15 percent of the cost of placing the advertisement. National advertising time was sold through national sales representatives, who received a commission based on advertising cost. Local advertising time was sold by each station's sales staff; again, the advertiser paid a commission. Networks generally sold about 80 percent of their available time slots in advance (called "upfront television ad sales"), and the rest was sold on the "scatter" market—the period that began after the start of the fall program season. Upfront market prices usually determined those in the scatter market because they influenced forces of supply and demand. Thus, upfront sales were indicators of the health of television industry revenues in the coming year.

Many contracts came with audience guarantees, so networks could be caught off guard by programs that did not meet expectations of audience appeal or viewership, leading advertisers to cancel their contracts. Some contracts included a "make-good" clause, by which advertisers were to receive "free" advertising time from the network on later programming if audience size for a contracted slot fell below a certain level. Advertisers could also cancel upfront contracts for no other reasons, leaving networks with more advertisement time to fill within the scatter market.

The Television Networks[4]

All of the U.S. networks were divisions of larger corporations. ABC was owned by Walt Disney Co., CBS Corp. had agreed to be acquired by Viacom Inc., Fox was a unit of News Corp., and NBC was owned by General Electric Co. WB was 75 percent owned by Time Warner Inc. and 25 percent owned by Tribune Co. UPN was a 50/50 joint venture of Chris-Craft Industries Inc. and Viacom Inc. ABC, CBS and NBC provided their roughly 650 station affiliates with about 22 hours of prime-time programming per week and a substantial amount of programming for other time periods. The terms of most network affiliation contracts ran from two years to 10 years. They paid affiliates for broadcasting their programming and national commercials—each network was thus able to reach virtually every significant U.S. television market.

The Fox network, established in 1996, had 211 affiliates and a prime-time audience reach of about 96 percent of American television homes. (Audience reach meant the percentage of TV-owning households in which a broadcast was available.)

In general, the Big Three networks' share of the prime-time television audience had declined over the past few decades. It had been whittled away by the growing popularity of cable television, the success of the 11-year-old Fox network, and most recently, by the explosion of alternative viewing choices made possible by new cable technologies and regulatory easing. One such technology offered consumers their personalized selection of channels. Instead of paying for a "package" of 200 channels, for example, each consumer could choose a personalized combination of channels and would be billed per selection. According to Neilsen Media Research in 1999, ABC, CBS and NBC collectively commanded a 91 percent share of the prime-time television audience in the 1978–79 season, and a 75 percent share in the 1986–87 season. In the most recent tele-

---

[4]Broadcasting & Cable Industry Survey, January 27, 2000.

vision season (September 1998 through May 1999), the Big Three's combined share was down to 45 percent of the television audience. By network, CBS's share of the prime-time audience was 16 percent, compared with 15 percent for NBC, 14 percent for ABC, and 12 percent for the Fox network. UPN (United Paramount Network) gathered a 5 percent share during its six hours of weekly programming, and the WB (Warner Brothers Television Network) network attracted 3 percent during its seven hours of weekly prime-time programming. Independent television stations took an 11 percent share, basic cable attracted 36 percent, and pay cable garnered 6 percent. (These figures added up to more than 100 percent due to differences in programming schedules and because of the "multiset" phenomenon, in which different sets in one home may be tuned to different channels.)

As competition had eaten into their audience shares while programming costs had escalated, TV networks were increasingly expecting their television station affiliates to help ease the profit squeeze. In the past several years, ABC, CBS, NBC and even Fox had been chipping away at the arrangements whereby they paid their affiliates to carry network programming. More recently, they had asked affiliates to help pay for costly sports rights packages and for renewal rights to certain hit programming.

In April 1999, the Fox network proposed a cut of 22 percent in its affiliate stations' local commercial slots; it rescinded 20 of the affiliates' 90 prime-time commercial units per week. The 200 affiliates protested strongly at first, but capitulated in late May 1999 on Fox's compromise plan. This plan would give affiliates first refusal rights on purchasing 20 time slots at below-market rates and would grant them 15 new prime-time units to sell locally. As part of the deal, Fox agreed not to take back any more slots, including slots that ran during NFL football games, for three years.

Fox would gain some US$70 million annually from the take-back, as opposed to the US$100 million it originally sought. And while affiliates were collectively losing that US$70 million a year, they would each get 15 more slots per week to sell, along with all the revenue generated.

From the start, some of the newer networks, UPN and WB, established more frugal associate relationships in which case compensation was rare. They charged their affiliates for certain event programming and provided fewer hours of costly prime-time programming than the established networks did. To expand their audience reach, the newer networks distributed their programming through cable, as well as across the airwaves.

In Canada, there existed three national television networks: Global, CTV and government-funded Canadian Broadcasting Corporation (CBC). Much of Canadian prime-time television programming originated from the United States.

Broadcast Television Stations[5]

The top 25 owners of U.S. television stations together controlled 36 percent of the more than 1,200 U.S. commercial television stations at the end of 1998, up from 33 percent in 1997 and 25 percent in 1996. In Canada, the CHUM Group was the majority owner of the largest group of television stations. Of this group, some stations were affiliated with different national networks and some were non-affiliated.

TV station revenues came primarily from three sources: national spot advertising sold to national and regional advertisers; advertising time sold to local advertisers; and network compensation payments (networks' payments to affiliates for broadcasting network commercials and programming). A station's competitive position depended on network affiliation, programming quality, management ability and technical factors. Its success relied on the public's response to its programs compared with competing entertainment, as this response affected ratings and, thus, revenues.

Television stations that served a given designated market area (DMA) competed for advertising sales with other broadcast and cable stations, plus other media such as newspapers and radio. Within each DMA, advertising rates depended primarily on the stations' program ratings, the time of day and the program's viewer demographics.

Television stations frequently made substantial financial commitments to guarantee their access to programs that would be syndicated in the future, requiring the station to purchase an entire program series.

As of year-end 1999, there were 1,616 full-power television stations in the United States. Of these, 1,243 were commercial stations and 373 were educational stations. In addition, a total of 2,194 low-power television stations were licensed to operate.

There was a contrast between U.S. and Canadian television stations. Whereas low-powered television stations in the United States served community channels and college markets, Canadian networks used low-powered television stations as "repeaters" to carry programming signals to rural parts of the country.

Cable Television Systems[6]

Cable system operators received signals from their program providers by several means: special antennas, microwave relay systems, Earth stations, and fiberoptic cables. The system used amplified the signals, combined them with locally originated programs and ancillary services, and distributed them to subscribers. "Cable providers have retransmit-

---

[5]Broadcasting & Cable Industry Survey, January 27, 2000.
[6]Broadcasting & Cable Industry Survey, January 27, 2000.

ted network broadcasts for years without having a contract or having to pay them any royalties. This is because the networks realized that the cable providers were extending their audience reach for them," stated David Spencer, an associate professor of film and media studies at the University of Western Ontario.

Although there were thousands of cable system operators in the United States, the industry had been dominated by the top 25 players for many years. At the end of May 1999, the top 25 cable operators served about 91 percent of the U.S. market's subscribers, up from 85 percent a year earlier. The 10 largest accounted for more than 71 percent of the 68 million cable subscribers, up from 45 percent in 1994. In Canada, Rogers Cablesystems was the major player, with roughly similar cable penetration in Canada compared with the United States.

Unlike broadcast television, cable system providers (cable providers) derived most of their revenues from monthly subscriber fees. In addition to recurring subscriber programming revenues, cable providers received revenues from installation charges, sales of pay-per-view movies and events, set-top converter rentals, remote control sales and rentals, advertising, carriage fees from home shopping channels and fees from companies presenting infomercials. In recent years, the industry had upgraded the technological capabilities of its broadband network so that cable providers could offer such new services as digital video, high-speed Internet access, local and long-distance telephone services, and commercial competitive local exchange carrier operations. High-definition television (HDTV), video on demand, and e-commerce were also among the newest offerings. Total revenues for U.S. cable system operators, including subscription fees, advertising, new services and other fees and charges, were expected to increase 15 percent in 2000 to US$15.3 billion, with projections for annual 15.4 percent growth rates through 2004.

Cable providers' advertising revenues continued to grow rapidly as well, expected to increase by 27 percent in 2000, and expecting to advance 22 percent on average each year through 2004. By January 2000, cable was available to more than 30,000 U.S. communities, serving nearly 68 percent of the roughly 102.68 million U.S. households with television.

Cable's growth over the past 15 years had hurt broadcast television by fostering the creation of dozens of new cable networks that battled for advertising dollars. At the same time, it also helped broadcast television networks by providing clear reception for weak stations.

Syndication Deals

Content producers were free to sell and syndicate their programs to competing and international stations.

Spencer explained,

> This would help the producer recoup the cost of producing the program. Alliance Atlantis (a Canadian syndication content provider) could sell the rights to put "Traders" (their Canadian syndicated show) on air to Global, at which time Global sells advertising and recovers the costs. Alliance then could also sell syndication to CBS, who in turn recoups its costs through advertising. The only caveat is that if Global and CBS aired the same show at the same time, the Canadian television stations carrying Global's signal would be forced to substitute U.S. advertising for Canadian-only advertising.[7]

Regardless of network affiliation, all broadcast stations obtained some programs from independent sources. These programs were mainly syndicated TV shows (some of which had previously aired on a major network) and syndicated feature films that were either made for network TV or previously shown in theatres and on cable television.

Although network audiences were analysed to estimate the future value and potential profitability of program syndication (a program licensed for reruns after it had been aired), there was no assurance that a successful network program would continue to be profitable once syndicated.

Syndicators sometimes sold broadcast stations a license to air a syndicated program, allowing the purchase station to sell the advertising slots and keep the revenues; no barter element was involved. The cash price of such programming varied, depending on its perceived desirability and the number of times it was to be aired. Syndicators also offered programs to stations on a barter basis. Although stations did not pay fees to get such programming, the syndicators often sold most of the associated advertising, keeping the revenues for themselves. This arrangement gave purchasing stations fewer advertisement slots, but reduced their programming slots. A third option was the cash-plus-barter sale, a combination of the first two options. In recent years, barter and cash-plus-barter deals were becoming more prevalent. These exchanges provided programming to stations without requiring as much upfront cash as a direct sale. Of course, they also reduced the amount of advertising time that stations could sell, although the direct impact on broadcasters' operating income was believed to be neutral. Program distributors that acquired airtime by barter must then compete with television stations and broadcasting networks to sell their available slots to advertisers.[8]

---

[7]David Spencer, Interview, September 28, 2000.
[8]Broadcasting & Cable Industry Survey, January 27, 2000.

Substitute Advertising Media to Broadcast Television

Broadcast networks and cable operators alike were seeing significantly greater competition from alternative technologies. Digitalization of the television signal (which was now analog) allowed for the broadcast and transmission of high-definition television (HDTV), with its incredibly sharp and detailed pictures. Under the current schedule mandated by the FCC, all television signals had to be transmitted digitally by May 1, 2002. By mid-1999, TV stations covering nearly 45 percent of U.S. homes had been converted to the digital format—the advent of digital television allowed cable providers to tout the crystal-clear picture that had been trumpeted by direct broadcast satellite providers in their marketing campaigns.

Digital television also made it possible for cable providers to transmit more than one signal per channel by means of a technology called broadband compression. This capability, which functioned by condensing numerous signals into one bandwidth, was probably more important to cable providers and broadcasters than picture clarity, allowing a 60-channel cable system to hold 510 channels by giving 50 channels a compression factor of 10 and using the remaining 10 channels for other revenue-producing services involving phones, computers, music and other features. One drawback of this technology, however, was that as more channels were added, the picture quality diminished.

If consumers demanded sharper, clearer picture quality than cable could offer, they would subscribe to Direct Broadcast Satellite service (DBS). DBS systems provided higher picture quality and more programming choice than cable did, but both factors were becoming less advantageous with the cable industry's current rollout of digital broadband capabilities. Thus, DBS's penetration of the cable market had been relatively minor. One shortcoming of DBS was that it was costly— the consumer had to bear the cost of the DBS dish as well as its installation and maintenance. With cable, equipment costs and maintenance were borne by the cable system operator. Another disadvantage was that in most markets, DBS subscribers could not receive locally originated over-the-air broadcast signals; to receive those channels, they had to put up rabbit-ear antennae or subscribe to cable. In addition, DBS reception could be lost or badly disturbed in severe weather—for these reasons, roughly one-fourth of DBS subscribers also subscribed to cable. In 1999, lawmakers eased the rules that currently prevented satellite companies from offering local stations, putting DBS on a more equal footing with cable. According to Neilsen Market Research, the number of DBS subscribers grew from 2.1 million in 1996 to 11.3 million in 1999.

Radio was expected to continue exhibiting stronger growth than broadcast television, enjoying 10.4 percent annual revenue growth through 2004. As the U.S. business environment changed in response to deregulation in telecommunications and advances in technology, advertisers in various segments were expected to continue to intensify their marketing programs to keep up with the competition.

Alliances between Cable Providers and Broadcasters

The Big Three networks had long considered forming formal alliances with cable providers prior to 1999 as a means to reach wider audiences, taking action only in the past year or two, due to the increased pace of audience erosion as digital television replaced analog television. Fox and the newer networks (UPN, WB, and PAX) had already drawn on cable's reach by forming affiliate relationships with cable channels. In June 1999, NBC reached an agreement with AT&T, the new cable giant, under which AT&T would carry NBC's cable and broadcast programming, including an Olympics package and HDTV signals through 2009. The companies did not disclose financial terms, but NBC stated that the pact would increase distribution of its CNBC and MSNBC cable-news channels from 50 million homes to more than 66 million homes in three years. It would also allow NBC to carry the 2000 Olympics over cable as well as network TV.

Regulation

Government oversight of broadcasting and cable services fell primarily under the jurisdiction of the Federal Communications Commission (FCC) in the United States, and the Canadian Radio and Television Commission (CRTC) in Canada. The FCC was created through the Communications Act of 1934 and regulated all interstate and international communications by wire and radio. The CRTC had regulated Canadian airwaves since 1968. Canadian ownership regulations prevented foreign nationals from owning more than a 25 percent controlling stake in networks or television stations. This ruling had largely dissuaded the U.S. broadcasting players from taking a significant equity stake in any Canadian broadcast properties.

The U.S. radio and television industries were transformed during the 1990s by such landmark legislation as the Telecommunications Act of 1996, rule changes by the FCC, and other recent federal legislation. Most of the recent legislation was designed to boost competition and to level the playing field. One major effect of these new laws has been widespread and continuing consolidation in the media arena. Most recently, in August 1999, the FCC revised its local market television ownership rules—the TV duopoly rule and the radio and television cross-ownership (or "one-to-a-market") rule—to permit ownership of two television stations within the same market and to permit cross-ownership of multiple radio stations at the same time.

These rules changes have led and would continue to lead consolidation in the marketplace, allowing for the centralization of similar functions and the ability for the growing conglomerates to offer larger audiences and wider advertising reach to clients.

In Canada, the situation had been different, stated Spencer:

> We have had extremely restrictive media regulations in Canada since 1932. The CRTC sought to bring all media under the umbrella of Canadian nationalism. This started with the Canadian content rules—30 percent of all content on AM Radio and 55 percent of prime-time radio and television content have to be Canadian. But there are ways to minimize that restriction because content is counted on a rolling average. Therefore, if a Canadian station picked up Wednesday Night Hockey (three-hour broadcast), news and current affairs, plus a Canadian syndicated television series, it would have its quota for the week.

But the CRTC decided in 1996 not to regulate media activities on the Internet, beginning a series of announcements that led industry observers to note that the Canadian media industry was also moving towards deregulation.[9] For example, cable was never treated as a part of the broadcasting system in Canada until amendments were made to the Canadian Broadcasting Act of 1968. Until then, cable was regarded simply as a method by which television signals could be distributed to a wider audience without physical interference. Spencer explained:

> Since most of the television products that appeared between the first cable system and the revised Canadian Broadcasting Act of 1968 were produced and distributed by networks, the networks were only too happy to have expansion of their signals instead of setting up a series of low-power relay transmitters in remote areas. If nothing else, the retransmission enhanced advertising rates for the networks.
>
> The copyright issue first began to become a problem in the United States when Hollywood insisted on royalty payments based on distribution. The U.S. networks refused, claiming that the only audience they should pay for was the audience that they had been licensed to serve—that referred to the audience within the broadcast contour, not those collected on cable.
>
> At least in Canada, the CRTC declared with the 1968 Broadcast Act that cable was in effect a member of the broadcasting community. But here, the definition gets cloudy. In effect, the CRTC stated that there were two ways to approach the definition of "broadcasting." First, providing to consumers cable-specific channels, such as Rogers Cable 13 in London, subjected cable operators to the same conditions that any broadcaster, off air or off cable, had

---

[9]David Spencer, Interview, September 28, 2000.

to meet. However, the retransmission of network signals was not considered broadcasting. So in effect, the CRTC stated that cable operators were not stealing product when they retransmitted a signal, and that was that. The U.S. industry disagrees.

Cable operators often retransmitted network signals to audiences already able to receive network broadcasts via affiliated television stations. Therefore, if a U.S. or Canadian broadcaster has already paid for the rights to broadcast the program across the country, why should cable be subject to pay more to retransmit the signal to the same audience?

Consolidation and Convergence

Media giants were emerging. By being the only willing investors in new media and entertainment technologies, software and delivery systems, the industry giants such as the major network broadcasters (ABC, NBC, CBS and Fox) were expected to gain further control of the shape and focus of the media and entertainment industry in the decades to come. In a vicious circle of market power and access to capital, these industry giants, because of their market share and purchasing power, would continue to strengthen their financial and market prospects and further reinforce their powerful gatekeeper positions well into the 21st century. But they offered enormous benefits to consumers, since their fiscal power would allow them to efficiently develop and implement new technologies.[10]

Breaking into the Industry—A Traditional Approach (Pre-Internet)

Starting a traditional television network was theoretically simple. First, one had to have programs, preferably something unique and highly appealing to a mass audience. Next, one would need to get local TV stations to agree to act as affiliates. If enough affiliates were lined up, one could sell advertising time to advertisers. Then, an arrangement with a common carrier company (AT&T, Bell) would be needed to transmit programs to the affiliates. Getting the programs would be fairly easy, although it was the most expensive part. Very few program producers were likely to go to the considerable expense of producing shows without payment in advance, or at least guaranteed. One alternative was to contract with the party that owned the rights to a sports event, for example. Usually the rights could be obtained for a modest advance fee, with the balance to be paid if and when the event actually was used.

---

[10]Michael N. Garin, and Thomas A. Redmond, "The Changing Economic Structures and Relationships among Entertainment Industry Participants in the 21st Century," Charles M. Firestone, Editor, *Television for the 21st Century—The Next Wave,* 1993, p. 34.

Lining up affiliates was the hardest part of forming a new network. Since there were not many independent stations, and the more successful ones were profitable with their usual programming (syndicated old movies and off-network shows), they were not eager to give up their time for an uncertain venture.[11]

For an aspiring new cable system operator entrant, Spencer outlined the Canadian rules of entry:

> A new player must apply to the CRTC, and if the application is accepted, the licensee plays under the same rules as any other cable operator. However, there are virtually no areas of the country not serviced by cable or by satellite through operations such as Bell ExpressVu. The activity then in this area deals largely with companies buying out other companies.

Theoretically, a new cable operator entrant would need to negotiate rights and carriage fees to pay for certain cable programs, but could (at least in Canada) legally retransmit network television signals.

A New Media Alternative

iCraveTV's founders had two options: work within the existing framework and seek to negotiate Internet rights from syndicators, or pirate network signals and launch the site. Ian McCallum offered:

> Fiber is being installed at about the rate of 2,400 kilometers a minute. About 11 percent of office workers have high-speed access. We expect there to be 10 million homes passed by mid-2001, and 30 million four years later. In the first quarter, cable modem access jumped 44 percent and DSL grew by 183 percent. We expect growth rates in North America to slow to 4 percent and in the rest of the world to be about 11 percent for the next five years. Angus Reid Group has predicted that by the end of 2000, there will be 450 million people on the Internet. China alone jumped from 6 million to 10 million since February.
>
> When cable television's copper lines were laid down throughout North American neighborhoods, about 40 percent of homes in the service areas subscribed. That figure currently stood at about 70 percent of households; about half of that number subscribe to additional tiers amounting to a total of 220 per cent of pay to basic. (Basic U.S. monthly cable was $29 and per-tier pricing is about $8.) We know that studies have been done to show the online movie viewer profiles, which look very encouraging. Pay-per-view still has a way to go, but the Internet may eventually break through some of the problems experienced in the cable environment.

---

[11]Stuart M. DeLuca, *Television's Transformation for the Next 25 Years,* 1980, p. 135.

The Concept of "Companion Television"

iCraveTV did not perceive itself to replace television consumption. McCallum mentioned,

> Companion Television is designed to be part of the online computer experience. It converges continuous live and archival television onto the computer screen. A viewer sitting 18 inches away from their computer, could choose from one of three screen formats: 3″ × 5″ to full screen. The quality is expected to improve as throughput of the online world improves.

McCallum coined the term "extension market" to emphasize that iCraveTV would take television programming to places it had not been before—computer screens in the office, student computers in residences, bedrooms of youths, offices—anywhere, in fact, where one possessed an online computer. He continued:

> We spent a couple of million dollars on equipment (antennae, receivers, servers, digitizers and an operations centre) and around Cdn$13 million in telecom commitments. In addition, we have commissioned two-and-a-half OC3 telecom pipes. To give you an idea of what that means, all of Toronto's traffic to the United States passes along three OC3s.

iCraveTV's Revenue Model

The founders intended iCraveTV to realize 60 percent of revenues from service subscription fees and 40 percent from online banner advertisement sales. iCraveTV's advertising revenue assumptions were based on management experience and industry information concerning rates and inventories in the cable industry, with the difference being that iCraveTV could insert commercials as well as run ad banners into viewer content. Furthermore, some of the ad banners would be below the picture and therefore would be viewed for an entire 30 seconds.

A Different Audient Served versus Traditional Broadcast Television

McCallum felt strongly that he would not be in competition with existing television stations. This was the view that he presented to the public on iCraveTV's relationship with traditional broadcast television:

> This service is not, I want to emphasize, to compete with over-the-air broadcasting. Anyone who has seen video on a computer monitor will know that it is not a substitute for television. Typically, the video picture takes up only a small portion of a computer monitor that is itself small compared to current television screens, and if the video is enlarged, it loses resolution. We expect the technology, and so the quality of the picture, to improve, but it will not in the foreseeable future improve to the point where someone who owns a television set—which includes, of course, far more people than own computers—will want to watch a TV show on a computer rather than on TV.

Instead, iCraveTV serves a different audience. It serves those who cannot receive broadcast television, such as those in the shadow of the huge CN broadcast tower in Toronto, and those in universities and offices who cannot receive broadcast television and do not have cable access. And it serves those who are working on a computer and would like to be able to view a television program in a corner of their screen. In these ways we provide a real service to some people, but it is not a service that provides any competition to over-the-air broadcasters or cable or satellite retransmitters. This is confirmed by the limited capacity of the video server used by iCraveTV: we can serve no more than about 4,000 viewers at a time. This is hardly a threat to television broadcasters with their tens of millions of viewers, and the technology will not permit it to become such a threat, even if we wanted to, which we do not. In the future, we hope to use technological improvements to serve millions of consumers. In fact, within months, we expect to have this capability to serve millions.

The Issue of Royalty Payments for Re-transmitted Signals

According to Canadian copyright laws, iCraveTV would be permitted to retransmit to Canadians any U.S. programming already carried on Canadian cable channels and to sell advertising on those shows. Spencer commented:

> Rogers Cable Television regularly substitutes commercial messages when retransmitting A&E, TNN and other signals. So in effect, they are using a foreign product for domestic gain. As well, cable operators are required to black out U.S. television signals and transmit only the Canadian signal when the U.S. networks and the Canadian stations or networks are broadcasting the same program at the same time. However, once a company starts rebroadcasting Canadian signals and selling advertising in those signals, it is acting like a broadcaster. Even though the CRTC has decided that it will not regulate the Internet, programming copyright laws are still in effect.

McCallum commented:

> iCraveTV was launched to provide TV retransmission to Canadian viewers, to pay royalties to copyright holders, including Buffalo, New York broadcasters and international program producers, with payments to be made according to tariffs to be established by the Canadian Copyright Board in negotiation with the broadcasters, iCraveTV and similar companies, and to generate revenues based on banner advertising. Except for the latter point, it will be similar to Canadian cable companies. By this means the Canadian government had established a technologically independent means to cut through the Gordian Knot of conflicting, dispersed or ill-defined rights and thereby to provide what no contracts could provide—the flow of revenue from the viewers/advertisers, through iCraveTV to broadcasters and program producers.

Initially iCraveTV will be established using best available security techniques to contain the service within Canada. However, U.S. rights holders might be concerned that these techniques are inadequate to stop their programming from entering the U.S. market.[12]

McCallum knew that measures had to be taken to at least attempt to prevent U.S. users from accessing the Canadian site. One option was to require the user to enter a three-digit Canadian telephone area code in order to confirm that they were located in Canada.

Conclusion

For McCallum and Craig, several issues remained unresolved as they moved towards the launch of iCraveTV. First, they believed that no broadcasting rights for current television programs existed. They could either negotiate those rights from each of the content syndicators, or attempt to pay Internet royalties for the programming if a suitable tariff were to be retroactively negotiated by broadcasters and the Canadian Copyright Board.

iCraveTV might be able to retransmit to Canadians the same programs already being retransmitted by the cable operators, but what if American audiences gained access to the Internet retransmission? In spite of these issues, McCallum and Craig planned to implement a "viral marketing" campaign to boost awareness a week before the launch date. It seemed as though they had a great idea and an untapped niche. Now they had to figure out how to capitalize on it.

---

[12]Ian McCallum, Presentation to the Congress Judiciary Committee, June 15, 2000.

Open Text Preferred Listings

By Professor Sid L. Huff and Mike Wade

It was June 20, 1996, and the marketing team at Open Text Corporation in Waterloo, Ontario, were putting the finishing touches on the new "Preferred Listings" service. Senior management had to decide whether to incorporate this service into the company's main product, the Open Text Index, an Internet search engine.

Open Text Corporation

Open Text Corporation was born in the aftermath of a project to index and catalogue the 60 million words and 2.4 million quotations contained in the Oxford English Dictionary (OED). OED project manager, Tim Bray, and two University of Waterloo professors, Frank Tompa and

Gaston Gonnet, formed Open Text after the project ended in 1989. In its early days, Open Text was, according to Bray, a "low-key, academics-in-the-garage kind of operation" with a superior product, the software used to index the OED, but without the marketing or management skills required to exploit it. Potential clients had trouble imagining any new uses for the product. "When we showed people the OED, they said, 'This is good stuff, but we don't have a dictionary.' " Bray notes, "As computer scientists, no matter how hard we tried to explain the benefits, we couldn't do it."

In 1994, the company brought Tom Jenkins in as president. The 36-year-old electrical engineer had worked in a number of high-tech companies. He had a technical background (his name is on several patents for integrated circuit designs), but his main contribution to the company came from his experience as a sales and marketing manager. When Jenkins got the call, Open Text was just one product, the direct descendant of the OED's search engine. It was a product without a market, and without any change, the venture seemed doomed. But unbeknownst to Jenkins or anyone else at Open Text, the company was actually well positioned to take advantage of the unexpected growth in global networking.

"The Internet came out of nowhere and surprised everybody," said Bray. "Partly through design and, to be honest, partly through accident, our software's technical characteristics applied beautifully to the Internet." Bray recalled the exact moment Open Text changed course. In November 1994, a speaker at a conference that Bray was attending made an observation about the World Wide Web (WWW). He said, "The truth may be out there, but without help, you'll never find it." At that moment the "penny dropped" for Bray—the Web needed a search engine! "I was so excited, I was physically shaking for a couple of days, because I could see right away how it could be done."

Bray's idea was to send robotic software agents crawling through cyberspace, following tens of thousands of links and finding millions of pages of text, then bring them home and index them. Users would be able to search this vast catalogue of information by using key words. The retrieved information would be ranked according to relevancy with the most relevant result at the top of the list. Users could then find the best-fit material they wanted quickly and efficiently.

IVEY Mike Wade and Professor Sid L. Huff prepared this case solely to provide material for class discussion. The authors do not intend to illustrate either effective or ineffective handling of a managerial situation. The authors may have disguised certain names and other identifying information to protect confidentiality.

EXHIBIT 1   Internet Catalogues and Search Engines

Internet catalogues and search engines are two tools available for Internet users to cut through the vast amount of information on the World Wide Web (WWW). Even though they approach the task differently, both have their uses depending on the nature of the information being sought.

Internet catalogues such as Yahoo are essentially searchable directories. Designed in a tree structure, they allow users to delve deeper and deeper into a particular category, until the desired topic is isolated. At the lowest level, the user receives a series of links relating to the chosen topic. Most Internet catalogues don't actually index the linked web pages. An advantage of this structure is that searches can be refined to include only those topics of interest to the user. Disadvantages are that searches can be slow if there are many branches to go down, and imprecise if directory categories don't mesh perfectly with the categories users are looking for.

Search engines such as Open Text Index are vast databases, holding millions of web pages. These databases can be searched using key words as search criterion. When a search is initiated, the search engine goes through its database of web pages and responds with the most appropriate results. Most search engines respond to search requests quickly, and since many search engines index all the words on a web page, the level of detail is very high. A disadvantage of search engines is the high number of search results that are inappropriate to the search criteria. It is not uncommon for a search engine to retrieve hundreds of thousands of search results, 99 percent of which are useless, i.e. a high signal-to-noise ratio.

As Open Text worked to get an indexing software package together for the WWW, it became obvious that others were working toward the same goal. In April 1995, Open Text launched the Open Text Index on the WWW. The Open Text Index was initially designed to showcase the company's information management and indexing software. The product was a huge hit with Internet users as it was easy to use, free and comprehensive.

By the end of 1995, the Open Text Index was getting half a million visits per day and was routinely mentioned in the press as one of the top search engines on the Internet. It became so successful that Open Text management decided to run the Open Text Index as a for-profit center by selling online space to advertisers.

Open Text had many early successes, most notably the exposure it received thanks to its partnership with Yahoo, the definitive WWW catalogue. In the fall of 1995, Open Text agreed to be the main indexing agent and search engine associated with the Yahoo index, a service it agreed to provide free of charge. Management felt that the exposure and recognition Open Text would receive due to its collaboration with Yahoo would justify the running costs. See Exhibit 1 for a description of the difference between a catalogue and a search engine.

EXHIBIT 2   Open Text Stock Chart 15.1.96–15.6.96

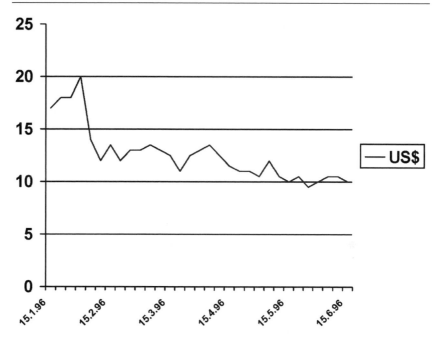

In January of 1996, Open Text raised US$69 million in a successful initial public offering (IPO) and joined the NASDAQ index. The stock initially soared but lost value in the following months. Chinks in the Open Text armor started to appear by April 1996. Netscape, who had offered Open Text a spot on its home page, one of the most visited sites on the net, decided to go with other search engines. Newer search engines such as Altavista and Excite had developed superior products. From being one of the pioneers, the Open Text Index was becoming a "me-too" search engine. A deep blow came in early June 1996, when Yahoo cancelled its arrangement with the Open Text Index and, instead, signed a long-term agreement with Altavista to provide its search services. Management felt that the positive brand exposure generated from working with Yahoo did not justify the cost of running the service. Open Text stock dropped by $1 on the news. See Exhibit 2 for share price data for the period.

World Wide Web Search Engines

In June 1996, there were a number of search engines on the WWW. The big names, in order of popularity were Altavista, Excite, Webcrawler, Lycos, Open Text Index and Infoseek. "Meta" search engines, which would submit a search request to a number of search engines concurrently, were also in existence. All search engines basically did the same

---

EXHIBIT 3   What Is a "Spider"?

A "spider" or "web robot" is a program that traverses the Web's hypertext structure, retrieves web pages, indexes them in a database, and then recursively retrieves all documents linked to those web pages. The name "spider" is a bit misleading as it gives the impression that the software itself moves between sites like a virus. This is not the case. A spider simply visits sites by requesting documents from them. This is different from an "autonomous agent," which does travel between sites, deciding when to move and what to do. Autonomous agents can only travel between special servers and are currently not widespread on the Internet.

Spiders allow search engines and other databases to be updated automatically at regular intervals, so that "dead" links in the databases can be detected and removed. Spiders operate continually over prolonged periods of time, often months. To speed up operations, many spiders feature parallel retrieval, resulting in a consistently high use of bandwidth in the immediate proximity. Consequently, some sites do not like to be visited by spiders. To stop a spider from visiting a site, or part of a site, a special file called a robot.txt file can be inserted on the web server.

In general, spiders start from a historical list of Uniform Resource Locators (URLs), especially of documents with many links elsewhere, such as server lists, "What's New" pages, and the most popular sites on the Web. Most search engines and indexing services also allow users to submit URLs manually, which will then be queued and visited by the spider. Sometimes other sources for URLs are used, such as scanning through Usenet postings, published mailing list archives, and so on.

The amount of data a spider indexes depends on the particular spider. Some spiders index just the text in the title section of the web page's underlying code, or the titles plus the first few paragraphs of text. Others parse the entire page, including hidden tags and all text, and apply weightings to different components. In practice, most spiders end up indexing and storing almost everything they come across.

---

thing in slightly different ways. Using "spiders," they combed the WWW by travelling from link to link, indexing the pages they found along the way. See Exhibit 3 for a description of how spiders work. Pages could also be submitted to the indexes by programmers. Some engines only indexed a portion of each web page; others indexed the whole thing, every word on every page. Most search engines allowed users to run advanced searches using Boolean operators such as AND, OR, NEAR and NOT. These helped users to refine searches. Nevertheless, often a search would result in thousands of hits, many of which were not useful to the user, resulting in a high signal-to-noise ratio. See Exhibit 4 for a comparison of the top search engines.

All search engines received revenue by selling advertising space on their web pages. It was generally understood in the industry that rev-

EXHIBIT 4   World Wide Web Search Engines

The following chart describes some differences among various WWW search engines.

Category	Altavista	Excite	Webcrawler	Lycos	Open Text	Infoseek
Case sensitive?	Y	N	N	N	N	Y
Considers phrases?	Y	N	Y	N	Y	Y
Required term operator	+	+	N	N	N	+
Prohibited term operator	−	−	N	N	N	−
Results ranking?	Y	Y	Y	Y	Y	Y
Controllable results ranking?	Y	N	N	Y	N	N
Booleans allowed?	Y	Y	Y	N	Y	N
Proximity operators allowed?	Y(10)	N	Y(range)	N	Y(80)	Y(100)
Subject (directory) searching?	N	Y	Y	Y	N	Y
Refine based on first search?	N	Y	N	N	Y	N
Controllable display format?	Y	N	Y	Y	N	N

enue from this type of advertising was not sufficient to cover operating costs. The search engines ran at a loss in the hope of operating profitably in the future.

Preferred Listings

The Open Text Index, like other search engines, made its money from advertising revenue. Advertisers "bought" certain words so that when users included a bought word in their search strings, the advertiser's banner appeared at the top of the page over the search results. For example, a hotel chain might buy the word "travel." If an Internet user ran a search including the word "travel," the hotel chain's advertising banner would appear above the results of the search. In the case of the Open Text index, advertisers would be charged five cents each time their word was included in a search request.

The marketing team in Waterloo believed that the potential to earn revenue from the Open Text Index was underrealized. In response to many requests from advertisers, they came up with the idea of Preferred Listings.

By buying a Preferred Listing, advertisers would be guaranteed to appear at the top of the retrieved lists of relevant web pages. So, for a fee, a link to the web page of the same hotel chain mentioned earlier would appear at the top of the search results list. This differed from the banner advertising model in a number of ways. For one thing, the paid-for link would look similar to other non-paid-for search results. Also, more than one advertiser could buy each target word.

The top 10 spots on the search result list for each target word would be sold at a sliding fee scale. The number one spot would go for US$20,000 while the number 10 spot could be purchased for US$2,000. The paid-for spots could be renewed at six month intervals. To make the user aware that the paid-for place would not necessarily be the most relevant, the marketing department decided that it would be fair to mark the paid-for spots clearly as advertising space. This was done using a special icon that would appear next to the paid-for spot. If all 10 of the top spots were bought, then the 11th spot would actually be the most relevant result of the search.

The potential for revenue generation using Preferred Listings was significant. If a word was completely bought it would generate US$110,000 for the company every six months. If the company could completely sell just 100 words, it would generate US$22,000,000 in revenue in the first year or more than 20 times the previous year's revenue from traditionally placed banner ads.

There was some speculation that allowing advertisers to buy spots on the list of retrieved search results would not be received well by the Internet community. The *de facto* standard for WWW search engines was for the search retrieval list to be organized by relevancy. The most relevant items would be returned first, and the least relevant would appear last. It was not clear how the Internet community would react if this standard was altered.

Proponents of the plan likened the scheme to the Yellow Pages, where advertisers paid for larger and more prominent listings. Opponents noted that, unlike the Yellow Pages which lists in alphabetical order, a WWW search engine is *expected* to list by relevancy.

The technology to add preferred listings to the Open Text index was in place. In addition, many advertisers had shown interest in the service. Senior management had to decide whether or not to go ahead.

Euro-Arab Management School

By Professor Sid L. Huff and Mike Wade

Tawfik Jelassi, dean of Academic Affaires of the Euro-Arab Management School (EAMS), stared past the Al-Hambra palace toward the distant snow-capped Sierra Nevada mountains on Spain's southern coast. The town of Granada, where he was located, was rich in cultural and political history. For centuries it had been regarded as a crucial bridge between the Arab and European worlds. Indeed, this was one of the main reasons that the European Union, along with the League of Arab States and the Spanish government, had decided to locate the joint management school in this Andalusian center.

It was January 1999, and Jelassi pondered the year ahead. Even though EAMS had been operating for over three years, this would be the first year the school would take in students, through its partner institutions, for its Euro-Arab Management Diploma. He felt the school was ready for this step, although some lingering doubts did remain. Could a business school which counted only 14 full-time staff members on its payroll, from the janitor to the director, really compete with established academic institutions? Could a truly "virtual" multinational organization be managed effectively? Had management education really come to the point where students would accept the learning model proposed by EAMS?

The Euro-Arab Management School

The Euro-Arab Management School (EAMS) was formed in 1995 by the European Union (EU). The idea for the school developed from a Euro-Arab dialogue as a way to further develop economic relations between Europe and the Arab World. The school was referred to in the Action Program of the EU's 1995 Barcelona Declaration in reference to its contribution to the development of human resources, especially in the fields of professional training and educational technologies. The venture was initially funded 100 per cent by the EU, but had the full support of the Arab League and the Spanish Government. In 1999, the Arab League and the Spanish Government also financially contributed to the School project. The EAMS mission was to prepare, through different educational, training and research activities, competent managers from the Arab world and Europe.

The EAMS was owned by the Euro-Arab Foundation, a trust consisting of representatives from the EU Commission, the European Parliament, the Arab League and the Spanish Government. The owners of the trust appointed a board of trustees to oversee the EAMS governance structure. The board appointed a governing council consisting of representatives of the EU Commission and the Spanish Government Min-

IVEY Mike Wade prepared this case under the supervision of Professor Sid L. Huff solely to provide material for class discussion. The authors do not intend to illustrate either effective or ineffective handling of a managerial situation. The authors may have disguised certain names and other identifying information to protect confidentiality.

istry of Education and Ministry of Foreign Affairs. This body, in turn, appointed the Executive Committee of the school, the group which managed the school on a day-to-day basis. The Executive Committee consisted of the director and the dean of Academic Affairs. The committee shared much of the managerial responsibility for the school with two other bodies, the Council of Partner Institutions, which approved the delivery of EAMS programs in partner institutions, and the Academic Council, which granted the diplomas and degrees, set the admission and assessment policies and controlled the quality of the content and its delivery. For a schematic representation of EAMS's governing structure, refer to Exhibit 1.

The school's mission statement stated that the goal of the EAMS was to ". . . deliver managers/entrepreneurs capable of working within the Euro-Arab marketplace, equipped with the skills to function in a rapidly changing business environment . . ." and to ". . . extend the understanding of managerial, economic and social issues that confront Arab and European managers in dealing with each other." The school would offer a "train-the-trainers" program, a one-year management diploma, a one-year MBA program and various executive education seminars and customized programs to students and executives in the 15 countries of the EU and the 22 countries of the Arab League.

It was determined that, even though the management school would be located in Spain, educational programs would be offered throughout Europe and the Arab World. There was considerable debate early on as to the most efficient method of accomplishing this. It was considered impractical to establish a physical infrastructure in multiple locations. The cost of building and staffing multiple campuses was prohibitive. Other models were considered, including various self-directed learning options such as web-based education, correspondence courses and the like. However, it was felt that priority should be placed on some form of interaction between students and EAMS tutors and professors. After much consideration, a model was adopted that combined self-directed learning with local tutorship by EAMS-trained and certified trainers.

The Master in Management Development Program

The Governing Council of EAMS decided to work in collaboration with academic institutions throughout Europe and the Arab world to oversee the local delivery of EAMS programs. EAMS would train tutors from these partner institutions at its Granada facility. The tutors, who were typically junior business professors or business Ph.D. students, would meet for five modules, each lasting three weeks during the one-year program. The tutors would learn skills in bicultural (Euro-Arab) management and be exposed to EAMS's pedagogical structure and course content. Between sessions in Granada, the tutors would have to complete various pedagogical projects and assignments. Upon passing

EXHIBIT 1　Euro-Arab Management School's Governance Structure

the course, tutors would be awarded a Master in Management Development Programme (MMDP) diploma. They would then return to their institutions to act as tutors to students taking EAMS courses locally in their native countries.

The role of the tutor was different from that of a teacher. Tutors did not teach EAMS programs directly, but acted as "facilitators" or "helpers" to students. Students received the course material either by mail or through the World Wide Web (WWW). Students would work independently on the course material and meet with the tutor usually once per week for three hours or for a whole day every two weeks. The tutor would answer questions about the course material and provide advice on particular approaches or directions for projects and assignments. The tutors would also lead students in case analysis. Case-based learning was prioritized in the EAMS system.

Another key function of the tutors was to help students appreciate the "cultural dimensions" of the course material. An essential part of the program was to provide students with an appreciation of the similarities and differences between European and Arab cultures. Part of the tutor's responsibility was to facilitate this type of learning.

EAMS began taking in students for its MMDP (train-the-trainers program) in October 1995. Students came to Granada for five three-week modules throughout the 10 months of the academic year. Each module was organized around a particular theme, such as "bicultural learning" or "managing a pedagogical project." EAMS picked up all the expenses of the admitted MMDP participants. This included tuition fees, travel between Granada and their home institutions (typically five round-trip air tickets), accommodation and a small weekly per diem rate while studying in Granada.

Most of the faculty would also travel to Granada to conduct the sessions, often for a week or a few days at a time. This was necessary since EAMS's staff was kept to a minimum (EAMS had 14 employees in December 1998). Instructors came from all over the world, although most worked for European academic institutions. The future tutors would typically receive instruction from 15 to 20 instructors during the year-long MMDP. All courses were conducted in English.

Three batches of tutors had graduated by the end of 1998. These three groups represented 55 tutors from 18 institutions in 13 countries throughout Europe and the Arab World. A fourth group of 18 tutors was set to graduate in late 1999. A fifth MMDP was set to begin in January 2000. By December 1999, EAMS would have graduated 73 tutors from 27 institutions in 16 countries, eight of which were Arab and eight of which were European. See Exhibit 2 for a list of these institutions and countries.

Student Programs

Once the tutors were in place throughout Europe and the Arab world, student courses could begin. The first course for students, the Euro-Arab Management Diploma (EAMD), was scheduled to be launched in October 1999. The EAMD was a 10-month management training course, which included, among others, modules on: communications skills, managing people, conflict management, human resource management, planning techniques, organizational design, change manage-

EXHIBIT 2   List of EAMS Partner Institutions

Algeria:	Institute Supérieur de Gestion, Algiers
	Institute Supérieur de Gestion d'Annaba (ISGA), Annaba
Egypt:	TEAM International, Cairo
Finland:	Åbo Akademi University, Turku
France:	Ecole Supérieure de Commerce (ESC), Toulouse
Germany:	Hochschule Bremen
Italy:	Scuola di Amministrazione Aziendale (SAA), University of Turin
Jordan:	Applied Science University, Amman
	Institute of Public Administration, Amman
	Jerash University, Amman
Lebanon:	TEAM International, Beirut
Morocco:	Ecole Nationale de Commerce et de Gestion (ENCG), Settat
	Groupe Ecole Supérieure d'Informatique et de Gestion (ESIG), Casablanca
	Groupe des Hautes Estudes Commerciales et Informatiques (HECI), Casablanca
	Institut des Hautes Etudes de Management (HEM), Casablanca
Palestine:	Al-Azhar University of Gaza, Gaza
	Hebron University, Hebron
	Islamic University of Gaza, Gaza
Saudi Arabia:	Arab Development Institute (ADI), Al-Khobar
	TEAM International, Ryadh
Spain:	Escuela de Administratión de las Empresas (ESADE), Barcelona
Sweden:	Uppsala University, Uppsala
Tunisia:	Ecole Supérieure de Commerce (ESC), Tunis
	Institut des hautes Etudes Commerciales (IHEC), Carthage
	Institut Supérieur de Gestion (ISG), Tunis
U.K.:	School of Business, University of Bradford, Bradford

ment, operations, marketing, information systems, data analysis, accounting and budgeting. Special emphasis was placed on bicultural contextual learning. In addition to regular course work, students would complete various projects and case analyses. Students would meet with tutors in their native countries often during the program. The EAMD was estimated to require 450 hours of self-study time and 110 hours of study time with a tutor (three hours a week for nine months). In addition to course work, there was a major project component, which was estimated to add an additional 250 hours to the time required to complete the course, making a total of 810 hours to receive a EAMD.

In order to complete the EAMD, students had to attend at least 90 per cent of classroom sessions with the tutor. Assessment of the student would be made by the tutor monthly on a five-point scale (strong pass, pass, bare pass, bare fail, fail). The tutor also assessed project work. An EAMS-designed final exam would be administered by the tutor at the end of the course. Students must pass this exam in order to pass the course. Students who passed the final exam and completed their projects with a passing grade, and regularly attended tutor sessions, would be referred to the Academic Council, which made the final decision on whether or not to award the EAMD to the student.

For admission into the EAMD program, candidates had to hold an undergraduate university degree, have two years of work experience, be proficient in English and pass the EAMD Admission test. Candidates who failed to fulfill any of these requirements might still be admitted in exceptional circumstances with special permission from the EAMS Executive Committee and the Academic Council. The EAMD targeted managers and entrepreneurs working or intending to work in a Euro-Arab context. Students who successfully completed the EAMD, or managers with substantial and related work experience could apply to the Euro-Arab Masters in Business Administration program (EAMBA). The EAMBA was a one-year course designed around a "business process" approach to learning in contrast to the "functional area" approach adopted by most business schools. The functional area approach, which was characterized by learning from distinct perspectives such as marketing, finance, information systems, organizational behavior and so on, was not considered fully representative of actual business practices. The business process approach analyzed a process, such as a new product launch or an expansion option, from a variety of perspectives. The consequences of business decisions on all functional areas were to be studied concurrently. Case-based learning lent itself particularly well to this style of learning. It would be taught partly in Granada and partly in the student's native country utilizing the same methodology as the EAMD program, namely tutor-facilitated self-study. The first EAMBA program was scheduled to be launched in September 2000.

Tuition fees for students taking the EAMD program would be collected by partner institutions. For example, students taking an EAMS course in Finland would pay tuition fees to the EAMS's partner institution in that country. That institution, in turn, would transfer a "franchising fee" back to EAMS, typically 20 percent of the gross tuition amount. EAMS recommended tuition fees for the EAMD program to be between 3,000 and 4,000 Euros (about US$3,500 to $4,600), although a certain amount of variability in this rate was expected to reflect local market conditions. While rates for the EAMBA program had yet to be finalized, the tuition was expected to be around US$16,000.

In addition to the flagship EAMD and EAMBA programs, the EAMS offered public, as well as company-specific, executive education seminars that focused on bicultural management (Euro-Arab). EAMS also conducted research activities primarily from its Granada headquarters. Research in 1998 focused on two areas, banking and finance and information technology and telecommunications. See Exhibit 3 for a schematic diagram of the EAMS learning model.

EXHIBIT 3   The Euro-Arab Management School Education Delivery Process

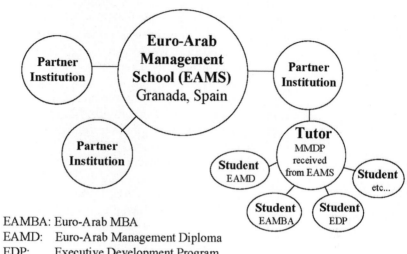

EAMBA: Euro-Arab MBA
EAMD: Euro-Arab Management Diploma
EDP: Executive Development Program
MMDP: Master of Management Development Program

Academic Quality

A concern with any virtual learning model is to ensure consistent quality of education. In an attempt to ensure the quality of its programs, EAMS set up an Academic Council consisting of internationally recognized management education experts from Arab and European countries. This body examined the EAMS academic plan, pedagogical standards, admission policies, assessment guidelines, granting of degrees, and so on. Furthermore, the Academic Council decided that it would individually audit partner institutions and tutors on an ongoing basis to enforce and ensure a homogeneous quality throughout the EAMS network of partner institutions. More specifically, the Academic Council evaluated, by means of an EAMD validation subcommittee, the local delivery of the Diploma, the provision of services and student performance. The subcommittee validated the EAMD on a regular basis and consisted of the dean of Academic Affairs and two members of the Academic Council provided that they were not from the local Partner Institution or its home country. The validation subcommittee reported back in writing to the EAMS Academic Council, placing particular emphasis on adherence to the due process and on the quality and extent of tutoring. It would thus visit the different Partner Institutions, attend tutorial sessions, and talk to tutors and students, thereby ensuring the quality of the tutoring at the Partner Institution.

Competition

The EAMS was not the only institution offering business education programs on a "virtual" basis. A number of universities had begun to offer various forms of distance learning options for students who wished to study remotely. The most established option offered by many institutions was distance learning through correspondence courses. These programs typically followed a self-learning model where students would receive learning material and assignments from an institution, often by mail, which they would complete and send back to the institution for marking. Correspondence courses usually involved minimal direct contact between students and faculty. Time periods for completion of these courses were often flexible.

The U.S.-based research organization, The Gartner Group, estimated that demand for online training would increase 10 percent per year between 1998 and 2000, to $12 billion. Another research organization, Quality Dynamics, also based in the U.S., predicted that half of all corporate training would be delivered via technology by 2000.

Recently, many institutions had modified the traditional correspondence course learning model to take advantage of the speed, interactivity and ubiquity of the World Wide Web (WWW). Learning material was being posted on websites rather than being mailed, and students were given the option of returning assignments by e-mail, and even corresponding with faculty through interactive means such as "chat" programs or video-conferencing. Other institutions had begun to offer full videoconferencing MBA programs, where students would gather in small groups in remote locations and conduct classes with students from other remote locations and faculty, through the use of cameras, microphones and TV monitors.

The trend toward the "virtual MBA" was being led by business schools in North America; yet by the end of 1998 some European universities had also begun to offer distance learning options. A number of schools in the U.K., such as the Open University, Brunel University, Henley Management College, the University of Warwick and Leicester University, had established accredited MBA programs which were administered remotely, mostly using some form of web-based learning. Some continental schools were also offering MBA programs on a "virtual" basis. This list included the Virtual University of Hagen in Germany and the Open University of the Netherlands. In addition to schools offering accredited programs, there were many academic and quasi-academic institutions that offered MBA programs and other management degrees and diplomas over the WWW.

Tawfik Jelassi was comforted by the fact that the mix of self-study, IT-based distance education and tutored learning, as adopted by EAMS, was unique in Europe. Also, EAMS was the only business school tailored to an Euro-Arab audience. Clearly, there were many students, of both Arab and European descent, who were interested in a bicultural (Euro-Arab) management education. Now that tutors were in place throughout Europe and the Arab world, these students would be able to study in their native countries through the EAMS systems. But how would they adapt to EAMS's distance learning model? And how would EAMS adapt to the inevitable changes and developments which would occur as new courses and new students entered the system?

Index

H